The Rise of the States

The Johns Hopkins University
Studies in Historical and Political Science
120th Series (2002)

1. Wendy A. Woloson

*Refined Tastes: Sugar, Confectionery,
and Consumers in Nineteenth-Century America*

2. Jon C. Teaford

*The Rise of the States:
Evolution of American State Government*

3. Carol Collier Frick

*Dressing Renaissance Florence:
Honorable Families, Economics, and Tailors*

The Rise of the States

EVOLUTION OF AMERICAN STATE GOVERNMENT

Jon C. Teaford

The Johns Hopkins University Press

Baltimore and London

© 2002 The Johns Hopkins University Press

All rights reserved. Published 2002

Printed in the United States of America on acid-free paper

9 8 7 6 5 4 3 2 1

The Johns Hopkins University Press

2715 North Charles Street

Baltimore, Maryland 21218-4363

www.press.jhu.edu

Library of Congress Cataloging-in-Publication Data
Teaford, Jon C.
The rise of the states : evolution of American state government/Jon C. Teaford.
    p. cm.
Includes bibliographical references (p.) and index.
ISBN 0-8018-6888-2 (hardcover : alk. paper) — ISBN 0-8018-6889-0
(pbk. : alk. paper)
1. State governments—United States—History. 2. Federal
government—United States—History. I. Title.
jk311.T43 2002
320.473'049'0904—dc21

                                                    2001003739

A catalog record for this book is available from the British Library.

Contents

The Rise of the States

1

~~~

A Flawed Prognosis

Iɴ 1888 the great British observer of American government James Bryce
wrote, "The truth is that the State has shrivelled. . . . It does not interest its
citizens as it once did." Eighteen years later U.S. Secretary of State Elihu Root
warned that if the states continued to neglect the needs of their citizenry,
"sooner or later constructions of the Constitution [would] be found to vest
power where it [would] be exercised—in the national government." In 1933,
during the nation's worst economic depression, a leading expert on public
administration, Luther Gulick, claimed that Root's dire prediction had come
true: "The American state is finished. I do not predict that the states will go,
but affirm that they have gone." At the close of the 1940s, Washington correspondent Roscoe Drummond made a similar assertion: "Our federal system of
states no longer exists and has no more chance of being brought back into existence than an apple pie can be put back on the apple tree." And in the 1960s a
discouraged defender of state power, Senator Everett Dirksen of Illinois, conceded that if the prevailing trend continued, "the only people interested in state
boundaries [would] be Rand-McNally."[1]

From the late nineteenth century through the 1960s, the prognosis for state
government was grim. In every decade distinguished observers pronounced
the states either dead or dying. Moreover, many commentators regretted what
little life was supposedly left in the forty-eight or fifty commonwealths. The
state was deemed a painful and useless element of the nation's body politic, like
a burst appendix, that threatened the life of democratic rule if not removed. In
1939 the renowned political scientist Harold Laski wrote of "the obsolescence
of federalism" and pleaded for recognition that "the federal form of state [was]
unsuitable to the stage of economic and social development that America
ha[d] reached." The dispersion of power among the states did not "provide
for sufficient rapidity of action; it inhibit[ed] the emergence of necessary
standards of uniformity," and it left "the backward areas a restraint, at once
parasitic and poisonous, on those which [sought] to move forward."[2] A decade

later, journalist Robert S. Allen compiled *Our Sovereign State,* in which he leveled his most venomous rhetorical blows at the states. Barring no holds, Allen wrote: "State government is the tawdriest, most incompetent, and most stultifying unit of the nation's political structure. . . . Venality, open domination and manipulation by vested interests, unspeakable callousness in the care of the sick, aged, and unfortunate, criminal negligence in law enforcement, crass deprivation of primary constitutional rights, obfuscation, adolescence, obstructionism, incompetence, and even outright dictatorship" were characteristic of state government. In a torrent of passionate prose, Allen condemned "the stifling inadequacies and imbecilities of state government," a system of rule that was "moribund, corrosive, and deadening" as well as "riddled with senescence, incompetence, mediocrity, ineffectualness, corruption, and tawdriness. It pollutes instead of purifies; destroys and obstructs instead of building and improving."[3]

Even those who viewed Allen's rhetoric as excessive recognized that state government had a tarnished reputation. In his influential *Storm over the States,* published in 1967, Governor Terry Sanford of North Carolina admitted to "the many virtues in the systems of state government" but sought "to sound the trumpet for others who would labor to improve the states' effectiveness." Unlike some earlier authorities, Sanford did not pronounce the states dead or dying. "There is medicine to cure the illness and put the states back on their feet," Sanford assured his readers.[4] Yet even the optimistic governor believed the patient needed a strong tonic.

Basically, the state appeared to be the runt in the American governmental litter, with its more raucous siblings, national and city government, squealing for the bulk of the attention and the cash. From the late nineteenth century through the 1960s, a prevailing centripetal force seemed to be drawing ever-increasing power to the national government. The rising magnitude of interstate commerce and the growing muscle of corporate capitalism demanded a strong central government to regulate the economy. Moreover, the successive crises of economic depression, World War II, and cold war focused attention on Washington, D.C. Events in Albany, Tallahassee, and Sacramento appeared trivial compared to the worldwide economic, military, and ideological threats facing the federal executive and Congress. By the 1950s and 1960s, the only time state action made headlines nationwide was when a racist governor stood in a schoolhouse door, futilely attempting to thwart the national dream of equal opportunity.

Meanwhile, a seemingly unremitting wave of urbanization produced a network of giant cities, many of which were more populous than the puny commonwealths of upper New England or such sovereign but relatively uninhab-ited states as Wyoming, Montana, and Idaho. Observers might have attacked city governments as corrupt or incompetent, but few dismissed them as insignificant. Every politically conscious American of the first half of the twen-tieth century had heard of New York City's Tammany Hall, but very few knew of Nevada's Boss George Wingfield. In the modern industrialized world, the national government and the great municipalities appeared to be the polities of the future. In fact, by the 1960s trendy policy gurus talked and wrote of a federal-urban axis, a new alliance between the national government and the cities that would bypass the anachronistic states.

Among academics, the field of state government lay relatively fallow during the period from 1920 to 1965. At the beginning of the twentieth century, reform-minded scholars filled books and periodicals with the latest reports from such bastions of progressivism as Wisconsin and California. But after World War I interest waned, and by midcentury the study of state government consumed the energies of fewer political scientists. International and domestic policies emanating from Washington, D.C., or Moscow were of top priority. Kremli-nologists commanded the attention of the nation; experts on state sales tax legislation won fewer listeners.

Meanwhile, historians cared even less for state government than their col-leagues in political science departments. Some wrote of state-level reforms during the Progressive era, and professors authored a number of political his-tories of individual states, focusing on campaigns and political rhetoric more than the actual development of government. Others studied the states and the New Deal, yet their focus was on the application or reception of federal poli-cies and initiatives in the states.[5] The states were significant only insofar as they reacted to the federal overlord. The evolution of state government as a whole was neglected, and individual state histories were deemed "local" and never commanded as much respect as national chronicles. Generally, American his-tory texts emphasized the growth of the republic and the progressive consoli-dation of the nation. They told how the United States gradually became more united. The defeat of states' rights in the Civil War and the failure of state efforts during the Great Depression were monumental landmarks in the rise of the nation, and the great figures of the national pageant, men like Abraham Lincoln and Franklin Roosevelt, used their power to consign the states to a subordinate place. Through the mid–twentieth century, then, state govern-ment had few suitors. Journalists reviled it, most political scientists judged it homely and unworthy of their attentions, and historians hardly seemed to notice it.

During the 1970s and 1980s, however, the ugly duckling of state government suddenly seemed more swanlike. In 1972 the iconoclastic political scientist Ira Sharkansky published *The Maligned States,* in which he bluntly told the reader: "This book is *not* one more tirade against the states. . . . If any segment of government promises the resources to meet the most pressing of our social problems," Sharkansky wrote, "it is the states." According to him, the states did not "deserve to be the whipping boy of commentators who believe[d] things should be better."[6] That same year, John E. Bebout urged his fellow academics to study "the emerging state governments."[7] And in 1975 Peter F. Drucker discounted premature reports of the death of state government, announcing boldly, "The patient has refused to die." Instead, it had "undergone a renaissance," leading Drucker to proclaim a "resurgence of state government."[8]

In the last quarter of the twentieth century, the rebirth of the states was heralded in dozens of insightful books and articles. Ronald Reagan's "New Federalism" followed close on the heels of Richard Nixon's "New Federalism," reinforcing the earlier president's policy of returning power to the states and drawing attention to the actions of governors and legislatures. Scholars described the dramatic, but often unnoticed, transformation of the states into dynamic governmental units as a "quiet revolution" or a "silent revolution." By 1989 Carl Van Horn of Rutgers University announced that the states were "arguably the most responsive, innovative, and effective level of government in the American federal system."[9] During the 1990s even some "big-government" liberals were claiming that devolution of power to the states might not spell doom to cherished policies. In *The American Prospect: A Journal for the Liberal Imagination,* contributors were explaining to troubled readers why states could realize liberal goals and assuring them that decentralization did not necessarily equate with conservativism.[10] Unreconstructed centralizers such as Harvard's John D. Donahue still warned of "disunited states," but by the late 1990s his work could be dismissed as "a rather elegiac yearning for federal power of the sort one might expect from a Rooseveltian academic in . . . Clintonian times."[11]

During the last decades of the twentieth century, state-level politicians also won new respect. In the late 1970s, political scientist Larry Sabato found that the American governorship had been transformed. According to him, it was "reasonably clear to American political observers that a greater percentage of the nation's governors" were "capable, creative, forward-looking, and experienced."[12] Scholars and journalists alike accorded new respect to the chief executives of the fifty states, reporting on their innovative proposals to improve everything from education to the economy. Others wrote of the professionalization of the state legislatures. A new breed of full-time legislators supported by expert staffs seemed a marked improvement over the farmers and small-town lawyers who had previously descended on state capitals every two years to clumsily patch together statutes.

State government and the study of state-level leaders and policies had thus become respectable. The putrefying carcass of state rule had returned to life, and in the wake of this purported resurrection, political scientists were making up for past neglect. Yet historians were less interested in the subject, and the evolution of state government was only dimly perceived. In a short article historian Morton Keller presented the novel argument that state power did not need to "be resurrected because it never died."[13] Few other scholars of American history, however, appeared to care whether the states were reborn or simply victims of a false prognosis. Broad generalizations about the changing role of the federal government seemed to suffice for most history texts.

This study attempts to build upon Keller's argument and remedy past neglect. Recognizing the significance of the states in American history, it surveys the development of state government from the 1890s to the 1980s. During this century modern American state government emerged. Whereas the nineteenth-century state was spare, with little administrative muscle, during the course of the twentieth century, the state expanded beyond recognition, becoming a governmental gargantuan in comparison with its earlier self. During the first century of the nation's history, internal improvement projects drove states to bankruptcy, and a civil war relegated the doctrine of states' rights to a secondary place in the nation's creed. But during the nation's second century, the states emerged as dynamic molders of domestic policy and vital providers of government services.

In this book I argue that previous reports of the states' death and rebirth have been exaggerated. Rather than slumbering for the first seven decades of the twentieth century, then suddenly springing to life under the leadership of a new breed of bright and vigorous governors, the states have been vital actors from the 1890s onward. The image of foot-dragging hayseeds in provincial capitals blocking change and thwarting omniscient dynamos in Washington, D.C., needs to be discarded. Though state government did change notably in the 1970s and 1980s, it also changed markedly in the 1920s and 1930s. The vitality characteristic of the last quarter of the twentieth century was not a new phenomenon. Instead, the states continually adapted. A quiet revolution had been under way ever since the close of the nineteenth century. Moreover, the proportion of glad-handing mediocrities inhabiting the governor's mansions probably did not change dramatically throughout the course of the twentieth century. Many able, farsighted figures won the governor's chair in the first seven decades of the century, and criminal and impeachment proceedings against governors occasionally blemished the reputation of the office during the era of the states' "renaissance." In other words, I contend that the states, for better or worse, have been very much alive throughout the twentieth century. They did not die, and their "rebirth" is thus a misnomer. They have not always been successful, and in retrospect their actions might occasionally appear offensive or foolish. But they were not hibernating for decades until finally awakened in the 1970s. They were consistently major actors in American history.

Given the continuing significance of the states, some understanding of their expanding role is called for. And this study will identify and trace certain general trends. Basically, the rise of state government was a product of the tension between two views of government that were influential in twentieth-century American thinking. Twentieth-century state government balanced a rising devotion to expertise and managerial efficiency and persistent fears of concentrated national authority, fears that were endemic to American thought. These twin forces in large part determined the direction and growth of state rule.

During the early twentieth century, an emerging commitment to professionalism, expertise, efficiency, and "scientific" management gave rise to reform at both the state and federal levels. Belief in administrative reform and professionalism in government promoted centralization of authority, the creation of a nonpartisan bureaucracy, the concentration of power in the hands of the executive, and the development of legislative expertise. The result was a wide range of structural reforms in state government. Efforts to secure the executive budget, restructure the executive branch, and establish legislative reference bureaus, for example, reflected the influence of the administrative reformers and their call for efficiency and expertise in government. Moreover, the development of legislative expertise, the rationalization and concentration of administrative authority under the governors, and the transfer of power from elected local officials to expert state bureaucracies remained persistent themes in the evolution of state government. Enthusiasm for the gospel of efficiency might have waned after the first decades of the century, but its message continued to influence policymakers. Throughout the twentieth century, the state response to new challenges was professionalization and centralization. When faced with the demands of the automobile age, the crisis of economic depression, or the imperatives of educating millions of baby boomers, the states responded by shifting responsibility from local units to state-level administrators.

As policymakers curbed the authority of local, partisan amateurs and moved responsibility up the governmental ladder to state capitals, they greatly expanded the role of the state. This shift from delegation to control was a notable theme in the history of twentieth-century state government. In the nineteenth century, state legislatures authorized townships, counties, cities, school districts, business corporations, and trustees of educational and charitable institutions to take action and exercised little supervision or control. In the twentieth century, state governments increasingly intervened and often took direct charge. Local road supervisors, township assessors, one-room-school districts, and justices of the peace untutored in the law were no longer thought adequate, and the states transferred the construction and maintenance of highways to professionals in state highway departments, assumed a larger share of the responsibility for levying and collecting taxes, shouldered a growing portion of school expenses while also imposing professional educational standards on local districts, and fixed higher professional standards for local jurists.

Yet, at the same time, a persistent fear and misgiving about concentrated authority and centralized rule limited the shifts in government responsibility and notably preserved and expanded the role of the states in the face of growing federal authority. Although the trend was toward centralized expert administration, national policymakers repeatedly refrained from taking direct charge of major state functions. Federal highway acts bolstered the authority of an emerging corps of professional state highway engineers and pressured recalcitrant states to give up the localized, amateur road-building practices of the past. The federal government did not, however, assume direct control of highway construction or ownership of the highways. Members of Congress expressed their fears of national control and opted for the carrot of funds to secure professional standards rather than assuming primary responsibility for highways. This reluctance to centralize responsibility in Washington is also evident in the field of education. The federal government remained a minor element in education during the first two-thirds of the century, and throughout the century schooling was primarily a state and local function, with the state assuming an ever-larger role. Even when the federal government assumed major responsibility for a new function, as it did with welfare and income maintenance during the 1930s, it opted to work through the states. The federal government generally did not choose the model of central control exemplified by the postal service, with Washington monopolizing responsibility to the exclusion of state action. Instead, the cooperative relationship embodied in the federal highway acts was the norm. In part this was due to financial considerations. Contrary to common belief, the federal treasury was not a bottomless pit, and federal budget makers burdened by the expenses arising from world wars and cold wars could not afford to pursue many policies without state matching funds. Concentrated authority in Washington thus strained both the national treasury and the nation's devotion to dispersed power.

Actually, fears of centralization of authority in the hands of the federal government spurred the state governments into reforming themselves in line with prevailing twentieth-century notions of professionalism and administrative efficiency. Throughout the century, advocates of "modernization" warned that if state government did not reform and did not impose professional standards on localities, the federal government would intervene, and decentralized rule would disappear. The specter of federal expansion was a catalyst for change, a prod for expanding the states' roles and revising their legislative, executive, and financial structures.

The bottom line is that state government in the twentieth century was not an increasingly irrelevant relic of the parochialism of the past. Instead, it was admirably suited to a century in which a growing belief in expertise and professional administration and standards had to accommodate a traditional suspicion of central control and concentrated authority. The supposed renaissance of state government during the last quarter of the century was not simply a consequence of more competent governors and more professional postreapportionment legislatures; it was the culmination of decades of change during which the convergence of centralizing reforms and decentralizing inhibitions left the state governments with expanded duties and "modernized" structures.

Throughout the twentieth century, then, the states were very much alive. They were assuming greater control over localities, expanding their functions, imposing professional standards, adapting their tax structures, reorganizing their bureaucracies, and joining in cooperative efforts to improve themselves. Perhaps nothing was more indicative of their continuing vitality than their growing revenues. Although everyone noted and many criticized the increasingly heavy tax burden imposed by the federal government, the own-source revenues of state governments actually grew at a faster pace than federal revenues (see table 1). In other words, if one considers only the revenues raised by the states themselves, excluding intergovernmental payments from the federal government, the states outpaced the federal government in revenue growth. During the 1940s, federal revenues did increase at a markedly higher rate than state receipts. Clearly, the demands of World War II forced Uncle Sam to dig deep into the pockets of the taxpayers. In the 1950s the pace of federal and state revenue growth was almost identical. But during every other period, the states' own-source revenue growth greatly exceeded the rate of increase for the federal government. During World War I, federal revenues soared, but in the 1920s the creation of new state taxes to finance highway construction caused state income to rise more rapidly than federal receipts. Although many observers claimed that the economic depression exposed the fiscal inferiority of the states, between the late 1920s and 1940 state-level tax reforms swelled state revenues at a pace exceeding the income growth of the federal government. And in the 1960s, 1970s, and 1980s, the pattern was the same. An inability to raise money did not doom the states to obsolescence. Instead, they coped quite handsomely with rising financial demands and surpassed even the federal authorities in their ability to discover and exploit new sources of revenue.

Given the flawed prognosis of those who pronounced the states dead or dying, it is necessary to reexamine twentieth-century state government and discover its actual condition. The states as well as the federal government have made history, and this study attempts to recount part of that history. It does not, of course, describe every state program or all areas of policy. The breadth of state action discourages such a comprehensive approach. Yet this work does present the major developments in the evolution of the modern American states.

Table 1. Federal and Own-Source State Revenues 1902–1990

Year	Federal (in millions of $)	Percent Change	Own-Source State (in millions of $)	Percent Change
1902	653	—	183	—
1913	962	+47.3	360	+96.7
1927	4,469	+364.6	1,994	+453.9
1940	7,000	+56.6	5,012	+151.4
1950	43,527	+521.8	11,480	+129.1
1960	99,800	+129.3	26,094	+127.2
1970	205,562	+106.0	68,691	+163.2
1980	565,477	+175.1	212,636	+209.6
1990	1,154,596	+104.2	505,843	+137.9
1902–90		+176,714.1		+276,316.4

Sources: U.S. Bureau of the Census, Historical Statistics of the United States, Colonial Times to 1970, Bicentennial Edition, (Washington, D.C.: Government Printing Office, 1975); U.S. Bureau of the Census, Historical Statistics on Governmental Finances and Employment (Washington, D.C.: Government Printing Office, 1985); U.S. Bureau of the Census, Government Finances: 1989–90 (Washington, D.C.: Government Printing Office, 1991)

This is not, however, a history of federalism during the period 1890 to 1990. The focus is not on the changing relations between the national government and the states or the allocation of power within the federal system. That would require equal emphasis on both sides of the federal equation, the national government and the states. This study instead concentrates primarily on the lesser-known half and seeks to demonstrate that America's federal system has not simply been a top-down operation with Washington, D.C., taking the initiative and the states following behind. The American federal system has included two dynamic halves, each one interacting with the other and determining the course of government. By emphasizing the states, I do not intend to deny the expanding role of the federal government in the twentieth century. Too often Americans have conceived of federalism as a zero-sum game: any time the federal government scores, it deletes points from the states. In fact, government power is not a finite constant so that one element's gain is another's loss. Instead, state expansion and federal expansion have proceeded simultaneously. The rise of the states does not imply the fall of the national government, nor should the growth of Washington's role necessarily mean a decline in the state's position.

As the federal government has adapted, so have the states. Moreover, they have been more than laboratories of democracy, testing programs that could later be applied nationwide by authorities in Washington. They have been significant as the factories of government as well as the laboratories. For better or worse, the twentieth-century states produced and implemented many of the programs and policies that changed American life. Demands for administrative reform and a new level of expertise in government transformed the structure of state rule and also shifted control from county seats to state capitals. Yet traditional misgivings kept the centripetal force in American politics from reducing the states to antique nonentities in a consolidated nation ruled from Washington. State government survived and expanded, regulating and servicing the American populace in manifold ways. The states were too vital and alive to be ignored.

2

A New Era in State Government

EFFICIENCY was among the watchwords of the early twentieth century. Journals published articles on scientific management, and with stopwatch in hand, efficiency experts attempted to boost industrial productivity. Social workers and a corps of pioneering sociologists collected volumes of data to serve as the foundation of a new science of social uplift that would supposedly ensure the efficient application of aid to the poor and discover a formula for curing the ills of the industrial age. Meanwhile, progressive reformers campaigned for businesslike, efficient government. Whereas a previous generation of good-government reformers had emphasized honorable intentions and upright character, early-twentieth-century crusaders believed those were not enough. Honesty alone was not sufficient; government also had to operate efficiently.

Although proponents of the cause differed somewhat in their definition of the term, all believed that efficiency implied a new level of rationality, planning, and expertise that would ensure more effective services, preferably at lower costs. Basically, government needed to operate more effectively, maximizing its social output and minimizing its expenses. According to reformers espousing economy and efficiency, government could only do so by relying on expert administrators who would impose system on the ramshackle structure of rule and rationally plan for the future. The sleepy pace and hayseed rule of the county court houses and rural town halls were no longer sufficient. Nor was the wasteful partisan cronyism of the urban boss. In the industrial era, state government needed to operate like an efficient machine, and rubes, party hacks, and part-time solons could not be trusted with the controls.

Given this attitude, centralization of authority in the hands of the state executive branch was among the most notable trends of the period. Rather than continuing the traditional policy of distributing authority to local governments, courts, and independent boards of trustees, the tendency of the age was to refocus power and assert unprecedented supervision and control. During the late nineteenth and early twentieth centuries, some states did grant "home rule" powers to local governments, allowing them to draft their own charters and choose whether to accept the commission, city-manager, or mayor-council form of government.[1] Yet, while there was much talk of home rule, the states were extending their administrative control, attempting to weave the loose threads of government into a stronger fabric of rule.

A variety of interests demanded that the states tighten their hold on government and eschew the long-standing practice of delegating authority without adequate oversight. Critics of big business crusaded for state supervision of corporations, corporations preferred state regulation to municipal intervention, and friends of labor urged the states to assert administrative control over the welfare of injured workers rather than leaving them to the mercy of a judiciary devoted to outdated common law principles. Bicyclists and the growing corps of automobile owners wanted the states to take charge of the roadways, and an emerging body of professional state highway engineers sought to substitute their expertise for the trial-and-error efforts of the farmers and storekeepers who had traditionally taken on the task of township road supervisor. Meanwhile, foes of wasteful spending called for increased state control of the institutions of higher education. Rather than perpetuating mutually destructive rivalries between the principal public universities within each state, solons were expected to impose new structures of governance that would ensure a coordination of academic policy. Dispersed, unregulated authority was not deemed conducive to "scientific" administration. Thus the states needed to take charge.

Although critics might have questioned the ability of the state to answer these demands, legislators, governors, and state administrators did act, introducing and implementing new policies. The forces of decentralized rule did not quietly disappear, and in some cases they continued to pose a serious barrier to effective state rule. But in capitols across the country, policymakers were gradually remaking state government and proving wrong those who considered the subnational polity an endangered species, withering from obsolescence.

The Executive and the Legislature

Among the significant developments in this new era of state government was the changing status of the executive and legislative branches. Discontent with traditional practices was producing a gradual shift in power, with the legislature falling into the shadows and the governor winning the spotlight. Pre-eminently loyal to the parochial desires of their districts, legislators seemed to represent the localism and dispersed authority of the past. Chosen by a state-wide electorate, the governors enjoyed a mandate from the people as a whole and appeared to be the appropriate figures to achieve a new level of central supervision. Legislators supposedly spoke for interests and factions; governors were leaders with a broader vision. Given this prevailing image of the two branches, the executive gradually assumed new prominence in the structure of state government, a tendency that would continue through much of the twen-tieth century.

Indicative of disenchantment with the legislative branch were the constitu-tional restrictions imposed on state solons during the second half of the nine-teenth century. During the first half of the century, most state legislatures met in annual sessions of unrestricted length. By 1900, however, only Massachu-setts, Rhode Island, New York, New Jersey, South Carolina, and Georgia re-tained the annual legislative session.[2] Elsewhere the biennial legislature was the norm, as framers of state constitutions became convinced that one meeting every two years was sufficient and preferable. Furthermore, in a majority of states the constitutions capped the length of these sessions. For example, Mon-tana, Nevada, and Utah imposed an absolute limit of sixty days on the bien-nial meetings, whereas Colorado imposed a ninety-day cap and Wyoming required legislators to complete their business in forty days.[3]

These restrictions reflected a prevailing concern that legislatures produced too many laws and would commit manifold mischief if allowed to meet too often or too long. "One of the faults most commonly found in the legislatures," wrote reformer Edwin Godkin in 1897, "is the fault of doing too much. I do not think I exaggerate in saying that all the busier States in America . . . witness every meeting of the state legislature with anxiety and alarm."[4] In 1904 another observer called "this craze for law collecting" "an American mania" like the "craze for bric-a-brac."[5] And in 1913 Alabama's Governor Emmet O'Neal reit-erated these sentiments, recognizing that a revulsion against excessive law-making underlay the restrictions on legislative sessions. "We have come to believe that the legislature, like a strong man inflamed by violent passion and dominated by wicked influences," O'Neal remarked, "was likely to 'run amuck' trampling down the interests of the just and the unjust alike; and hence we have sought not to reform the patient, but to lessen his capacity for evil, by shackling his limbs and putting him in a strait-jacket."[6]

Yet the biennial session of limited duration did not necessarily produce less legislation than annual gatherings of unrestricted length; instead, it simply generated laws more hurriedly. One critic after another lambasted the lack of serious deliberation in the state legislatures and the mad rush to enact laws in the last days of each session. "That the legislature lacks time is axiomatic," observed a 1904 study of state legislatures. "From every hamlet in the state, from every township and city, from every corporation office flows a stream of bills to the honorable representatives of the various districts, and on the mad current of this stream are rushed forward bills, members, and public."[7] During the 1890s the average session of a state legislature produced about 350 acts and resolutions, and in succeeding years the output would not decline.[8] The 1911 session laws of California filled 2,000 pages, and even relatively uninhabited Idaho could claim 810 pages of enactments that year.[9]

This hasty mass production of laws supposedly resulted in an unprecedented sloppiness. The Montana session laws of 1907 were so full of errors that the secretary of state, who compiled them, issued a disclaimer that "neither this office nor the printer employed in the work [was] responsible for spelling or punctuation." A measure intended to outlaw the sale of diseased meat instead prohibited butchers from selling "deceased" meat, seemingly requiring Montanans to purchase only live animals for their dinner tables.[10] Kansas governor George H. Hodges expressed a common sentiment of the time when he deplored "lawmaking in hot haste," resulting in "a lot of more or less crude and illy-digested laws, some of which are puzzles for even learned jurists to interpret."[11]

Some commentators also took exception to the personnel engaged in this rapid-fire lawmaking. In 1897 Edwin Godkin complained it was "well-nigh impossible" to convince "a man of serious knowledge on any subject" to serve in the house or senate, and he contended that legislatures were "mainly composed of very poor men, with no reputation to maintain or political future to look after."[12] Seven years later, another commentator concluded that "expert knowledge, judicious temperament, and great wisdom" were not "apparent in bulk in any state legislature." Instead, the legislatures were "composed of average men, possessed of human weaknesses, prejudices, and passions."[13]

Such comments, however, perhaps reflected the arrogance of the authors rather than the reality of America's corps of lawmakers. State legislators were most often successful farmers or ambitious lawyers, better educated than the average American and chosen to serve because they commanded some degree of prestige or esteem within their communities. Generally lawyers outnumbered farmers in the state senate, whereas the opposite was often true in the state house. On the average the farmer-legislator was at least ten years older than the lawyer-legislator.[14] For farmers, a term in the legislature capped their careers; it was a token of respect bestowed on successful agriculturists in their fifties. For lawyers, however, legislative service was more often an early step in their climb to success, a means for securing greater recognition and more lucrative clients.

Though younger on the average, lawyers were more likely to hold leadership positions than their agrarian colleagues. Nationwide, 58 percent of the men serving as state house speakers during the period 1897 to 1910 were lawyers; 4 percent were farmers.[15] Throughout the nation, the speaker of the house of representatives was the most powerful legislative figure. He determined who served on what committees, who chaired those committees, who would be recognized in floor debate, and to which committees legislation was referred. He thus held the power of life and death over bills. And a member of the legal profession most often wielded this power.

Few, however, wielded legislative power for long. The turnover rate was high among state legislators, for most had no intention of becoming permanent fixtures in the state capitol. At the turn of the century, about two-thirds of all state lawmakers were serving their first term in the legislature. There was considerable variation among the states, with only 6.5 percent of Vermont's house members having served in a prior session as compared with 62.5 percent of Rhode Island's representatives.[16] But turnover was the norm, and career legislators were virtually unknown. Even the legislative leaders did not enjoy great seniority. According to a nationwide survey, 68 percent of all state speakers from the period 1897 to 1910 served three or fewer terms in the legislature, and 85 percent held the speaker's chair for a single term.[17]

Lawmaking was not, then, an occupation or a career. Legislative service represented a brief interlude in the lives of citizens whose chief interest was their law practice, farm, or business. At the close of each sixty- or ninety-day session, the citizen lawmakers went home to resume their interrupted careers, and many never returned to the senate or house chambers.

When they went home, it was most often to small towns or rural areas. Already in 1900 many legislatures were malapportioned, giving the village and the farm a disproportionate influence in the state capitols and depriving the large cities of their full voice in state policymaking. The apportionment of representation was especially skewed in the older states of the Northeast. Vermont allocated a single representative to each of its 246 towns regardless of population, so that Somerset with 61 residents enjoyed equal representation in the lower house with Burlington, a community of 14,590 inhabitants. Similarly, Connecticut's constitution of 1818 specified that each town would forever retain its existing representation. By the 1890s the three largest Connecticut cities, with more than one-fourth of the state's population, elected only 6 of the 251 representatives in the lower house.[18] In 1901 Connecticut's governor noted that it was "theoretically possible for less than 20 percent of the people to elect a clear majority of both branches of the general assembly, and so secure absolute control of the entire state government."[19]

Newer constitutions also curbed the power of the rapidly growing cities. New York's constitution of 1894 blocked an anticipated takeover of state government by New York City and the then-independent city of Brooklyn by specifically forbidding any two adjacent counties from electing more than one-half of all state senators.[20] Arguing against apportionment on the basis of population alone, constitutional convention delegate Elihu Root claimed that if the principle were "pushed to its logical conclusion, every county, every city, every town, every village, every man in the state of New York [would become] subject to the absolute domination and control of the delegation from New York" City. He favored "the principle which ha[d] been adopted in a large number of the states . . . that the small and widely scattered communities, with their feeble power comparatively," should through "the distribution of representation, be put upon an equal footing . . . with the concentrated power of the cities."[21] Not all states adhered to Root's formula for curbing urban power. In Louisiana New Orleans actually was slightly overrepresented in the legislature.[22] Yet the prevailing pattern of apportionment was not favorable to the nation's largest cities.

During the early twentieth century, the state legislatures thus seemed in many ways to be running counter to the trends in the nation as a whole. Although the nation was becoming increasingly urban, the legislative seats were apportioned to preserve the power of dying backwater towns in New England and elsewhere. An infatuation with professionalism and expertise was increasingly evident as Americans pursued the goal of scientific efficiency. Yet the legislatures clung to the nineteenth-century tradition of rotation in office. Amateurs made laws and even presided from the house rostrum in an age when professional organizations were imposing stricter educational and licensing requirements on a wide variety of occupations. Legislatures operated more effectively than their severest critics claimed, but still their image clashed with the prevailing attitudes of the era. And this clash would mar the reputation of the state legislatures throughout the first two-thirds of the twentieth century.

As the legislature lost prestige, the governors gained in stature. For the states' executives were emerging as powerful initiators of policy and self-proclaimed tribunes of all the people. In the late 1880s, James Bryce dismissed the state governor as "not yet a nonentity," claiming that "in more than one

State a sort of perfume from the old days linger[ed] round the office."[23] Yet Bryce clearly believed that the pleasant aroma could not linger much longer. By 1910 he and many others thought otherwise. That year the Englishman remarked, "Of late years the tendency seems to have been for the power and influence and authority of the State Governor to increase and be revivified — ... increased in this sense; that your people seem to be looking more and more to your Governor as the representative of the consciousness and conscience of the people."[24]

Similar observations appeared with increasing frequency in academic journals and popular periodicals during the first two decades of the century as the emergence of the governor as chief state legislator became apparent to commentators throughout the nation. "Governor after Governor has been making himself the chief fountain of legislation in his State," wrote Gamaliel Bradford in the *Nation.* And in a letter to the *New York Evening Post,* Bradford praised the emerging potential of the chief executive, proclaiming, "Reform of the state government must be the work of the governor. The object of the legislature" was to maintain the status quo and "keep the governor in subjection, and the people in ignorance."[25] Since the legislature could not lead the citizenry toward a more progressive future, the executive had to become the Moses of state government, the policymaker guiding his people to the promised land. In 1912 John Mathews of the University of Illinois expressed the prevailing academic opinion when he wrote of "the new role of the governor" and "the increasing influence of the governor over legislation." Basic to this transformation was the governors' emerging role as spokespersons of public opinion and their exploitation of public anger to force legislative action. "No matter how jealous a legislature may be of its own prerogatives, no matter how incapable it may be of being bulldozed, wheedled, or cajoled by threats or intimidation on the part the governor," Mathews wrote, "it cannot withstand the force of pitiless publicity wielded by a vigorous, independent, and courageous governor, supported by the pressure of intelligent and aroused public opinion." Mathews believed it was "the function of the governor to keep [public opinion] aroused by a continuous and relentless application of repeated doses of publicity throughout the whole course of legislation."[26]

A number of contemporary governors were conforming to the pattern Mathews identified and fueling the enthusiasm of Bradford and others who hoped for a reform messiah. During his term as governor of New York from 1899 to 1901, Theodore Roosevelt was characteristically vigorous in the pursuit of a legislative program. In his autobiography he remarked, "More than half of my work as governor was in the direction of getting needed and important legislation."[27] Charles Evans Hughes, New York's chief executive from 1907 to 1910, also pushed a reform agenda through the state legislature, stirring cries of "government by executive usurpation," though he claimed it was "government by public opinion after discussion." Hughes characterized the governor as "the representative of the people as a whole," as compared to the legislator who pandered to the parochial interests of his district. "The general sentiment must find a voice, and in the course of our experience the people have come to look to the chief executive for that voice," the New York leader argued. "By his authority to recommend measures which he believes to be of general importance and by his freedom to support his recommendations with argument and appeal, [the governor] commands a position of influence which is not embarrassed by district limitations."[28] In adjacent New Jersey, Governor Woodrow Wilson became the preeminent promoter of the new gubernatorial role. In 1911 Governor Wilson echoed Hughes when he observed, "The whole country, since it cannot decipher the methods of its legislation, is clamoring for leadership; and a new role, which to many persons seems a little less than unconstitutional, is thrust upon our executives."[29]

Governors in the Midwest and the West were also claiming to be the oracles of public opinion with an obligation to propose reform programs and ensure their passage by the legislature. Serving as governor of Wisconsin from 1901 to 1906, Robert LaFollette conceived of his administration as a crusade to right the wrongs of the past, and any legislator who stood in his way was regarded as both morally corrupt and an enemy of the people. "I freely admit that as governor I used all the power and prestige of the office to secure the legislation that had been promised to the people," he confided in his autobiography.[30] California's Governor Hiram Johnson was equally sure of the righteousness of his cause, viewing the office of governor not primarily as a ceremonial or administrative post but as a means for applying the pressure of public opinion on the legislature and thereby securing legislation that would free Californians from the grip of the big corporations.

Throughout the nation governors perceived that their influence as lawmakers was increasing and recognized that gubernatorial recommendations generally carried considerable weight. In 1907, when preparing their study of the American executive, John H. Finley and John F. Sanderson surveyed the nation's governors on the question of the executive's power to initiate and secure legislation. Generally the responding governors reported that their initiative in legislation was "of increasing influence and importance" and that their recommendations had "great weight, not only with the legislature, but with the people." One executive replied that "of 53 matters proposed by the governor, 43 were acted upon favorably," and another claimed that "with few exceptions, during the last two sessions of the legislature, executive recommendations were enacted into law."[31] The governors were, in large part, setting the legislative agenda, and no single person was more important in securing a desired law than the executive.

Enhancing the governors' legislative clout was their veto power. In 1909 Rhode Island's governor acquired the power to disapprove legislation, leaving only one state, North Carolina, which did not grant its executive the veto. North Carolina retained this distinction for virtually the entire twentieth century. By 1917 thirty-six of the forty-eight states had empowered their governors to veto not only entire acts but also individual items in appropriation measures.[32] Since the president of the United States did not enjoy the item veto, state executives actually wielded greater disapproval power than their federal counterpart.

Moreover, legislators had to regard this executive power seriously. Although state legislatures could override their governors' vetoes by an extraordinary majority, most often two-thirds, in many states such overrides were rare or nonexistent. For example, during the period 1875 to 1973, New York's governors vetoed 23,627 bills; not one veto of a full bill was overridden.[33] Similarly, in Illinois from 1870 through 1915, governors vetoed 297 bills, and only two were passed over the executive's objection. Of the 236 vetoes from 1896 through 1915, none were overridden.[34] Some governors who proved especially offensive to legislators were not so fortunate and suffered the humiliation of repeated overrides. But generally the governor's word was final. Bolstering the effectiveness of the executive's veto power was the fact that most important legislation was passed in the final few days of the legislative session. By the time these significant measures reached the governor's desk, the legislature had adjourned and thus had no opportunity to overturn the executive's ruling.

But governors could also impress the full benefit of their wisdom upon legislators by simply threatening to disapprove measures. In fact, many observers regarded the potential veto as more significant in the lawmaking process than the governor's actual veto. At the Massachusetts Constitutional Convention of 1917–18, Josiah Quincy expressed a prevailing view when he noted, "The potential veto shapes legislative action so constantly that the actual veto does not have to be used very frequently in practice."[35] There was no physical separation of powers at the state level, as there was in the federal government. The governor's office was in the same building as the legislative chambers; the executive branch did not operate out of a White House compound a mile away from the legislative branch. Consequently, there was ready communication between legislative leaders and governors, and everyone on the floor of the legislature knew that the person with the power to kill every piece of legislation being considered was just downstairs and closely monitoring the house and senate proceedings. Through administration spokespersons in the legislature, governors expressed their views and made it clear what amendments to bills were necessary if the legislation was to receive the governor's signature.

Overall, then, governors were emerging as the policy leaders and chief legislators of their states. Executives such as Hughes, LaFollette, and Johnson campaigned not primarily as nominees of a political party but as leaders of a policy crusade. Presenting themselves as spokespersons of an angry populace, they claimed to have a mandate for change and were not reluctant to appeal over the head of the legislature to the people themselves for support in realizing their legislative program. Through public appeals and the veto power, they had considerable clout, constituting themselves as virtually a third house of the legislature. And some felt that they were the most important house.

This heightened executive initiative in policymaking encouraged a centripetal trend in state government. Legislators fought primarily to gain favors for their constituents. They battled to secure additional funds for state institutions in their districts and additional powers and privileges for their hometown municipalities. For them the state was a distributor of money and power; it was not expected to administer but to authorize others to do so. Governors, however, viewed themselves as representatives of the whole state and as such were less sympathetic to the parochialism of the legislators. The state existed to serve the interests of the people as a whole, not simply to delegate powers to cities and counties or allocate funds to whichever institutions shouted the loudest. To ensure the commonweal, state coordination and administration was necessary. According to the new breed of governors, state government had to take charge and work for the welfare of the people at large.

Business and Labor

Topping the reform agenda were proposals to limit the outrages of business corporations and protect the consumer and worker. Most notably at the state level, policymakers sought to create state public utility commissions and workers' compensation programs. These reforms would supposedly correct the imbalance of power between big business and the exploited laborer and customer. According to proponents, such regulatory schemes would shift the power of the state to the side of the little guy and achieve a new level of economic justice. But these reforms not only checked the power of the private sector; they also shifted authority from localities, judges, and juries to state administrative agencies. Acclaimed by their supporters as achieving a new level of government regulation of business, these programs also marked an advance in state administrative power.

The new state public utility commissions built on past efforts to regulate transportation lines but also deviated markedly from traditional practices. For decades the states had attempted to check the supposedly rapacious practices of railroads, with Massachusetts creating a pioneering rail commission in 1869. During the next three decades, a number of states assumed the power to fix maximum rail rates, but other public utilities remained unregulated or subject to the regulatory power of the municipalities. Franchise agreements between municipalities and public utility companies imposed some obligations on purveyors of gas, electric, streetcar, and telephone services. Yet by the first decade of the twentieth century, reformers in cities across the country had declared war on the utilities, demanding better service and lower rates. Stories abounded of corrupt deals between city council members and public utilities as city fathers reportedly sold the privilege of laying tracks and mains along and under the municipal thoroughfares in exchange for handsome bribes. Angered by the irresponsible behavior of the utilities, a growing number of urban leaders were joining the crusade for municipal ownership of public utilities. In 1905 Edward F. Dunne won the Chicago mayor's race running on a municipal ownership platform, and expressing similar beliefs, William Randolph Hearst lost the New York City mayoral election by a narrow margin. Meanwhile, Cleveland's Mayor Tom Johnson was gaining nationwide fame because of his crusade for a municipally owned streetcar system. City hall appeared on the verge of taking control of public utilities, as a growing corps of municipal leaders were intent on purchasing some services and regulating those that remained in private hands.

During the decade 1907 to 1917, however, the state governments headed off the move toward municipal control of utilities and assumed the regulatory function for themselves. At first the utility companies feared state regulatory commissions, but they soon rallied behind state regulation as a preferable alternative to municipal control. Utility magnates came to realize that state regulation not only restricted corporate freedom but also reined in the municipalities and curbed their ability to demand or harass. In their eyes, state regulation was a lesser evil than municipal ownership or a periodic shakedown by bribe-hungry city council members or local political bosses. Moreover, a growing number of commentators claimed that utility regulation required a level of expertise and coordination that most municipalities could not provide.

Consequently, one state after another refused to delegate additional regulatory responsibility to local units. The states retained the authority to regulate and exercised it through administrative agencies.

In 1907 New York and Wisconsin achieved the distinction of creating the first state public utility commissions. Led by newly elected governor Charles Evans Hughes, the legislative battle for reform in New York commanded attention from observers nationwide. Before running for governor, Hughes had served as special counsel to a legislative investigatory committee examining the gas companies, and the findings of that committee had stirred public indignation in the Empire State and a private resolve in Hughes to impose stringent state regulation of the utility corporations. New York utility moguls lined up in opposition to a strong state regulatory commission, for as Hughes recalled, "the corporations and their legislative henchmen were determined to make impossible the conferring of such an aggregation of powers."[36] The *New York Times* likewise reported that the corporations were planning "to punch holes in the bill and to emasculate or eliminate its most vital provisions."[37] New York City's Democratic legislative delegation joined the battle, rebelling at what it deemed a violation of the principle of home rule. In the opinion of those lawmakers, the city's public utilities should be regulated by the city, not the state. President Theodore Roosevelt, however, pressured Republican legislators to line up solidly behind the proposal of the Republican governor, and Hughes's regulatory scheme passed both houses of the legislature. Meanwhile, Wisconsin lawmakers were transforming that state's Railroad Commission into a public utilities commission by authorizing it to regulate not only rail lines but also heat, light, telephone, telegraph, and streetcar companies as well as waterworks.

The New York and Wisconsin laws were innovative measures that would inspire proponents of public utility regulation in other states. New York's law actually created two public utility commissions, both appointed by the governor. The one commission regulated utilities in New York City, and the other, known as the upstate commission, was responsible for the rest of the state. Moreover, in 1910 the upstate commission was assigned responsibility for regulating telephone and telegraph services throughout the state, including New York City. Both commissions had the power to fix maximum rates and order improvements in service. In addition, they had to approve all franchises, all new services and extensions of services, all issuances of stock or bonds, and all sales or mergers of utility corporations. Wisconsin's Railroad Commission had equally broad authority. Especially controversial was the Wisconsin commission's control over not only private corporations but also municipally owned lighting plants, waterworks, and other utilities. The state of Wisconsin was protecting the public from the malfeasance of both local government and the private entrepreneur.

Other states soon emulated the examples of Wisconsin and New York. By the close of 1912, fifteen states had provided for state regulation of public utilities, and during the next year seven more were added to the list.[38] In 1909 the contagion of regulation spread across New York's borders to adjoining Vermont, where the legislature created a state public utility commission. The powerful New England Telephone and Telegraph Company did nothing to block the reform, but the many small independent telephone companies in the state attacked the commission proposal, believing it would favor their larger rival.[39] This was a precursor to coming events in other states. The large and supposedly rapacious utilities that the proposed commissions were intended to control were withdrawing any opposition to the reform.

When Illinois framed its public utilities law in 1913, there was no longer serious disagreement over the desirability of government regulation. That was conceded. Debate focused on which government should regulate—state or local. Chicagoans sought to ensure that municipal authorities regulated the Windy City's utilities; others favored a single state commission to regulate all utilities throughout Illinois. As finally enacted, the public utilities bill denied Chicago and other cities a "home rule" exemption from state supervision and instead authorized comprehensive state control of all utility companies. Chicago leaders urged Governor Edward F. Dunne to veto the act. Yet because of "a crying demand for the control of all of these utilities as the result of the rapacity of many of them, and their scandalous exploitation of the public in the past," Dunne felt compelled to allow the measure to stand.[40] Many Chicago leaders were outraged. Charles Merriam, professor of political science at the University of Chicago and a former mayoral candidate, claimed the legislature's action was "as daring a raid as a pirate crew ever made upon a rich and defenseless city." According to Merriam, the bill authorizing state regulation "was passed in the interest of public utility corporations, and was the crowning climax of the corporation legislation" in Illinois. State supervision survived, however, and the forces of local home rule were repelled.[41]

Elsewhere the same debate was raging, with proponents of municipal supervision conducting a largely unsuccessful campaign against state centralization. Confronted with a proposal for state supervision, the Minnesota Home Rule League responded by issuing a blistering report on the powerful Railroad Commission in neighboring Wisconsin. The league concluded that the "inspiration for state regulation [came] from the public utility companies to be regulated" and that "state regulation ha[d] not given the people the benefit of as favorable rates, nor as good service, as many cities with home rule powers ha[d] secured for themselves."[42] Local leaders in the Keystone State organized the Municipal Home Rule League of Pennsylvania, dedicated to effecting "amendment or repeal of the public service company law and such other laws or parts of laws as affect the inherent and constitutional rights of municipalities and the people in their self-government."[43] Although he admitted that the state public utilities commission had been "a great benefit to New York," New York City mayor John Purroy Mitchel believed a state commission grew "remote and in a measure intangible" and for that reason "thought sympathetically of a plan to establish a local commission, which [would] be responsible to the people of the city, which [would] speak the voice and interest of the people of the locality and be alive to the demands and necessities of the community."[44]

Self-interested corporations were not the only supporters of state supervision. Many leaders with impeccably progressive credentials believed that the state should not delegate the important responsibility of utility regulation to localities. For example, LaFollette progressives in Wisconsin, including Railroad Commission chair Balthasar H. Meyer, stood staunchly behind the broad powers of the Railroad Commission, believing central control was necessary given the economic and technological realities of the age. Meyer believed that the state regulatory commissions were created in reaction to "the relative or absolute failure of cities to perform such functions" and "the inability of cities to accomplish anything at all in the way of insuring to the public reasonably adequate service at reasonable rates." This was in part due to corruption in local government. "The ostensible cry may be the invasion of 'home rule,'" Meyer remarked, "but in reality it is frequently only the wail of the local politician who can no longer rest comfortably on the backs of the utilities in order to accomplish his selfish if not corrupt desires." Moreover, most municipalities could not handle the task. "Very few cities in any of our States can afford to establish and maintain properly equipped laboratories, make expensive statistical compilations bearing upon every branch of service, organize and maintain staffs of men skilled along the various lines of engineering, statistics, etc."[45]

Halford Erickson, LaFollette's labor commissioner and a member of the Wisconsin Railroad Commission, seconded Meyer's views and emphasized that many utilities no longer served a single municipality but operated over a broader area. Consequently, state regulation was necessary since "regulation in order to be effective [had to] be coextensive with the operations of the utility which [was] to be controlled." Of the 333 telephone exchanges in Wisconsin, 294 served both rural and urban customers. Similarly, of the 277 electric, gas, and water utilities replying to a commission survey, 106 operated beyond the limits of a single municipality, with one company providing service in more than twenty cities and villages as well as in the surrounding countryside.[46] Given the interurban nature of many utilities, Erickson believed that they could not be subject to municipal control. To ensure reasonable service and fares throughout the companies' utility networks, the state had to act.

Others also noted the limits of local supervision. Milo R. Maltbie of the New York state public utility commission recognized that "with electric lines encircling several counties, . . . with natural gas mains extending from one end of the state to the other, . . . the problem assume[d] a complexity never before realized."[47] Clyde L. King, an economist at the University of Pennsylvania and an expert on utility regulation, concluded, "As the more difficult problems of utility regulation are State-wide problems, they can be adequately coped with only, by State commissions."[48] Minnesota's Governor Adolph O. Eberhart presented an especially thorough defense of state control of public utilities, claiming that "telephones, telegraphs, electric and steam railroads [were] all intermunicipal and [could] not possibly for lack of jurisdiction be regulated by the municipalities." He emphasized further that most cities could not afford to maintain the expert staff necessary to regulate utilities. Even though Minneapolis, Saint Paul, and Duluth might be able to foot the bill, he asked, "Why should the taxpayers of those cities pay for three sets of experts and equipment when one set is not only sufficient but can serve all the cities better?"[49]

Devotees of municipal regulation blustered and fumed, but the centralizers were ascendant. During the second decade of the twentieth century, regulation of public utilities became a standard state function as legislators and governors acceded to arguments for uniform, expert state administration and deviated from the localism of the past. The states were responding to change, yielding to proponents of central control such as Meyer. The *New York Times* stated, "In all these years, when the corporations have been coming to their estate of power and wealth, the States that created them have been slothful and weak." The *Times* believed that state public utility legislation reflected "a reawakening of State pride and the sense of State duty."[50] Disregarding laissez-faire and localism, the states were resolving to exercise a new function and expand their administrative role.

But the public utility commissions were not the only signs of an expanding sense of state duty. At the same time that the states were centralizing control over the gas, electric, telephone, and streetcar companies, they were also developing administrative agencies to bring order to the awarding of compensation to injured workers. Rather than leave this to the chance of a court verdict,

states endeavored to rationalize the procedure, enhancing the economic security of both employee and employer. No longer delegating the resolution of
injury claims to the courts, the states were taking charge and fashioning the
administrative structure of workers' compensation programs.

Before 1910 workers seeking compensation from their employers for on-
the-job injuries had to turn to the courts, where they faced an uphill battle. In
the courts employers benefited from three common law defenses. First was the
assumption-of-risk defense, meaning that workers assumed the ordinary risk
incident to their jobs. If injured owing to this risk, they could not collect damages. Second, they had to cope with the contributory negligence defense. When
workers' injuries could be in any way traced to their own negligence, they
could not recover any compensation. Third, they had to overcome the fellow-
servant doctrine. According to this rule, a maimed worker could not collect
from an employer if the worker's injury resulted from the negligence of a fellow worker. In other words, it was difficult to prove an employer's liability. The
system was skewed to favor management.

Yet by the first decade of the twentieth century, employers were growing
increasingly nervous over the issue of liability. If the injured worker overcame
the common law defenses and proved employer liability, sympathetic juries
might well award heavy damages that could ruin a small business. Furthermore, popular opposition to the common law defenses was growing, and legislatures threatened to weaken or eliminate these legal bulwarks so valuable to
the employer. In addition, clashes over on-the-job injuries were fueling already
fiery employer-employee relations. Employers might avoid the payment of damages, but they reaped an ample fund of ill will from uncompensated injuries.

Thus, by that time a broad range of concerned citizens were attacking the
traditional reliance on court proceedings. Personal injury cases were costly to
the public and seemed to benefit primarily ambulance-chasing lawyers. Criticizing the "enormous social and economic waste" of the traditional approach,
one New York authority reported that "every year about 60 percent of the time
of the jury trial and the first appeal courts in New York [was] occupied by the
consideration of accident cases." A Minnesota business leader similarly asserted that the citizens of Minneapolis's Hennepin County had "paid out more
money in the cost of trials of personal injury cases in that county than the total
amount of the verdicts which were recovered by plaintiffs." Repeatedly critics
argued that lengthy litigation proved costly to both employee and employer. In
1910 the Minnesota Bureau of Labor, Industries and Commerce concluded that
a "fundamental evil" of the existing system was "its slowness and uncertainty."
Widows, orphans, and injured workers had to "wait for the slow processes of

the law to work out their salvation," and "at best their chances of success [were] a mere gamble."[51]

Litigation was a poor means for providing financial support to victims of industrial accidents, and proponents of workers' compensation schemes sought to eliminate this reliance on trials and juries. A Wisconsin reformer asked point-blank, "For what is a workmen's compensation act enacted if not to decrease litigation?" And the Wisconsin Supreme Court recognized the stupidity of relying on personal injury suits. "To speak of the common-law personal injury action as a remedy for this problem is to jest with serious subjects, to give a stone to one who asks for bread," the court observed. "The terrible economic waste, the overwhelming temptation to the commission of perjury and the relatively small proportion of the sums recovered which comes to the injured parties in such actions, condemn them as wholly inadequate to meet the difficulty."[52]

Recognizing the validity of such criticisms, a number of state legislatures authorized investigatory committees to examine the problem and consider European procedures for compensating injured workers. In 1909, at the behest of Governor Hughes, New York's solons created such a commission, which was expected to conduct a "special and expert inquiry into the question relating to employer's liability and compensation for workmen's injuries."[53] That same year Minnesota and Wisconsin also created investigatory commissions, and these midwestern investigators met with their New York counterparts at a conference in Atlantic City in July 1909 to share information and exchange ideas.[54] In 1910 eight additional states created commissions to consider the question, and nine more did so in 1911.[55] The campaign for workers' compensation, like that for state regulation of public utilities, was rapidly spreading across the nation as one state after another confronted the flaws in the existing system and considered solutions.

The investigations soon produced legislation; New York led the way in 1910. Ten more states, ranging from New Hampshire in the East to California in the West, adopted workers' compensation acts the following year. By 1915 thirty-one of the forty-eight states could boast of such laws, and five years later forty-two states had taken action.[56] During the second decade of the century, only six states, all in the South, failed to enact compensation legislation. The laws differed in details, but they all eliminated the requirement that an injured worker prove employer negligence to collect compensation. No matter who was at fault, every employee was entitled to compensation for injuries incurred from on-the-job accidents. Since no proof of liability was necessary, there would no longer be inordinate delays in the awarding of aid to workers or their survivors, and legal expenses would be reduced. Some states, such as Ohio, Washington, and Wyoming, compensated workers from a state insurance fund to which employers contributed. In other states, employers could procure insurance from private casualty companies or mutual employer associations. But the principal goal in each of the states was compensation for the worker with as little waste of time and money as possible.

To administer the plan, most states relied on industrial boards or commissions that were empowered to settle all claims. In 1915 twenty-four of the thirty-one workers' compensation states had such boards. But in seven states workers had to turn to the courts to settle claims.[57] Since this latter procedure could again lead to unnecessary expense and delay, most advocates of workers' compensation criticized those states which continued to rely on the courts. For example, New Jersey's compensation law provided for court administration and consequently was found wanting. In 1915 a committee of the American Association for Labor Legislation exposed the New Jersey situation, reporting that "in many cases no compensation whatever was paid[,] petitions to the courts had frequently resulted in irregular settlements[, and] often injured workmen had been induced to settle for amounts less than they were entitled to receive under the law, and judges had approved such settlements."[58]

The prevailing trend was toward reliance on a state administrative agency rather than the courts. Most states embraced the administrative commission option in their original workers' compensation legislation, and others were gradually to recognize the limitations of court procedure. For example, in 1921 Minnesota shifted responsibility for the administration of the workers' compensation law from the district courts to a newly created industrial commission.[59] Though one of the first states to enact compensation legislation, Kansas did not provide for commission administration of the scheme until 1927.[60] Finally, however, slow and costly court procedure yielded to state administrative control.

Through both the workers' compensation programs and the public utility commissions, then, the states were asserting unprecedented central supervision in an attempt to impose uniformity and rationalize policy outcomes. Public utilities were not to be left to the mercies of the many municipalities, and injured workers were not to be subject to the caprice of a multitude of juries hearing cases across the state. Expert commissions staffed by specialists in utility regulation and workers' compensation law would endeavor to ensure some order and predictability in the fixing of rates and service standards and the awarding of compensation. This was the ideal emerging in the early twentieth century. The administrative agencies did not always realize the goal of a fairer, more just economic system. But the prevailing opinion among policymakers was that state administrators could more nearly approach that goal than local governments or the courts.

Highways

By 1890 America's rutted and sometimes impassable roadways were perhaps the most obvious reminders of the shortcomings of amateur, decentralized rule. States had delegated responsibility for highways to counties, townships, or road districts as well as authorizing private corporations to construct toll roads as profit-making enterprises. Virtually none of the rural thoroughfares were satisfactory arteries of transportation, but from 1840 to 1890 the development of a dense web of rail lines had lessened the need to rely on the inadequate highways. At the close of the century, however, the states were shifting course, withdrawing the carte blanche formerly granted localities and asserting new control over road construction and maintenance. The public was demanding better highways, and the states felt compelled to take charge and ensure a higher level of expertise and coordination. Just as state administrators were gaining the upper hand in utility regulation and workers' compensation programs, they were also assuming control of rural thoroughfares, contributing to the overall centripetal trend in state government.

This shift toward state control of highways was a product of the good-roads movement that swept the nation during the 1890s. Disgusted by the condition of roadways, a diverse group of citizens agitated for reform. Merchants and railroad corporations believed better roads would boost business, channeling increased quantities of farm products to trading centers and rail facilities and enabling farmers to shop more often in the county seat. Educators and clergy claimed that improved thoroughfares would increase attendance at schools and churches, thereby upgrading the moral, spiritual, and intellectual life of rural America. Especially energetic in their efforts to upgrade roadways was the growing corps of bicyclists, who exerted pressure on lawmakers through their national organization, the League of American Wheelmen. In 1894 the New Jersey state commissioner of public roads acknowledged "the valuable assistance of the League of American Wheelmen, who from the date of their organization began an agitation for better roads through the State" and whose "persistent demand and numerous publications, distributed with a liberality seldom equaled, ha[d] done much to bring about the movement for 'good roads.'"[61] Cyclists wanted smooth, passable rural roads, so they could satisfy their bicycling passion and pedal throughout the countryside. The deplorable state of rural roads was an obstacle to their mobility, and in the opinion of the League of American Wheelmen, it was an obstacle that had to be removed.

Cyclists and other good-roads advocates laid much of the blame for the poor condition of highways on incompetent local authorities. In 1893 a Massachusetts commission on the improvement of highways emphasized that lack of expertise among local road officials. "These officers who have charge of the highways have at present no other sources of information as to their art save that which may be traditional in the locality," the commission reported. And given the short tenure of most local road officials, they were not likely to learn much from experience. Referring to this turnover in office, the Massachusetts commissioners concluded, "If this method had been devised to secure the perpetuation of bad roads, it could not have been more effectively adapted to the end."[62] At the International Good Roads Congress of 1901, a Pennsylvania official described the system of local road supervisors in his state as characterized by "the selection, not of the fittest, but of the most unfit." Localities chose men who were "willing to stand out on the public roads for a dollar and a half a day and watch two or three other men do nothing."[63]

Throughout the nation good-roads proponents concurred with this judgment and claimed that most money spent on rural thoroughfares was wasted. In 1894 New Jersey's commissioner of public roads claimed that local expenditures were "practically thrown away." He argued that the chief drawback of township control of highways was "the lack of any practical, contiguous system of building and maintaining different portions of the same road where it [ran] into or across two or three townships."[64] A decent roadway might become a rutted path at the township line, for the quality of the thoroughfare depended on the locality. Rhode Island's Board of Public Roads similarly emphasized that local spending failed to provide a continuous stretch of first-rate highway. Centralization would ensure "not here a rich town and good roads, and next a poor town with bad roads, but ... main thoroughfares ... of the same standard, open to all."[65] In 1896 California's Bureau of Highways also reported on the waste of local road funds, claiming that they had been used to "pay political debts" or "about election times to further political interests." Moreover, the bureau discovered that in several counties officials hired for road jobs "those owing them for merchandise, food, board, or drinks."[66] If deadbeats could not pay their bar bills, a local saloon keeper–road supervisor could put them on the county payroll and thereby ensure remuneration.

Local control was thus indicted on a number of counts. It perpetuated amateur efforts at road building and stymied expert direction. It wasted money and was unsystematic. Adequate development of long stretches of highway was virtually impossible if each locality retained its independent authority to approve and fund construction and repairs. And local control was conducive to petty corruption as township and county road supervisors profited from their handling of the public's money. Thus, by the close of the nineteenth century, the traditional system of road administration seemed old-fashioned. The diverse interests that rallied in support of the good-roads movement demanded the application of state-financed expertise and the creation of highways worthy of the modern age.

The mounting complaints and agitation produced legislative results, with seven states launching a highway program in the 1890s. In 1891 the New Jersey legislature led the way by enacting a state-aid law, and three years later it created the post of commissioner of public roads. Under New Jersey's program, the state paid one-third of the cost of state-aid roads, and the county financed the other two-thirds, less one-tenth, which would be paid by the property holders abutting the roadway. Previously townships had financed all public roads in New Jersey, but now the larger units of the county and state were to assume the burden for state-aid thoroughfares. Other state-aid measures followed in Vermont in 1892, Massachusetts in 1893, Connecticut two years later, and New York in 1898. The state's share of construction costs varied, the trend being for the state to shoulder an increasing portion of the expense. For example, in 1895 Connecticut agreed to pay one-third of the costs, but in 1897 the legislature increased the state's share to one-half. In 1899, in a message to the legislature, Connecticut's governor lamented about the plight of "the poorer towns of the state . . . already burdened in keeping open and making passable their many miles of highways" and urged that the state increase its contribution to three-fourths.[67] The legislature complied with the request, boosting the state's share to three-fourths for poor towns and two-thirds for more affluent communities.

Yet the states attached strings to their aid, requiring localities to submit to state supervision. State road authorities had to approve the surveys and construction specifications for state-aid roads. These highways had to meet state standards, for the states did not intend to perpetuate the long-standing tradition of incompetent work and wasted expenditures. This central supervision, however, did not deter localities from participating in the program. Already in 1894 New Jersey's state commissioner reported demands for aid "from more than half of the counties in the State," and the specifications then on file absorbed the existing "annual State allowance for two years in advance."[68] Similarly, according to the Connecticut highway commissioner's report for 1900, 159 of the 168 towns in the state had participated in the program during the first 5½ years of its existence.[69]

After 1900 the forces of state control gathered further momentum and secured additional highway legislation throughout the nation. By 1905 nineteen states had some sort of central road agency, and the principle of state action was taking root not only along the east and west coasts but also in such states as Michigan, Ohio, Illinois, and Iowa.[70] Some of this legislation only opened the door slightly to state supervision, appropriating funds for the development of state expertise but authorizing little state control. For example, the Illinois Highway Commission created in 1905 was empowered primarily to investigate and experiment, with the state highway engineer devoting his time to the preparation of instructive bulletins and the laying out of experimental roads intended to promote local effort. Not until 1913 did Illinois authorize a comprehensive system of state-aid highways.[71] Likewise, as established in 1904, the Iowa Highway Commission was largely an educational and research agency. Operating as an adjunct of Iowa's land-grant college in Ames, the commission explained in its 1906 report, "It is the aim and desire of the commission to build up an engineering bureau of practical men who can go into any part of the State at the call of the proper authorities to help them in whatever work they have in hand."[72]

Adding to the clout of the good-roads cause during these years was the growing number of automobile owners. In 1901 New York imposed the first state license fee on automobiles and collected a mere $954 that year. By 1909 there were 294,000 licensed automobiles in the United States, and in 1914 the figure was up to 1,711,000. By this latter date, forty-six of the forty-eight states levied license fees, producing a total of $12 million, most of which was earmarked for funding highway construction. Between 1904 and 1914, state and local expenditures for highways rose threefold, from $80 million to $240 million.[73]

State engineers needed every dollar of this increased sum, for the wave of new automobiles added significantly to the financial and technical problems of road builders. "The advent of the automobile has doubled the expense of maintaining the state highways," the Massachusetts Highway Commission reported in 1908.[74] But if the state commissions were challenged, local authorities proved totally inadequate. Township road supervisors who were incompetent to accommodate horse and bicycle traffic were clearly ill suited to the automobile age. The need for centralized control was more pressing than ever before.

Responding to these demands, some states were committing munificent sums to highways and supplanting localities as the primary source of road funds. In 1904 Maryland lawmakers authorized a state-aid program and an annual appropriation of $200,000 to pay half the cost of state-aid roads. Two years later, Maryland began work on a highway linking Baltimore and Washington, D.C., to be known as State Road 1, and in 1908 the legislature authorized a state system of main arteries to be financed solely by the state. To fund this ambitious scheme, in 1908 Maryland solons approved a $5 million bond issue, two years later authorized another $1 million in bonds, and in 1912 gave their imprimatur to an additional debt of $3.17 million. In 1911 Maryland's state government expended a total of $7 million, of which $2.6 million was for roads. As a result of this progressive centralization of authority, by 1913 the Maryland state government spent two and a half times as much for roads as Maryland's local governments, making it one of three states in which state funding for highways exceeded local funding.[75]

New York was one of the other two states in which state government shouldered the bulk of road financing. In fact, New York's effort dwarfed that of its fellow commonwealths. In 1905 the voters approved a $50 million bond issue for highway construction and in 1912 a second $50 million issue. By comparison, in 1906 the state's total expenditures amounted to only $30 million.[76] New York road builders were discovering what their colleagues in other states would soon realize. The states were assuming a costly responsibility that ate up ever-increasing appropriations and could produce a mounting public debt. By centralizing highway construction, state governments were embarking on a program that would bloat state budgets and impose an awesome burden on state finances.

By the second decade of the twentieth century, a growing number of state highway officials and good-roads advocates believed that the federal government should relieve some of this burden by contributing to the road-building effort. The federal Constitution specifically authorized the national government to establish post roads, and during the early nineteenth century Congress had taken full responsibility for the funding and construction of the National Road, which linked the eastern seaboard with the trans-Appalachian West. But after the 1830s, the federal government largely withdrew from the business of road building. In 1893 Congress created the Office of Road Inquiry in the Department of Agriculture, which was to investigate road-building techniques and disseminate information on the subject. Renamed the Bureau of Public Roads, this agency continued to pursue its educational and research efforts during the first decade of the twentieth century, but federal financing for highway construction was not forthcoming. The American Automobile Association, founded in 1902, lobbied for federal funding, organizing the first Federal Aid Convention in Washington, D.C., in January 1912. The following year a second convention stepped up the pressure as the various good-roads groups joined in an effort to pry open the federal treasury.

Perhaps the most significant advocate of federal aid was the American Association of State Highway Officials. For years state highway engineers had discussed the creation of a professional organization for sharing information and promoting road construction, but early in 1914 a few state officials decided it was time to take action. George P. Coleman, Virginia's highway commissioner, wrote to his colleagues urging the founding of such an association, which would advance the interests of the officials and enable them to "work as a unit for national help." In November 1914 the association was formally organized, and the following month representatives of the state highway departments met in Washington, D.C., "to assist in drafting a bill to be presented to Congress, which [would] embody a plan of Federal cooperation in road construction."[77] During the following year the association's members arrived at a consensus and submitted a proposed bill to Congress, which became the basis for the Federal-Aid Road Act of 1916.

This act provided for $75 million in federal highway funds to be distributed among the states over the next five years. Each state would have to match the federal contribution with an equal sum, so altogether $150 million in state and federal funds would be allocated for road construction. The states would be in charge of planning and constructing the federal-aid highways, subject to federal approval and inspection. To qualify for the funding, however, each state had to maintain a highway department that would be responsible for implementing the program. Thirty-three states already had state highway departments sufficient to qualify for the aid, but this federal legislation would force the other fifteen states, mostly in the South and the West, to join the majority and centralize their road efforts.[78] If a state continued to delegate all responsibility for roads to its county officials and refused to establish a modern state highway program, it would have to forgo its share of the federal largesse.

Thus the state highway officials profited in two ways from the act they sponsored. They received federal funds, which were especially welcome in the smaller, less affluent commonwealths. But they also achieved their goal of enhanced central control by professional road builders, for the federal legislation required that the states and not the localities assume primary responsibility for highway development. Since New Jersey's pioneering legislation of 1891, state highway officials had gradually tightened their grasp on road building. In 1916 the Association of State Highway Officials confirmed the triumph of the state over the locality in the Federal-Aid Road Act. Contemporaries recognized that federal financing was a boon to state highway centralizers. Before the passage of the 1916 act, a good-roads advocate noted "the importance of state management in any scheme of Federal aid," observing that "all of the measures which ha[d] received attention by Congress provide[d] as a requisite to Federal aid the existence of a highway department for each state participating in the benefits of such legislation." "It must be evident," the commentator continued, "that a well-organized state highway department affords just the agency for direct supervision of improvements financed jointly by the state and the nation."[79] Following the adoption of the act, the federal Office of Public Roads also emphasized the law's contribution to centralization at the state level. "The most important outcome of this Federal legislation was the enactment of State laws providing effective State control of a large measure of road work," reported the director of that office in 1917.[80]

During the quarter-century from 1891 to 1916, then, the state highway officials gradually expanded their authority over local governments and assumed primary responsibility for road construction. These state officials also drew the federal government into the business of road building and in the process enhanced the role of the state highway departments. The Federal-Aid Road Act of 1916 was not an example of unwanted aggression by a Congress hostile to states' rights. The federal government was a welcome ally in the ongoing effort to strengthen the position of state engineers vis-à-vis local governments. In question was the willingness of the federal government to provide a meaningful cash contribution. Spread over forty-eight states and five years, $75 million was not a lavish appropriation. New York, though ready to accept the federal money, would received only $3.76 million under the new federal law, hardly a munificent sum for a state that had already contracted $100 million in highway debt.[81] During the 1920s state highway officials would discover whether the federal government was a generous or a frugal ally.

Higher Education

As state administrators were relieving municipalities of their responsibility for public utilities and counties of their control over highways, there was a growing desire for the states to assert a new degree of supervision also over their disparate institutions of higher education. In the nineteenth century, state legislatures created scores of public colleges and universities but left the governance of these schools in the hands of boards of trustees who were more dedicated to the perceived interests of the institution than to those of the state. Each college and university followed a narrow path of self-interest, and no one seemed to be guarding the commonweal effectively.

This was especially evident in the duplication of programs at state institutions. Every university and college aspired to greatness, and in the minds of most higher education administrators, greatness meant a broad range of academic programs worthy of a true university. Few of the agricultural colleges created under the Morrill Act of 1862 were satisfied to remain institutes solely for plow handlers; they sought academic respectability by expanding into other fields traditionally reserved to liberal arts universities. Though created to offer only two-year teacher training programs, many state normal schools dreamed of becoming four-year institutions granting college degrees and duplicating the efforts of the state university. Meanwhile, liberal arts universities were eager to expand their offerings and award degrees in engineering, home economics, and other "applied science" fields. As a result, sparsely populated states that could scarcely support one college found themselves financing two undersized engineering programs, one at the state agricultural college and the other at the university. One state after another was funding the academic aspirations of every ambitious institution, without regard for the interests of the burdened taxpayer.

During the early twentieth century, state lawmakers grew increasingly restive with this narrow-minded pursuit of glory, for the financial burden of higher education was growing rapidly as colleges and universities ate up an ever-larger share of the state's funds. State expenditures for Iowa's three competing institutions rose ninefold between 1895 and 1914, whereas total state expenditures increased only fourfold. Likewise, in Kansas the state's outlay for the university, the agricultural college, and four normal schools soared ninefold over the same period as compared to an overall doubling of state spending.[82] Not everywhere was the increase so dramatic, but for the nation as a whole, the share of state expenditures devoted to higher education rose from 7 percent in 1902 to 10 percent in 1922.[83] Enrollments were rising rapidly and accounted for much of this increase. But state legislators attributed some of the burden to the waste arising from unnecessary duplication of effort.

This was not a problem in every state. Some states did not maintain a separate agricultural college but instead assigned the teaching of agriculture to the state university. Most states checked the ambitions of their normal schools and carefully restricted them to the training of elementary school teachers. For example, the University of Wisconsin at Madison had no rivals in Wisconsin. All branches of higher learning were taught at the university, and the state's normal schools were made to know their inferior place within the educational structure. California, Illinois, Minnesota, and Nebraska likewise maintained a single university responsible for all education above the normal-school level.

A number of eastern states had no state university but only an agricultural college and thus were spared the problem of duplication. But twenty-three states operated two or more state institutions granting college degrees.[84]

To the increasing distress of legislators and educational experts, these colleges too often battled fiercely for distinction and money. In 1916 a report of the federal Bureau of Education asserted that, given the existence of two or more state institutions, it was "the responsibility of the State . . . to make a coherent plan to prevent conflict." The need for such a state plan was "the major problem in educational administration in the United States."[85] This was the emerging consensus of the early twentieth century. The states had to take charge, impose some coordination, and curb the rampant parochialism of the individual institutions of higher education.

Iowa was among the states responding to this imperative. The state maintained a liberal arts university at Iowa City, an agricultural land-grant college at Ames, and a teacher-training institute at Cedar Falls. Both the university and the agricultural college offered engineering programs and graduate work in the sciences. In 1909 the normal school at Cedar Falls secured the more elevated title of teachers college, and as such it offered a full four-year course of study, including liberal arts courses, and awarded a bachelor's degree in education. Meanwhile, the university at Iowa City also maintained a school of education, which duplicated the offerings in Cedar Falls.

With each institution clamoring for ever-increasing appropriations and none willing to cede an inch of curricular ground, the state's legislators grew increasingly exasperated and in 1904 created a joint committee to study the problem of unified control. Known as the Whipple Committee, this investigating body submitted a blistering report in 1906. "The governing boards and the presidents and faculties of each of our educational institutions press their respective claims upon the legislature without regard to the needs of the other institutions," the committee observed. "A spirit of rivalry is engendered that is, in many respects, detrimental to the educational interests of the state." According to the Whipple Committee, "the problem [was] how to bring about harmony of action and uniformity of methods at [the state] educational institutions [and] secure to the state good and efficient management."[86] The committee's answer was to eliminate each institution's governing board and to place the three schools under a single central policymaking body. Iowa would then have a system of higher education moving with concerted effort in one direction, not three competing institutions obsessed with their own fortunes and oblivious to the broader interests of the state as a whole. Just as the state needed to coordinate road construction and ensure that highways met at the county lines, so the state also had to coordinate higher education and ensure that curricular lines met. A coordinated system of higher education was just as necessary as a coordinated network of roadways, and both required the state to assume greater control than it had in the past. Not everyone agreed with the Whipple Committee, and the president and faculty of the state college in Ames were especially outspoken in their opposition to any loss of autonomy.[87] But in 1909 the legislature approved a new governing system, placing the three institutions under a single board of education composed of nine gubernatorial appointees.

The result was not a new era of harmony, for in 1912 the board presented a controversial scheme to reduce wasteful duplication. Most notably, the board recommended terminating all engineering programs at Iowa City and making Ames solely responsible for engineering education in the state. Iowa City, however, was to gain a monopoly on home economics and on advanced work in the pure sciences; Cedar Falls would be restricted to a three-year program and would no longer be able to compete with the university in offering a four-year bachelor of education course of study. With unusual accord, all three schools agreed that the board's plan was totally unacceptable. Alumni angrily denounced the board's effort to prune programs from their beloved alma maters, and both candidates for governor rejected the proposed changes. The legislature urged the board to retreat, and in 1913 it complied with this request. In a pattern that was to become increasingly familiar throughout the nation, state efforts to check the empire building of their colleges and universities were stymied. Whereas the states had overcome the objections of municipalities to central regulation of public utilities and local obstructions to a centralized highway program, they would prove less successful in overcoming educational parochialism.

State highway officials had enlisted the help of the federal government in overcoming localism, but such a strategy did not succeed with regard to higher education. In 1915 the board of education asked the federal commissioner of education to conduct a survey of higher education in Iowa, and the federal report submitted in 1916 recommended a thoroughgoing effort to eliminate the chronic overlapping of functions. Agreeing with the board's recommendations of 1912, the federal survey held that "the continuance of two schools of engineering" was "uneconomical and indefensible." It argued further that "the atmosphere of the institution at Cedar Falls [was] not unequivocally collegiate," and thus the students receiving "training there for the bachelor's degree [were] likely to miss certain valuable elements in such training." The federal investigators spared no words in expressing their disgust for the rivalry among Iowa's institutions. The interinstitutional bitterness and suspicion was "a devastating blight fastened upon the whole educational system of the State" and "the principal cause of the State's educational woes."[88]

Alumni, faculty, and administrators were no more willing to heed the federal experts than they were their own state board. Duplication and hostility persisted, and during the early 1920s personal enmity between the presidents of the Ames and Iowa City institutions precluded harmonious cooperation. The central board of education remained in charge of Iowa's institutions of higher learning and in many ways proved an effective governing body. But the bitter conflict of 1912 and the triumph of institutional self-interest over state-wide coordination demonstrated that the state could not pull the reins on its colleges and universities and expect an obedient response. In 1912 the board of education had tugged at the reins, and the schools at Ames, Iowa City, and Cedar Falls had continued to gallop off in various directions.

Iowa's experience attracted considerable attention in higher education circles, for the situation in that state presented a classic example of the problems of overlapping responsibilities and seemed a portent of future problems elsewhere. "What has happened in Iowa with reference to duplication will in the future take place in other states where the university, the agricultural college, the school of mines, and the normal schools, having the scope of teachers' colleges, exist," wrote the president of the University of Wisconsin in 1911.[89] Iowa was not an unusual case. Instead, the Iowa scenario was already being repeated in other states.

For example, the frontier state of Montana was struggling to achieve coordination among its university in Missoula, its agricultural college in Bozeman, its school of mines in Butte, and its normal school in Dillon. With a population of only 376,000 and a total of 141 engineering students in 1911, Montana maintained three separate engineering programs, one each at the university, the agricultural college, and the school of mines.[90] Taxpayers complained of the wasteful duplication, and President E. B. Craighead of the university campaigned unsuccessfully for the consolidation of all the schools into one enlarged institution at Missoula. Boosters in Bozeman, Butte, and Dillon understandably balked at this solution, yet virtually everyone recognized that Montana suffered from an excess of state institutions.

In 1909 Montana's legislature placed all four of the schools under a single board of education and four years later created a consolidated University of Montana to be headed by a chancellor with offices in the state capital of Helena. Each campus would survive with a separate president and a local governing board, but the chancellor would be in charge of the system as a whole and provide overarching coordination.[91] The new scheme, however, did not permanently check the centrifugal forces dominating Montana education. Responding to pressure from areas of the state that lacked institutions of higher education, during the 1920s Montana's legislature created two additional institutions, Eastern Montana College in Billings and Northern Montana College in Havre. Local sentiment prevailed, and the result was six institutions of higher education in a state that could barely support one.

Other states also tried to assert central control over their institutions of higher education, though support for the movement was not universal. In 1905 the Florida legislature abolished the six existing state schools of higher education, all low-grade institutions barely deserving the title of college. The state replaced them with four new institutions, all under a single board of control. To safeguard against undue local influence, no member of this central board could be from a county in which any of the institutions were located. Though a policy clash soon led to the dismissal of the state university president, the scheme of central supervision seemed an improvement over the old pattern of dispersed control. By the beginning of the second decade of the twentieth century, the new state university president said that under no circumstances would he want to "go back to the independent boards and their scrambles at each meeting of the legislature for support of their respective institutions."[92] In 1913 Idaho's legislature established a state board of education to serve as the sole governing board of the state's institutions, and this body was to appoint a commissioner of education to ensure professional oversight. Imposing a degree of central supervision unusual in the United States, the Idaho plan was, according to one expert observer, "a fairly close approximation to the European Ministry of Education."[93] To the west in Oregon, the legislature of 1909 authorized a board of higher curricula with "the exclusive purpose and object" of determining "what courses of study or departments, if any, shall be duplicated in the higher institutions of Oregon" and to "define the courses of study . . . to be offered and conducted by each such institution." In its initial orders, however, the board indicated its reluctance to act too boldly when it basically authorized the continuation of existing programs, permitting both the university and the agricultural college to maintain departments of civil and electrical engineering.[94] Similarly, in Washington the creation of a Joint Board of Higher Curricula marked only a temporary truce in the turf battles between the university in Seattle and the land-grant college in Pullman.

Despite the bad news from a number of states, the notion of central coordination remained a serious topic of debate and a source of contention in the educational politics of states throughout the nation. Between 1896 and 1913, South Dakota, Kansas, Georgia, Mississippi, and West Virginia, as well as the states previously discussed, all established central coordinating boards for their colleges and universities. Moreover, Virginia created a commission to consider methods for achieving a "harmonious education system," and North Dakota likewise appointed an investigatory body to consider "the unifying and systematizing of the educational system," the "removal of unnecessary duplication," and the prevention of "any unseemly competition" among the state's institutions.[95]

The experiences of Iowa and Montana, however, were representative of the problems that educational centralizers faced throughout the nation. In 1912 university president E. B. Craighead lamented, "Consolidation or even administrative unification of Montana's higher institutions seems to be a dream, not to be realized because of the strength of the forces of localism."[96] And his statement applied to any number of other states as well. Highway officials were making headway in achieving their dream of a state highway system, but Craighead's dream was less readily realized. Localism was indeed an obstacle that states would continue to encounter when formulating higher education policy. In the coming decades, state policymakers would persist in their struggle for some degree of coordination among the institutions of higher education, attempting to realize an acceptable balance between institutional autonomy and the needs of the state as a whole. The pioneers of the early twentieth century had explored the problem and established some tentative programs, but they had not tamed the wilderness.

Yet during the early twentieth century, the tendency was already toward tighter state control. In the field of higher education, as in highway development, public utility regulation, and workers' compensation, the past pattern of permissive delegation of authority was gradually yielding to state administration and supervision. Localism persisted, but from the 1890s to 1920 the states were asserting new authority and in the process reversing the traditional dispersion of power. Motivated in part by the prevailing gospel of efficiency, legislators and governors were centralizing responsibility in the hands of state administrators. But changing technology was also rendering past practices obsolete. Utility companies were servicing regions rather than municipalities; workers were using hazardous machinery, not simple tools; automobile owners were demanding through highways in place of rutted country lanes; and universities required increasingly expensive equipment and facilities for engineering laboratories, which made duplication a costly proposition. The twentieth century demanded a more dynamic state government, and the states were responding to that demand by adopting a new course of concentrated authority.

3

Financing the Emerging State

I N HIS INTRODUCTORY ADDRESS to the National Conference on Taxation in 1901, renowned economist Edwin R. A. Seligman summed up the problem facing state policymakers: "Democracy must spend much—will spend ever more—but it should spend intelligently."[1] The functions of government were expanding, and the public revenues to pay for these new services had to expand accordingly. But turn-of-the-century leaders did not believe profligacy was an inevitable by-product of expanding government. Efficiency-minded reformers claimed that through expert administration state government could indeed spend more while also spending more wisely. As in the case of public utility regulation and highway construction, the states could achieve this goal by curbing the authority of locally elected amateurs. If expert administrators succeeded in restraining parochial, shortsighted legislators and untutored, untrustworthy county assessors, they supposedly would be able to raise and disburse revenues with optimum efficiency.

Given the shortcomings of the general property tax, the need for expert help and state intervention seemed especially critical. The chief source of state and local revenues, this tax was the object of unremitting criticism. Scores of committees struggled to revise the system of property taxation, and a multitude of experts and lawmakers debated alternative means of raising funds. The hoary structure of property taxation was the focus of fiscal policymakers in every state. For them the issue was whether the general property tax could be salvaged or should be discarded.

Central to the struggle over efficient disbursement was the idea of the "scientific" budget. Rather than continuing to have every state institution and legislator drain the treasury through scores of ill-considered appropriation measures, state-level reformers sought a rational mechanism for ensuring that each element of government received what it deserved. In accord with the growing power and esteem of state governors, executive supervision of appropriations seemed the solution. By 1920 the executive budget, presented by the governor but fashioned with the aid of budget experts, was the favorite panacea of every student of public finance. Through this enlightened procedure, the states would supposedly achieve the much-sought goal of spending efficiently.

From the 1890s to the early 1920s, then, the fiscal structure of America's states adapted to the perceived needs of the period. State lawmakers in Albany and Springfield did not vegetate, mindlessly perpetuating the errors of the past. Nor did they succeed in exorcising all the inherited fiscal demons. But they did adopt financial reforms that would be vital to the later development of state government.

The Faulty Revenue Structure

At the close of the nineteenth century, the general property tax was the mainstay of the states. Although policymakers were already devising some alternative sources of revenue, in 1902 the property levy still produced 53 percent of all state tax receipts.[2] Theoretically, it applied to all property, both real and personal, tangible and intangible. Thus the property tax was a levy on one's house and farm as well as such tangible personal property as furniture, pianos, livestock, watches, and unsold merchandise on store shelves. It also applied to so-called intangibles, for example, money, stocks, and bonds. In other words, it was a tax on every kind of property within the state, and only charitable, religious, educational, and governmental institutions were exempt. Most state constitutions required that this property be taxed at an uniform rate. To prevent favored treatment for certain categories of property or property holders, the framers of mid- and late-nineteenth-century state constitutions had specified that the legislature levy the same rate on watches and bonds, cows and office buildings, and vacant land and machinery.

In the minds of many, this application of a single tax rate to all classes of property was grossly unfair. A fifteen-mill tax on stocks, bonds, or bank accounts that earned 4.5 percent interest in fact deprived the owner of one-third of the income earned from such intangibles. Yet this same fifteen-mill impost amounted to only a seventy-five-dollar annual tax on a house and lot valued at five thousand dollars. The tax was uniform, but the burden did not appear to be equal, and critics denounced the levies on intangible property as confiscatory. Attacking the heavy imposts on the profits from intangibles, in 1897 the Massachusetts Tax Commission remarked: "No civilized country ever imposed with success an income tax (in ordinary times) of more than 3 percent, or at the most 5 percent. Can we expect to collect honestly, equally, effectively 33⅓ percent?"[3] Twelve years later, the Kentucky Tax Commission observed, "When a man is required to list a bond for taxation . . . and realizes that . . . the tax will take from 50 to 75 percent of the income from the bond, he must be a man of an unusual degree of patriotism and of an unusually urgent conscience to submit to this tax . . . without looking around for some method of escape."[4] And in 1910 a special committee of the International Tax Association concluded, "When . . . securities that bear say 4 percent interest are made subject to a 2 or 3 percent tax on their market or face value, the moral sense revolts at this practical confiscation of so large a share of the income."[5]

In fact, every state found the tax on intangibles unenforceable. Faced with the threat of a confiscatory levy, holders of intangible personal property simply evaded the tax. Each year they failed to report their intangible holdings to the tax assessors. Unlike a house, 160 acres of farmland, or a herd of cattle, stocks, bonds, and money were relatively invisible, and assessors had a difficult time proving their existence. As the New Jersey State Board of Equalization noted in its 1908 report, "while the tangible is hard enough to rate, it is practically impossible to rate the intangible, except by inquisitorial methods that public opinion will not sanction."[6] "It is extremely rare that any private individual is assessed for property of this class," the California tax commission of 1906 reported: "Only in the case of an estate in probate or of money in the hands of trustees who are afraid to prejudice the interests of their dependents by any attempt to evade the law is there any regular assessment of such property."[7] Tax expert Edwin Seligman agreed that it was futile to "attempt to enforce the taxation of intangible personalty. . . . Its only result has been to produce not revenue, but dishonesty."[8] Many complained that widespread evasion of taxes on intangible personal property especially burdened farmers. Farmers' wealth was in their lands, and land was eminently visible. Whereas urban holders of stocks and bonds could evade their share of taxes, farmers could not hide their property.

But much tangible personal property, such as household furnishings or goods on store shelves, also escaped taxation. Few honestly declared their household goods, and most assessors were not energetic in uncovering untaxed beds or pianos. In 1906 California's tax commission found that "the value of furniture returned [was] only $21,726,000, which [was] only $13 apiece for each man, woman, and child in the State; barely enough to buy a bed and bedding."[9] Another investigator reported that in Illinois "the total assessment for house and office furniture in 1913 was less than in 1873; and the total 'full value' assessment was less than $10 per capita."[10] Moreover, tax rolls revealed a mysterious paucity of watches, and the valuation of merchants' inventories fell far short of true worth. Despite the extraordinary growth in commerce and industry during the previous half-century, in 1908 an Ohio tax commission found: "The merchants' and manufacturers' stocks returned for taxation last year were about the same as during the period of the civil war."[11]

The elected local tax assessors themselves undermined the property tax system by seeking to ensure that their locality bore as small a share of the state tax burden as possible. Thus, they not only ignored both intangible and tangible personal property; they also undervalued real estate. By reducing their assessments to a lower level than those of other counties or townships, assessors could shift the cost of state government from their own constituents to taxpayers elsewhere in the state. In 1902 a West Virginia tax commission commented that it was in "the interest of every county that its assessments [should] be kept as low as possible" so that "the share contributed by the county to the State treasury should be made as low as possible in comparison with that furnished by other counties."[12] Six years later, an Ohio tax commission remarked on the "disposition on the part of local taxing authorities to reduce valuations in their own communities in order to make certain that other communities [were] bearing at least their full share of the cost of maintaining the state government."[13] State boards of equalization were responsible for correcting the valuation totals reported by the counties and thereby ensuring that counties could not escape their fair share of the state tax burden. But the perfunctory adjustments of such boards were no remedy. With good reason everyone believed that real estate assessments were uneven, and most sought to ensure that they, and not their neighbor, benefited from the inequities.

In the minds of many critics, local assessors were both unfaithful servants of the law and incompetent. Given the heightened demands and economic complexity of the twentieth century, this unprofessional, parochial body of elected officials no longer seemed an adequate foundation for the state tax structure. "Managers of private business would not think for a moment of placing an important function requiring technical knowledge and skill in the hands of temporary, inefficient and irresponsible employees or agents," wrote Kansas tax commissioner Samuel Howe; "but what is condemned by the industrial and commercial world is quietly permitted by the public." States tolerated "planless and headless and therefore loose and haphazard methods" rather than insisting on "a *business* of assessment and taxation founded in efficiency."[14] A 1913 report investigating the tax structure of Utah seconded Howe's views and emphasized the low public esteem accorded the office of assessor. "In nominating conventions it is usually the last place filled," the Utahans reported, "and the nominee is more likely to be chosen because of the particular section from which he came, or on account of his past services to the party ... rather than because of his especial fitness for the office." That the political hacks who served as assessors performed as well as they did was "due more to good luck than to good management."[15] In 1912 a special report on taxes in Iowa similarly spared few words in condemning "the hopelessly decentralized and inefficient system of local assessment."[16]

According to experts in the universities and many policymakers in the state capitols, county and township assessors, like county and township road officials, were not competent to deal with the demands of a new era. The tax system was like the road network in suffering from nineteenth-century localism. In Iowa, Utah, Kansas, and their sister states, lawmakers needed to overcome such localism and bring the tax structure into the twentieth century. In 1916 Charles J. Bullock, professor of economics at Harvard University, proclaimed the prevailing expert opinion when he wrote, "Under a purely local system of administration there never was and never will be a generally satisfactory assessment of either income or property."[17]

By the early twentieth century, then, the perceived sins of the general property tax were manifold. In 1914 a student of the general property tax in Illinois concluded that "a complete list of its defects would include infractions of almost every commandment in the fiscal decalogue."[18] Constitutional provisions requiring uniform and equal taxation of all property in fact produced a system plagued by inequality. Intangible property, if discovered, bore a heavier burden than tangible, but little intangible property was listed. Consequently, the prevailing rule of dishonesty ensured that wealthy holders of money and securities bore a light tax load. Much tangible personalty also escaped taxation, and a combination of independence and incompetence ensured that assessors did not treat real estate uniformly. The system seemed designed to encourage cheating, and the most successful cheaters paid the least. In practice, the general property tax was a levy on honesty; those who had the most of that rare commodity paid the most.

Not only was the general property tax a blight on the past and the present; it also appeared to offer little hope for the future. The states needed more money, and the flawed property tax could not generate the necessary funds. Intangible wealth was growing at a much faster pace than tangible, yet tax collectors could not reach this invisible property. In 1870 the intangible property listed on the grand duplicate of Ohio was valued at $136 million; in 1906 the intangible total had risen to only $148 million. The sum actually declined between 1890 and 1906.[19] During the period from 1870 to 1906, industrialization transformed Ohio, and great magnates like Cleveland's John D. Rockefeller and Mark Hanna accumulated multimillion-dollar fortunes. Yet according to the tax rolls, the total value of cash, stocks, and bonds had remained virtually constant. If Ohio or any other state was to finance new functions and services, it had to reach the previously unreachable intangible wealth. As state investigators throughout the nation realized, the general property tax was not likely to provide the desired payoffs. "While the real and personal property of the State are in reality increasing as rapidly as the population and the necessary expenses of government," a West Virginia tax commission observed in 1902, "the assessments of real and personal property . . . do not furnish a true record of our increase in wealth, and . . . will not produce revenues commensurate with the needs of the State."[20] In 1909 a Kentucky investigatory commission came to the same conclusion. The general property tax did "not produce sufficient revenue for the proper support of the State and local governments" and could not "be made to produce sufficient revenue, in spite of constantly increasing the tax rate."[21] Perhaps the most damning of all the indictments was that the general property tax would not produce enough money. A "bad" tax that proved sufficiently lucrative might be tolerated; one that offered little prospect for adequate growth deserved condemnation.

The Triad of Tax Reform

Given the imperative need for change, there was no shortage of proposed remedies. Experts in academia and members of investigatory commissions focused primarily on three options, however. First, they proposed repeal of the requirement that all property be taxed uniformly. Instead of uniformity, they urged a classification of property, with each class taxed at a different rate, appropriate to the nature of the property. Second, they advocated greater central control of assessment and taxation. As in the case of highways, state experts should supplement or supplant local amateurs to ensure coordinated and efficient administration of state laws. Third, many experts and investigators suggested separation of tax sources. In other words, the state should draw on new and different sources of revenue, leaving the general property tax to the localities. From the 1890s to the 1920s this triad of reform dominated debate over state taxation; and despite institutional inertia, the state tax structure did change.

Abolition of the requirement for uniform taxation of all property seemed a logical first step in the restructuring of the state tax system. Proponents of this reform believed that if intangibles could be taxed at a lower rate than real estate, more taxpayers would report their cash holdings and securities. Despite the lower rate of taxation, total revenues from intangibles would rise, and the moral blight of widespread tax evasion would be eradicated. Among the leading advocates of classification was Harvard's Charles Bullock, who argued, "If we are to continue to tax property, . . . it is under modern conditions imperative that we should classify property in a scientific manner and pass from a general to a classified property tax."[22] Other tax experts concurred, and by a unanimous vote, in 1907 the first meeting of the National Tax Conference resolved: "That all state constitutions requiring the same taxation of all property, or otherwise imposing restraints upon the reasonable classification of property, should be amended by the repeal of such restrictive provisions."[23]

As early as 1885, Pennsylvania adopted a special tax on intangibles, and Maryland followed suit in 1896. In both states the assessed valuation of stocks, bonds, and money soared after the adoption of the lower tax rates as holders of intangible property realized that the price of honesty had dropped. During the second decade of the twentieth century, the list of states imposing classified property taxes increased markedly, with Minnesota and Iowa leading the way in 1911. Rhode Island adopted a low-rate intangibles tax in 1912, Virginia in 1914, North Dakota in 1915, Kentucky and Oklahoma in 1917, and Montana and South Dakota in 1919. By 1925 sixteen states had chosen the option of a low-rate levy on intangibles.[24]

No state embraced classification so fully as Minnesota. That state not only taxed intangibles separately but also adopted a scheme establishing four additional classes of property, each assessed at a different rate. Iron ore was assessed at 50 percent of its true value, urban real estate at 40 percent, rural real estate as well as machinery, livestock, and merchandise at 33⅓ percent, and clothing and household items at 25 percent. Ignoring the previous requirement of uniform taxation, local assessors had already been assessing these classes of property at different levels. Thus the Minnesota legislation simply legalized existing practice.[25]

Although Minnesotans rallied behind the reform, classification faced serious obstacles during the early twentieth century. In most states, adoption of such a scheme required a constitutional amendment repealing existing provisions that mandated uniform and equal treatment of property. And such amendments had to win the approval of an electorate suspicious of new taxes. Moreover, as an Oregon investigating committee noted, "to the casual understanding nothing seems fairer than the principle that all taxation shall be equal and uniform."[26] Many uninformed voters might balk at the prospect of authorizing unequal taxes. Given these difficulties, a number of proposed classification amendments suffered defeat. For example, in November 1914 classification amendments failed at the polls in Kansas, Nebraska, Ohio, North Carolina, and Oregon.

Some classification amendments did succeed, however, and in every state adopting the low-rate tax, the amount of intangible property on the tax rolls increased markedly. In 1910 in Minnesota the assessed value of intangibles was

$13.9 million; in 1912, a year after adoption of the low-rate tax, the figure soared to $135.4 million, and by 1920 it was up to $437.6 million. In 1910 only 6,200 Minnesotans paid a tax on intangible property; ten years later, 127,500 did so. The assessed-value figures for Iowa were $194.2 million in 1910 and $627.6 million in 1920; in Kentucky the value of declared intangibles rose from $72 million in 1915 to $364 million in 1919.[27] The tax collector was reaching property that owners had previously concealed, and the number of dishonest Minnesotans had dropped by 120,000.

Yet classification was not an unalloyed success. In some states the increase in assessed value did not compensate for the drop in tax rate, and income from intangibles actually declined under the low-rate scheme. In other words, a three-mill tax on $100 million in intangibles proved less lucrative than a thirty-mill levy on $20 million of money and securities. Iowa tax expert Professor J. E. Brindley wrote that in his state "it [was] safe to say that the amount of revenue was decreased by at least one half as a result of the new law." In 1925 another student of intangible taxes found that in Kentucky "the tax ha[d] been . . . inferior to the former general property rate, so far as receipts [were] concerned."[28]

Moreover, some intangibles continued to evade taxation. According to expert opinion, Minnesota could boast of the best-administered intangibles tax. But even in that model state, a prominent tax official admitted that no more than 45 to 50 percent of the intangible property was listed on the tax rolls.[29] Similarly, fourteen years after adoption of Iowa's intangibles tax, Professor Brindley estimated that less than half of that state's intangibles were taxed.[30] Classification had reduced the incidence of evasion but had not eliminated it. Overall, the results were mixed. Commentators admitted that classification was a decided advance over past practices, but it was no solution.

Those who evaluated classification all agreed that central supervision was necessary to achieve any level of success. Just as highway engineers and public utility regulators felt that the complexities of modern technology required the states to step in and impose central control over localities, most tax reformers believed that a fairer, more lucrative revenue structure required firm intervention by state officials. Some local assessors were incompetent, and most assessed according to their own peculiar rules. Such local diversity was no longer tolerable; central control was imperative.

Responding to this sentiment, state legislatures throughout the nation created state tax commissions or tax commissioners. Between 1843 and 1893, legislatures established at least twenty-seven temporary commissions to investigate tax problems.[31] But not until 1891 did Indiana authorize the first modern permanent tax commission, and Indiana's example would spawn many imitators. By 1918 thirty-five states had such tax agencies.[32] Usually the boards consisted of three commissioners appointed by the governor, but some states opted for a single commissioner to oversee the revenue structure.

The purpose of the commission or commissioner was generally threefold. First, the officials were to review state tax laws and procedures and recommend changes. The commissions, then, were intended to be permanent generators of change. Second, they were to assess certain corporate property such as railroads and public utilities that were beyond the capacity of local assessors to handle. Third, and perhaps most significant, the state commissions were to supervise local assessors, ensuring uniform procedures and compliance with state tax laws. The local assessors had formerly been a law unto themselves, but the state tax commissioners were expected to end that abuse of power. According to the president of the Michigan State Board of Tax Commissioners, the purpose of his body "was to ingraft into the Constitution and laws of the State pertaining to assessments, nerve and blood and spinal marrow" and to halt the "rot and decay" that resulted when there was no state agency to enforce the statutes.[33]

Not only was the tax commission to crack down on local assessors; it was also to offer them expert advice and guidance. C. R. Jackson, president of the Washington State Board of Tax Commissioners, said his board was "to advise assessors . . . as to their duties, to interpret the law in disputed cases, to visit, confer with and assist the assessors in the state in order that a just and equitable assessment . . . be obtained." According to Jackson, "certain uniform rules [could] be laid down for the assessors and their deputies and yet the detail work of assessment [could] be done by men familiar with local conditions and values."[34] Professor Thomas S. Adams of the Wisconsin Tax Commission characterized the agency as "a great central reserve of expert aid." Such a commission was essential to "securing efficient administration," because it was "impossible for each local government to maintain the necessary experts."[35] Like the state highway department and the state public utility commission, the state tax commission was supposed to supply the expertise necessary for the efficient operation of government in the modern age. Once again state lawmakers had found local government inadequate to shoulder the technical demands of the twentieth century, and they had intervened to create a state overseer.

Though the energy and effectiveness of the central authorities varied from one state to the next, commissions throughout the nation organized conferences for local assessors, compiled instructive manuals on assessment procedures, provided standard assessment forms, and generally endeavored to bring some method and uniformity to the assessment process. Their efforts reaped rewards in the form of higher assessed valuations, and in a number of states the increase in the valuation figures was especially dramatic. During the first year of the Michigan tax board's existence, the state's total assessed valuation rose from $968 million to $1.34 billion; in West Virginia the first-year increase was from $277 million to $875 million; and in Kansas valuations soared almost sixfold as a result of the tax commission's campaign to ensure assessment of property at "actual value in money," instead of at some variable percentage of monetary value.[36]

Yet the tax commissions had not transformed the general property tax into a fair and efficient generator of revenue. For the commissions had not solved the problem of taxing intangibles. "The figures for intangible personal property reveal most clearly the failure of the uniform rule, even under centralized administration," observed economist Harley Lutz in his study of state commissions. "The total assessment of intangibles has usually stood still, or has increased but slowly, while many of the individual items have declined."[37] In other words, the commissions had improved the assessment of houses, farms, and railroads. They were valued more fairly than in the past. But the state commissions had not solved the problem of taxing money and securities.

Many experts realized that this shortcoming was not the fault of the commissions but of the general property tax itself. An increasing number of policymakers were suggesting that the states end their reliance on the property tax and turn to new sources of revenue. They proposed that the property tax remain the chief support of local government but not of the states. By thus separating the sources of revenue for the states and localities, the states would eliminate the local incentive to keep assessments as low as possible. Local assessors returned low figures for their counties and townships to ensure that their constituents bore the lightest possible share of the state tax burden. If there were no state property tax, then there would be no contest among localities to see which could win the prize for underassessment. A low county assessment would simply require a higher county tax rate, so no one would benefit if all property in the county were assessed at less than true value.

During the late nineteenth century, some eastern states had already abandoned the general property tax for state purposes. From 1877 to 1921 Delaware did not levy a state property tax, and by the 1880s Pennsylvania also had assigned the general property tax exclusively to its local governments. From 1890 to 1909 Connecticut eschewed a general property tax for state revenue. And from 1902 to 1905 New York imposed only a small levy on property and no levy at all from 1906 to 1910 and in 1914 and 1916.[38]

Eastern state lawmakers did not abandon the general property tax in a conscious effort to separate state and local sources, however. Instead, each of these states developed new sources of revenue and consequently no longer needed to impose a state property levy. Delaware was able to reap at least 20 percent of its annual revenues from license fees and franchise taxes on the many corporations that chose to take advantage of that state's permissive incorporation laws.[39] Corporation taxes also sustained Pennsylvania's treasury, whereas New York pioneered a long list of levies, demonstrating to the other states myriad modes for picking the pockets of the citizenry. For example, by the first decade of the twentieth century, an inheritance tax produced one-fifth of the state's tax revenues. But New York also imposed a corporate franchise tax, a corporation organization tax, a foreign corporation license fee, a stock transfer tax, and a mortgage recording tax. Among the most lucrative of the imposts was the liquor license levy, which provided about one-third of state revenues during the first decade of the century.[40] Lawmakers in Albany were proving that a state need not rely on property levies. They could live without the much-maligned general property tax.

In California policymakers consciously embraced the ideal of separation of sources. They did not gradually adopt new state taxes and concurrently phase out the state property levy. Instead, they viewed separation as a quick remedy to the ills of the property tax and in one stroke shifted from the general property tax to an alternate revenue structure. Thus California became the test case for the principle of separation of sources. If the plan worked in California, it would win adherents in other states as well.

California's separation scheme was a product of the special Commission on Revenue and Taxation appointed in 1905. The commission consisted of the governor, two state senators, two assemblymen, and Carl C. Plehn, professor of finance at the University of California. Plehn, in fact, was the chief author of the plan presented in the commission's report of 1906, and he would remain the principal advocate and defender of the California experiment. According to the 1906 report, "the separation of State from local taxation as to sources of revenue ha[d] come to be generally recognized as the one feasible pathway for tax reform." Specifically, the commission proposed that the counties and other local governments should "tax only the private or individual real estate and tangible property within their boundaries, property . . . which [was] clearly and distinctly localized." The state should "tax all those industries, and classes of property sometimes called 'corporate,'" for such property extended "over many communities, serve[d] all, and all contribute[d] to its income."[41] The commission said that "separation would abolish the chief incentive to and cause for undervaluations and remove the chief source of the existence of discrimina-tions." For "a large part of the inequalities in the assessment ha[d] their origin in the attempt of assessors to save part of the State burden to the county by undervaluation," and without a state burden, one county no longer would need to shift it to another.[42]

The California tax commission further believed that only the state could effectively assess and tax corporate property; localities were simply incapable of shouldering the task. "The taxation of public-service corporations, . . . whose business pervades the whole State, can not be adequately handled by the local assessors," the commissioners argued. "In every case, in order to obtain any sort of equality, uniformity, and justice in the treatment of these great corpo-rations, it is necessary to call in the assistance of a State board."[43] Carl Plehn later admitted that "the reason for recommending separation which was most conclusive with the commission was the incessant political activity of the public utilities." So long as each county or city assessed public utility prop-erty, the public utility corporations were, in effect, ready targets for extortion by corrupt local officials. And the corporations paid off to the local political machines. "Anything they could save in taxes provided a fund for the 'ma-chines,'" Plehn explained.[44]

Separation in California would, then, supposedly correct the problem of underassessment by removing the incentive for such a practice. It would also shift responsibility for taxation of public utility corporations to the state, curb-ing political corruption at the local level and presumably ensuring more effec-tive administration of the levies. It seemed a well-laid plan for righting the state's taxation wrongs.

Responding to the commission's report, in 1909 the California legislature approved a resolution for a constitutional amendment permitting the sepa-ration-of-sources scheme, which won voter approval by a large majority in November 1910. Under the new plan, the state levied a 4 percent levy on the gross earnings of electric and steam railroads and gas and electric companies, a 3.5 percent tax on the gross earnings of telephone and telegraph companies, a 1.5 percent levy on the gross premiums of insurance companies, and addi-tional imposts on railroad car and express companies and banks. Other than a modest temporary property levy earmarked to fund the upcoming Panama-Pacific Exposition, the state imposed no general property tax, leaving that levy to the localities.[45] As the 1906 commission proposed, corporation taxes were expected to fund the state, and the general property tax was the mainstay of local government.

California's experiment, however, was at best only a partial success. Most seriously, the corporation taxes proved insufficient to finance expanding state functions and services, leaving the state in a fiscal bind every biennium. In 1917 the State Tax Commission reported that the new system "failed as a revenue producer . . . and would have resulted in financial paralysis for the state had it not been for the fact that the legislature responded to Governor [Hiram] Johnson's recommendations by increasing the rates upon the gross earnings of corporations, first at the session of 1913 and again at the session of 1915."[46] In 1915 Newton W. Thompson, the president pro tem of the state senate, complained, "It was soon evident that the revenues of the state were dependent almost entirely upon general business conditions and the prosperity of those utilities taxed directly for its support." A downturn in utility revenues meant a drop in state funds. Moreover, by 1915 both Senator Thompson and Carl Plehn had realized that the state public utility commission's efforts to secure railroad, electric, telephone, and gas rate reductions cut the gross earnings of utilities and state revenues. In other words, by protecting its private consumers, the state was robbing itself of funds needed to finance the public utility commission and other state agencies.[47] Within a few years after implementation of the California plan, lawmakers and economists alike agreed that the corporate taxes were too inelastic to fund the fast-growing state government. California needed a broader tax base.

Other states also complained that the corporation and inheritance taxes were not proving flexible enough to satisfy the growing appetite of the states for cash. In 1909 Connecticut's cash-strapped legislature had to authorize a state property levy for the first time in almost twenty years. After suspending the tax for 1912 and 1913, Connecticut lawmakers renewed it for 1914 and for 1915, and in the latter year it accounted for 17 percent of the state's total receipts. In 1921 Delaware likewise reinstituted the state property tax after forty-five years of surviving without it. From 1916 to 1928 New York again relied on the state property levy, and in the first half of the 1920s, it produced about one-fifth of the Empire State's tax revenues.[48] Like classification and centralization, separation might have made state tax structures more equitable and fair, but like the other reforms, it was not a panacea. The alternate revenue sources were simply inadequate to meet growing state demands. The 1929 report of the California Tax Commission asserted, "The conclusion is inescapable that, although the adoption of the plan of separation of sources did bring about a substantial improvement as compared with the situation which existed previously, the course chosen far from being 'the one feasible pathway to tax reform' has proved to be a blind alley."[49]

The Income Tax

State policymakers and tax experts were in accord about the flaws of the general property tax, but by the second decade of the twentieth century they also doubted that the triad of classification, centralization, and separation would cure the ills plaguing the state tax structure. What was needed was a tax that could be more effectively administered than the general property tax and that was more elastic than public utility imposts. It needed to reach the growing wealth derived from intangible property, and its burden should rest equitably on the citizenry. The experts and lawmakers were to find this magic solution to the revenue dilemma in the income tax. The income tax was the greatest contribution of the state tax reform movement. By 1920 most commentators agreed that it was the best answer to the states' problems, and during the course of the twentieth century it would be a major element in the transformation of the state revenue structure.

During the nineteenth century, several states experimented with the income tax, and by 1910 a total of seventeen states had at one time imposed the levy, though all but five had abandoned it.[50] Like the levy on personal property, it seemed impossible to enforce. Local officials were in charge of assessing incomes but had to rely on the taxpayers' own listing of their incomes. Taxpayers were no more likely to list their incomes honestly than their intangible property, and locally elected assessors were not willing to ferret out the true resources of the voters in their communities. Thus, evasion and lax enforcement were the rule. Revenues from the tax were therefore insignificant. In 1898 North Carolina's yield was less than $3,900, and according to a student of that state's tax system, "in considerably more than one-half of the counties of the state, no person was reported as in possession of a taxable income!"[51] In 1899 only two of Louisiana's fifty-nine counties reported taxable incomes, which yielded a grand total of $104 for the state.[52]

Given the past record, virtually all tax experts rejected the income tax as an unrealistic option for revenue-hungry states. At the University of Wisconsin, Delos Kinsman prepared a doctoral dissertation on state income taxes, publishing his findings in 1903. "The experience of the States with the income tax warrants the conclusion that the tax, as employed by them, has been unquestionably a failure," Kinsman reported. "It has satisfied neither the demands for justice nor the need of revenue." He deemed it theoretically sound, but its failure had "been due to the administration of the laws." Moreover, since Kinsman believed taxpayer self-assessment was a necessary facet of any such tax in

America, he grimly concluded, "A general State income tax must be a failure."[53] The California tax commission of 1906, guided by Professor Carl Plehn, was even more critical of the income tax. The commission bluntly proclaimed, "A general income tax is un-American. Our people have so much respect for labor that what is won by honest toil is regarded as sacred and not to be reduced by direct taxation." Based on the experiences of other states, Plehn and his colleagues also categorized the tax as "a failure, being evaded, disliked, laxly enforced, and yielding small returns."[54] In 1911 University of Wisconsin economist Thomas S. Adams summed up prevailing opinion when he wrote, "Today the economists of this country have lined up in opposition to the state income tax in an array so nearly unanimous that the outside world would be justified in asserting that current American political economy is against the income tax."[55]

Adams was, in fact, the one economist not lined up in array against the state income tax. Since the late 1890s, the LaFollette reform faction had sought a means of taxing Wisconsin's intangible personal property to thereby relieve the burden on the state's farmers. Adams and state tax commissioner Nils P. Haugen believed an income tax was the solution, and in 1908 they and their reform allies succeeded in placing an income tax amendment to Wisconsin's constitution on the ballot. The state's voters concurred with the reformers, approving the amendment by a more than two-to-one margin. Not until 1911, however, was the legislature able to agree on an income tax bill, and the following year the state began collecting the new levy. Meanwhile, Adams had joined Haugen on the state tax commission, where he was instrumental in implementing Wisconsin's great experiment. The 1911 law provided for a graduated tax on personal and corporate incomes ranging from 1 to 6 percent. Liberal exemptions ensured that the working class would not bear any additional burdens. "The man who depends on his manual labor for a living will pay no income tax whatsoever," Haugen explained. Wisconsin's law did "not assess anybody unless he ha[d] some net revenue above the mere needs of existence."[56]

The Wisconsin levy differed from previous state income taxes in two significant ways. First, the state did not depend on locally elected officials to administer the law. Instead, under the Wisconsin statute, the state tax commission appointed forty-one assessors in accord with civil service regulations. These nonpolitical state civil servants were in charge of the assessment of incomes, and they were responsible to the state, not to the local electorate. As Professor Adams proudly declared, "They are divorced from local pressure, from local control, and left free to assess and administer their office as their conscience may dictate, prodded by a resolute tax commission."[57] Second, the

Wisconsin statute required that businesses report the incomes of employees, the dividends of shareholders, and interest payments to bondholders. Thus assessors did not need to rely solely on the honesty of the individual taxpayer in determining tax liability. If taxpayers falsely reported their salaries, dividends, or interest payments, the state could catch the culprits by checking their returns against the information submitted by businesses. Unlike previous state income tax laws, then, Wisconsin's measure did not depend on local administration or faith in the honesty of the taxpayer. It provided for a centralized system designed to discover income and tax it.

The Wisconsin system worked. In 1912 the net yield of the tax was more than $2 million, a dramatic improvement over the $2,000 collected from the income tax in a state such as North Carolina. It also reached intangible wealth, which previously had evaded taxation, and thus shifted more of the state's tax bill to the affluent. Reporting on the first assessment of incomes in one of the state's largest counties, Nils Haugen remarked, "Less than 5 percent of the people of Dane county will pay any income tax [and] seventeen wealthy men will pay 24 percent of all income taxes in the county."[58] Dismissing fears that the tax would drive business from the state, Adams reported that "not a single instance was found in which an industry had left the state on account of the income tax, or had failed to locate in Wisconsin because of the tax."[59] To the surprise of many students of taxation, the best-laid plans of Wisconsin's tax reformers had produced the intended results.

Wisconsin's success transformed views on state taxation. Adams and Haugen had proved that the states had the administrative capacity to effectively tax incomes. Because it taxed according to ability to pay, the income levy, in theory, had always been a most desirable option. Practice, however, had not conformed to theory. Now Wisconsin had joined theory and practice, producing a new alternative for the states.

Within a few years after Wisconsin's breakthrough, some states were ready to follow its example. In 1915 Connecticut imposed a corporate income tax, and the following year Massachusetts adopted a personal income tax. In 1917 Delaware opted for a 1 percent flat-rate tax on personal incomes, Missouri imposed a personal and corporate income tax, and Montana instituted an income levy on corporations. That same year, New York imposed a corporate income tax, adding an individual income levy in 1919. In one state after another, the income tax paid off: in 1917 Connecticut collected $3.2 million and Massachusetts collected $12.1 million. During the first eight months that the New York corporate income tax was in effect, the state collected $14.8 million, and even the modest impost in little Delaware garnered $395,000 in 1918. In 1920 the state personal and corporate income taxes produced $36 million for New York, constituting one-third of the total state revenues.[60]

Basic to the success of the income tax in New York, Massachusetts, and Connecticut, as in Wisconsin, was an unprecedented centralization of authority. Appointed state civil servants were the key players in the new structure of taxation. Writing of the Massachusetts tax, economist Harley Lutz remarked, "It would be fatal to the successful administration of such a tax law if those in contact with the taxpayers could be in any degree influenced by local, or partisan, or business or other reasons."[61] In other words, a state income tax necessitated an end to pervasive localism and administration by elected partisans. The tax collector had to be an obdurate servant of the state and not a compliant friend or neighbor.

Convinced of the merits of the new tax, in 1921 a committee of the National Tax Association chaired by Charles Bullock submitted a model state income tax act to guide the work of fiscal policymakers in capitals throughout the nation. This model act as well as the experience of Wisconsin, Massachusetts, and New York influenced additional states to accept an up-to-date plan for income taxation. In 1919 North Dakota had adopted a defective income tax measure, which yielded little revenue, but in 1923 it enacted a new law based on the National Tax Association's model act and achieved better results. Similarly, Mississippi's income tax law of 1912 relied on local administration, with predictably dismal consequences. But in 1924 Mississippi recognized its error and substituted a more centralized structure that reaped the needed revenue. In 1921 North Carolina likewise adopted its first modern income tax measure; it was producing more than $4 million annually by 1924. And in 1922 South Carolina joined the band of states embracing the Wisconsin experience and the advice of the National Tax Association. By 1922 thirteen states had adopted income taxation, and income taxes accounted for almost 11 percent of all state tax revenues in the United States. Nationwide, the general property tax still contributed 37 percent of state tax receipts, but this was down from 53 percent in 1902.[62] The state tax structure was changing, but past practices were not readily discarded. Tax reformers were making inroads against the hated general property tax, but they had not vanquished their foe.

By the 1920s, however, the advantages of the income tax were apparent. It was an elastic producer of revenue. With an income tax, a state could separate the sources of state and local government and still collect enough money to provide for expanding services and functions. Moreover, the income tax reached intangible wealth and forced holders of stocks and bonds to pay their fair share. And it balanced the tax burden, relieving farmers of a disproportionate responsibility for the cost of state government. All of the early supporters of the income tax viewed it as a levy on city dwellers that touched farmers lightly. In 1912 Milwaukee accounted for 19.5 percent of the general property valuation of Wisconsin yet contributed 42.0 percent of the income tax receipts. Only 68 farmers in Dane County, Wisconsin, paid income taxes, as compared with 170 clerks and bookkeepers.[63] In 1926 only 173 planters in the entire state paid Mississippi's income tax, although 3,368 merchants and 5,256 clerks did so.[64] The following year, in overwhelmingly rural North Dakota, farmers contributed only 7 percent of the state income tax receipts.[65] With their wealth largely in the form of land, cash-poor farmers benefited from the provisions exempting the lower income brackets from taxation. Instead, the income tax forced salaried workers and investors to pay a greater share of the cost of state government. An elastic tax that reached intangible wealth and spared the farmer, the state income tax seemed an answer to reformers' prayers.

Budget Reform

Rising expenditures and the emerging belief in state-level expertise put pressure not only on the tax structure but also on the appropriation process. Tax reform alone was not sufficient; equally necessary, in the minds of many policymakers, was the introduction of "scientific" budget practices. Without such practices, the money raised by new taxes would be squandered and the reputation of state government further blemished. Economy and efficiency were the lodestar of early-twentieth-century politics, and to achieve this much-vaunted goal, many commentators believed that the states had to enhance executive budgetary authority and develop expert staffs to review appropriation proposals.

Stirring reformers to action was the prevailing chaos in statehouses across the nation. The typical legislative session was a free-for-all for funds. Governors did not submit comprehensive and coordinated budgets with recommendations for the funding of each agency and with estimated revenues balancing expenditures. Instead, each state institution or department submitted its own estimate of its future expenditures, and each battled to win that sum. According to a veteran California politician, the appropriation process of the first decade of the twentieth century was "a blind scramble on the part of the various institutions and departments of the state in an endeavor to secure as large a portion as possible of whatever money might happen to be in the treasury."[66] Moreover, individual legislators were not reluctant to propose additional bills funding their own pet projects. The result was a mass of disparate spending measures. The Massachusetts legislature passed 100 to 150 appropriation bills per year; in each regular session of the Michigan legislature, 50 to 75 appropriation bills were passed; and in the 1913 session, Illinois's lawmakers approved 94 separate appropriation measures, which filled 116 pages in the volume of session laws.[67] Expressing disdain for the helter-skelter procedure, California's tax commission reported that no attempt was "made to consider scientifically the state's fiscal policy as a whole. Regular appropriations, special appropriations and deficiency bills were thrown into the legislative hopper in haphazard fashion, with little or no thought of where the money was to come from."[68]

Most legislators were unprepared to judge intelligently the requests of the army of money seekers. An investigatory committee in Michigan found that even the lawmakers who sponsored appropriation bills did so blindly at the request of department heads. The legislators were "not furnished with adequate information resulting from a proper investigation of financial needs, nor with a comparative statement of past expenditures with amounts requested for the same activity." Before endorsing an appropriation for a state institution, a legislative committee might visit the facility. Yet this too was insufficient. "As a usual thing," the Michigan committee observed, "the time spent by the committee at the institution is wholly inadequate for getting anything but meager information, and most of that is furnished by the executive officer of the institution."[69] In the state of Washington, ill-informed legislators were also the norm. "The legislator has nothing before him giving him accurate information as to the needs of a particular department or function by showing the actual cost of operation in the past and what values were received for outlay," observed a Washington critic.[70]

When the legislature adjourned, however, the appropriation process was not over. Governors could veto appropriation bills and thereby pare spending and reduce the deficits resulting from careless legislative procedure. Furthermore, armed with the item veto, most governors could disallow individual items in appropriation measures if they did not choose to veto the entire bill. Thus the governor could strike any provision that appeared wasteful or unnecessary.

Numerous governors used their veto as a device for enforcing responsible fiscal behavior. In 1903 New York's Governor Benjamin Odell disallowed $1,757,675 in appropriations, and the following year he slashed $2,255,323, or about one-tenth of the state's annual operating budget. In 1911 Governor John Dix of New York vetoed forty single-item appropriation bills amounting to $4,360,598; he disallowed 115 items in other bills, thereby eliminating an additional $3,158,170 in expenditures. The resulting total of $7.5 million constituted 17.5 percent of all appropriations approved by the legislature that year.[71] During the biennium 1903–5, Governor Richard Yates of Illinois disallowed almost

$1 million of the $15.5 million in appropriations. In 1913 Illinois's Governor Edward Dunne vetoed items totaling $1.04 million, and two years later he slashed items amounting to $1.93 million, or about 4 percent of the total state appropriations.[72] In 1911 the *Detroit News* wrote that Michigan's Governor Chase Osborn had "gone through the items of institutional appropriations very carefully," and he had "stricken out here and there until the aggregate elimination [reached] a total of nearly a million dollars." Osborn was meticulous in excising the legislature's appropriations, deleting even the smallest items that aroused his suspicion. In the appropriation bill for the State Board of Fish Commissioners, he vetoed four items of less than $100 and three additional items of less than $300.[73]

Yet these slashing governors had to act without the aid of budget experts and without a body of data to support their actions. There was no executive budget office to analyze appropriations and consider whether legislative spending measures exceeded necessity. Instead, governors cut on the basis of their personal perceptions of what seemed wasteful or improper. Some state executives balked at the thought of blindly slashing state appropriations. In 1911, when confronted by a mass of appropriation bills requiring his signature, California's new governor, Hiram Johnson, asked for data regarding the necessity of the appropriations and the adequacy of state revenues. No such data existed, and Johnson was forced to sign the measures, ignorant of their possible faults. "Such a proceeding as this is a disgrace to the people of an intelligent commonwealth," commented the angry governor.[74]

By 1911 a growing number of state leaders agreed with Johnson. Lacking an independent bureau staffed by budget experts, neither the governor nor the legislature had any neutral source of information regarding how much should be spent and for what purposes. Lawmakers had to depend on the testimony of self-interested department heads and institution chieftains. Just as the general property tax depended on holders of personal property to list accurately their possessions, the appropriation process depended on state administrators to report their needs truthfully. The structures of both revenues and appropriations were built on the shaky foundation of trust. And in the minds of most observers, that trust seemed misplaced. Legislators and governors needed a statement of financial requirements and fiscal priorities based on data gathered by personnel who would not profit from false reporting. Such a budget document could effectively chart the course of state policy during the biennium.

During the second decade of the twentieth century, the cries for reform were to produce noteworthy changes. Throughout the nation, states attempted to centralize and rationalize authority over the budget. As in the case of state highway departments, public utility commissions, and tax commissions, the idea was to place authority in the hands of expert officials representing the interests of the state as a whole. These officials could supposedly rise above the parochialism that had long plagued America's states and ensure a level of unbiased professionalism. Rather than allowing legislators representing local interests and popular, smooth-talking institution heads to drain the treasury without central control or plan, these officials were to impose some unity and direction on the appropriation procedure. As with other reforms of the period, the "scientific" budget process sought to tighten the loose structure of state rule and discard the makeshift and amateurish government procedures of the past.

In the United States the modern budget movement actually began at the municipal level. As early as 1899, the National Municipal League's model municipal incorporation act provided that each year the mayor "submit to the Council the annual budget of current expenses of the city."[75] After its creation in 1906, the New York Bureau of Municipal Research led the cause of budget reform, and one of its first reports was "Making a Municipal Budget," published in 1907. The bureau was able to influence New York City's budgetary practices, and one reformer characterized the nation's largest municipality during the early twentieth century as "a veritable laboratory in financial administration, affording experience for the education of the whole country in the significance of the budget."[76]

One person who became aware of the significance of the budget was President William Howard Taft. Eager to bring order to the national government, in 1910 Taft appointed the Commission of Economy and Efficiency, headed by Frederick A. Cleveland, director of the New York Bureau of Municipal Research. Among the reports issued by the commission was "The Need for a National Budget," which President Taft submitted to Congress in June 1912. The commission proposed that the president present annually a "definite business and financial program" for Congress to act upon.[77] Congress, however, responded coolly to the notion of an executive budget and tabled the proposal. Not until 1921, after virtually all of the states had taken action, did the federal government embrace an executive budget and Congress authorize the creation of the Bureau of the Budget. Although the national Congress refused to abandon traditional procedures and ignored the findings of Cleveland and his colleagues, the commission's report received a good deal of publicity and spurred state lawmakers to reconsider their wayward practices.

While Taft's commission was still considering procedural shortcomings at the national level, two states took action and pioneered budgetary reforms. In 1911 California and Wisconsin created boards to oversee state finances and prepare budgets. California's Board of Control consisted of three appointees of the governor, who held office at his pleasure. Wisconsin's Board of Public Affairs comprised the governor, the secretary of state, the chairs of the senate and assembly finance committees, and three gubernatorial appointees, removable by the chief executive. The governor chaired the board. Moreover, both boards had staffs to aid in their financial investigations. California's board had charge of a newly created department of public accounting, which was authorized to employ three "skillful accountants . . . well versed in public accounting," who could require from state officers "financial and statistical reports" and had the power to examine "all accounts and all financial affairs" of such officers.[78] Wisconsin law prescribed that the Board of Public Affairs appoint a secretary who was to be "a man of experience and character that qualif[ied] him to direct investigations into the operation of public bodies and into the business and financial methods employed by them." In addition, the Wisconsin board employed a permanent corps of accountants and was required by law to audit annually all state departments.[79]

In preparing their state budgets, the two boards followed a procedure that was common to later budgetary agencies as well. During the summer of even-numbered years, each state department and institution was to compile its estimate of expenses for the coming biennium and submit it to the boards. During the following fall, the boards conducted hearings on the estimates, the California board inviting the state controller to join in its deliberations. The boards revised the estimates after these hearings and compiled their budgets, which were submitted to the legislatures when they convened in January of odd-numbered years. The respective legislatures had the final say in funding decisions and could ignore the submitted budget. But in both states the board enjoyed the respect of the legislatures. In Wisconsin the finance chairs of the legislature served on the Board of Public Affairs, and the submitted budget had passed their scrutiny as well as that of the veto-wielding governor. In California Governor Hiram Johnson warned the first legislature confronted by a Board of Control budget that solons who disregarded the board's recommendations would do so in vain. "These appropriations which have been studied and approved by the Board of Control and State Controller, acting as a budget commission, will receive executive sanction," Johnson announced. "Those which have not been approved by the budget commission will fail."[80] Through use of his veto power, Johnson would ensure that the legislature added nothing to the board's budget.

Leaders in Wisconsin and California were not reluctant to boast of their new budget agencies and preach the message of scientific budgeting to the other states. Contrasting behavior under the new system with that under the old, the chair of California's Board of Control claimed that in the legislative session of 1913, "no promises of jobs or of anything else were made for the simple reason that the Governor and Board of Control had assumed responsibility for the entire budget and the heads of departments and institutions realized that the securing of proper appropriations was no longer a contest in trickery and ward heeling strategy."[81] Not only had virtue supposedly triumphed, but so had economy. According to the California Tax Commission's report of 1917, "the great, outstanding result of this budget system [was] that the state ha[d] been able, during the past six years, to meet the greatest growth in its history with the smallest percentage of increase in appropriations."[82] Similarly, Wisconsin's Governor Philipp observed that "the adoption of the budget system ha[d] made it necessary for all financial affairs of the state to be conducted in a manner which [was] open and above board," and "the lobbying which department heads and even employees formerly indulged in ha[d] been eliminated." Moreover, the Wisconsin governor asserted that it was "a well-known fact" that "the budget system ha[d] resulted in the saving of money to the people of the state."[83] From California and Wisconsin the message was much the same. The budget system had eradicated skullduggery and achieved economy.

Impressed by such testimony, reformers in other states demanded adoption of a budget system. In 1914 the Iowa legislature's Committee on Retrenchment and Reform urged that "the Governor should, aided by careful individual investigation, make up a budget showing the needs of the state, to be in the hands of the members of the legislature immediately upon convening."[84] That same year, Minnesota's Efficiency and Economy Commission recommended a budget system as well, and in 1915 the Committee on Finances, Revenues and Expenditures of the New York Constitutional Convention favored adoption of a constitutional amendment providing for a budget. The New Yorkers emphasized the folly of the existing system of generous legislative appropriations pared by gubernatorial veto. "Instead of the man who is to spend the money presenting to the body which is to grant the money his request for their final decision, the latter body, in substance, draw their check in blank and present it to the executive for him to determine how much of it he cares to use." In 1916 the Massachusetts Commission on Economy and Efficiency concurred wholeheartedly in the growing wave of support for a budget, and in December of that year Colorado's Survey Committee of State Affairs recommended that the governor submit a budget to each regular session of the legislature. To aid the governor, the Coloradans suggested the creation of "a permanent budget and efficiency commissioner, with the necessary expert staff, qualified to make all necessary studies of every branch of the state government's activities with the object of using the results of such studies in the revision of estimates of departments, boards, institutions, etc., and the compilation of the budget."[85]

Across the country the budget was a popular cause, resulting in a mounting number of budget laws. By 1921 forty-six of the forty-eight states had formally provided for a budgetary procedure. One state, Arkansas, designated a special legislative committee to prepare the budget, but all of the other forty-five states allocated this function, at least in part, to a body outside the legislature. Twenty-one states followed the examples of California and Wisconsin and created boards or commissions to prepare the budget. Of these boards, thirteen were composed solely of administrative officials, most often the governor and such elected financial officers as the comptroller and treasurer. Some of these thirteen, however, replicated the California model and comprised gubernatorial appointees. Eight of the state boards imitated Wisconsin and included both legislative and administrative officers. In each of these states, the chairs of the house and senate appropriation committees were board members.[86]

Yet by the early 1920s, most public administration experts had turned against the idea of a budget board and were advocating the executive budget. Consequently, as of 1921 twenty-four states had adopted this option. Under the executive budget plan, responsibility for recommending a program of state expenditures rested solely with the governor. The chief executive could rely on the expertise of a budget director and staff of accountants, but the budget was to represent the governor's judgment and priorities. Chosen by a statewide electorate, the governor was the representative of all the people, and advocates of the executive budget plan believed this spokesperson for the people should have absolute charge of formulating the blueprint for future expenditures. In addition, no other official had such a comprehensive vision of the commonweal. Governors were not simply financial officers such as treasurers or comptrollers. Instead, they were theoretically responsible for a broad range of public activities and were best suited to recommend budgets for all departments and institutions. Moreover, by dividing budgetary authority among a half dozen officials, the board option minimized accountability. By focusing responsibility on the ultimate tribune of the people, the executive budget plan made the governor clearly accountable, and in the next election voters could cast their ballots accordingly. Many commentators viewed these arguments in favor of the executive budget plan as unassailable. In 1924 the Efficiency Commission of Kentucky pronounced: "The right and propriety of the Governor's position as the executive who makes the budget recommendations is obvious. Any limitation upon the Governor's power in this connection should . . . be regarded as contrary to the fundamental scheme of our government."[87] And at the close of the 1920s, the leading expert on budget reform, A. E. Buck, asserted that "American writers on the budget . . . ha[d] practically without exception endorsed the executive type of budget making authority."[88]

An early leader in the effort to bolster the governor's budgetary authority was the state of Maryland. Maryland's legislative session of 1914 was a model of fiscal irresponsibility, generating a financial crisis that became a campaign issue in the gubernatorial election of 1915. The Democrats and their gubernatorial candidate, Emerson Harrington, pledged the adoption of a budget system. The party's convention also named a committee of distinguished citizens to frame a budget bill. Heading the committee was the eminent political scientist Frank J. Goodnow, who was then president of Johns Hopkins University and had been a member of the Taft Commission. The Goodnow Commission drafted a bill that assigned responsibility for preparing the budget to the governor, rejecting an alternate proposal to designate the Board of Public Works, composed of the governor, the comptroller, and the treasurer, as the state's budget commission. "We have felt that to make use of the Board of Public Works as a Budget Commission would have the disadvantage of dissipating personal responsibility for financial propositions," Goodnow and his colleagues explained.[89]

Moreover, under the Goodnow Commission plan, the legislature was forbidden to revise the governor's budget bill except to eliminate or reduce items. In other words, the governor's budget set an upper limit, and the legislature had to accept that limit. The Goodnow Commission claimed that "the weakness of all American financial methods . . . was to be found in the practice to which all American legislative bodies [were] addicted of adding either to the amounts demanded by the administrative departments, or to the items for which appropriations were asked."[90] Maryland's executive budgetary procedure was, then, expected to prevent the spending addicts in the house and senate from further draining the public treasury.

Harrington and the Democrats triumphed at the polls in 1915, and the legislature of 1916 quickly acted to implement the Goodnow plan. With only minor changes, the plan was presented to the voters as a constitutional amendment, and in November 1916 it carried by a two-to-one margin. The first budget prepared under the new plan received only cursory legislative review as the state's solons seemed to abdicate authority for appropriations to the governor. "What had taken the governor three months for preparation," Harrington observed, "the ways and means committee passed upon in practically two or three sittings, each of very short duration." The legislature approved the $12 million budget after striking only one item of $2,000.[91] In 1917 both Utah and New Mexico adopted similar plans that also forbade the legislature to increase items within the governor's budget, and in 1918 Governor Harrington proudly proclaimed that Maryland's scheme had "been more than favorably mentioned by expert economists or fiscal authorities of the country."[92]

But Maryland was not to be the model for most executive budget states. Instead, Illinois soon assumed an envied place in the vanguard of reform. In 1917 that state adopted a civil administration code that reorganized the executive branch and provided for an executive budget. Like most states, Illinois did not follow Maryland's example and forbid the legislature to increase items in the submitted budget. Thus the Illinois law imposed less restraint on the legislative branch. It was regarded as an advance, however, because it established a Department of Finance under the control of the governor to provide expert assistance in the formulation of the budget. Ideally, the executive budget was not to be a compilation of department estimates submitted by an uninformed governor. It was to be the product of thorough investigation, and Illinois's Department of Finance was designed to ensure knowledgeable budget preparation. In 1918 budget reformer William F. Willoughby concluded that the Illinois budget law represented "the furthest advance that ha[d] yet been made by any government in the United States towards the adoption of a budgetary system."[93]

Willoughby and others found Illinois's Department of Finance especially laudable because of the shortcomings in many other states. Although one state after another enacted budget legislation, too often the reforms seemed to have little real substance, largely because of the lack of an expert budget staff. For example, in 1915 Minnesota's legislature approved an executive budget act, and two years later Governor J. A. A. Burnquist presented recommendations for the coming biennium. In 1919, however, Burnquist submitted the unrevised departmental requests together with a two-page message explaining that the governor agreed with the departmental estimates and did not recommend any revisions. In 1921 and 1923, Minnesota's governor likewise transmitted the estimates without any suggested changes. The state's executives repeatedly complained that they could not provide a true budget as opposed to a listing of estimates because they did not have a budget staff. "In order that Minnesota may have an up-to-date budget system, the Governor should be given the help necessary for the careful preparation of a budget," Burnquist informed the legislature in 1919. "This can be done most simply and expeditiously by providing a budget officer who shall devote all his time to the study of the finances of the State." In 1925 Minnesota did finally create a Commission of Administration and Finance, which would supposedly provide "facilities for a scientific preparation of a budget."[94] But before the mid-1920s, Minnesota lacked the budget technicians necessary to ensure such a "scientific" endeavor.

Other states also lacked adequate personnel and machinery. Kentucky's budget law of 1918 did not provide any staff to assist the Budget Appropriation Commission. The commission imposed on the Assistant Auditor of Public Accounts to perform some clerical chores, but this overworked official could not fulfill the expectations of budget reformers. In 1924 the state's Efficiency Commission deplored "the absence of any staff that [could] give its full and undivided attention to the special technical problems of budget making." Budget problems were "highly technical" and could only be handled by someone who could "devote a great deal of time and thought to them."[95] Ohio did employ a full-time budget commissioner to aid the governor, but even in that state budget-making suffered from inadequate investigation and data collection. In 1921 the Joint Legislative Committee on Administrative Reorganization questioned whether the budget commissioners had been ferreting out the figures necessary to scientific budgeting. "In past years," the committee reported, "appropriations made to the budget commissioner for traveling expenses have been allowed to lapse, to large extent, and no record was obtainable in his office of visits made to departments, institutions, etc., and what findings and recommendations resulted."[96] The budget commissioner was seemingly sitting in Columbus doing little to discover the costs and needs of state institutions.

States were, then, gradually moving toward realization of budget systems, just as they were gradually reforming their tax structures. Throughout the nation state lawmakers were tightening the reins and checking previous anarchy in taxation and appropriation. They were attempting to shift the tax burden to those who had long evaded the demands of the state, and they were endeavoring to crack down on the smooth-talking institution heads who had traditionally received more than they deserved. In 1924 Kentucky's Efficiency Commission lamented, "Governmental *control*... is a science which as yet has hardly begun to attract the attention of the members of the Legislature, the Governor, the Auditor of Public Accounts, and other central administrative agents of the people."[97] This science of governmental control underlay the financial reforms of the early twentieth century. And despite its slow progress in Kentucky, it was making notable headway in such states as Wisconsin and California. The limp hand of state government so characteristic of the nineteenth century was yielding to a firmer grasp. State tax commissions were imposing some strictures on local assessors, income tax assessors were forcing holders of intangible property to pay their fair share, and state budget officers were forcing some order on the appropriation process. Kentucky's efficiency commissioners might have despaired, but the science of governmental control was gradually transforming state rule.

4

〜๑〜

Restructuring State Government

URING THE FIRST DECADES of the twentieth century, calls for efficiency and scientific management generated not only reforms in state finances but also changes in the structure of state government. New taxes and scientific budgeting were not enough. The whole lawmaking and administrative process was under scrutiny, and in the minds of many Americans, it was found wanting. State government seemed to require renovation, and reformers campaigned for a variety of proposals to ensure greater expertise and a more rational administrative structure. The lines of authority linking administrative agencies and governors had to be clearly defined, and lawmakers had to be better informed and benefit from the expertise of an emerging body of social scientists. Special-interest commissions had to answer to that representative of all the people, the state governor, and special-interest lobbyists had to yield their role as the font of legislative information to supposedly disinterested researchers. Governors and legislators also needed to learn from the experiences of other states and act cooperatively to adopt policies and laws that reflected the wisdom of legal experts and the nation's best minds. If the states did not cooperate for their mutual benefit, the threat of a federal takeover seemed imminent.

Yet many Americans no longer wanted to rely solely on legislators to make law. Instead, they sought to transform the lawmaking process by allowing the voters themselves to legislate through initiative and referendum. During the twentieth century, there were persistent efforts to produce more expert, professional legislatures. At the same time, however, the electorate remained suspicious of their lawmakers, and initiative and referendum provided one way to curb the power of not-always-trustworthy solons. While tuning up the engine of the state legislatures, the electorate did not neglect the brakes. A new element of direct democracy was the result.

Despite stereotypes to the contrary, then, state government was not a collection of complacent farmers and small-town lawyers gathering in sleepy

capitals where they perpetuated the errors of the past and remained indifferent to changing expectations or fresh notions of democratic rule. Certainly a
fair share of dinosaurs stalked statehouse corridors. But unthinking tradition-
alists did not necessarily have the upper hand. At the state level, proposals for
change were abundant and criticisms of the existing system were commonplace. Scores of commissions and committees considered how to restructure
and improve the state polity, applying a microscope to the status quo and iden-
tifying the various flaws and failures. Change was manifest in the states, and
early-twentieth-century policymakers were busy tinkering with the structure
of rule.

Administrative Reorganization

The focus of much attention was the executive branch and the administrative structure of the state. During the second decade of the twentieth century,
demands for administrative reorganization swept the nation as an increasing
number of governors, scholars, and journalists viewed renovation of the executive branch as a prerequisite for achieving economy and efficiency. Specifically,
reformers attacked the multitude of irresponsible state commissions and
boards and called for a limited number of departments headed by gubernatorial appointees subject to the governor's removal power. During the late
nineteenth and early twentieth centuries, legislatures created scores of often
overlapping commissions whose members duplicated the tasks of other boards
and were not subject to the control of the governors or removable by them. A
public health board or agriculture commission could be virtually a government unto itself. Under the reform scheme, governors would become the focus
of state administration, for they would appoint and remove the principal administrators and could be held accountable for the actions of these subor-
dinates. Accountability, in turn, would foster economy and efficiency, for a
profligate or incompetent governor would win few votes at the polls. Only
executives who maintained an efficient administrative apparatus and produced the best possible government services at the least possible cost would
supposedly face a bright political future.

By the close of the first decade of the twentieth century, governors were
growing increasingly dismayed that this wave of reform had not yet engulfed
the states. In his 1909 inaugural address, New York's Governor Charles Evans
Hughes repeated what was becoming a commonplace sentiment: "The practice
of withdrawing appointive administrative officers from direct responsibility to
the executive head of the State, who is directly accountable to the people is of

doubtful wisdom." A year later, in his annual message to the legislature, Hughes again expressed his belief that "it would be an improvement . . . in state administration if the executive responsibility were centered in the governor who should appoint a cabinet of administrative heads, accountable to him."[1] At a national meeting of governors in 1911, Alabama's Emmet O'Neal won the generous applause of his fellow chief executives when he criticized the weakening of gubernatorial powers "by a multiplicity of boards and departments" over which the governor "exercise[d] but scant authority." Because governors could not supervise or control state boards or commissions, "the executive and administrative business of the State [was] conducted without harmony, unity of action, efficiency, economy or system. No great business corporation," O'Neal remarked, "would long escape bankruptcy that tolerated such an utter lack of system and business methods."[2]

Action at the national level finally jump-started the state legislatures into responding to the complaints of their governors. President Taft's Commission on Economy and Efficiency, appointed in 1910, not only studied the adoption of scientific budgeting but also investigated the administrative machinery of the nation's executive branch. Taft specifically directed the commission to study the administrative structure "with a view to the assignment of each activity to the agency best fitted for its performance, to the avoidance of duplication of plan and work, [and] to the integration of all administrative agencies of the government . . . into a unified organization."[3] Although the commission reported diligently on the administrative disarray at the national level, Congress took no action. Yet state lawmakers were inspired to create their own economy and efficiency commissions to right the well-known flaws in state administration. Consequently, from 1911 to America's entry into World War I in 1917, fifteen states established such commissions. Maintaining its reputation for innovative rule, Wisconsin led the way in 1911, but the large states of New York, Pennsylvania, and Illinois followed suit during the next two years, lending their prestige to the movement.[4] Moreover, throughout the country, candidates for public office found that the battle cry of economy and efficiency won votes from the tax-weary electorate. By the onset of World War I, administrative reorganization had become a popular crusade.

Everywhere the efficiency investigators told dire tales of disarray. In 1913 the New York Committee of Inquiry reported: "The business of the State can reasonably be said to be run without any systematic plan whatever. Each department is conducted as an independent enterprise, and there is no effort at cooperation." In 1915 New York's newly created Department of Efficiency and Economy, together with the Bureau of Municipal Research, issued a seven-hundred-page survey of the state's government, which uncovered a total of 169 state agencies. According to the survey, the state's administrative structure had "grown up from year to year" and had not developed "according to any studied plan of scientific and economic needs." Among the 169 agencies were 108 boards, many of which "were created for similar purposes and . . . perform[ed] functions for which there already existed at the time of their creation fully organized departments of the government."[5]

Elsewhere the situation was much the same. "Everyone familiar with our government knows that we have too many State boards and commissions," New Jersey's Governor James F. Fielder wrote, "and that not only could we lessen the number and thereby economize in the expense of administration, but that greater efficiency would follow a consolidation of departments whose work is along similar lines." The New Jersey efficiency commission reported, "It has been the practice in this state to organize a separate commission for each new phase of work." To support its argument, the commission noted that New Jersey already had "two Washington Commissions—one a Washington Crossing Commission and the other a Washington Rock Commission." For the "preservation and improvement of the oyster industry," New Jersey maintained five separate commissions or bureaus, all of which were ineffective in stemming the decline in the value of oyster production.[6] Likewise, Minnesota's Efficiency and Economy Commission found the state's government "incoherent," with "a multitude of disconnected, unaffiliated departments and bureaus, over which neither the governor nor the legislature nor the people have effective control." To remedy this, the commission proposed six executive departments headed by gubernatorial appointees. "Instead of fifty or sixty independent governments, there will be one State Administration," the commission reported.[7]

Thousands of pages of surveys and a score of commissions, however, did not necessarily produce immediate or dramatic change. Economy and efficiency sounded admirable, but if reorganization plans threatened one's job or a favored agency, then the efficiency experts had gone too far. Writing of reforms to promote efficiency, the New Jersey commission found: "While [a state official] is loud in his praises of what can be accomplished along such lines, he is, at the same time, strong in his denunciation of the application of it to his particular department."[8] After criticizing the legislature for failing to act, New Jersey's commission did achieve a partial reorganization of the state government. In 1915 New Jersey lawmakers authorized four new departments to perform the services formerly handled by nineteen separate agencies. And in 1916 and 1918 the process of consolidation continued, most notably through the creation of a department of charities and corrections responsible for all the state's prisons, asylums, and hospitals.[9]

Illinois, however, won praise for implementing the first comprehensive program of administrative reorganization. In 1913 the legislature created a committee "to investigate all departments of the State government . . . with a view of securing . . . such reorganization that [would] promote greater efficiency and greater economy." The committee hired John A. Fairlie, professor of political science at the University of Illinois, to direct the investigation and conduct a series of public hearings in Springfield and Chicago. Issued in 1915, the committee's report repeated the standard complaints heard in one state after another: "A condition of disorganization and confusion exists in the executive departments of the State government which necessarily produces inefficiency and waste in the State services." Any attempt to chart the relationships among the executive branch agencies "would have resulted in an utterly unintelligible diagram." Approximately 130 executive agencies existed, with 34 new state boards, commissions, and offices created from 1909 to 1913, including such specialized agencies as the Stallion Registration Board, the Mine Rescue Station Commission, and the State Inspector of Apiaries. Though the governor had the power to appoint and remove officials, "the very number of separate offices [made] impossible the exercise of any adequate control" by the chief executive. Consequently, each body was "left to determine its own action." In accord with prevailing expert opinion, the committee, guided by Professor Fairlie, recommended "the reorganization and consolidation of more than a hundred separate State offices, boards and commissions into a limited number of executive departments, the chief authority in each department to be appointed by the Governor . . . and to be responsible to the Governor for the conduct of the department."[10]

In the gubernatorial election of 1916, the successful Republican candidate, Frank O. Lowden, ran on a platform dedicated to administrative reorganization and pledged to realizing the goals of the efficiency and economy commission. A millionaire business mogul, Lowden was accustomed to being in command. "I am a good deal of a monarchist when it comes to execution," he once admitted.[11] With a desire to be in complete charge of the executive branch and to run Illinois's government like an efficient business, the new governor convinced the 1917 legislature to approve a reorganization scheme embodied in an act called the Civil Administration Code. This code consolidated the approximately 130 boards, commissions, and bureaus into nine departments, each headed by a gubernatorial appointee. The plan was much the same as that proposed for Minnesota, but in Illinois it was actually implemented.

Moreover, Governor Lowden did not regret his advocacy of the plan. In 1919 he said of this "revolution in government" that it had "more than justified all the expectations that were formed concerning it." According to Lowden, "the governor [was] in daily contact with his administration in all its activities. Unity and harmony of administration ha[d] been attained, and vigor and energy of administration enhanced."[12] In other words, under the new plan the governor was in charge and knew what was happening in his departments. Someone was holding the reins of government and ensuring that it moved in one direction.

In 1919 Nebraska and Idaho followed Illinois's example, adopting thoroughgoing reorganization schemes. The 1918 platform of Nebraska's Republican Party announced forthrightly, "We favor the enactment of a Civil Administrative Code in this state . . . providing for the consolidation of the boards, institutions, commissions, and different departments and agencies of government, thereby eliminating useless offices and positions and avoiding the overlapping functions thereof." Elected on this platform, the incoming governor, Samuel R. McKelvie, likewise denounced "the confusion of authority and responsibility . . . as a menace to good government." Consequently, he pushed a reorganization plan through the legislature, thereby eliminating eleven boards and commissions and creating in their stead six departments headed by gubernatorial appointees. The result, according to McKelvie, was "simple, responsible organization and up-to-date administrative methods for the departments under the Governor, supplanting the confused, irresponsible and multifarious commission and board organizations."[13] In Idaho fifty-one departments, boards, and bureaus were erased from the chart of administrative organization and their functions placed under nine departments directed by gubernatorial appointees, who formed the executive's cabinet. Idaho's Governor D. W. Davis proudly proclaimed "the dawn of a new era in civil administration" and an end to "the red tape and costly duplication of the past."[14]

The momentum for administrative reform increased during the 1920s, as the ideals of economy and efficiency proved increasingly popular with voters and ambitious elected officials. Frank Lowden's success as an administrative reformer made him a leading candidate for the Republican presidential nomination in 1920, and other governors also won applause at home and nationwide as effective advocates of up-to-date, streamlined government. In 1921 Michigan's Governor Alex J. Groesbeck secured passage of a reorganization scheme and established his reputation as a dynamic executive, a reputation that ensured him three terms as governor. "Nobody knew where the other fellow was going," Groesbeck said of the state's administration prior to reform. "There was no way by which even the governor could get a proper perspective on the whole job to be done."[15] Meanwhile, in 1925 New York's Governor Alfred E. Smith secured passage of a constitutional amendment mandating administrative reform, and a committee headed by the eminent former governor, Charles Evans Hughes, drew up a statute reorganizing the Empire State's executive branch. Battling an obstructive Republican legislature, the Democrat Smith garnered laurels from good-government advocates nationwide for the difficult task of taming the administrative structure of the nation's largest state.[16] In Virginia Governor Harry Byrd likewise sponsored a comprehensive administrative restructuring. His success at achieving "business-like" government made him the most admired governor in the South and was a significant building block in the foundation of a political organization that would rule Virginia through the 1960s.[17] Others joined Lowden, Groesbeck, Smith, and Byrd in this popular movement, and by the close of the 1920s seventeen states had adopted reorganization schemes.

Some, however, questioned the centralization of authority in the governor's office and perceived dangers in the new reorganization schemes. Most notably, special-interest groups that had traditionally controlled commissions or boards feared that centralization would result in too much political interference. As early as 1913, the esteemed public health expert Dr. Charles Chapin urged that control over state health matters remain in the hands of a long-term board, composed largely of physicians, which should appoint the state's chief health officer. "The only reason that is advanced in favor of appointment by the governor is the somewhat theoretical one that all executive power should be lodged in the chief executive so as to fix responsibility," Chapin noted. Yet unfortunately, the governor was "a partisan and often too much at home in the pernicious methods of practical politics." "When the utopian day arrives in which the governor, in his appointments, will ignore all claims to office except fitness," Chapin concluded, "it may be well to transfer to him all executive appointments, but until then the states in which the state health officer is selected by the board of health had better cling to this method."[18] When Ohio's legislature was considering reorganization in 1921, the Ohio Public Health Council presented much the same argument, claiming that a health executive should be "chosen for fitness and kept in office as long as he renders effective service" and should not need to give attention "to the changing conditions of political affairs." A gubernatorial appointee would remain in charge of the health department only so long as the governor, elected to a two-year term, stayed in office. Effective health service, however, supposedly required continuity in office and immunity from shifting political fortunes. Thus, in 1916 the Minnesota Commission on Public Health argued in favor of appointment by boards, claiming, "The assurance of permanency of tenure is essential in order to secure high grade men in academic and scientific positions."[19]

Public welfare professionals believed that they too needed to be insulated from gubernatorial control. In 1922 a public welfare group attacked the much-vaunted Illinois reorganization reform, arguing that "any system which [did] not insure a continuity of service of experienced and competent heads of departments and institutions [was] a defective and undesirable system." That same year, a participant at the National Conference of Social Work concurred with this criticism. Attacking "the political scientists and the efficiency experts" who had not shown how to eliminate partisan influence, this devotee of public welfare professionalism would "not admit the necessity or even the desirability of concentrating authority and responsibility in all matters pertaining to human welfare in a single executive who in the nature of things [was] the leader of the dominant political party of the state."[20]

These various critics all touched upon a fundamental shortcoming of the administrative reformers. Blindly devoted to a neat diagram of government with clear lines of authority, the reformers failed to recognize that rule by a supposedly confusing array of boards and commissions might not have been all bad. The commissions accommodated the spokespersons for various interests. They permitted those who had a special interest, and purportedly a special expertise, in a government service to have a disproportionate voice in the administration of that service. In this case administrative efficiency and expertise were not necessarily allies. Enhanced executive power would not invariably result in the most professional administration. Furthermore, in states where sectional divisions were strong, commission rule permitted representation from every area of the state. Administrative reformers assumed that the governor spoke for all of the people of the state and thus should be the focus of power. Public health specialists, however, believed the governor represented the Republican or Democratic party rather than the health profession. And downstaters might view their executive as a suspect upstater rather than a sterling tribune for all of the state's citizenry. Although administrative reorganization might have saved some money, a neat pyramidal scheme with the governor at the apex and clear lines of authority stretching to the base was not everyone's perfect solution.

Tinkering with the administrative structure and rearranging departments and commissions remained a favorite pastime of state-level reformers, however. Administrative restructuring would characterize the 1930s as well as the 1920s, with nine additional states adopting reorganization statutes between 1930 and 1937. State leaders were not satisfied with inherited practices or procedures. They were not invariably shortsighted, lethargic, reactionaries resistant to change and disinterested in "modernizing" government. Instead, they adapted the executive structure, seeking to reach the elusive goals of economy and efficiency.

Legislative Reference Services

In a further effort to attain these goals, state leaders of the early twentieth century endeavored to introduce a new level of expertise in the lawmaking process. Throughout the twentieth century there was a persistent tension between the old ideal of the part-time, citizen legislature and newer ideas of a full-time, professional lawmaking body. Most wanted to retain representation by friends and neighbors who served for a few months each biennium and received nominal pay. Yet at the same time there was a growing desire that these friends and neighbors become better informed and enjoy expert advice and aid. Consequently, between 1900 and 1920 a number of states embraced the idea of a legislative reference service that could gather information on policy issues and aid lawmakers in drafting statutes. Rather than allowing novice legislators to wander ignorantly through the lawmaking process, with adverse consequences for the states, the legislative reference services offered expert guidance. Thus, the citizen legislator survived, but the part-time lawmaker was to have the assistance of a disinterested professional staff.

The generally acknowledged father of legislative reference work was Charles McCarthy of Wisconsin. McCarthy launched his legislative reference work in 1901. That year, the library of the Wisconsin Historical Society was moved from the capitol to the society's headquarters on the university campus. Recognizing the need for a small reference collection close at hand to the legislators, the secretary of the Free Library Commission secured an appropriation of fifteen hundred dollars to provide "for the use and information of the legislature, the several state departments, and such other citizens as may desire to consult the same, a working library . . . of the several public documents of this and other states, and to purchase . . . standard works of use and reference." McCarthy was appointed the "document cataloger" of this collection, and henceforth until his death in 1921, he was the preeminent crusader for legislative reference work throughout the nation.[21]

McCarthy championed legislative reference services as needed antidotes to the amateurish, sloppy lawmaking so prevalent in American statehouses. The chief cause of faulty statutory construction was a lack of information and expert aid. "The legislator is a busy man; he has no time to read," McCarthy remarked. "We can be of the greatest service to him, if we index, digest and make as clear as possible all kinds of information." If a legislative reference service did not provide help and information, then lobbyists would do so, thereby gaining dangerous influence over harried lawmakers who were often "deceived by those . . . seeking the accomplishment of their own selfish ends." Private interests maintained bureaus of information for legislators, but McCarthy urged the creation of "public information bureaus open to private and public interests alike."[22]

McCarthy's bureau also included a bill-drafting department staffed by lawyers who knew how to frame, revise, and amend bills. To ensure that these attorneys served the legislators and did not insert their personal views into the bills they drafted, McCarthy enforced strict rules governing the preparation of legislation. No bill was to be drafted "without specific detailed written instructions from a member of the Legislature," and "the draftsman [could] make no suggestions as to the contents of the bills." McCarthy emphasized, "Our work is merely clerical and technical. We cannot furnish ideas." In both the library work and bill drafting, McCarthy's staff was expected to remain neutral about policy issues. Legislative reference bureaus had to be "absolutely non-political and non-partisan."[23]

The Wisconsin bureau chief believed that services such as his could prove the salvation of state government. "There is a widespread agitation at the present time for centralization and nationalization," McCarthy noted, "a movement which strives to have one after another of the state functions absorbed by the national government." But he believed that as "state laws . . . gradually improved, a great deal of this agitation [would] cease." Thus McCarthy concluded, "The only means of saving . . . state government, the only means of keeping the federal government at Washington from controlling our affairs, is to make our state laws better and better." To make them better, states had "to use scientific methods" in lawmaking such as provided by the legislative reference services.[24]

Not everyone shared McCarthy's enthusiasm for the legislative reference service. Despite McCarthy's public pronouncements about the need for his staff to remain neutral, he was a widely acknowledged champion of the La-Follette reform program and openly lobbied for greater state funding for the university where he was an adjunct faculty member. Such action stirred resentment, and in 1907 a LaFollette foe in the legislature attacked a special appropriation for McCarthy's library, proclaiming, "If this bill passes we may be creating the biggest and most dangerous lobby that ever was known."[25] By the time of the 1914 gubernatorial election, criticism of McCarthy had mounted to the point where his life's work was threatened. Conservative Republicans united in an attack on McCarthy's "bill factory" and targeted specifically its formidable chief. Meanwhile, the Democratic platform pledged to "make the reference library a purely reference library for reference uses by the legislature and other public officials and prohibit every officer and employee thereof from directly or indirectly initiating, preparing, drawing, recommending or assisting in passing any legislative bill."[26]

Despite this opposition, Wisconsin's legislative reference library survived. Republican Emanuel Philipp won the election and in a message to the legislature criticized McCarthy's bureau as exercising "an undue influence upon legislation."[27] The legislature, however, had grown dependent on the reference service and its bill-drafting department, and consequently the grumbling failed to produce adverse legislative action. At times McCarthy might not have behaved with appropriate servility, but he and his staff had proved indispensable to too many members of the assembly and the senate.

McCarthy's efforts not only secured his agency a permanent place in Wisconsin lawmaking; they also reaped a flock of imitators. In 1904 California's state library established a legislative reference section, and two years later Indiana's State Library Board did likewise, appointing as permanent director a man who had been trained by Charles McCarthy. In 1907 seven states joined the movement; six more did so in the biennium of 1909–10. By 1917 thirty-three states, representing all sections of the country, had established legislative reference services.[28]

Pioneering reference librarians in other states embraced and disseminated the views of their Wisconsin colleague. Indiana's C. B. Lester spread the gospel by preaching the necessity of "making available for the legislator all that knowledge which he need[ed]" and of providing it "quickly and accurately."[29] Nebraska's Addison E. Sheldon seconded this idea, defining his reference bureau as an institution that gave "condensed, comprehensive, impartial, accurate information on any subject under the sun upon five minutes notice."[30] In Georgia the state library sold the McCarthy message by writing to every legislative committee chair and offering to aid them in assembling needed data. According to state librarian Maud B. Cobb, the Georgia solons were "clearly surprised at the gratuitous service and deeply grateful for it." So grateful, in fact, that they authorized a permanent legislative reference department, which after three years of service was described by Cobb as "the most virile phase of state library work" and as "dynamite to the sluggish."[31]

In some states these dynamic bureaus not only served the legislature while it was meeting but also acted as the research arms of special investigatory committees that prepared legislation between sessions. For example, between 1912 and 1915, Nebraska's reference bureau provided the research staff for special commissions on workers' compensation, tax reform, school law revision, forestation, and reform of legislative procedure. In 1912–13 Indiana's bureau prepared the report of the Industrial Education Commission, and two years later it aided special committees in codifying the state's health and mining laws. In 1917 the Hoosier agency was in charge of gathering and compiling information for a proposed state constitutional convention; the Illinois reference service collected volumes of data and material on state government problems to aid delegates to that state's constitutional convention of 1919–20.[32]

The dynamism of the most active agencies was not always appreciated, and McCarthy was not the only reference bureau director who was accused of injecting personal views into the legislation drafted. In most states, however, there was little danger that the legislative reference bureau would become too powerful. The greater danger was that it would lapse into dormancy. In 1925 John H. Leek of the University of Oklahoma estimated that only ten or fifteen of the thirty-three existing services were "substantial." That same year, the Wisconsin Legislative Reference Library circulated a questionnaire to services throughout the nation and on the basis of the replies concluded that at least one-third of the reference agencies were nominal.[33] With little funding, some services seemed to consist of one possibly knowledgeable reference librarian in the state library. The degree to which the bureaus aided in the drafting of legislation varied greatly. A survey of the 1929 sessions found that virtually all the bills introduced in Wisconsin's legislature were drafted under the legislative reference library's supervision, and 90 percent or more of the bills in Pennsylvania, Illinois, and Indiana were products of the reference bureaus of those states. Yet North Dakota replied, "We draft very few bills."[34] And the North Dakota case was not unique. As with administrative reorganization and tax reform, some states embraced the movement to modernize less vigorously than others. Less affluent states simply donned the garb of reform as cheaply as possible by designating a compiler of newspaper clippings as their expert staff.

Nonetheless, the legislative reference movement marked a beginning in the gradual professionalization of the state legislature. Voters and solons alike were slow to abandon the ideal of the citizen lawmaker; but throughout the twentieth century, critics of state government claimed that professional lawmaking was a prerequisite for the survival and vitality of the states. At the beginning of the twentieth century, Charles McCarthy was already promoting expert staff assistance as a defensive bulwark against aggression by a power-hungry national government. Robert Whitten, chief of the New York legislative reference department, wanted to go even further than the Wisconsin reformer. In 1908 he suggested that legislative committees "employ experts of all kinds— engineers, accountants, economists, physicians, actuaries, and in fact specialists of every class . . . capable of disinterested scientific investigation."[35] Such futuristic innovations were not yet possible. The trend toward expert staff assistance had begun, however; the drift toward professionalism was under way.

Initiative and Referendum

Expert assistance was one solution to the problem of an amateur legislature dependent on the advice and guidance of private interest lobbyists. Another means of righting legislative wrongs was to bestow lawmaking power directly on the people. In the minds of many Americans, state government was faltering as corporate lobbyists and allied political bosses applied their stranglehold on the body politic. Only the combined power of the people through a system of direct democracy seemed sufficient to free the states from greedy clutches. Acting on this belief, voters in one state after another approved constitutional amendments permitting citizens to initiate and adopt laws through petition and popular referendum. To undo the mischief of the state legislatures, the reform amendments also permitted voters to demand referenda on controversial bills. Like the administrative reorganization schemes and the legislative reference bureaus, these initiative and referendum measures exemplified the adaptation of the states to the perceived needs of the age. The intent, however, was not to enhance legislative authority or bureaucratic efficacy. It was to provide an end run around suspect lawmakers and administrators.

Actually, at the turn of the century, the practice of popular referenda was already well established at the state level. Every state but Delaware required a popular vote on constitutional amendment proposals, and such propositions appeared frequently on the ballot. Between 1901 and 1908, the states submitted about four hundred constitutional propositions to voters. Moreover, in some states other significant measures required voter approval. For example, Michigan's constitution of 1850 mandated submission of all general banking laws to the electorate. The Illinois constitution of 1870 required that all changes in the banking laws, as well as any measures increasing the state indebtedness above a specific limit, be approved by the voters.[36] Thus, at the state level, the referendum was part of the governing tradition.

At the close of the nineteenth century, however, some vocal malcontents were launching a campaign to expand direct democracy in the states. Among the leaders of the cause was James W. Sullivan, a typographer and labor union activist, who had visited Switzerland and become acquainted with the system of direct democracy in that country. In 1892 Sullivan's book *Direct Legislation* was published, selling ten thousand to fifteen thousand copies annually until 1895. This work extolled the virtues of initiative and referendum to readers throughout the nation, and in 1896 Sullivan helped found the National Direct Legislation League. The *Arena,* a reform journal edited by Benjamin O. Flower, also took up the cause, further publicizing the possibility of direct democracy.[37]

Meanwhile, supported by labor groups and the increasingly powerful Populist movement, South Dakota critics of the status quo were pursuing a campaign that would lead to adoption of the first initiative and referendum scheme in America. In the 1896 election, an alliance of Populists and Democrats won a majority in the legislature, and the following year, South Dakota's lawmakers approved the placement of an initiative and referendum amendment on the ballot. Voters endorsed the constitutional change by a large margin. Many South Dakotans apparently agreed with Governor Andrew Lee's views on the reform. "I can see that the occupation of the lobbyist will be gone under direct legislation," Lee wrote to a leader in the national movement for direct democracy. "When he is compelled to appeal his case directly to the voters of the State and submit his designs to the scrutiny of public discussion, he will conclude that his game is not worth the pains, and thus about the worst, most selfish and demoralizing phase of our political system will be at once removed."[38]

The South Dakota initiative and referendum procedure as finally adopted would supplement and curb representative rule but not supplant it. Upon petition of at least 5 percent of the voters, any proposal could be placed on the ballot, and if approved by the electorate, it would become law. Five percent of the voters could also demand a referendum on bills enacted by the legislature, and a majority of the electorate could thereby veto legislative actions. This referendum procedure did not apply to any law that the legislature designated as "necessary for the immediate preservation of the public peace, health or safety or support of the State government and its existing public institutions."[39]

Despite the enthusiasm for the reform, South Dakota voters were slow to make use of their new power. Moreover, by taking advantage of the emergency exemption, the legislature limited the opportunities for invoking a referendum. In 1913 supporters of direct legislation estimated that the legislature had designated 40 percent of the measures enacted in South Dakota during the past decade as emergency laws and consequently not subject to repeal by the electorate.[40] In any case, not until 1908 did South Dakotans finally apply the reins to representative rule, placing one initiated measure on the ballot and referring three laws adopted by the previous legislature. During the following two decades, thirteen more initiated measures appeared on the ballot as well as sixteen additional referred laws. Of the fourteen measures initiated from 1908 to 1928, only two won voter approval, but of the nineteen laws referred during this period, thirteen were vetoed by the electorate.[41] Thus, South Dakotans were exercising their lawmaking authority, though they did so sparingly. As compared to the hundreds of bills enacted by each legislature, the number of initiated and referred bills were few.

Because of this rather limited use of direct democracy, South Dakota did not win fame as the premier exponent of initiative and referendum. Instead, this honor went to Oregon. Leading the movement in Oregon was William S. U'Ren, who had organized that state's Direct Legislation League in 1892. As a state legislator in the 1890s, he pushed for an initiative and referendum amendment to Oregon's constitution; and as in South Dakota, farmer and labor organizations rallied behind the movement, which promised to free government from the iron grip of big-business lobbyists. In an editorial backing the reform, Oregon's leading newspaper argued that under the referendum plan, "no predatory measure could be carried before the people. The legislative lobbyist would be put out of business." Direct democracy would prove an obstacle "to surreptitious legislation; to legislation in particular interests; to partisan machine legislation, and to boss rule."[42] As in South Dakota, supporters of direct legislation believed it would open the closed world of lawmaking and break the monopoly of power enjoyed by the lobbyist and the political boss. It would ensure that Oregon's government was truly government by the people.

In 1902 an initiative and referendum amendment finally appeared on the Oregon ballot, and it carried by an eleven-to-one margin. According to one observer, Oregonians rallied behind the amendment because they "felt the government was getting away from them and they desired a more direct control, both in the making of laws and in their enforcement, than they enjoyed." But another claimed that "a great many people did not know what they were voting for." U'Ren's sales pitch had been so effective that the newspapers, many state leaders, and both political parties had lined up behind the reform, and many uninformed voters were "simply following the rest."[43] These two interpretations of the 1902 returns summed up the clashing views that would dominate debate over the merits of direct legislation. Some viewed the voter as an alert tribune of the public interest, ready to curb injustice if given the means to do so. Others regarded the electorate as incapable of understanding difficult issues and easily swayed by molders of public opinion. Giving lawmaking powers to these impressionable voters would threaten the stability of state government and nurture demagoguery.

The Oregon scheme was similar to that of South Dakota. Eight percent of the voters could place an initiated proposal on the ballot, and 5 percent could require a referendum on a legislative act, excepting those laws "necessary for the immediate preservation of the public peace, health or safety." Three months before each election, the secretary of state was to issue a pamphlet containing the text of each initiated and referred measure, with any arguments for and against the measure provided by advocates and opponents. Each voter in the state was to receive this pamphlet, and thus he supposedly would have ample opportunity to become informed about the issues.[44]

Oregon voters soon found that keeping informed was not to be an easy task. Although only 2 issues appeared on the ballot in 1904, two years later 11 initiative and referendum measures confronted the electorate. By 1908, the number of ballot propositions had risen to 19; in 1910 the figure reached 32, and in 1912 it peaked at 37 before falling to 29 in 1914. Between 1904 and 1919, Oregonians voted on a total of 170 statewide issues, including 105 initiated measures. Unlike South Dakotans, Oregon residents used their new power to the fullest, leading the *Portland Oregonian* to complain that the reform encouraged "every group of hobbyists, every lot of people burning with whimsical notions to propose initiative measures or to interpose objections through referendum appeal."[45]

Among the ballot issues were some measures of only local interest and others of statewide significance. For example, on the 1910 ballot were six proposals to create new counties and two bills to change the boundaries of Portland's Multnomah County.[46] Yet in each general election, Oregonians also passed judgment on proposals vital to the long-term crusade against political boss rule and corporate privilege. In 1904 voters approved an initiated measure creating a direct primary for nominating candidates, thereby practically eliminating the party convention. "This law killed the political party bosses and destroyed their machines, both State and municipal," U'Ren proudly reported.[47] In 1906 the electorate endorsed an initiated constitutional amendment granting home rule to cities, two years later it authorized recall of public officials, and in 1910 it adopted a presidential preference primary. All these measures were intended to enhance the power of the people at the expense of the professional politician. To end corporate tax dodging, in 1906 Oregonians adopted initiated measures that imposed gross earnings levies on express, telegraph, telephone, and railroad car companies. That same year, the electorate approved a bill forbidding railroads to grant free transportation to public officials and thereby seek to win their favor.

Though such propositions conformed to William U'Ren's view of the public interest, other measures were clearly intended to serve special interests. In 1906 the owners of a toll road sought to profit from direct democracy by initiating a bill that provided for the state's purchase of their road. Four years later, Rogue River fishermen dedicated to preserving their share of the salmon used the ballot to make war on cannery interests on the lower Columbia River. Casualty companies and "ambulance chasing" attorneys turned to the referendum in their battle against a workers' compensation act that threatened their livelihoods.[48] Perhaps most notoriously, the town of Cottage Grove attempted to refer the University of Oregon's appropriation bill to the electorate in retaliation for opposition in the university's home town of Eugene to creation of a new county with Cottage Grove as county seat. In 1912 an irate Oregonian concluded, "The machinery of direct legislation has fallen into the hands of dishonest men who for money and spite have abused the privilege of direct legislation and who in the name of the people have misrepresented our citizenship and brought disgrace upon our state."[49]

Despite these criticisms, Oregon residents remained dedicated to the reform. In 1912 the *Oregonian* concluded that initiative and referendum were "here to stay. The People rule . . . in Oregon . . ., and they have no wish or desire or purpose to go back to old methods."[50] Flaws notwithstanding, direct democracy seemed to enhance the power of the people, and the people were not about to relinquish their newly won clout. By the second decade of the twentieth century, direct legislation was a sacrosanct fixture of Oregon's governing process.

Many residents of other states were eager to follow Oregon's example. By 1919 twenty states had adopted both initiative and referendum, and two additional states had adopted referendum only. The procedures were especially popular in the West, where every state but Wyoming embraced either initiative or referendum or both. In the Great Plains both of the Dakotas, Nebraska, and Oklahoma incorporated initiative and referendum provisions in their constitutions. Among the states of the industrial Midwest, Michigan, Ohio, and Missouri were converts to the cause, but in the former Confederacy only Arkansas and Mississippi accepted the reform. The New England states of Maine and Massachusetts adopted initiative and referendum, and Maryland accepted referendum alone.[51] Generally, the farther east a state was located, the less enthusiasm there was for the cause. Oregon was the premier exponent of the movement, and the states nearest it were most likely to fall prey to the lure of direct legislation.

In all of these states, the arguments presented in favor of initiative and referendum were much the same as in South Dakota and Oregon. In 1907 Missouri's reform governor Joseph Folk endorsed the reform, claiming that it was "of much importance in the final elimination of corruption and the establishment of true representative government." Embracing the widely felt hatred of corrupt lobbyists, Folk said of direct legislation, "It puts an effective stop to bribery in legislative halls, for bribery of legislators would be useless where the people are the final arbiter of a measure."[52] In California reform governor Hiram Johnson deemed direct legislation a means for breaking the powerful grip of lobbyists employed by the Southern Pacific Railroad. "The first step in our design to preserve and perpetuate popular government shall be the adoption of the initiative, the referendum, and the recall," Johnson proclaimed in his inaugural address of 1911. Expressing his belief in direct democracy, the California governor boldly announced, "No man is better in government than any other man." Johnson's father, the longtime legislative spokesperson of the Southern Pacific Railroad, thought otherwise and graphically expressed the sentiments of foes of direct democracy when he cried, "The voice of the people is not the voice of God, for the voice of the people sent Jesus to the cross."[53] In Arkansas Governor George W. Donaghey championed the cause of direct legislation as an antidote to corruption in the legislature.[54] Similarly, Colorado's Governor John F. Shaforth made initiative and referendum a vital plank in his platform dedicated to freeing Colorado from the supposed bondage of political bosses and corporate interests.[55] Writing in 1912, a Maine professor summed up the general view of initiative and referendum: "The people of Maine . . . look upon [it] as a safeguard against ill-advised and corrupt legislation, as a check upon the lobby and the power of the old-time political boss."[56]

The format of the initiative and referendum laws in all of these states was similar, with a specified number or percentage of the voters able to place a new proposal on the ballot or refer an act of the legislature to the electorate. But the use of these procedures differed markedly from one state to another. California, Arizona, and Colorado, like Oregon, made extensive use of direct legislation, and between 1912 and 1918 voters in California passed judgment on 30 initiated measures, whereas Arizonans and Coloradans voted on 33 and 41 initiated proposals respectively. In contrast, from 1908 to 1918, 9 initiated measures appeared on the ballot in Montana and only 1 in Maine.[57] In some states legislatures frequently attached an emergency clause to statutes, thereby exempting them from referral to the voters. But elsewhere solons refrained from such tactics and did not significantly limit the right to referral. Writing in 1914, an Arkansas observer noted that "the last legislature manifested a strong tendency to prevent reference," though he found it difficult "to discover any fixed principle in the use of the emergency clause."[58] Any measure could be an "emergency" bill if it was fortunate enough to be so designated. Thus, although the referendum allowed voters to curb the power of the legislature, in Arkansas and elsewhere the emergency exemption permitted legislatures to check the power of the people.

Application of initiative and referendum differed from state to state, but by 1920 there was nationwide agreement that the procedures were not perfect solutions to the problem of representative rule. Special interests exploited the reforms, and business, farm, and labor organizations had a clear advantage in manipulating direct democracy. They had the money necessary to hire a corps of circulators to gather the requisite signatures and to pay for newspaper advertising prior to the election. An Oregon newspaper had claimed that initiative and referendum made "every man his own legislature."[59] But in fact, not every man could afford the privilege. Moreover, by the close of the second decade of the twentieth century, it had become clear that voters were not always competent to handle the complex issues presented to them. When confused or ignorant, they often chose not to vote on a question, leaving resolution of the issue to a minority of the electorate. And as the elder Johnson noted, the voice of an ignorant or selfish people could yield decisions about as meritorious as that of the Good Friday mob. Yet in the states that had adopted initiative and referendum, voters were not willing to revoke the procedures and grant a monopoly on lawmaking to the legislature. Initiative and referendum were flawed, but in the minds of the electorate they were not as flawed as the system that existed before their adoption.

Direct legislation thus survived, a legal expression of the people's lack of faith in their chosen representatives. This skepticism about the state legislature was, in fact, a continuing feature of the twentieth century, and it yielded two strands of reform, one seeking to infuse expertise into the lawmaking process and the other endeavoring to ensure a healthy dose of popular control. The legislative reference services exemplified the first and the initiative and referendum the second. During the early twentieth century, there was as yet no conflict between these two strands; political reformers could simultaneously embrace professional lawmaking and the sovereign right of the people to intervene. In later decades, however, the tension would grow between expertise in government and the power of the people. To what extent should law be a product of expert staff and professional legislators, and to what extent should lawmaking remain close to the people? Were all people equally capable of governing, as Hiram Johnson claimed, or should authority be entrusted to those most knowledgeable and experienced? These were questions that continued to trouble the states throughout the twentieth century. Achieving a desirable balance in the lawmaking process was a goal not readily attained.

Interstate Cooperation

State leaders of the early twentieth century not only sought to enhance the role of the people in the lawmaking process; they also sought to preserve the role of the states themselves in policymaking through new mechanisms of interstate cooperation. Rail lines reached throughout the nation, facilitating an ever-increasing volume of interstate commerce, and huge corporations transacted business from Maine to California. Given these facts of modern economic life, the states seemed increasingly obsolete as governing units. Economic realities demanded uniform nationwide regulation and thus an expanding role for the federal government. The states could, however, counter a feared federal monopoly on lawmaking by adopting uniform legislation based on the latest expert opinion. If representatives of the states could frame such model uniform statutes and the legislatures then enact them, a resort to national legislation would prove unnecessary. But to achieve this degree of cooperation and uniform action, the states had to establish certain structures for coordinated effort. During the 1890s and the first two decades of the twentieth century, such structures emerged and promoted an unprecedented degree of interstate cooperation. Yet the experience of the early twentieth century also revealed obstacles to united action. The states existed and would survive as significant lawmakers because the nation was not uniform and on many subjects the people did not want uniform laws. Instead, they wanted laws tailored to the needs and desires of their specific state.

In 1907 two innovative plans for cooperation reflected the growing desire for uniform state legislation. First, William G. Jordan, a former editor of *Saturday Evening Post,* authored a brief pamphlet that called for creation of a "House of Governors" to "promote uniform legislation on vital questions, to conserve states rights, [and] to lessen centralization." Under Jordan's scheme, the governors of all the states would convene for two or three weeks each year to consider proposals for uniform state legislation. The individual legislatures would then enact the statutes proposed by the House of Governors.[60] If the states acted in concert, they would forestall further expansion of national power and guarantee their preeminent position in the federal system.

The second scheme was the handiwork of Charles A. L. Reed of the University of Cincinnati. Speaking at the conference of the National Tax Association in November 1907, Reed proposed a Council of States "to formulate standard bills . . . of pressing importance, and submit them for enactment in uniform terms by the state legislatures." Reed proposed not a conclave of governors but rather a council of delegates chosen by each of the states. Otherwise, Reed and Jordan generally agreed. Like Jordan, the Cincinnati professor regarded interstate cooperation as absolutely necessary to stem the extension of federal power. "It becomes convincingly obvious," Reed explained, "that the States, unless they take some step that they have not yet taken for the wise and more uniform exercise of certain of their present functions, are destined to forfeit an important part of both the revenues and the influence that they now enjoy." Emphasizing the threat of "federal aggression," Reed issued "a warning to the states" that they needed to take cooperative action for the sake of self-preservation.[61]

The following year, the nation's governors did meet for the first time, yet not at their own behest but at the invitation of President Theodore Roosevelt. Roosevelt organized a White House gathering of all the governors to promote a goal that he strongly embraced—the conservation of natural resources. The Governor's Conference of 1908 was, then, a presidential initiative to secure gubernatorial support for a national policy. Commenting on the conference, the *Nation* observed, "We may be very sure that Mr. Roosevelt had no notion of erecting a new political organism." This was no House of Governors. Instead, the conclave was "one of those devices to collect and express public opinion and to forward good causes."[62]

The 1908 gathering, however, jump-started the movement for an annual gubernatorial convention, and in January 1910 governors from thirty states again convened in Washington, D.C. But this time the meeting was called by the governors themselves. President William Howard Taft addressed the meeting, yet he emphasized that he and the arrangements committee agreed that the conference sessions should not be at the White House as in 1908 but at "a neutral place," the New Willard Hotel. "This is a movement among the Governors to have some sort of permanent arrangement that shall bring them here without suggestion from anyone but the Governors themselves," Taft told the assembled state executives.[63]

In his comments to the governors, the chief organizer of the conference, Governor Augustus E. Willson of Kentucky, attempted to define the nature of this assembly. William G. Jordan was serving as unofficial secretary to the conference, but Willson made it clear that the governors were not in Washington to implement Jordan's scheme. "This meeting has no legal authority whatever," Willson asserted. "It is not a house of Governors. It is simply a conference of Governors." The conference was intended to serve the common interests of the people and "for the common pleasure of the Governors." Opening the door for a degree of socializing alien to the plans of Jordan and Reed, Willson concluded: "We shall reserve the right to have a meeting that doesn't amount to anything except having a good time together if we want to; but it is likely that such a gathering of men as this will bring forth something, on many occasions, that will be useful to our country."[64] In other words, the governors conference would at the very least offer the assembled executives a good time and probably would also yield some serious benefits.

Following the Kentucky governor's introductory remarks, Governor Charles Evans Hughes of New York further attempted to define the "scope and purpose" of the governors conference. "It is not sought . . . to create another agency of government or to invest a body such as this with governmental functions," Hughes explained. Instead, the advantage of the conference was "in the formation of common sentiment" among the governors, resulting in "greater uniformity of State action and better State Government." Hughes believed that it was impossible for the governors "to undertake the drafting of uniform laws," but their "united consideration" of proposed uniform statutes would "bring these matters into deserved prominence and supply for the progress of uniform legislation a much needed impetus." Moreover, the governors could learn from a valuable "interchange of State experience." Hughes conceived of the states as "constituting a laboratory of experimentation in free institutions."[65] The governors' conferences would permit those in charge of the laboratories to share their findings to the mutual benefit of all.

The 1910 attendees seemed to agree with Hughes. None of the governors present stepped forth to implement the plans of Jordan and Reed. Rather, the governors conferences were to be conclaves of business and pleasure where the nation's executives could become acquainted with one another and with what was happening in the various states. The annual meetings would promote a degree of uniformity, but they would not be weapons aimed at destroying the diversity of the states. They were forums of congeniality and discussion, not coercion and dictation.

At their 1912 conference, the state executives agreed upon "Articles of Organization" that would incorporate the views of Governors Willson and Hughes. Article 3 stated, "The functions of the Governors' Conference shall be to meet yearly for an exchange of views and experience on subjects of general importance to the people of the several states, the promotion of greater uniformity in state legislation and the attainment of greater efficiency in state administration."[66] Again the governors did not endorse an innovative house of governors or council of states but only a modest, extraconstitutional adjustment to the federal system. The Governors' Conference was to be an annual gathering dedicated to sharing professional information and realizing the prevailing early-twentieth-century goal of efficiency.

During the next decade, the governors' conferences would continue to play a modest, rather than a revolutionary, role in American government. Attendance was less than perfect, reflecting the limited significance of the institution. At the 1914 conference, only sixteen states were represented, with fourteen governors present. The next year, representatives of twenty-six states were in attendance, including twenty governors and fifteen former governors. And in 1916 twenty-three states participated, with seventeen sitting governors present.[67] State executives thus felt no compulsion to attend the conferences. If their schedules permitted and they had some interest in interstate cooperation, they might participate. Yet the conferences remained largely a pleasurable combination of social gathering and discussion group. They were informative and attracted the attention of the most conscientious and knowledgeable governors, but a majority of state executives did not attend.

The Governors' Conference was not the only agency for interstate cooperation. By the second decade of the twentieth century, there were a number of organizations composed of state officials and policymakers that served as channels for the sharing of information and the promotion of a modicum of uniformity. They were among the many professional organizations that developed during the late nineteenth and early twentieth centuries, and they shared with those groups a desire to agree upon uniform professional standards. As early as 1883, the directors of the state bureaus of labor statistics agreed to meet for "candid discussion." Four years later, Philadelphia hosted the first convention of state factory inspectors, largely at the behest of Henry Dorn, Ohio's chief inspector of workshops and factories. According to Dorn, the meeting was "for the purpose of comparing notes" and availing oneself "of the experience and suggestions of others." In 1914 the factory inspectors and labor statisticians merged into the Association of Government Labor Officials of the United States and Canada. The new organization's constitution reflected the growing demand for concerted state action and pledged the association "to secure uniform labor legislation."[68] Meanwhile, in 1907 the National Tax Association held its first meeting, answering a call by Ohio's Governor Andrew L. Harris "to secure the application of correct economic and business principles in all tax legislation, and thus develop a high degree of uniformity in the tax laws of the several states."[69] Seven years later, the emerging corps of state highway engineers formed the influential American Association of State Highway Officials for their mutual edification and to impose professional standards of road construction throughout the nation.[70]

Perhaps the most ambitious promoter of interstate cooperation was the National Conference of Commissioners on Uniform State Laws. As early as 1881, the Alabama State Bar Association created a committee to correspond with bar associations in other states for the purpose of encouraging uniform state legislation, especially with regard to marriage and divorce, negotiable instruments, conveyance of land, and attestation of wills. Acknowledging the "desirability of uniformity in the laws of the several States," in 1889 the American Bar Association appointed a special committee on uniform legislation, and the following year, New York's legislature authorized the governor to name three "Commissioners for the Promotion of Uniformity of Legislation in the

United States" to consider the best means for achieving concerted legislative action among the states. As a result of these initiatives, the first National Conference of Commissioners of Uniform State Laws was held in Saratoga Springs, New York, in 1892, with representatives of nine states present.[71] Henceforth, each year commissioners appointed by their respective governors or legislatures met to consider and draft uniform acts. On returning home, they were expected to submit the proposed statutes to their legislatures, which ideally would adopt the standard acts and thus further the cause of legal uniformity. By 1909 forty-four of the forty-six states had appointed commissioners for the annual conference, and the assembled commissioners had approved seventeen acts for legislative consideration during the conference's seventeen-year history.[72]

The following year, however, marked the high point of enthusiasm for the uniform legislation movement. In 1910 the National Civic Federation, an elite reform organization whose membership list read like the who's who of the nation, organized a Conference on Uniform State Legislation in Washington, D.C. It was planned to coincide with the Governors' Conference then meeting in the nation's capital, so 31 governors as well as 750 delegates representing forty-four states were present to promote the cause of uniform laws. President Taft spoke to the conference, as did Alton B. Parker, the Democratic candidate for president in 1904 and the chair of the National Civic Federation's Committee on Uniform Legislation. The *National Civic Federation Review* reported that the "speakers frequently asserted that this effort of the Federation to secure uniformity of legislation among the States [was] the greatest voluntary, non-political movement ever undertaken in this country." To stir action, supporters of the cause repeatedly warned that the states had to embrace uniform legislation in order to thwart the expansion of federal power. Labor leader and National Civic Federation vice president Samuel Gompers predicted, "Either the Federal Government, as a matter of industrial and commercial necessity, will exercise the powers which constitutionally belong to the States, or, if that is to be avoided, the States must move toward acting with the greater degree of uniformity necessary to the successful and lawful conduct of industry and commerce." Similarly, Indiana Governor Thomas R. Marshall warned, "Unless the States respond to this movement and meet the need of it, sooner or later we shall find ourselves hopelessly in the grip of the [federal] government where the people will be compelled to act for the relief which we deny them."[73] In 1910 the only choice appeared to be uniform state action or an ever-more-powerful federal government feeding on the prerogatives formerly belonging to the states.

The dire warnings produced only limited action, however. By 1919 every state but Georgia had adopted the Uniform Negotiable Instruments Act drafted by the conference of commissioners in 1896, and forty-four states and territories had approved the Uniform Warehouse Receipts Act framed in 1906. But none of the other twenty-eight acts drafted by the conference since 1892 had won the approval of a majority of the states. In the twenty-seven years since its drafting in 1892, the Uniform Execution of Wills Act had been adopted in only six jurisdictions, and the Uniform Insurance Policies Act framed in 1901 was not on the statute books in any state.[74] Frustrated by the diversity of state regulatory measures, insurance companies yearned for uniform legislation, and yet state legislatures consistently balked at adopting a single nationwide standard.

By the close of the second decade of the twentieth century, it was clear that the prospects for uniform state legislation were limited. Legislatures could rally behind a single statute on negotiable instruments or warehouse receipts because such a measure stirred little excitement or controversy, except perhaps among a few members of the American Bar Association. Most voters did not even know what negotiable instruments were. But when the conference of commissioners drafted uniform laws on child labor and workers' compensation, as it did in 1911 and 1914, respectively, it was dealing with well-publicized topics of popular concern, and it could not realistically expect to achieve a consensus among the states. In 1910 Alton B. Parker recognized the limits to the movement when he remarked, "We do not aim at absolute uniformity of law throughout the States, but a wise and conservative uniformity."[75] Despite the expectations of the most ardent devotees of uniformity, only cautious and conservative change was possible. On most subjects the states could not be convinced to accept a single legal standard.

This was especially evident in the crusade for uniform divorce laws. During the late nineteenth and early twentieth centuries, divorce laws varied greatly among the states. Some states, such as South Carolina and New York, sought to uphold the sanctity of marriage by making it difficult or impossible to obtain a divorce. The Dakotas and Nevada, however, offered lax procedures, which attracted divorce seekers to those states and enriched local lawyers and hotel owners. One could thus thwart the efforts of some jurisdictions to uphold morality by temporarily moving to Sioux Falls or Reno. Defenders of the family and holy matrimony deplored this situation and desired a tough uniform standard. Responding to these concerns, the 1899 Conference of Commissioners on Uniform State Laws was devoted exclusively to the question of divorce statutes. The president of the conference remarked "that the laws concerning divorce were the most important of the subjects that called the Conference into being [and] that a treatment of the subject was most urgently demanded by public opinion."[76] Despite these urgent demands, the 1899 conference was unable to agree on a uniform measure. At the call of Pennsylvania governor Samuel W. Pennypacker, a National Congress on Uniform Divorce Law met in 1906 with delegates from forty-two of the forty-five states. This congress produced a uniform divorce act that the Conference of Commissioners on Uniform State Laws approved the following year. Yet by 1916 only three states, Delaware, New Jersey, and Wisconsin, had adopted the uniform standard.[77]

Nationwide consensus on the subject of divorce proved impossible. At the Governors' Conference of January 1910, Governor Martin S. Ansel of South Carolina announced bluntly, "We have no divorce law in South Carolina and we will never have it."[78] At the conference two years later, Nevada's Governor Tasker Oddie told his fellow executives, "The declaration that divorce is inherently an evil cannot be substantiated." The bachelor governor explained, "We have advanced in intelligence beyond the idea that there is anything essentially holy, and therefore morally irrevocable, in a marriage which would . . . condemn a pure woman to a lifelong unwholesome existence with a diseased and bestial husband." Given such extremes of opinion, there was no possibility of uniformity. South Carolina was dedicated to never permitting divorce, whereas Nevada's governor spoke of "rational modern divorce laws" that were in "keeping with modern conditions."[79]

Advocates of uniform legislation thus had to face the grim realities. They lived in the United States of America, not the Uniform States of America. The Conference of Commissioners on Uniform State Law, the Governors' Conference, and the other organizations of state officials and policymakers opened new channels for consultation and cooperation, but they did not eradicate the differences among the states. The nation was heterogeneous, and no group of commissioners could homogenize the moral views of the forty-eight states and produce a blend satisfactory to all. In fact, if the states were to be Charles Evans Hughes's laboratories of experimentation, they needed the freedom to pursue different courses and test different policies. In 1910 Nebraska's Governor Ashton C. Shallenberger questioned the prevailing "desire for unification or standardization" when he observed that uniformity was "very often only another name for mediocrity." Rather than accepting the lowest common denominator, the states should seek to enact "the very best laws possible upon any given subject."[80] Diversity, rather than uniformity, was conducive to this search for excellence.

Despite the shortcomings of the movement for uniform legislation, the impetus for interstate cooperation and consultation would not wane. During the course of the twentieth century, organizations and institutions promoting interstate links would proliferate. Governors and other state officials would continue to share information in their search for professional standards and coordinated, if not uniform, action. Just as the goals of legislative professionalism and administrative efficiency would remain on state agendas, the drive for interstate cooperation would persist and contribute to the making of the modern American state. The structural tinkering of the period 1900 to 1920 was only the beginning of a century-long effort to tune up the mechanism of state government.

5

Adapting to the Automobile Age

"NOT KINGS, nor Congresses, nor courts, nor constables, nor ships, nor soldiers, but roads rule the world," Governor Theodore Bilbo told the Mississippi legislature in January 1928. "Permanent highways are . . . the exodus from stagnation in any society, the call from savagery in the tribe, the high priest of prosperity."[1] In this paean to highways, Bilbo was expressing graphically the prevailing attitude of the 1920s. Automobiles were no longer toys for the rich; they were essential to the mobility of millions of Americans. But the growing army of automobile owners could not maximize the return from their investment in Fords or Chevrolets without a network of hard-surfaced highways. Thus, they clamored for modern roads, and any state or locality that failed to respond to these demands for concrete and asphalt arteries was deemed woefully behind the times. During a decade devoted to the worship of material success, smooth, durable roads were the emblem of prosperity and the antithesis of stagnation.

In one state after another, roads ruled the civic agenda. Each aspirant for the governor's office promised to lift the state out of the mud, and incumbents loudly boasted of the road mileage surfaced during their administrations. Voters rallied behind bond issues for new highways, and legislators jockeyed to secure road improvements for their districts. To satisfy the recreation needs of the automobile-borne, some states also planned comprehensive park systems, and the movement's pioneers promoted professional standards for park development through a national organization of state park advocates. No one questioned the belief that government had a sacred duty to serve the motorist, for the automobile age had definitely arrived.

These new obligations, moreover, transformed state government and elevated it to a position of unprecedented significance. For the burden of responding to the automobile fell primarily on state government. Washington, D.C., provided expert advice but relatively little money. And state highway officials and park developers became even more convinced than ever before that localities lacked the competence to shoulder the demands of the new age. With the federal government failing to expand its role and local governments unable to do so, the states filled the gap and assumed the task of financing and constructing highways and parks. In the process, the states had to revamp their revenue structures and rely on new forms of taxation. The state ledgers of 1929 were radically different from those of 1917, for the automobile age imposed massive new expectations on the states, and they quickly responded with new means of raising revenue.

During the 1920s, then, the demands of the motorist translated into expanded state authority. Seeking to achieve statewide networks of highways and parks developed in accord with prevailing professional standards, policymakers perpetuated the trend toward centralization and supervision by state-level administrators so evident during the previous two decades. The localities were perceived as inadequate to the task, and the federal government was unwilling to assume the primary responsibility, so the states took action.

Developing the Highway System

During the first few years after passage of the Federal-Aid Act of 1916, the pace of change was halting. The minority of states without highway departments conformed to the desires of the American Association of State Highway Officials (AASHO) and created road agencies. But federal money did not flow freely to the states, and the pace of federal-aid construction was discouraging. Dedicated to scrupulous supervision, the Bureau of Public Roads moved slowly in approving federal-aid proposals submitted by the states, and the nation's entry into World War I in April 1917 restricted the availability of construction materials. The war effort took priority over road building. In 1918 the states contributed at least an estimated $66.4 million for road construction, whereas the federal contribution was only $2.1 million, less than the amount expended by the single state of Oregon. Moreover, in late 1918 and early 1919, voters approved almost $225 million in state highway bonds, including $60 million in Illinois and $50 million each in Pennsylvania and Michigan.[2] The electorate clearly wanted highway construction, and the sooner the better.

Frustrated by delays in Washington, D.C., highway advocates were losing faith in the Bureau of Public Roads and the scheme of state-federal cooperation embodied in the 1916 act. The Chamber of Commerce of the United States and a wide range of other organizations joined the American Automobile Association in lobbying for the creation of a federal highway commission that would be directly responsible for the building of a national system of major thoroughfares. The federal government rather than the states would build and own the principal interstate highways, and an independent federal commission would supplant the Bureau of Public Roads, a subordinate agency within the Department of Agriculture. In 1918 the editor of *Engineering News-Record* observed, "Sentiment has been growing all over the country in favor of the construction and maintenance by the Federal Government of a highway system that shall transcend state bounds and that shall do nationally what state control has done within state borders—place the through routes under a single competent authority." Expressing the feelings of those who favored a national highway commission, he asked: "The states have highway departments. Why not a United States highway department? The states have highway systems. Why not a Federal highway system?"[3]

With a greater dedication to the expeditious construction of interstate highways than to the preservation of states' prerogatives, many state highway engineers even favored a national system that would eliminate the obstacles involved in working through the states. The 1918 convention of the AASHO was torn over the subject, and when the issue came to a vote, the result was an exact tie and a consequent delay in any action.[4] As late as 1920, the president of the AASHO, who was employed as chief engineer of Maine's state highway commission, continued to favor "a system of Federal highways" and "the creation of a Cabinet position or a strong commission to look after this work." Remembering "the dissension that occurred . . . when this matter was under discussion two years" earlier, however, he was muted in his comments, claiming he would "very much dislike to see a repetition of that."[5]

The engineer from Maine needed to be wary, for the opponents of a national commission had mobilized their forces and achieved the upper hand by 1920. Among the leading foes of a national system was Thomas H. MacDonald, chief engineer of the Iowa State Highway Commission until his appointment as chief of the federal Bureau of Public Roads in 1919. While still Iowa's chief engineer, he disparaged the "disposition in some quarters to overlook existing agencies and to pass responsibility for undertaking the super-program of road improvement demanded along to the Federal Government." He believed the aid scheme embodied in the act of 1916 was "a worthy and suitable foundation" and that the act itself was "as liberal a measure as [could] be expected." Any rules or regulations "productive of delays or embarrassments or misunderstandings between the State and Federal departments . . . should be eliminated in conference."[6] Upon assuming his federal post, MacDonald remained dedicated to these views and successfully endeavored to remove the embarrassments and misunderstandings that had slowed project approval under his predecessor. At MacDonald's urging, the secretary of agriculture now permitted states to begin construction upon receiving approval from the bureau's district engineers. State engineers did not need to wait for the bureau's Washington officials to complete a project review. This decentralization policy, combined with the end of wartime restrictions on the shipment and use of construction material, expedited the highway programs and relieved tensions between the state departments and the federal bureau. By mid-1920 MacDonald could confidently boast of the "outstanding results of federal aid."[7]

Others seconded MacDonald's views. In 1919 Secretary of Agriculture David Houston was "unable to see the need for the creation of a separate Federal highway commission" or the wisdom of replacing the existing "cooperative program" with a scheme to provide for a limited number of federally owned interstate highways. Protecting his bureaucratic turf, he believed that "nothing material would be gained by the proposed change" and that "many complications would be introduced."[8] The Kansas highway department agreed and took a lead in convincing other state highway engineers to remain loyal to MacDonald, the Bureau of Public Roads, and state construction and ownership of federal-aid roads. At the AASHO national convention of 1919, the Kansans triumphed, securing a resolution endorsing the existing system of federal-state cooperation and rejecting the notion of federally owned or constructed highways.[9] An Illinois state engineer expressed the prevailing opinion when he wrote that "it would be more desirable to all concerned if the respective States had complete control of all State and Federal highways with such general supervision from the [national] Government on all Federal highways to insure that the roads in each State would connect at the State lines" and to see that the federal money was spent to construct roads suitable to expected traffic.[10]

Political realities also were running counter to the idea of nationally owned highways and a national commission. Rather than sharing the expense with the states, the federal government would have to pay the complete cost of the proposed national system. Neither the incoming president, Warren Harding, nor Congress was eager to foot the awesome bill for such a scheme.[11] Moreover, the notion of national construction and ownership offended many congressional foes of centralized authority. Texas representative Sam Rayburn protested that he was "sick and tired of the Federal government's everlasting sticking its hand into the affairs of [his] state. [He was] against any building up of more bureaucracies in Washington to reach out into the states and tell people what they shall and what they shall not do."[12] For many lawmakers, big government was a bogey, and nationally constructed and owned highways smacked of an un-American concentration of power.

Consequently, when the provisions of the Federal-Aid Act of 1916 expired in 1921, Congress did not choose the path of greater centralization but instead continued the policy of state-federal cooperation. The Federal Highway Act of

1921 perpetuated the principles of the 1916 law, though it provided that federal aid could only be expended on a predetermined system of major roads, that system to constitute no more than 7 percent of the total road mileage in the state. In other words, federal money could not be used to finance construction of minor country roads. It was for highways that would carry interstate or intercounty traffic, and the state highway departments would submit a list of such roads to the Bureau of Public Roads for its approval. Construction and maintenance of these federally aided highways were to be under the direct control of the state highway departments and not delegated to local authorities. Thus, in 1921 as in 1916, federal legislation bolstered the authority of state highway officials and further weakened local units, a goal much desired by the AASHO. The fifty-fifty matching requirement of the 1916 law was retained, and administration of the program remained in the hands of Thomas MacDonald and the Department of Agriculture.

The Federal Highway Act of 1921 permanently determined the role of the federal and state governments in road construction. In the United States, the federal government would provide some financial aid and ensure professional standards, but it would not construct or own highways. The building of highways was to be a state responsibility, and the new thoroughfares were to be state property. In the twentieth century, unlike the early nineteenth century, there was to be no National Road. The states were in charge of constructing the highways of the automobile age.

Furthermore, during the 1920s it became apparent that the states were going to shoulder a disproportionate share of the cost of paving over America. Though the number of automobiles and trucks soared during the decade, the federal government's financial commitment did not increase. For 1922 Congress appropriated $75 million for the highway program, for 1923 reduced the sum to $50 million, increased it to $65 million for 1924, and for the years 1925 through 1930 returned to the $75 million figure. From 1921 through 1930 the states spent $7.9 billion on roads, only $839 million of which came from the federal government. In addition, the federal share of state road expenditures progressively declined during the decade, dropping from 20 percent in 1920 to less than 8 percent in 1930.[13] The demand for new and better roads was rising, but the federal government did not respond to these heightened demands. Instead, the states had to take up the slack and step up their contributions.

Not only were state and local governments solely responsible for funding the 93 percent of mileage not in the federal-aid system; the states also provided more than the required 50 percent contribution to federal highways. For the highways improved with federal aid during the fiscal years 1927, 1928, and 1929, the federal government provided only 44.5 percent, 43 percent, and 42 percent, respectively, of the funding.[14] Moreover, the impatient states proceeded to construct thousands of miles of federal highways without any federal funding. In its annual report for 1927, the Bureau of Public Roads explained that "for several years the unaided efforts of the States ha[d] resulted in the improvement of a greater mileage than ha[d] been built with Federal aid, and the major portion of this unaided State work ha[d] been applied to the improvement of the roads of the Federal-aid system." The bureau reported, "The independent State work tends to increase, and for each mile improved with Federal cooperation there are now nearly 2 miles that are built by the States alone."[15] The wealthier states of the northeastern quadrant of the nation were most likely to proceed with construction of the federal-aid highway system without awaiting funds from Washington. Of the system mileage completed in New England in 1925, only 26 percent received federal aid, and only 19 percent of the mileage in the east north central states was federally funded. By comparison, the figures for the poor or sparsely populated states of the east south central and Rocky Mountain regions were 94 percent and 88 percent respectively.[16] Basically, federal funding was insufficient, and the wealthier states moved ahead on their own.

Throughout the 1920s, then, the federal government's response to the automotive revolution was lukewarm. Thomas MacDonald, working closely with his fellow engineers in the AASHO, shared the latest findings in highway research and provided an expertise that was especially welcome in the poorer, more backward states. But Washington was freer with advice than it was with dollars. In 1924 a member of the National Tax Association committee on highway finance observed correctly, "Federal aid . . . has its greatest value not in its amount but in the standards it sets up." Five years later, a committee of the Chamber of Commerce of the United States likewise concluded, "The present value of federal aid is measured not so much by the size of contributions as by . . . the experience and wisdom of the Bureau of Public Roads in guiding the state highway departments to sound programming, design and construction methods." State officials pointed out that the federal government's role as benefactor was exaggerated. "The impression which seems to be quite general that the Federal Government pays fifty per cent of the total cost of any Federal aided improvement is erroneous," remarked Michigan's highway commissioner in 1926. And four years later, that state's highway chieftain reiterated this notion when he spoke on financing highway construction and maintenance. "Michigan's federal aid allotment each year amounts to approximately $2,200,000," he noted, "which is not sufficient even to maintain the roads on our federal system."[17] The bottom line was that at least half of the federal-aid highways were being built by the states without federal aid.

During these years the nation's political leadership was adverse to increasing the federal contribution. The tightfisted Calvin Coolidge regarded the highway program as a violation of American principles of federalism and an undesirable drain on the nation's treasury. He referred to the federal-state sharing of costs as "one insidious practice which sugar-coat[ed] the dose of Federal intrusion." The president further concluded, "When the National Treasury contributes half, there is a temptation to extravagance by the State." Thus both the principles of federalism and public finance purportedly required an end to aid from Washington, and in his 1925 budget message, Coolidge characteristically recommended a reform that "would operate to diminish the amount of Federal contribution."[18]

Coolidge's stance was indicative of the limited tolerance for the existing system of federal funding. During the 1920s, the political climate was not favorable to further federal aid. Faced with this reality, the states had to shoulder the burden of accommodating the automobile and the truck. Before 1916 state policymakers had concluded that localities were inadequate to the task of building principal highways. Now the states had to recognize that the federal government was not up to the task of financing more than a small portion of the bill.

Consequently, the crusade for improved roads suitable for the automobile age was to be conducted largely at the state level. In one state after another, governors campaigned on the promise that they would pull their commonwealths out of the mud; and after two or four years in office, each governor loudly boasted of the miles of pavement laid during his or her administration. For example, Michigan's great road-builder was Governor Alex J. Groesbeck, who presided over the state from 1921 to 1927. Not until 1919 had Michigan's legislature authorized the state to take direct charge of the construction and maintenance of the trunk-line network, having relied until that time on state aid to local governments to achieve road-building goals. That same year, Michigan's voters approved a $50 million highway bond issue. Thus, when Groesbeck took office, the money and authority were available to pave Michigan's roads, and the governor was dedicated to the task. "It must be conceded," he observed to the legislature in 1926, "that the paving, widening and general improvement of our trunk line system constitute the most important work the state is engaged in." Nothing could be permitted to interfere with this important work. To ensure a ready supply of cement necessary to keep the state's concrete highway program on schedule, in 1923 Michigan purchased its own cement plant. Three years later, Groesbeck boasted, "Not once since we acquired the . . . cement plant has a single construction job been delayed because cement was not delivered promptly." In fact, five to six hundred miles of concrete pavement were laid each year during Groesbeck's administration, and by the end of his tenure as governor, Michigan had improved more than sixty-five hundred miles of the trunk-line system, including gravel and macadam roads as well as concrete highways.[19] Moreover, in 1925 Michigan assumed complete responsibility for major highways when the legislature finally relieved the counties and townships of any share of the costs of constructing or maintaining trunk-line or federal-aid roads. Completing a gradual process of centralization that began with a state-aid law in 1905, the 1925 legislation made the building and care of primary roadways solely a state responsibility.

Groesbeck also implemented the Wider Woodward project, a scheme to widen the state's busiest road, Woodward Avenue. At a time when the federal Bureau of Public Roads was mandating only an eighteen-foot-wide pavement for federal-aid highways, the state of Michigan laid two parallel strips of concrete, each forty-four feet wide, from Detroit to Pontiac. The resulting thoroughfare won the title of "the world's first super-highway."[20]

In Illinois the exemplar of the good-roads governor was Len Small, who led the state from 1921 to 1929. "Illinois leads the world . . . and its 7,000 miles of completed concrete pavement exceed the mileage of any other state in the Union," Small proudly proclaimed in 1928.[21] In 1924 alone, the Small administration was able to take credit for the construction of 1,229 miles of hard-surfaced roads.[22] But hard pavements were not only a means of boosting the commercial fortunes of Illinois; they were also a tool for enhancing the political fortunes of Len Small. Counties that lined up behind Small on election day were more likely to be pulled out of the mud than those who backed an opponent. If an area wanted hard-surfaced roads, political loyalty was the price it had to pay to the Small administration.[23]

Dedicated to creating an apolitical, professional highway department, some state executives eschewed this mix of paving and politics. Acclaimed the "Road Building Governor," Austin Peay of Tennessee could take pride in the thousands of miles of hard-surfaced highways constructed during the four and a half years he served as chief executive.[24] Even more noteworthy was his refusal to follow Tennessee tradition and play politics with his public works program. Responding to one job seeker, Peay wrote: "We had a slush of politics before the present administration, with the result that the people were securing no roads. Nothing is more sure than the disruption of highway activities by politics." And he did not trade roads for votes. "I cannot make promises for the sake of votes," he wrote one mayor. "That has been the ruin of road building in many states." Peay firmly believed that he had to "leave the road locations to the Highway Department. It is their business and for me to attempt it would be to demoralize our road building completely."[25]

Later Tennessee governors were not so deferential to the professional wisdom of highway department officials. Nor were their counterparts in some other states, where governors used promises of highways to win the support of local political leaders and legislators. The pattern was not uniform throughout the nation, but in many states the advent of the automobile and the paved highway added to the arsenal of gubernatorial weapons and accelerated the already evident trend toward executive ascendancy within state government.

Owing to the combined pressure of the motoring public and the federal Bureau of Public Roads, the 1920s also witnessed an acceleration of the trend toward centralization. Just as Michigan's state officials assumed control over the trunk-line system in 1919, other highway engineers, especially in the South, fought to overcome localism and enhance state control. As early as 1911, Oklahoma had established a state highway department, but not until 1924 did Oklahoma lawmakers respond to pressure from the federal bureau and actually shift responsibility for constructing and maintaining highways from the counties to the state. Similarly, in 1925 the Texas legislature finally authorized its state highway department to have "exclusive and direct control" of all federal-aid projects. The state authorities could improve all other sections of the state highway system "either with or without county aid." By the fiscal year 1931–32, the monthly average number of employees of the Texas state highway department was ninety-five hundred, and in the latter year the state broke ground for an eight-story office building to house the expanding agency.[26] In 1930 federal threats to cut off aid forced Mississippi's legislature to give the state highway commission "complete control and supervision, with full power and authority to locate, relocate, widen, alter, change, straighten, construct, or reconstruct any and all roads on the State Highway System."[27] A decade behind most of the other states, Mississippi was now poised to perfect its highway program.

Although it had fallen behind most of its fellow states, Mississippi could take solace from the events transpiring in neighboring Arkansas. For that state represented the worst in state highway development. Dedicated to local rule but restricted by a constitution that prohibited counties to borrow except to refund debt, the state of Arkansas opted to rely on hundreds of local improvement districts to build its roads. Each of these districts had the power to tax and borrow, and each operated with little state supervision or coordination. "If roads in the different districts connected," wrote one critic of the scheme, "it was largely accidental."[28] Moreover, the district commissioners rarely knew much about road building or public finance. Those who did understand government finance too often seemed to use that knowledge to line their own pockets.

By the early 1920s, this recklessly decentralized scheme was the object of bitter attack. "Personally I will say that this road business has turned out to be the greatest disaster that has ever befallen the people of Arkansas," remarked Governor Thomas C. McRae in 1921. "The whole thing is a scandal and a shame and the odor of it reaches to heaven." A justice of the Arkansas Supreme Court said that millions of dollars had been spent on roads that began nowhere and ended nowhere.[29] The federal secretary of agriculture ordered an investigation of the Arkansas situation, and it predictably uncovered substantial evidence of incompetence and unsatisfactory road maintenance. Consequently, in January 1923 the federal government suspended road aid to Arkansas until the state reformed its procedures. The result was the Harrelson Act, which enhanced the powers of the state highway commission and charged it with responsibility for the construction and maintenance of the state highway system. Arkansas's problems, however, persisted. In 1927 the state assumed the burdensome road district debt as well as committing itself to borrowing $13 million annually for the next four years to finance further highway construction. As a result, between 1926 and 1930 the state debt soared from $3 million to $120 million. This increase proved ominous, for during the depression of the 1930s, Arkansas won the dubious distinction of being the only state that defaulted on its debt.[30] In the course of the 1920s, the state and its road districts had borrowed millions for roads but had remarkably little to show for the massive expenditures. Motoring through Arkansas was still an adventure fraught with peril for one's tires, for the state had generated more conflict and complaints than concrete pavements.

Arkansas was the anomaly, however, not the norm. Between 1921 and 1931, the surfaced mileage under state control in the United States rose from 84,000 to 258,000; and by the latter date, one could drive throughout the Northeast and the Midwest on paved highways. In large type on its 1931 road map, the Iowa Highway Commission proudly announced: "Motorist. Get This, Once for All — IOWA IS NO LONGER A MUD ROAD STATE!"[31] This was a boast a majority of American states could make. With remarkable rapidity the states had constructed a web of paved highways to replace the dirt roads prevalent just twenty years earlier. The pace of development had been uneven, with Michigan pioneering the construction of superhighways and Mississippi barely entering the age of concrete pavement. In fact, the highway programs of the 1920s pointed up one of the flaws in twentieth-century federalism. Some states were more than able to shoulder the demands of the age with no help from Washington, D.C., whereas others were too poor or sparsely populated to handle the task, even with persistent prodding from the federal government.

Federal intervention did not close the gap between the rich and the poor. The financial contribution from Washington was relatively minor as compared with the state funds expended. During the 1920s the states, not the federal government, paid for the paving of America. The federal Bureau of Public Roads did, however, reinforce the existing trend toward state centralization and professional administration. Throughout the 1920s, as in the Federal-Aid Act of 1916, the federal bureau's chief contribution was to encourage the concentration of authority in state highway departments. Arkansas's road districts were vestiges of past localism and pariahs to centralizers in Little Rock and Washington. The states were not only to pay for their state highway systems; they, and not the localities, were to build them.

Financing the Highway System

The creation of the state highway systems carried a heavy bill, forcing legislators to confront the problem of where to get the money. During the decade following World War I, however, state policymakers successfully overcame this problem and funded a public works program of gargantuan proportions. Whereas in 1914 state highway departments allocated only $24 million, by 1919 this figure was up to $107 million, and in 1929 it reached $910 million.[32] At the beginning of the 1930s, then, state highway building and maintenance was a billion-dollar-a-year business, and the states proved capable of funding this enterprise. Through borrowing and new forms of taxation, they were able to meet the financial challenge of the automobile. Moreover, through experimenting with new taxes, the states opened the door to a radical change in their revenue structures that would prove vital in the future.

The quickest way to raise ample sums to finance a grand network of highways was through borrowing. After the passage of the Federal-Aid Act of 1916, this option appealed to many state lawmakers, and throughout the nation bond proposals appeared on the ballot. Whereas in 1915 there were $115 million in state road bonds outstanding, by 1922 state issues totaled $346 million, with Illinois, Pennsylvania, Michigan, and California committing themselves to a large share of the debt. Borrowing continued throughout the 1920s, with $1.43 billion in state road bond issues outstanding by 1931.[33]

Yet borrowing was not the preferred solution in every state. Between 1894 and 1928 only thirty-one of the forty-eight states issued state highway and bridge bonds, the remaining seventeen eschewing a policy of indebtedness. Moreover, the proportion of road funds derived from borrowing did not increase during the course of the 1920s. Whereas the sale of bonds and notes

accounted for 19 percent of state highway income in 1923, by 1928 it only constituted 14 percent of the total.[34] The pattern was not uniform—some states,
such as Arkansas, assumed a burdensome highway debt during the late 1920s—
but overall, the forces dedicated to pay-as-you-go financing seemed to gain
ground in the course of the decade.

The reluctance to borrow meant, however, that states had to generate massive current revenues. Everywhere the citizenry wanted modern roads, and if
the state did not borrow the money to pay for these improvements, they needed
to raise it through taxation. Beginning with New York in 1901, the states
imposed license or registration fees, and this proved a handsome source of
revenue as the number of automobiles soared and the states periodically raised
the fees. In 1909 the average license tax was only $3.20, but by 1923 it was up to
$12.50. Overall, registration or license tax revenues rose from $12.4 million in
1914 to $51.5 million four years later, $122.5 million in 1921, and $288.3 million
in 1926. Although the rate of increase slowed in the late 1920s, the registration
tax remained the largest source of state highway revenues through 1928, generating approximately one-fourth of highway income during the middle and
late 1920s.[35]

One advantage of this tax was that it placed the burden of highway costs on
the users. During the 1920s it became an axiom of public finance that automobile and truck owners should pay the cost of roads; the revenues should not
come from the state's general fund, derived from property, business, or income
taxes. In 1923 *Engineering News-Record* summed up the attitude of highway
experts when it editorialized: "It is the user who must pay. And with 14,000,000
motor vehicles being used the payment has to be large."[36] A. R. Hirst, state
highway engineer of Wisconsin, likewise urged Americans to brush their "brains
clear of cobwebs, obsessions, prejudices and bunkum, and calmly recognize
that when [they] bought and insist upon operating fourteen million or more
motor vehicles, [they] bought also a highway expenditure of billions of dollars,
just as much a part of the cost of those motor vehicles as . . . their tires, their
engines, and their supplies."[37] That is, motorists demanded highways, but they
were also expected to pay for them. Registration or license fees helped realize
this expectation.

The burden of the registration fee was not necessarily proportional to the
use of the highways, however. Most of these fees were based on the horsepower
or weight of a vehicle rather than the number of miles driven on the state's
thoroughfares. A high-powered Cadillac that remained in the garage paid a
considerably higher license fee than an inexpensive, low-horsepower Ford that
cruised the highways daily. Recognizing this, states were increasingly attracted

to another user levy, the gasoline tax. "The motor fuel tax . . . in our opinion is by far the most scientific impost upon motor vehicles," wrote A. R. Hirst in 1923. For it "meter[ed] highway service and the benefits received from the use of highways" and "approximate[d] toll gate results without the infirmities of toll gate procedure."[38] Moreover, the gasoline tax, unlike the license fee, shifted some of the burden of financing to out-of-state travelers who wore out the pavements and purchased fuel but were registered in their home states. In 1922, in a sales pitch for the fuel tax, the California Highway Commission reported, "It will bring a large new revenue into the state from out-of-state cars that are attracted to California by the state's highway system, and which now enjoy the state's roads without contributing either to the cost of their construction or their upkeep."[39] Since a tax that soaked nonvoters was inherently appealing to elected officials, the gasoline levy enjoyed a definite advantage among legislators. In fact, the motor fuel impost was to spread rapidly throughout the country and reveal to state lawmakers the lucrative potential of consumption taxes. Once the gasoline levy conquered the nation, state finances would never again be the same.

As early as 1914, Congress considered a tax on motor fuel, and the following year President Woodrow Wilson proposed a gasoline levy. Yet the federal government took no action, and the states moved in to mine this new mother lode of revenues. In February 1919, Oregon led the way with a one-cent-per-gallon impost, and during the following two months Colorado and North Dakota also adopted one-cent levies and New Mexico imposed a two-cent tax.[40] In 1921 sixteen states had already imposed the tax, by 1923 the figure was up to thirty-five, and two years later forty-four states were garnering the benefits of an impost on motor fuel. When New York's legislature approved a gasoline levy in 1929, it brought the number of taxing states to the full complement of forty-eight. Thus, within a single decade, the impost became a fixture of every state's finances. "The history of this tax is unprecedented," wrote political scientist F. G. Crawford in 1930. "In ten years it has swept the country."[41]

States not only adopted the levy; they also readily raised the rate of taxation. Whereas in 1921 fifteen of the sixteen gasoline-tax states imposed a rate of one cent per gallon, four years later only three of the forty-four taxing states had such a low rate. By 1929 the largest bloc of states levied a four-cent-per-gallon tax, with Florida, Georgia, and South Carolina imposing the highest rate, six cents per gallon. In only four states did the rate remain unchanged from 1925 to 1930; in the other forty-four, legislators could not resist reaping ever larger revenues through tax hikes.[42]

With gasoline consumption rising as well as tax rates, the proceeds from the motor-fuel impost soared. In 1919 it earned $1 million, by 1924 the net receipts nationwide were $80 million, and in 1929 the figure was $431 million.[43] In the latter year, state gasoline-tax revenues surpassed motor vehicle registration receipts for the first time and were almost six times as great as the federal appropriation for highway aid.

Given such figures, it was not surprising that legislators and state highway officials were fond of the newfound tax. Remarkably, however, even the taxpayers did not oppose the levy but instead welcomed it. Since in most states the motor-fuel tax receipts were earmarked solely for roads and sold to the public as necessary to highway construction, motorists yearning for smooth, continuous pavements embraced the impost as a means to a much-desired end. Remarking in 1926 on the ready acceptance of the gasoline levy, the chief collector of the motor fuel impost in Tennessee exclaimed, "Who ever heard, before, of a popular tax?"[44] Four years later, F. G. Crawford commented on the gasoline levy: "As yet no adverse reaction is discernible. The appetite of the taxpayers for highways seems to be insatiable."[45]

Moreover, rate increases failed to stir taxpayer revolts or stem the flow of traffic. When New Mexico raised its tax from three cents per gallon to five cents, critics of the hike expressed fears that tourists would avoid the state and New Mexicans would opt to consume less gasoline. But during the first year the higher rate was in effect, the total gallons consumed rose 23 percent and tourism increased 20 percent as 700,000 auto-borne visitors experienced the state's attractions. This latter figure was especially significant because the state highway engineer estimated that no less than one-third of the gasoline tax was derived from out-of-state visitors.[46] Other states reported similar experiences. In response to a survey of state highway agencies, the South Carolina department replied, "Year following increase in tax from three cents to five cents, [gasoline] sales increased in greater proportion than automobile registration." Wyoming's department answered succinctly, "Increase in tax does not result in reduced sales."[47]

But the gasoline levy proved acceptable not simply because its receipts were dedicated to a popular program. It also enjoyed the advantage of being relatively imperceptible, for it amounted to only twenty or thirty cents added to the price of gasoline each time a motorist fueled up. "The tax is paid in a manner that is unobtrusive and convenient," the National Tax Association's committee on motor vehicle taxation commented in its 1930 report. "This is peculiarly noticeable in comparison with the motor-registration tax, which is characteristically paid in one large sum rather than through the year as the vehicle is driven."[48] The gasoline levy deprived taxpayers of their spare change; the registration fee emptied their wallets once each year. Furthermore, the motor fuel impost was especially easy to bear because the price of gasoline was declining throughout much of the 1920s. The price, including taxes, averaged 29.38 cents per gallon in 1920, fell to 20.94 cents in 1924, climbed briefly to 23.38 cents in 1926, and then dropped to 16.98 cents in 1931.[49] Even with the tax, motorists were paying less at the pump.

Adding to the attractiveness of the gasoline tax was the low cost of collection. The states collected the tax from wholesale distributors who then passed it on to the consumer. Since there were relatively few wholesalers, the collection procedure was simple and inexpensive. During the first six years the gasoline tax was in effect, Oregon garnered $9.8 million at an expense of $20,802.15, or .2 percent of the total receipts.[50] Such figures were typical, with some states even reporting no cost of collection. In these cases the work was performed by existing clerks in the office of the auditor or the tax commission at no added expense to the state. As late as 1931, Oklahoma assigned the task to one office manager and two stenographers, who handled returns of almost $1 million per month.[51] "The gasoline tax is probably the most economical tax to collect," concluded F. G. Crawford.[52] During the 1920s, every expert seconded this opinion.

By the close of the 1920s, the states had largely solved their highway financing problems. "The gasoline tax has taken the country by storm," wrote one observer in 1929, and indeed, the new levy seemingly had worked a financial miracle.[53] Moreover, most lawmakers understood the message of this miracle — states could profit from taxes on consumption. In 1921 Iowa adopted the first sales tax on tobacco products, and by 1929 seven other states had followed its lead and were imposing a levy on cigarettes and cigars. As yet, however, few legislators were prepared to consider a general retail sales tax. An impost on thousands of retailers could prove considerably more difficult to collect and administer than a levy on a few wholesale distributors of gasoline. In any case, so long as the prosperity of the 1920s persisted, there was no urgent need for such a major innovation. But the gasoline levy opened the door to change, and during the 1930s the states were forced to pass through that door and fashion a new taxing structure.

State Parks

As more Americans purchased automobiles, they began to search the map for motoring destinations, and increasingly they expected the states to supply such destinations in the form of state parks. "Not until many of our good roads were built and used by millions of automobiles was there a keen demand for these outdoor areas of larger spaces and wild attire," wrote Michigan's superintendent of state parks in 1930.[54] In other words, once the pavements were laid, the states had to further placate the people by embarking on schemes to preserve the beaches, forests, and scenic attractions of the countryside and open them to the public. As in the case of highway development, the states accepted this challenge and with varying degrees of success launched park programs.

Some state parks predated the automobile. During the late nineteenth century, California maintained the Yosemite Valley as a state preserve, finally transferring it to the federal government in 1905 when it became part of the surrounding national park. In 1885 New York dedicated the Niagara State Reservation along the banks of the famous falls, and during the 1880s New York also launched its long-term policy of preserving the giant Adirondacks forest. Meanwhile, Mackinac Island became Michigan's first state park, and in 1891 Minnesota established Itasca Lake State Park to protect the headwaters of the Mississippi River.[55] Yet before 1900 no state considered creating a system of parks with nature preserves distributed throughout the state for the uplift and recreation of the citizenry. Instead, a few states acted to protect major natural landmarks such as Niagara Falls and the source of the Mississippi.

The state park movement accelerated somewhat after the turn of the century. A scattering of states began to purchase sites, sometimes of historical as well as natural significance, and state park commissions joined the list of public agencies. In 1904 North Dakota's state historical society launched a program of acquiring historic sites, which became the nucleus of a park network. With seven parks distributed throughout the state, in 1920 the society's secretary could boast, "North Dakota is peculiarly fortunate in having already made a beginning for what will soon become an unexcelled system of state parks."[56] In 1907 Wisconsin's legislature authorized the creation of a state park board, which hired the nationally known landscape architect John Nolen to survey the state's natural wonders. By 1910 the state had purchased thirty-eight hundred acres of parkland and eight miles of lakeshore, leading Nolen to proclaim that "in state parks the real lead . . . [had to] be accorded to Wisconsin."[57] Immediately to the south, the Illinois legislature of 1909 authorized a commission to "investigate and report on the preservation of certain lands for public parks for the State of Illinois." In 1911 the purchase of the dramatic Starved Rock site launched Illinois's system.[58] And in 1913 Connecticut established a state park commission, which acquired twenty park sites by the close of 1919.[59]

Perhaps the most noteworthy park pioneer of the second decade of the twentieth century, however, was Indiana's Richard Lieber. A leading figure in the park movement, Lieber guided the Hoosier state's efforts from 1916 to 1933 and during the 1920s and 1930s was a fixture at national conferences on park development. To commemorate the one-hundredth anniversary of Indiana's statehood in 1916, Lieber convinced the legislature to establish the first two state parks. He claimed that "the chief purpose of State Parks [was] to refresh and strengthen and renew tired people and fit them for the common round of daily life." But recognizing the hardheaded practicality of state leaders, he also noted that there was "a cash value in scenery, an income to be derived from excursionists." Referring to the oft-cited function of a park to provide fresh air and breathing space, Lieber observed that "the so-called 'Lungs' of a people ha[d] from a given view point a most convincing resemblance to a fat purse."[60]

As Lieber soon discovered, however, automobile access was increasingly significant to the success of these lucrative lungs. In part because of poor roadways, one of Indiana's original parks lagged in number of visitors and proved a disappointment to Lieber and his supporters.[61] By 1920 the state park was not simply a public tract preserving natural beauty. It was a destination for motorists, and without adequate roads few motorists would experience the scenic wonders of Indiana or any other state.

In states throughout the nation, thousands of new automobiles thus meant more parks as well as more highways. Immediately after World War I, Iowa joined the list of park builders, embarking on an ambitious program of acquisition and development. "No other line of public work in Iowa in the last four years has shown such marvelous results as has that of the acquisition of state parks," wrote one proud Iowan in 1921.[62] Meanwhile, in 1919 Michigan's governor told the legislature, "With the advent of good roads, . . . thousands of tourists will be attracted to Michigan for the summer season." Consequently, he recommended that steps be taken "to acquire the land necessary to establish a great chain of State parks bordering [the state's] rivers and lakes." The legislature acquiesced, establishing the State Park Commission.[63] In South Dakota Governor Peter Norbeck's pet project was the development of Custer State Park in the Black Hills. Created in 1919, with sixty-one thousand acres it was one of the nation's largest preserves. Norbeck intended to attract not just rugged hikers but, more importantly, the growing army of vehicle-borne tourists. Exploring the virgin parklands, Governor Norbeck asked his state engineer, "Scovel, can you build a road through there?" The confident engineer answered, "If you can furnish me enough dynamite." The result was the Needles Highway, completed in 1922 and proclaimed "one of the most scenic roads in the west and one of the most famous, extending as it d[id] throughout the [park's] remarkable granite needles."[64] By 1928 there were one hundred miles of roads in Custer State Park, enabling motorists to experience nature without ever leaving their automobiles.

Meanwhile, the National Park Service and Congress were attempting to cope with mounting requests for the creation of natural preserves. Every locality was convinced that nature had blessed it with a scenic wonder worthy of national park status. To relieve the pressure on the federal authorities, National Park Director Stephen Mather called upon the states to assume a greater share of the burden and arranged a conference of state park enthusiasts to meet in Des Moines, Iowa, in January 1921. Two hundred delegates from twenty-five states attended and agreed to establish a permanent organization, the National Conference of State Parks. "I believe we should have comfortable camps all over the country," Mather told the assembled delegates, "so that the motorist could camp each night in a good scenic spot, preferably a state park." The conference embodied this goal in its slogan: "A State Park Every Hundred Miles."[65] From the beginning, then, this organization of state park enthusiasts aimed to accommodate the motorist. No longer did states seek to preserve only such scenic wonders as Niagara Falls. Now they sought to provide a park every one hundred miles, no matter whether the wonders of nature existed at such regular intervals. The needs of the motorist determined the goals of state park commissions.

The Des Moines conference chose Secretary of Interior John Barton Payne as the organization's first chairman, though Stephen Mather remained the guiding spirit of the conference until his death in 1930. Then Richard Lieber assumed command for twelve years, spreading abroad the state park gospel he had preached in Indiana. During the 1920s Mather conceived of the National Park Service as a facilitator for further state park development and as a clearinghouse for expert advice and useful information. Thus, Mather viewed his role as similar to that of Thomas MacDonald. In cooperation with energetic state officials like Lieber, he would urge states to embark on park programs and adhere to professional standards of park development.

There was one vital difference between Mather's role and MacDonald's. Though the federal government's financial contribution to highway construction was relatively small, still the Bureau of Public Road's $75 million annual appropriation was a sufficiently seductive carrot that MacDonald could lead the states in the direction he desired. Mather's agency granted no money to state government, and thus the park service director had to rely solely on his personal powers of persuasion. He could provide moral support and a helpful word but no cash.

In fact, the National Park Service was a supplicant for state funds rather than a generous benefactor. The nation's frugal lawmakers ordained that Mather's agency could not purchase land for park purposes. It could only create parks on public lands already owned by the federal government or on donated tracts. Since there were virtually no federal public lands east of the Mississippi River, the eastern states had to assume the task of acquiring national park sites and donating them to the federal government. During the late 1920s, North Carolina authorized a $2 million bond issue and Tennessee approved $1.5 million in bonds to finance the acquisition of the site for the Great Smokies National Park. With matching funds from John D. Rockefeller, Jr., these states finally deeded the land to the federal government in 1930. Meanwhile, the state of Virginia, with help from Rockefeller, was piecing together the site of Shenandoah National Park in the Blue Ridge Mountains.[66] These southern states succeeded in creating national parks, but both North Carolina and Tennessee skimped on state park development as a result. In order to subsidize the federal government, southern states, which were not among the wealthiest in the nation, diverted money that could have been used for state preserves.

When Mather faced the problem of preserving California's redwood forest, he was forced to rely on state rather than federal action for that project also. In 1918 Mather and a group of like-minded conservationists organized the Save-the-Redwoods League with the objective of creating both state and national parks encompassing a large portion of the redwood forests. The league failed to secure congressional authorization for a national preserve, but the state of California was more forthcoming. In 1921 the legislature appropriated three hundred thousand dollars to match private funds collected for the purchase of redwood tracts. Later in the decade, the state allocated additional funds. Consequently, the world's tallest tree, the 364-foot Founders' Tree, was to be found in Humboldt State Park, not in a national preserve.[67]

This same scenario was repeated in Indiana. Led by the noted landscape architect Jens Jensen, the Chicago-based Friends of the Native Landscape lobbied vigorously for a national park to preserve the Indiana dunes along Lake Michigan. A founding member of the Friends, Mather espoused the group's cause but reported to Congress that creation of such a park would entail a purchase price of $1.8 to $2.6 million. Faced with such figures, Congress took no action. Consequently, the Friends turned to Richard Lieber and the state of Indiana. In 1923 the Indiana legislature authorized a two-mill tax to provide about $1 million toward the purchase of the dunes, and Lieber, together with a committee of interested Chicagoans, collected private donations from wealthy benefactors. The result was Indiana Dunes State Park, created in 1925. Immediately popular, in the summer of 1927 it attracted 125,000 paid admissions, and by 1928 the state had acquired 2,185 acres of duneland and three and one-fourth miles of beach frontage.[68]

During the 1920s, then, the tight-fisted federal government could not be counted on to protect scenic treasures or provide parks every one hundred miles. The states had to take on that task, doing so with varying degrees of success. Some created extensive park systems that were admired by park experts throughout the nation. Others produced more rhetoric than actual parklands. And some of the poorest states made virtually no headway in the creation of state recreational sites.

Among the successful states was New York. By 1920 the Empire State already maintained an imperial domain including most notably the Catskill and Adirondack preserves. State officials had not yet sought to fashion a unified, coherent park program, however. Various commissions governed the disparate state-owned tracts, and no central authority guided further development. Led by Robert Moses, a committee of the New York State Association sought to remedy this situation, drafting a plan for a unified system and recommending a bond issue to fund the scheme. In a report submitted to the people, this civic organization proposed "a really comprehensive and unified state park plan which [would] take into consideration the anticipated growth of the state's population."[69] The *New York Times* endorsed the proposed "unified system" as a means of providing adequate parkland while also preventing "haphazard and wasteful expenditure."[70] New York's legislature agreed and in 1923 created the State Council of Parks, chaired by Robert Moses, to plan park development and recommend how much the state should appropriate for each of the regional commissions. There were eleven such regional bodies charged with overseeing the parks in their sections of the state, but the council was to coordinate state efforts. In November 1924 the voters approved a $15 million bond issue for park development by the largest majority ever given to a proposal in the state's history.

The New York park program reflected the trend toward state centralization evident throughout the twentieth century. Regional commissions could no longer govern their domains as they wished. Instead, they were responsible to a coordinating council chaired by Robert Moses. And Moses pulled hard on the reins, forcing the regional bodies to proceed in the direction he indicated. In coming decades, as an administrator of city and state programs, Moses became known for his love of power and his autocratic high-handedness. Already in the 1920s he was earning enemies as state park czar. Among those alienated was the chair of the Taconic State Park Commission, Franklin D. Roosevelt. Angered by the Council of State Park's refusal to allocate additional money to his regional commission, the future president wrote Governor Smith, "I am sorry to say . . . that Bob Moses has played fast and loose with the Taconic State Park Commission since the beginning."[71] But New York had opted for a "comprehensive and unified" park system, and this meant central control—for the time being, control by Robert Moses.

During the 1920s Robert Moses and New York State achieved notable results. From 1924 through 1928, twenty-eight new state parks were created, encompassing more than nineteen thousand acres. Chaired by Moses himself, the energetic Long Island State Park Commission acquired fifteen preserves during this five-year period, including eight miles of beachfront at Fire Island and Jones Beach. In a survey of state parks published in 1928, the executive secretary of the National Conference reported that New York had "the largest acreage and number of preserves in state parks, forests or similar areas of any state in the country."[72]

Meanwhile, California was seeking to match New York's success. As of 1923, California had only five state parks, all in the northern or central section of the state. The State Board of Forestry administered three of the parks, and two independent commissions governed the remaining preserves.[73] There was no unified, comprehensive park system with recreation areas distributed throughout the state. Preservation of the grand but endangered redwoods had been the principal motive for creating the state's few parks. Accommodating motoring tourists had been of secondary concern.

But in the second half of the 1920s, California was to fully embrace the state park movement and launch a program for a unified system of parks serving every section of the state. The chief lobbyist for this extension of state responsibility was the California State Parks Council, which enjoyed the backing of such conservationist groups as the Save-the-Redwoods League and the Sierra Club as well as the support of such motoring organizations as the Automobile Club of Southern California and the California State Automobile Association.[74] Responding to this pressure, in 1927 the legislature created a state park commission to act as the single governing authority for all of California's state parks. It ordered "a survey to determine what lands [were] suitable and desirable for the ultimate development of a comprehensive, well-balanced state park system."[75] To finance the purchase of parklands, California's lawmakers, in addition, approved the submission of a $6 million bond issue to the state's voters. In 1928 the electorate passed the issue by the overwhelming margin of 975,979 to 346,998. "Throughout the state there is enthusiasm for the establishment of a real state park system," reported an official of the National Conference at the time of the election.[76] Clearly, Californians were eager to acquire new parks and expand the state's role as a purveyor of recreation.

Among the first acts of the new park commission was the hiring of world-renowned landscape architect Frederick Law Olmsted, Jr., to conduct the mandated survey. Californians submitted more than 330 proposals for state park sites, and Olmsted's staff reviewed each, eliminating more than 200 because they were "lacking in qualities suitable for a state park[,] definitely more of local than of statewide value," or "too small or isolated," and possibly too expensive, to justify acquisition. Finally, Olmsted selected 79 projects that he regarded as the most worthy contenders for a share of the state's bond issue money. These included not only additional redwood forests but also twenty coastal tracts, as well as a long list of lake, mountain, desert, and historical sites.[77]

During the following decade, California created a system of parks based on Olmsted's recommendations. By 1937 the state owned seventy parks comprising three hundred thousand acres. Six million people visited the parks annually, taking advantage of this new service of state government.[78] California, like New York, had fulfilled the expectations of the National Conference and expanded the recreation opportunities of its citizenry.

Other states were less successful in establishing a system of parks. For example, Texas collected stray parcels of land for park purposes, but in sharp contrast to California, it failed to formulate a rational plan for park development. At the beginning of 1923, the state did not own a single park; in May of that year Governor Pat Neff called upon the legislature to create a parks board to solicit donations of land for recreation purposes. "By the establishment of a system of parks and camping places throughout the State," Neff told the legislature, "we will make of Texas the Mecca for automobile tourists and bequeath to posterity a most valuable legacy." By January 1925 private donors had offered the state board fifty-two tracts varying in size from ten acres to over one thousand acres. The 1925 legislature, however, refused to accept title to the donations unless private parties or local governments agreed to finance development and maintenance of the parklands, "so that the State [should] never be required to make appropriations therefore."[79] Two years later the legislature did finally accept twenty-four of the donated parcels but again failed to appropriate funds for development of the sites. Moreover, the donations were of widely varying value for park purposes. Many were relatively small tracts of no special scenic merit, whereas the Davis Mountains State Park was a large parcel that preserved a major wilderness site.[80]

In a number of other states, dreams also exceeded appropriations. A 1928 survey of state parks throughout the nation reported that the development of Minnesota's preserves had "been hindered seriously by insufficient appropriations." Minnesota's legislature had not made a general appropriation for a state system, but responding to local pressures, the lawmakers in Saint Paul had allocated money to individual parks. Some state-owned sites had received funds from county and municipal governments. Similarly, the 1928 survey found that

Washington state was "badly in need of sufficient appropriations to properly administer and develop her park system." Fines collected from violators of the motor vehicle laws in rural areas provided most of the funds for this system. Yet the combined sum of these fines was never adequate to support a first-rate park network.[81] Even in Indiana some questioned the wisdom of Richard Lieber's handiwork, claiming that parks were an unnecessary extravagance. One columnist criticized "the ridiculous proposition of a fine salary to Richard Lieber to hunt up a picnic ground here and there throughout the state." Arguing for limits on the expansion of state government, he observed: "We have gone away beyond taking care of the pauper and the infirm. We must provide all kinds of pleasures for the able-bodied, well-to-do golf players and automobile tourist. Where will it all end?"[82]

Most Hoosiers did not share this attitude, nor did the voters in New York and California, who overwhelmingly approved bond issues for park development. But many thrifty legislators and governors questioned whether their states could afford to pay for yet another service. Thus, some states developed enviable park systems, whereas others faltered. Texas lawmakers did not wish to commit the state to the financing of Governor Neff's scenic sites, and solons in Minnesota and Washington were not as openhanded as their counterparts elsewhere. The poorer southern states were especially slow to assume this new responsibility. "Nearly every state has a state park or a state forest," reported the 1928 survey, "but as yet Mississippi has neither."[83] Mississippi could take solace, however, from the fact that its southern neighbors were also in the rearguard of the state park movement. In other words, the states were not moving lockstep toward the goal of a state park system. New York and California were advancing toward that goal, Texas was off to a fumbling start, but Mississippi had not taken the first steps.

During the 1930s federal aid would enable the laggard states to catch up a bit. Under the direction of the National Park Service, the Civilian Conservation Corps (CCC) sent thousands of unemployed young men to state parks to clear trails, build shelter houses, and lay out campgrounds. Southern states that had taken little or no action with regard to park development now acquired tracts and took advantage of the federal government's offer of free labor. For example, in May 1934 Mississippi obtained the land for its first state park, a symbol of the spread of the park movement to even the poorest states.[84] States that had already acquired parks used CCC recruits to make needed improvements. Throughout the nation, the help was much appreciated. In 1935 Richard Lieber noted that "an enormous impetus" had been given to the state park movement "through the coming of the CCC camps." He considered these camps "a master stroke" that had "met with universal approval."[85] According to the superintendent of North Dakota's parks, the federal help was "of immeasurable value," and in adjacent Minnesota the state park director claimed that words could not "express the appreciation which the people of the State" owed the federal authorities.[86] Alabama's park director wrote of the "tremendous impetus" resulting from federal intervention, and a spokesperson for South Carolina expressed a typical southern sentiment when he proclaimed, "There is no doubt that the South Carolina park system was born through the wonderful emergency conservation program of the President."[87]

Yet the pioneering state park work of the years prior to 1933 was almost wholly the product of state effort. Though the federal government occasionally donated a military reservation or offered a parcel of public land to a state at a cut-rate price, Congress during the 1920s never appropriated funds to aid the purchase or development of state parks. Stephen Mather provided moral support but could offer little more. Thus, New York and California had to assume the task of satisfying the emerging recreational needs of their motorists. National parks preserved America's scenic wonders, but state parks were intended to answer the more prosaic demands of millions of auto-borne tourists seeking a place to camp or picnic. The states acted with varying degrees of success, and by the beginning of the 1930s a number had laid the foundations for extensive park networks.

Washington, D.C., was more generous in helping the states cope with highway development, though states and localities bore the bulk of the expense. Moreover, when federal aid proved insufficient, the wealthier eastern and midwestern states expedited construction by paying more than their share of the cost of the federal-aid highways. The thrift of Calvin Coolidge and likeminded congressmen forced the states to shoulder a disproportionate percentage of the funding and thereby satisfy the demands of a highway-hungry citizenry. The states could do so in large part because they had discovered a veritable money machine in the form of the gasoline tax. Both popular and lucrative, this tax was an answer to a state lawmaker's prayers.

The expectations of the motorist thus fostered an expansion of state authority. The states were not reluctant governments that shuddered at the thought of new functions and conceded defeat in the face of fresh challenges. Nor were they helpless wards of an openhanded, activist federal government. Instead, they acted decisively, and the wealthiest and most energetic were considerably more dedicated to expanding the public sector's role than were the Congress and the presidents of the 1920s. There were numerous examples of faltering state efforts, especially in the South. But overall, at the state level the 1920s was a decade of expanded responsibility. The states filled the gap created by perceptions of local incompetence and predilections for limited federal power.

6

Economic Depression and Accelerated Change

ACCORDING to standard American lore, the 1930s witnessed the failure of the states and the triumph of the federal government. Burdened by the exigencies of economic depression, backward state governments collapsed, and only the intervention of Washington, D.C., saved the nation from total debacle. Traditional Jeffersonian precepts about the superiority of decentralized rule and long-standing bugaboos about federal control had to yield as amateur lawmakers in state capitals and shortsighted, reactionary governors proved inadequate to handle the crisis engulfing America. Antiquated notions of federalism gave way to a new faith in the national government and its ability to tackle the problems confronting Americans. In other words, the great depression was the iceberg that sank the sovereign states, but fortunately the federal government was on hand to rescue the nation.

Yet this popular scenario does not accurately describe the realities of the 1930s. During the early 1930s, the entire nation was in a state of collapse. The private sector was in desperate condition as the gross national product dropped by almost one half between 1929 and 1933; one-quarter of the nation's workforce was unemployed by the latter year. Federal finances were seemingly out of control, with federal receipts plummeting by more than one-half from 1930 to 1932. In 1932 the federal government's expenditures were almost two and one-half times its total revenues, resulting in a deficit of proportions unprecedented in peacetime. Meanwhile, many localities were on the brink of bankruptcy, unable to provide relief for the unemployed or salaries for their employees. Moreover, President Herbert Hoover seemed no more successful in handling the crisis than many of the state governors. Neither the private nor the public sector appeared able to save the nation.

But once political leaders realized that the economic depression was not a momentary spell of bad times that would pass without public action, both the state and the federal governments mobilized and proved the efficacy of the public sector in a crisis. Rather than wallow in indecision and cling to outdated institutions and practices, state leaders responded with marked policy changes and embraced notable reforms. In fact, governmental change was arguably more dramatic at the state level than at the federal level.

Among the changes in state rule was an accelerated pace of centralization and a heightened emphasis on expertise. One of the persistent trends of twentieth-century state government was centralization of authority and deviation from the pattern of delegation prevalent in the nineteenth century. But during the 1930s this tendency increased markedly. The great loser of the 1930s was local government. Traditionally the chief providers of government services, localities could no longer shoulder this burden. They broke under the pressure of the depression, and the states had to come to their aid and assume greater responsibility for local functions. This was especially true of the principal local service—education. To save the schools, the states had to act, and they did so.

In addition the states pursued a variety of other reforms. The 1930s witnessed the culmination of the long-term drift away from state reliance on property taxes; state governments finally weaned themselves from that much-criticized tax and restructured their revenue systems. Reformers also sought to inject a new element of expertise into the state lawmaking process and to foster interstate cooperation and exchange of information. Economic crisis stirred new support for the reform agenda of earlier decades and promoted the long-term trend away from the amateur efforts of untutored assessors and parochial lawmakers.

Faced with economic hardship, some states also took unorthodox action to lure money and investment. In the past, states had adopted policies aimed at promoting growth, but from the 1930s onward, economic development was to assume a higher priority on the agenda of state policymakers. Laissez-faire was not sufficient; state action was necessary to spur flagging economies. This would become an article of faith among governors and legislators as the century progressed.

Overall, then, the states did respond creatively to the economic depression. At both state and federal levels, leaders were initially reluctant to abandon traditional notions, but harsh reality forced them to reconsider and experiment. As a result there was an expansion of both state and federal authority. Congress, however, hesitated to act assertively unless such action was tied to economic recovery. Relief and economic security were the preoccupations of lawmakers in Washington. Consequently, the states found it necessary to expand their roles in other areas, acting where localities were unable to shoulder the task and the federal government was unwilling to do so. During the 1930s the federal government was indeed extending its authority; and in the minds of many frustrated governors, this seemed to threaten state sovereignty. But in hindsight what the federal government did not do was just as significant as what it did do. The responsibilities it did not assume were to fall to the states.

The Centralizing States

Local government was at the bottom of the governmental heap and suffered the consequences of its lowly position. Throughout the first third of the twentieth century, it funded most public services, but lacking any sovereign power, it could not draw on new sources of revenue without the approval of the state legislatures. Moreover, many small municipalities and rural counties had weak tax bases and little commercial wealth. Yet these poorly endowed local units were charged with carrying out the primary tasks of government. During prosperous times, localities had been able to live with this incongruous juncture of limited power and wealth and broad responsibilities. But the depression exposed the shortcomings of a system that burdened the least competent elements of government with the heaviest duties. In the end, both state and federal governments had to intervene and shift the burden of responsibility up the ladder of government.

This need for state and federal intervention became especially evident as localities proved unable to cope with growing demands for relief for the unemployed. In Pennsylvania the local Poor Boards increased taxes by more than 50 percent between 1928 and 1932, but during these years the allocation per relief recipient dropped to only one-fifth of what it had been a decade earlier. Similarly, in New Jersey local expenditures for public assistance soared from $5.9 million in 1930 to $15.3 million in 1931, but still thousands of families needed additional aid as the economic depression worsened.[1] Though initially reluctant to usurp a local function, by 1931 some state leaders recognized that they had to aid the unemployed and to prevent localities from collapsing under the relief load. Thus, in August 1931 Governor Franklin Roosevelt of New York called the legislature into special session for the purpose of responding to the crisis. In his message to the lawmakers, he admitted that hitherto the state had principally aided "those who through accident or old age were permanently incapacitated." Yet Roosevelt claimed that "the same responsibility of the State undoubtedly applie[d] when widespread economic conditions rendere[d] large numbers of men and women incapable of supporting either themselves or their families." The Democratic governor argued further that New York state could not await action by the Republican-dominated federal government. "It is true that times may get better, it is true that the Federal Government may come forward with a definite constructive program on a truly large scale," Roosevelt told the solons. "The State of New York cannot wait for that. I face and you face and thirteen million people face the problem of providing immediate relief."[2] Aid was imperative, and localities were incapable of further action, whereas the federal government was unwilling to act. Consequently, the state had to fill the void. No longer was the state of New York responsible for only the incompetent and maimed. Roosevelt was expanding state responsibility to the victims of economic debacle.

New York's lawmakers agreed with Roosevelt and in September 1931 approved creation of the Temporary Emergency Relief Administration (TERA). Over the seven-month period from 1 November 1931 to 1 June 1932, this state agency was to distribute $20 million in state aid to localities for the purpose of unemployment relief. To fund the emergency program, the lawmakers authorized a 50 percent increase in the state income tax. Led by its executive director, Harry Hopkins, the TERA distributed its $20 million appropriation during the winter of 1931–32. Because of continuing hard times, however, the legislature felt compelled to appropriate another $5 million at the end of March 1932. And to finance further state aid, it authorized the submission of a $30 million bond issue to the state's voters in the November 1932 election. At that time New Yorkers overwhelmingly approved the borrowing proposal, ensuring even more funds for the state's unemployed.[3]

Across the Hudson River, New Jersey solons soon followed New York's example. In October 1931 a special session of the legislature appropriated almost $10 million for unemployment relief in a program to be administered by the State Emergency Relief Administration (SERA). Although this public assistance act recognized that "the providing of relief [was] the responsibility and function of local government," New Jersey's program resulted in a marked expansion of state control over a traditionally local function. If New Jersey localities were unable or unwilling to raise the funds necessary to qualify for state assistance, then the state would take over the administration of relief in those communities. During the first year of the program, a growing number of localities yielded the relief function to the state; by mid-1932 the SERA was both financing and administering public assistance in 128 communities, including some leading industrial centers. Whereas in 1931 the state paid only 7 percent of the public assistance bill in New Jersey, the following year it funded 50 percent of relief expenditures.[4] Beginning in 1933, the federal government became the chief source of relief funds in New Jersey, but throughout the remainder of the 1930s, the state's share of the assistance burden surpassed that of the localities.

Meanwhile, other states were also assuming new responsibility for public assistance. In November 1931 Rhode Island agreed to loan $2.5 million to localities to aid in unemployment relief, and that same month Governor Philip LaFollette called Wisconsin's lawmakers into special session to confront the economic emergency. They responded by increasing state income taxes approximately 100 percent for the coming year in order to finance poor relief. In December 1931 the Pennsylvania legislature appropriated $10 million in state aid to localities to fund assistance for the unemployed; and the following February, Illinois solons created the Illinois Emergency Relief Commission and appropriated $20 million for relief.[5]

Yet these efforts proved insufficient as the unemployment rolls mounted. At the end of February 1932, the TERA was funding relief for more than 160,000 New Yorkers, but 1.5 million in the state were out of work.[6] Moreover, most states were either unable or unwilling to emulate the New York example, leaving localities to bear the brunt of relief costs. Consequently, both states and localities were ultimately to turn to the federal government for help. From 1933 on, Washington was to shoulder the largest share of the relief burden, which had proved too awesome for authorities in either the state capitals or the county seats. The states served as the laboratory where New Deal relief programs were tested. For upon becoming president, Franklin Roosevelt was to apply the relief structure that he had tested in New York to the federal program. The TERA became the model for the Federal Emergency Relief Administration, and Harry Hopkins assumed the same job in Washington that he had held in Albany. In Washington as in Albany, Roosevelt was to rely on borrowing and increased income tax rates to fund his recovery programs. New York thus anticipated the federal effort, but it and its fellow states could not continue to bear the burden by themselves. Responsibility shifted to the federal government, and within a few years the function of poor relief moved quickly up the governmental ladder from the locality to the nation.

During the 1930s, however, the buck did not invariably stop in Washington, D.C. Instead, much local authority gravitated to the state capitals and never moved beyond them. Centralization of government was the prevailing tendency of the decade. But just as significant as the centralization in the national capital was the shifting of control to Raleigh, Columbus, and Sacramento. Though state leaders warned of federal aggression, the Congress and the president refrained from many areas of domestic policy. Thus throughout the nation, the states had to pick up the slack as localities faltered.

This was most evident in North Carolina. During the 1930s the Tarheel State gained a national reputation for its centralizing reforms as state officials endeavored to ensure the continuation and improvement of services traditionally performed by local units. Even during the 1920s, local governments in North Carolina were straining under the burden of heavy expenditures. A southern state with northern ambitions, North Carolina had embarked on an expensive highway-building program and had sought to bring its educational system up to par. Throughout the state miles of hard-surfaced roadways and hundreds of new brick schools testified to the high expectations of policymakers. Yet localities bore a large share of the cost of these improvements, resulting in awesome local debt obligations.

The onset of economic depression forced an end to the profligate ways of North Carolina's local units. As early as 1930, approximately thirty local governments defaulted on their interest payments, and as Governor O. Max Gardner noted, state officials "began to realize that [North Carolina] had a surfeit of spending." But the rate of default was not to peak until 1933, when 62 of the state's 100 counties and 152 of its 260 cities and towns failed to meet their interest payments.[7]

Responding to the mounting burden of debt and expenditure, in 1931 the state, at the behest of Governor Gardner, embarked on a scheme of radical centralization. To ensure state control over local borrowing, the 1931 legislature created the Local Government Commission, which was to review all local borrowing proposals. If the commission disapproved a borrowing proposal, the locality could not proceed with its bond issue unless the local electorate approved the issue in a local referendum. Voters, however, were unlikely to endorse borrowing schemes that the state deemed imprudent. Only once during the first ten years of the commission's history did local voters override the state agency's veto.[8] In addition, the state commission took on the marketing of all local bonds and notes. The negotiation of the terms of sale became a state rather than a local responsibility. And the commission also supervised the investment of local sinking funds, specifying the types of securities that could be purchased. Overall, state administrators took charge of local borrowing. Governor Gardner said of the reform, "It takes away from local units the power to endanger further the interests of their taxpayers."[9]

North Carolina's legislature also sought to protect local taxpayers by shifting responsibility for the maintenance of all rural roads to the state. At the beginning of the 1930s, county and township officials were responsible for forty-five thousand miles of rural thoroughfares. A state survey of these roads found, however, that local maintenance varied from excellent to deplorable.

Some counties invested too little in roadways, but others spent too much and squandered public funds. When Governor Gardner proposed that the state take over responsibility for maintenance of all rural roads, the initial outcry from local officials was loud and shrill. But as the depression worsened, hard-pressed North Carolina taxpayers welcomed the resultant drop in local property tax levies and shed few tears for county and township officials who seemed to be wasting public money. Consequently, in 1931 Governor Gardner won the legislative battle, and the state took charge of the maintenance of every rural thoroughfare. From the beginning of European settlement in North America, localities had been responsible for local roads, and as of 1931 they continued to be in the other forty-seven states. But North Carolina was pioneering a new level of centralization.

Local control of schools had also produced unequal services and was imposing a heavy property tax burden on depression-era North Carolinians. Consequently, schools joined borrowing and roads as a target in Governor Gardner's campaign of centralization. According to the state superintendent of public instruction, by 1931 "local taxes could not be collected and teachers and other employees in many instances were unpaid for a part of their services." Given the growing "complaints against high costs of education and high taxes," a number of candidates for the legislature were "ready to lay the axe severely to public education, some even advocating the closing of the schools for a year or two."[10] Rather than embrace this drastic option, lawmakers chose to relieve localities of a large portion of school expenses, and in 1931 the state assumed full responsibility for funding the six-month minimum school term mandated in the constitution.

Two years later the state assumed responsibility for funding an additional two months of school, guaranteeing an eight-month term throughout the state. Consequently, the state shouldered the bulk of the expense, with its share of school finances soaring from 1.4 percent in 1930 to 86.2 percent in 1936. This reform was a boon for the poorest rural districts, which had been unable to fund an extended term. "Now . . . each child in the State, no matter whether he lives in the richest community in some city or in the poorest in the remotest area of the State," the state superintendent boasted, "is provided with a school for eight months in the year."[11] The state was guaranteeing an unprecedented uniformity of educational opportunity.

But state control accompanied state funding. In the interest of economy and efficiency, a state commission redistricted North Carolina, reducing the number of school districts from 3,602 to 1,449. The state also reviewed all county and city school budgets and could disallow items deemed unnecessary or extravagant. The state specified the number of teachers per principal, the number of pupils per teacher, and the maximum salaries of school employees.[12] Rather than to allow the school system to collapse, the state intervened, but in doing so it relieved localities of much of their former authority over both funding and administration.

Within the first few years of the 1930s, then, North Carolina had applied the brakes to local government, taking charge of school funding, assuming full responsibility for rural roads, and exercising a greater degree of supervision over local borrowing. Labeling these reforms a "grand experiment," the state commissioner of revenue claimed that North Carolina's efforts at centralization were "as revolutionary as the times and conditions that produced them."[13] Economic debacle had yielded a New Deal in Washington, but as the commissioner recognized, it was also fomenting revolution in Raleigh.

Elsewhere state leaders were generally unable or unwilling to embark on such a drastic restructuring of responsibilities, but a financial crisis forced West Virginia to replicate the innovations adopted in North Carolina. Reeling under the weight of property taxes, in November 1932 depression-stricken West Virginians approved a tax limitation amendment to their constitution. By capping the total property tax burden, this amendment slashed the possible yield from property levies by approximately 50 percent. Since localities relied almost wholly on such levies, they were especially threatened by this change, and state leaders recognized that they had to take quick action to relieve the counties, municipalities, and school districts. Consequently, the 1933 legislature abolished the fifty-five county road departments and incorporated the thirty thousand miles of local roads into the state highway system. Henceforth there were no county roads in West Virginia; the state was responsible for all rural roads. Moreover, the lawmakers disbanded the 413 local school districts and created in their stead a county unit system with one school district per county. And the state shouldered the largest share of the education bill, its proportion of school funding rising from 7.7 percent in 1930 to 53.8 percent four years later.[14] Sponsoring these centralizing reforms, Governor Herman Guy Kump pronounced the 413 school districts to be "luxuries that [could] not be indulged in collectively during these times of stress."[15] West Virginians had cut the fiscal throat of local government, and now the state was compelled to come to the rescue and maintain schools and roads.

Although West Virginia and North Carolina experienced a degree of centralization not replicated in other states, virtually everywhere the tendency was toward increased reliance on state funding and increased regulation by state administrators. This was most pronounced in the field of education. Schooling had long been regarded as a state responsibility, but it was a responsibility that had been delegated to tens of thousands of local districts. For a half-century the list of state requirements and regulations had been growing, as state boards attempted to ensure a minimal level of instruction. But during the 1930s, state intervention in education accelerated at an unprecedented pace. The revolt against local school levies was not confined to North Carolina and West Virginia. Instead, throughout the nation taxpayers balked, and the states had to substitute their revenues for those of hard-pressed localities, thereby markedly enhancing their role in public education. Between 1930 and 1940, the state share of school funding increased in forty-four of the forty-eight states, soaring more than twenty percentage points in fourteen states. Overall, this state proportion rose from 16.9 percent at the beginning of the decade to 30.3 percent at its close.[16]

Across the nation states were intervening to keep schools open in the face of financial disaster at the local level. In 1932 Michigan's tax-weary voters approved a 15–mill property tax limitation amendment to their constitution; and as in West Virginia, public schooling was among the services most threatened by this reform. Consequently, the 1933 legislature increased the state's contribution to education, and two years later it more than doubled its allocation of funds to the public schools. Whereas the state accounted for one-fifth of school receipts in 1930, it was providing almost one-half of the revenues a decade later.[17] In 1933 Californians adopted an amendment that repealed a constitutional requirement that counties levy taxes for the support of schools. Responding to this expression of public opinion, the legislature abolished all county school taxes and appropriated state funds drawn largely from sales and franchise taxes to compensate for the loss.[18] That same year, among the principal reforms sponsored by Indiana's Governor Paul McNutt was a state subsidy of teachers' salaries, which both benefited the teachers and relieved local school districts of some of their financial burden.[19] In 1935 Ohio lawmakers created the State Foundation Program, which distributed state funds to each school district on the basis of per-pupil daily attendance. Additional aid was granted to districts unable to raise enough money to finance the minimum level of school funding as defined by the state. That is, the state assumed responsibility for subsidizing every district in the state and also established a floor on school funding, thereby guaranteeing that each child would receive at least a basic level of education. In two years state support for public schools rose from $13.5 million to $48.5 million; and over the course of the decade, the state's share of school funding soared tenfold from 3.6 percent in 1929–30 to 37.7 percent in 1939–40.[20]

State assumption of a growing share of the costs of public education did not necessarily mean halcyon days for the schools. During the depths of the depression, state aid was not sufficient to compensate for the decline in local revenues, and state intervention often took the form of wholesale cuts in teachers' salaries. In 1931 the North Carolina centralization scheme included a 10 percent reduction in the salary schedule of teachers, and two years later newly imposed state standards slashed the pay of school employees even further. North Carolina won accolades for its efforts to ensure uniform educational opportunities, but in 1933–34 it ranked forty-seventh out of the forty-eight states in average annual salaries of principals, supervisors, and teachers.[21] Uniformity in North Carolina meant uniformly low salaries. In 1933 West Virginia teachers likewise suffered a 12 percent average pay cut as the state sought to reduce costs to the bare bones and maximize economy and efficiency.[22] Overall, in the United States current expenditures for public schools fell 17.8 percent between 1929–30 and 1933–34, and the average salaries of teachers and principals dropped 13.6 percent.[23]

The situation was not as bleak as these figures would seem to indicate, however. From 1929 to 1933 the price index plummeted more than 20 percent, so the cuts in school funding were actually less than the rate of deflation. Moreover, at no time during the depression did the number of school employees in the United States drop below the figure for 1929; and between 1930 and 1940, average per-pupil expenditures in constant dollars rose from $239 to $286. In fact, by the mid-1930s teachers' salaries were again on the rise, in large part owing to the infusion of state money.[24] During the decade the number of states providing free textbooks also increased, as did funding for school bus transportation. Generally the states proved able to meet the educational crisis of depression, and in the process they markedly extended their responsibility for maintaining public schools.

Many educators believed that the federal government should also lend a hand and assume a major role in school financing. As early as 1931 an advisory committee appointed by President Herbert Hoover concluded that "the American people [were] justified in using their federal tax system to give financial aid to education in the states," but at that time Congress took no action to establish a program of large-scale federal aid.[25] Then in 1937 President Franklin Roosevelt charged another advisory committee with reviewing the subject of federal support for education. In February 1938 the committee issued an unqualified endorsement of federal aid, claiming that a national program was necessary to compensate for the inequalities among the states. In the poor states of Arkansas and Mississippi, state and local authorities spent about one-fourth as much per pupil as their counterparts in the wealthy commonwealths of New York and California. Given the wide disparity in resources among the states, equality of educational opportunity was impossible unless the federal treasury helped even the score. Consequently, the committee proposed new federal grants that would gradually increase from $72 million in 1939–40 to $202 million in 1944–45.[26]

In both 1938 and 1939, bills for implementing this recommendation were introduced in Congress. But these bills foundered, owing largely to conflict over the two issues of aid to parochial schools and federal control of public schooling. The advisory committee had recommended that federal funds be used to aid both public and nonpublic schools, a proposal that deeply offended believers in separation of church and state. Yet friends of parochial schools opposed a federal program that discriminated against religious institutions and the children attending them. Even more fundamental was the objection to creeping federal control. In the minds of many, federal money meant federal regulation and a loss of state and local autonomy. Although advocates of the aid scheme believed funding would not necessarily lead to centralization, most observers were not so confident that Washington could refrain from assuming command. "You can put authority over poor people at Washington; you can grant power to deal with the unemployed; you can give funds to relieve human misery caused by a flood, an earthquake, or a depression," wrote the dean of the Teachers College of Columbia University, "but, if you put schools in this class, no matter how great their need for aid may be, discretionary authority and power inevitably will grow at Washington."[27]

This viewpoint was to prevail, blighting the hopes of supporters of federal aid legislation. The federal government was able to assume a large share of the traditionally local function of providing relief for the poor and unemployed. During the 1930s Americans expected Washington to perform this duty, and the result was billions of dollars of federal aid to the distressed. But the field of education was not allocated to the federal government. In 1941–42 the federal government spent $34 million for public education, or only 1.4 percent of the total bill and just 4.4 percent of the states' combined contribution.[28] Localities were no more able to shoulder the full burden of education than they were to fund mounting relief costs. It was the states that were to assume growing responsibility for the traditionally local task of schooling.

The depression-era legacy of centralization thus enhanced the role not only of Washington but also of Albany, Springfield, and Austin. The federal government assumed additional duties, but the states did likewise. In the process the states moved further from the nineteenth-century tradition of delegated responsibility and dispersed authority. Economic depression compelled both the states and the federal government to take charge and exercise their authority as never before.

Financing the Expanded State

Basic to the expanded role of state governments in the 1930s was the states' ability to raise revenues. Dependent largely on much-maligned property taxes, local units enjoyed little financial flexibility. Counties, towns, and school districts were in a fiscal straightjacket, and state lawmakers were not willing to release them from their restraints. Instead, the states exploited their sovereign taxing power to find new sources of cash and distributed part of the proceeds to hard-pressed localities. In the course of this effort, legislators revolutionized state finances. Across the nation the state financial reports of 1940 bore little resemblance to those of 1930. In a single decade, the states revamped their taxing structures and adapted to the difficult times.

Underlying this financial upheaval was a widespread revulsion against the general property tax. Criticism of the property tax had been mounting for decades, but during the early depression years, a full-scale revolt against the tax threatened the solvency of state and local government. Tax delinquency rates soared as property owners could not or would not pay the hated levy. In Iowa the delinquency rate for rural acreage rose from 14 percent in 1929 to 37 percent in 1931 and 48 percent in 1932. By 1933 Oregon recorded a delinquency rate for all property of 44 percent, Michigan's rate was 41 percent, and Indiana and Washington failed to collect 30 percent of the sum levied.[29] Many farmers and homeowners simply were unable to pay the property tax, for their incomes had disappeared. Others, angered by what they regarded as government extravagance and wastefulness, refused to pay. In fact, a taxpayers' strike spread throughout the nation in 1933 as property owners protested the status quo by withholding their tax payments. Clearly the taxing structure required some radical remodeling.

Responding to public opinion, many governors were calling for tax reform and spending cuts to relieve the burden on property owners. In 1931 Kansas governor Harry Woodring spoke to the legislature of the need "to lift a part of the load . . . borne by real and tangible personal property, and so far as possible to distribute it to other forms of wealth which hitherto either in whole or in part ha[d] escaped the tax burden."[30] In July 1932 Governor William Conley called the West Virginia legislature into an "economy session" and urged "a limitation of tax rates upon all classes of property."[31] Five months later, incom-

ing governor Junius M. Futrell of Arkansas urged the adoption of a state constitutional amendment to secure the people "against financial ruin, and excessive and unjustified taxation."[32] Across the country scores of candidates in
the 1932 campaign promised to reduce expenses and relieve the tax burden.
This was the popular panacea for the problems confronting the hard-pressed
taxpayer.

These cries for change produced results. In 1932 and 1933 at least sixteen
states adopted either constitutional or statutory limits on property taxes.[33] For
example, in November 1932 Michigan voters approved a fifteen-mill tax limitation amendment, West Virginia's voters endorsed a tax limitation amendment by a seven-to-one margin, and Washington's electorate approved an
initiative measure to cap property taxes.[34] A year later Ohioans overwhelmingly backed a ten-mill amendment, the tax limit carrying every county in the
state.[35] In 1933 Iowa's legislature capped the combined property levies in all taxing districts in the state at 80 percent of their 1930 rate.[36] Similarly, at the behest
of Governor Alfred Landon, Kansas lawmakers adopted a tax-limit statute
with graduated ceilings for counties depending on their assessed valuations.[37]

Even in states that failed to impose limits, public opinion forced a reduction
in property tax rates. As a result of these limits and reductions, reliance on the
property levy declined markedly during the 1930s. Whereas property levies
contributed 63.1 percent of all state and local revenues in 1932, they accounted
for only 39.9 percent in 1942.[38] The drop was especially dramatic at the state
level. As late as 1925, the general property tax raised 24.3 percent of all state
receipts, but by 1932 this was down to 14.2 percent, five years later the figure
was 5.8 percent, and in 1942 it had fallen to 4.4 percent.[39] Although in 1931 the
property levy was second only to the gasoline tax as a source of state tax
receipts, by the close of the decade it was a relatively minor element of the state
tax structure. Adjusting to the fifteen-mill amendment, in 1933 Michigan
slashed its state property tax rate from 3.5 mills to 0.6 mill. Then in 1935 the
state abandoned altogether its property levy, relinquishing to localities the
entire fifteen mills allowable under the constitution.[40] In 1934 Illinois likewise
discontinued its general property levy, yielding to local units a source of revenue that the state had relied on since 1839.[41] Gradually other states turned from
this former mainstay of the tax system, and in 1947 Arkansas became the twentieth state to abandon the general property levy for state purposes.[42]

With the decline of the property tax, states faced the necessity of adopting
alternative levies. Despite all the rhetoric about budget slashing, lawmakers
could not avoid the basic costs of government and had to find new means for
funding them. Not only did they have to fund state functions; legislators had

to help out localities now deprived of a portion of their property tax revenues. The problem, then, was to replace the state property levy and to pick up the bill for some of the expenditures of local units traditionally dependent on property taxes.

Most economists advocated reliance on the income tax, since it distributed tax burdens according to ability to pay, imposing the greatest burdens on those who could most afford to shoulder them. Many public officials agreed. In his message to the legislature in 1931, Governor Charles W. Bryan of Nebraska contended that it was "equitable and fair to enact a reasonable income tax law for the purpose of reducing the taxes on farms and homes." That same year Utah's Governor George H. Dern told lawmakers, "A tax based upon income is undoubtedly the best if not the ideal method of taxing intangibles."[43] On taking office in January 1933, Kansas's Governor Landon urged a "reorganization of an antiquated tax system," including adoption of a state income tax so that "the tax on property [could] be proportionately reduced."[44]

This rhetoric translated into action, for during the 1930s one state after another adopted the income tax. As of 1930 fifteen states levied personal income taxes. Then in 1931 Idaho, Utah, and Vermont joined the list of states imposing income levies, and Ohio adopted a tax on income derived from intangibles. Two years later, seven states, including Landon's Kansas, imposed a levy on personal incomes, as did Iowa and Louisiana in 1934. South Dakota and California followed suit in 1935, Kentucky did so in 1936, and Colorado and Maryland embraced the income tax in 1937.[45] By the close of the 1930s, over two-thirds of the states taxed incomes, the number having more than doubled during a single decade. Reduction of the property tax was the clear motive behind many of the new levies; Louisiana's income tax law was designated "an act to provide property tax relief."[46] Moreover, localities shared in the new revenues. All of Minnesota's income tax proceeds were distributed to local school districts, and 75 percent of New Mexico's income tax collections and Utah's corporate tax receipts were earmarked for education, as was 40 percent of Montana's personal income tax revenues.[47]

This rise in the number of states imposing income taxes did not, however, increase that tax's share of total state collections. In 1930 income levies contributed 11 percent of all state tax receipts; ten years later, if one excluded unemployment compensation taxes funding the states' share of the Social Security system, the figure was still 11 percent.[48] Although it may have been equitable and just, apportioning the costs of government to those who could afford the burden, the state income tax was not an especially bountiful generator of revenues during the depression decade. As incomes plummeted during the early 1930s, so did income tax receipts. Despite emergency increases in the tax rate from 1931 through 1934, New York's personal income tax collections dropped from $85 million in 1929 to $24 million in 1933. Owing to generous exemptions, only the relatively well-to-do paid the New York tax, but during the early 1930s this class was an endangered species. Thus, the number of New York taxpayers fell from 432,900 in 1929 to 215,538 four years later.[49] For the nation as a whole, state income tax collections decreased from $233 million in 1930 to $121 million in 1933. If these figures were not enough of an indictment of the income tax, policymakers only had to turn to the federal government's experience for further proof of the danger of relying on such a levy during an economic depression. Federal income tax receipts fell 70 percent from $2.41 billion in 1930 to $747 million in 1933. By the latter date, the federal tobacco tax was producing more revenue than the personal income tax. In both 1932 and 1933, the federal deficit exceeded $2 billion as Washington spent more than double what it received.[50] One did not need to be an accountant to recognize that the sluggish income tax was the chief culprit in the federal government's funding problems.

The variability of income tax receipts led some state policymakers to question its merits as a replacement for the traditional property levy. In 1934 a special tax commission studying new sources of revenue for Connecticut reported that the "extreme variability of the revenues from a general personal income tax" was "a crucial weakness" and had "caused acute financial embarrassment to those states relying upon this source for a substantial part of their revenues."[51] Even those sympathetic to the state income tax recognized its instability as a producer of funds. "The returns from the income tax vary with the swing of the business cycle," admitted a member of Wisconsin's tax commission, "and at the very time when the revenues may be needed most the receipts may be far below normal."[52]

Not only was the income tax unstable; it also produced relatively little revenue in the poor agricultural states, whose residents had little income. Whereas New York could soak Wall Street financiers and corporate executives, Mississippi, Arkansas, and North and South Dakota were not so fortunate. Writing in 1935, economist James W. Martin observed, "Mississippi, with one of the highest rate structures to be found in any state, secures from income taxation roughly fourteen cents per capita, whereas New York state secures about $5.60 of revenue per capita." Though an advocate of the state income tax, Martin admitted, "This extreme variation in the effectiveness of income taxes in poor and rich communities presents a substantial problem for which no solution is apparent."[53]

Unfortunately, the states most willing to adopt the income tax were those that would benefit least from it. Popular among farmers who because their meager incomes were usually exempt from this new levy, the income tax was most widely adopted in the less populous, rural states of the West, the Great Plains, and the South. There was no general personal income tax in industrialized, urban New Jersey, Pennsylvania, Ohio, Michigan, and Illinois. Yet these were the very states that had incomes sufficient to render such a levy worthwhile. New York, the wealthiest state, retained its income tax, and in 1937 the Empire State accounted for 61 percent of all state personal income tax collections in the nation and for almost one-half of the corporate income tax receipts. Less populated, agricultural states collected much of the remainder. In 1936 Professor Harley L. Lutz summed up the reality of state income taxation: "So far as the actual revenue is concerned, any tax based on net income will always be a relatively futile gesture for some, possibly for a majority of the states."[54]

Given the limited potential of the state income tax during the depression decade, policymakers needed to turn to other levies in their search for funds. The alternative that proved most lucrative and reliable was the general sales tax. Adopted by financially strapped European nations in the wake of World War I, the sales tax was virtually unknown in the United States as late as 1930. During the 1920s investigatory commissions and economists studying state tax reform never discussed the sales tax as a possible future source of revenue. The income tax was assumed to be the correct alternative to the general property levy, and most experts predicted that the states would increasingly tap the incomes of the wealthy in their pursuit for additional receipts. Yet at the same time lawmakers were gradually turning to selective sales taxes, with eight states adopting an impost on cigarette sales during the 1920s.

The most productive consumption tax, of course, was the gasoline tax, and its extraordinary success demonstrated that levies on the sales of commodities could be highly lucrative. Even more important for depression-era lawmakers, the tax on gasoline produced revenues during bad times as well as good. State collections of gasoline taxes actually increased 20 percent between 1929 and 1933, a remarkable showing given the collapse of the economy. Receipts from the tax did dip 3 percent from 1931 to 1933, but still it proved an admirably reliable source of funds.[55] Recognizing this, the federal government adopted its first gasoline tax in 1932. The federal income tax had faltered seriously during the early depression years, so Congress followed the example of the states and turned to the more stable and depression-resistant levy on a commodity.

But the states were to go further and emulate the European nations by adopting a general tax on the sale of virtually all commodities. Mississippi was

the first to embrace this alternative, enacting a sales tax in 1932. Vying with
Arkansas for the dubious distinction of poorest state in the nation, Mississippi
was unable to raise sufficient revenues from its income tax, and as elsewhere
the property tax burden was deemed intolerable. On 1 January 1932 there was
only $1,326 in general funds in the state treasury, yet outstanding warrants
issued against this munificent sum totaled almost $6 million.[56] Early in its 1932
session, the legislature had to authorize the chair of the state tax commission
to borrow $750 just to pay for the postage stamps needed for mailing income
tax notices.[57]

To ensure the fiscal integrity of his state, incoming governor Mike Conner
urged the adoption of a general sales tax. The governor favored this measure
because it would not only pay the state's bills but also relieve the "inequitable
and oppressive tax burden which rest[ed] most heavily upon land." Moreover,
it would shift some of the cost of government to African Americans, who constituted one-half of the state's population but paid little property tax.[58] This
must have made the scheme more feasible politically, for legislators did not
need to fear retribution at the polls from disfranchised but newly burdened
blacks. Many Mississippi retailers were outraged by the proposal, but the governor stood his ground, rallied the legislators, and secured adoption of a 2 percent retail sales tax.

Conner's dedication paid off, the sales tax proving a boon to the hard-
pressed state government. During the first eight months it was in effect, the tax
yielded $1.7 million, a handsome sum for impoverished Mississippi. By 1937 it
was producing $5.9 million annually, or more than one-fifth of Mississippi's
total state revenues. By comparison, the state income tax yielded only $1.5 mil-
lion.[59] At the annual conference of the National Tax Association in October
1933, the chair of Mississippi's State Tax Commission, A. H. Stone, endorsed the
sales tax, reporting that it had "yielded more revenue than was anticipated"
and that opposition to it had "either disappeared or become dormant."[60] Four
months later, at the meeting of the National Association of State Tax Administrators, Stone was equally positive. "Don't let anybody tell you that a sales tax
isn't all right," he told the assembled administrators. "As long as you can make
it work, why, you can collect it and successfully."[61]

Lawmakers in other states were impressed and quickly joined Mississippi in
embracing the sales tax. In 1933 alone fourteen states adopted the general sales
tax, and at the close of the 1930s, twenty-three states were relying on this new
source of revenue. By 1935 the sales tax had surpassed the property levy as a
generator of state funds; as early as 1936, it was the second most lucrative
source of state tax receipts, behind only the gasoline tax. Although fewer states
imposed the sales tax than imposed the income tax, it consistently accounted

for a larger share of the combined state tax collections. In 1940 the states raised $499 million from the sales tax and $361 million from the personal and corporate income taxes combined.[62]

Despite the sale tax's contribution to state solvency, many commentators despised it. Most notably, it was attacked as a regressive tax, imposing a proportionately heavier burden on the poor than the rich. Economists almost universally condemned the sales tax and regarded state adoption of the new levy as a step backward in the evolution of public finance. A past president of the American Economic Association claimed that the sales tax was "one more attempt to put the whole burden of taxes on the poor. It violates every canon of taxation accepted by the civilized world for 150 years." Columbia University economist Robert Murray Haig seconded this view: "To propose the substitution of general sales taxes for taxes on real estate as a measure of relief for the small man is an insult to intelligence and an affront to common sense."[63]

Yet the sales tax was an expedient means to an end. The states needed money, and no levy could produce revenues in such quantity and so quickly as the sales tax. Most states collected the sales tax monthly, so as an emergency measure it was far superior to the income or property taxes, which were paid annually. The sales tax diverted cash into state coffers a mere thirty days after taking effect, and it produced that cash as long as the citizenry continued to buy. Given these facts, many reluctant lawmakers turned to the flawed impost simply because there was no other satisfactory alternative. In North Carolina A. J. Maxwell had campaigned for office on a platform rejecting the sales tax, but in early 1933 he was forced to admit, "The undesirable necessity for a sales tax had become progressively apparent as revenue yields have been shrinking every day since the General Assembly convened."[64] In California the situation was much the same. Said the cosponsor of that state's tax relief plan, "Neither the Legislature nor the State's constitutional officers would claim that the sales tax is perfect, but this fact remains: It was the only tax available which would raise the necessary money."[65] Describing the adoption of his state's sale tax, one Utahan reported, "Finally only the sales tax remained, and when all hope of solution of the problem in some other way had expired, enough votes were recruited to pass a retail sales tax."[66] University of Vermont economist Alfred G. Buehler summed up the situation: "The general sales tax has been adopted as an emergency revenue because its productivity has been considered more important than its unequal burdens, because expediency has been given greater weight than equity."[67]

In the end, the desire for cash prevailed over economic theory. To public officials responsible for paying the states' bills, the sales tax was a practical solution to funding problems and thus had to be embraced. Economists might gnash their teeth over the states' departure from sound principles of taxation, but for legislators the soundest tax was that which reliably produced revenue. The sales tax fit the bill.

Moreover, the states did not need to share this new source of cash with the federal government. In 1932 Congress refused to adopt a national sales tax, in part because of protests from those seeking to reserve this generator of revenue for the states. The ranking Democrat on the Senate Finance Committee was Mississippi's Pat Harrison, and he was dedicated to allowing his home state to collect its new levy on sales without the federal government poaching on this field of taxation. "There is a growing feeling that the sales tax should be left exclusively to the States," Harrison proclaimed. And others joined him in urging that the general sales tax remain solely a state benefactor. A Texas representative complained that a national levy on sales would "still further trample upon the rights of the States. Yes; enact it into law and further reduce your State to the status of a Province."[68] Henceforth the federal government would rely primarily on the income tax, supplemented by assorted excise levies. But Washington would not reap the rewards of a general sales tax.

Influenced by the adverse experience of the depression decade, the states, however, fashioned a more diverse tax system. The general sales tax ensured a degree of stability vital during economic downturns. In contrast, the income tax afforded an element of elasticity that would benefit state coffers during periods of prosperity. During the 1930s many states had not yet opted for this balanced structure of taxation, with some imposing one of these taxes but not the other. Yet income and sales taxes were in place in many states, and both were major elements of the emerging pattern of state finances. In addition to these taxes, the states imposed special imposts on cigarettes and alcohol, as well as the ever-lucrative gasoline levy. Meanwhile, the traditional property tax was left largely to local units of government. Since the 1890s tax commissions and experts had urged that the states rely less on the general property tax and exploit other sources of revenue. By 1940 lawmakers had largely achieved this goal. The result was a heterogeneous tax structure that would underlie state government for the remainder of the century.

Scheming for Economic Success

During the depression decade, state lawmakers not only accelerated the pace of centralization and tax reform; some also took extraordinary action to boost local economies. Such initiatives were not unprecedented. Before the Civil War, states had attempted to promote economic development through internal improvement programs that resulted in state-owned canal systems from New York to Illinois. But the actions of Nevada and Mississippi during the 1930s anticipated a new wave of state-sponsored economic promotion schemes in the second half of the twentieth century, when every ambitious common-wealth would create a development department and a tourism bureau. Both of these states had thus far proved to be losers in the contest for growth and development. Nevada was the least populous state, and Mississippi was perennially among the poorest. Yet during the depression both launched particularly imaginative schemes to lift themselves out of the doldrums, thereby revealing how states could effectively exploit their powers and status as sovereign entities. While federal policymakers were creating NRAs and WPAs, lawmakers in Nevada and Mississippi had their own ideas about how to achieve economic success. And in the case of Nevada, the state's leaders proved remarkably prescient, laying the foundation for a booming future.

Nevada had experienced booms in the past as successive discoveries of gold, silver, and copper had momentarily boosted the state's fortunes. Yet a bust had followed every boom, and by 1930 a mere 91,000 people lived in the state, an increase of only 29,000 over the figure fifty years earlier. Nevada was largely a desert wasteland with a population of less than half that of the next least inhabited state, Wyoming.

Since the turn of the century, however, Nevada had sought to profit from its status as a state. Legislators enacted lenient incorporation laws, though equally permissive Delaware and New Jersey proved more successful in attracting corporations than remote Nevada. The legislature had also repealed Nevada's inheritance tax, and by the mid-1930s, it was the only state not to impose such a levy. Consequently, it had become the official residence of some millionaires seeking to avoid taxation. But its chief state-induced enterprise was the divorce trade. In an age of restrictive divorce laws, Nevada accommodated many out-of-staters who sought to sever their bonds of matrimony as quickly as possible. In 1927 Nevada had reduced the necessary period of residence for divorce seekers to only three months, the lowest in the nation. As of 1928 the state was producing more than twenty-five hundred divorces annually, earning millions of dollars for the state's lawyers and for the hotels and dude ranches that housed divorce-seekers for the requisite three months.[69]

By 1931 Nevada's divorce trade was threatened, as both Idaho and Arkansas prepared to lower their residency requirements to three months. To beat out the competition, the Nevada legislature reduced the residency requirement to six weeks. Reporting on the change, a leading Nevada newspaper carried the headline: "Revival of Gold Rush Days Predicted. Beat This One, If You Can."[70]

But Nevadans were not to rely solely on divorce for their future prosperity. A growing number of the state's residents also favored the legalization of gambling. Illegal games of chance had flourished in the state for years, with law enforcement officers tolerating them in exchange for bribes. During the 1920s there was agitation among some Nevadans to end this hypocrisy and the resulting corruption by repealing the ban on gaming. Not until the onset of the depression, however, were proponents of legalized gambling able to win a majority of legislators to their side.

Hard times caused some to abandon their moral objections, for optimistic promoters believed that wide-open gaming could lure considerable out-of-state money to underdeveloped Nevada. In 1930 Thomas Carroll, a Las Vegas entrepreneur, ran newspaper advertisements that claimed that legalized gambling would make Nevada the "Playground of the United States." "We can," Carroll contended, "make wide-open gambling the biggest industry in the state, so that it with horse racing and tourist traffic, will bring more millions of dollars into Nevada than . . . any other industry we now have."[71] In November 1930 the Las Vegas Chamber of Commerce polled its members on the issue, and ninety respondents favored wide-open gambling; only thirty-seven supported a continued ban.[72] Business interests obviously seemed to think wide-open gambling was a good idea, and in the 1931 session of the legislature, lawmakers appeared to agree. Commenting on the attitude of state legislators, a newspaper correspondent observed, "Important economic and governmental considerations . . . outweigh the moral issue."[73] Nevada could profit from legalization of games of chance, and consequently legislators in 1931 removed the ban, making their state the only one in the nation to allow wide-open gambling.

Thus, in a single session the Nevada legislature had reaffirmed the state's reputation as a refuge for those seeking a divorce and had ignored the nation's prevailing moral standards and legalized gambling. "Nevada is embarking on what may be termed a 'legalized liberality,'" observed a Reno newspaper. "It represents a theory of social and business economics that was formerly thought to be inconsistent with the best interests of the state." Now, however, Nevadans were willing to experiment with a combination of "open gambling and easy divorce as a means of stimulating business."[74] Another newspaper commentary excused this legalized liberality when it observed, "No one denies that the 'business of divorce' has brought millions of dollars into the state annually, and no one is to be blamed for desiring to continue this income."[75]

As predicted, Nevada did profit from its waywardness. In 1931 the new law resulted in a record 5,260 divorces, and the following year 127 lawyers practiced in Reno, a city of only eighteen thousand residents.[76] This was approximately

six times the average number of attorneys for a town of that size. By the beginning of the 1940s, the income from the divorce trade was estimated to be as
high as $5 million per year.[77] The gambling law was not to produce dramatic
results until after World War II. Yet it did boost the state's meager economy
during the 1930s, as new clubs opened in both Reno and Las Vegas. Faced with
a history of economic failure and the onset of hard times nationwide, Nevadans opted to profit from the wages of sin. This was an economic strategy
that was already paying off in the 1930s, and after 1945 sin would prove a
mother lode far more lucrative than the state's legendary Comstock Lode.
Through exploiting its status as a sovereign state, Nevada was able to legalize
practices that were illegal elsewhere in the Union and reap the monetary
rewards of states' rights.

During the nineteenth century, Mississippi had sacrificed virtually everything, fighting under the banner of states' rights. It emerged from the Civil War
impoverished, and during succeeding decades it had not markedly improved
its fortunes. By the 1930s the average annual per capita income was only $212,
one-third the national average of $636.[78] Even among southern states, Missis-
sippi was economically backward. The per capita value of industrial plants was
only one-fourth the average for its fellow southern commonwealths.

Many Mississippians felt that it was time for a change. Moreover, they knew
that they could not wait for the federal government and the Brain Trust or
bureaucrats of the Roosevelt administration to act on their behalf. The state
had to assume the initiative. "If the South sits around and waits for Brain
Trusters and selfish Northern industrial interests' approval of industrial expansion here," remarked one newspaper, "we will never achieve our rightful place
in the industry of the nation."[79] The most notable adherent to this view was
Hugh L. White, who campaigned successfully for governor in 1935, promising
to promote the "greatest industrialization in this state that ha[d] ever been
known." In his inaugural address in January 1936, White declared that Mississippi had to "balance agriculture with industry."[80] The press picked up on this
phrase, and White's economic program soon became known as the Balance
Agriculture with Industry (BAWI) plan.

The scheme as proposed by White and adopted by the legislature permitted
local governments to finance the building of manufacturing facilities through
the issuance of bonds. Before localities could do so, however, they had to secure
the approval of a three-person state industrial commission that reviewed the
merits of the investment. The bond issue also had to win the approval of two-
thirds of the voters in a local referendum. In other words, local governments,
supervised by the state, were constructing and leasing facilities for manufac-

turers willing to move to Mississippi and aid in its economic development. Because it smacked of state socialism and diverted public funds to private corporations, this scheme appeared to violate Mississippi's constitution. Nevertheless, in a strained argument, the Mississippi Supreme Court upheld White's economic plan. "It is said, in effect, that the engaging by a state or its political subdivision in manufacturing enterprises is a complete departure from the concept our forefathers had of the powers and duties of the state and is a step toward socialism," observed the supreme court majority. Yet "every intervention of any consequence by the state and national government in the economic and social life of the citizen ha[d] been so branded," and the court refused to allow itself "to be subjected to the tyranny of symbols."[81] Cries of socialism would not, then, render the law unconstitutional. White's program of publicly subsidized manufacturing enterprises could proceed.

Some Mississippians, however, continued to question the ideological correctness of the scheme. "The thing was outright Socialism and should never have been attempted, much less held constitutional," complained one banker. Others were more pragmatic. Thus, a fellow banker remarked, "I'm so much concerned about real forms of Socialism that I can't worry much about that municipally owned but privately operated factory down the street." And a third banker presented a practical argument: "The BAWI plan was socialistic in its tendency, but it worked."[82]

The fact that BAWI seemed to work allayed many people's misgivings. Between 1936 and 1940 the program produced twelve new manufacturing facilities in the state. By mid-1943 these twelve employed 12,500 workers, or 14 percent of the total number of manufacturing employees in Mississippi, and accounted for 24 percent of the total manufacturing wages in the state. Much of this was due to the Ingalls Shipbuilding Corporation, which was attracted to Pascagoula and became the state's largest employer during World War II.[83] Twelve manufacturing plants might not have been an impressive yield by the standards of other more industrialized states, and they did not revolutionize Mississippi's economy overnight. In 1944 Mississippi still ranked last among the states in per capita income and value of manufactured products.[84] But BAWI had increased the momentum toward industrialization, and Governor White was later able to look back upon his scheme as a success. "I can sit back and grin about the daily accomplishments made under BAWI," he observed. "The plan was attacked as socialistic when it was first put into effect but now most people realize it has brought about a complete reversal of the state's economy."[85]

Furthermore, Mississippi's efforts were to become a model for other states, especially in the South. According to one student of state promotion of industrial development, "by introducing a system wherein the state sanctioned and supervised the use of municipal bonds to finance plant construction, the BAWI program lifted the curtain on an era of more competitive subsidization and broader state and local government involvement in industrial development efforts."[86] Another war between the states was about to break out; this one was to be fought over manufacturing plants, as each state sought to attract new jobs or least preserve those it had. During the post–World War II era, Sunbelt was to be pitted against Rustbelt, Georgia against New York, Texas against Ohio. In the late 1930s, Mississippi fired the first shot in the struggle, for BAWI marked the beginning of this new era of heightened state competition to achieve prosperity.

Both Mississippi and Nevada were taking extraordinary action to overcome the consequences of economic colonialism. These states had long been producers of raw materials that had enriched capitalists in New York and California but had reaped limited rewards for the miners and planters of the West and the South. Now they sought to reverse the flow of cash, and they were willing to defy orthodoxy to achieve their goal. Mississippi flirted with socialism and Nevada embraced sin. Moral and ideological inhibitions were not allowed to block the path to development. Neither moribund nor prostrate in the face of hard times, the poorest and least populous states were innovating in ways that shocked some but which could pay off in the future.

Such innovation was typical of state government during the 1930s. The economic depression not only changed the role of the federal government; it also forced notable adjustments at the state level. The states felt compelled to assume an unprecedented degree of responsibility for such traditionally local functions as education. To finance their new role, states restructured their tax systems and quickly turned to revenue sources previously untapped. At the state as well as the federal level, the 1930s was a decade of change. Although the new deal in the states often bore little resemblance to that in Washington, D.C., governors and legislators were fashioning original and untested programs. Imagination was not confined to the White House, the Roosevelt Brain Trust, or the District of Columbia. Policymakers in Albany, Raleigh, and Columbus were also fabricating schemes unprecedented in the history of American government. And in the case of both Nevada and Mississippi, state lawmakers were willing to deviate from ideological and moral norms to boost the economy of their undeveloped domains.

Interstate Cooperation

During the 1930s the issue of interstate cooperation was the focus of more discussion and attracted greater attention than at any other time in the twentieth century. In no other decade did the issue seem so pressing, for at no other time did governmental centralization appear to be accelerating at such a breakneck pace. The states faced a dynamic federal government, and in response they closed ranks to a degree unprecedented in the nation's history. They fashioned an interstate network to exchange information and ensure that state governments better conformed to the prevailing twentieth-century concern for greater expertise in government. By promoting such a network, the states reinforced their positions in the federal system.

The key figure in this movement for interstate cooperation was Henry W. Toll. A respected Denver attorney with a Harvard law degree, in 1922 he ran successfully for the Colorado state senate and was to serve in that body for eight years. At the time of his election, Toll was already considering plans for the creation of a national organization of state legislators that would work toward greater interstate cooperation. And during the next two decades he would realize this goal. For many years his interstate organization was virtually a one-man effort. But through persistence, dedication, and considerable sacrifice of his time and money, Toll was to succeed. In the process he established himself as one of the most significant figures in the history of twentieth-century federalism.

In December 1925 Toll took the first step in achieving his goal when he sent letters to each member of the legislature in all forty-eight states. This mass mailing to seventy-five hundred lawmakers proposed the organization of the American Legislators' Association, and to give the proposal more substance, Toll enclosed with each letter the first issue of the *American Legislator,* the organization's periodical. In early issues of the periodical, Toll spelled out the purpose of his organization. The April 1926 issue observed that "millions of Americans [were] dissatisfied with their legislatures and their legislation" because the bills were "unconsidered, inconsiderate, and unscientific" and the legislative procedure "expensive, cumbersome, lacking in perspective, and susceptible to lobbies." Moreover, many Americans criticized the legislatures' "failure to pass uniform laws concerning many subjects and [the] entire lack of interstate cooperation." To remedy these shortcomings, Toll proposed "the organization of the American Legislators' Association to bring information to the individual legislator, to promote uniform laws, and to establish a line of communication between specialists and legislators—between those who know best what the laws *should be* and those who decide what the laws *are.*"[87]

Toll thus envisioned a program of cooperation and mutual enlightenment. Working together, disparate state lawmakers from throughout the nation could supposedly lift the pall of disrepute shrouding legislatures and ensure that solons were better informed and more expert. At the association's first annual meeting, a state senator from Nevada aptly noted that the group was created "in order to form a more perfect union."[88] But Toll's approach for achieving such a union differed from that of the framers of the federal Constitution of 1787. Whereas the framers sought greater perfection through the imposition of an effective national government, Toll's organization endeavored to do so through an extraconstitutional exchange of information and ideas that would bolster the lawmaking capacity of the states. Toll and like-minded state lawmakers believed the federal Constitution was no longer sufficient; the American Legislators' Association was a necessary supplement to ensure an effective federal system.

Yet during the late 1920s the American Legislators' Association was largely a figment of Henry Toll's imagination. It was run from Toll's Denver law office, with his office staff helping with the correspondence. He paid a large part of the bills from his own pocket. Although Toll publicized the group as a nationwide organization embracing all seventy-five hundred state legislators, in reality the association consisted of one truly active member and a few scattered sympathizers.

This was evident in the annual meetings of the late 1920s. The first gathering was held in Denver in July 1926, following the American Bar Association convention in that city. Toll hoped that many lawyer-legislators drawn to the bar convention would remain in Denver long enough to attend the association's initial meeting. This strategy proved moderately successful, for legislators from ten states did gather in the Colorado state senate chamber and formally organize the American Legislators' Association. Predictably, Henry Toll was elected president.[89] The following year, Toll sent notices to all the state legislators announcing the second annual meeting, to be held in Buffalo. Yet only five people—four reporters and Toll himself—appeared at the assigned meeting place in Buffalo's Hotel Lafayette.[90] A later account of the organization's early history reported that at the time of the failed Buffalo gathering, Toll's "dream seemed to be dead. . . . The following years were full of discouragement," and the association "ceased to function except for the continuing activities of the original organizer and his secretary."[91] No numbers of the association's periodical appeared in 1927 or 1928, and Toll later characterized his organization during these years as "a forlorn venture, doomed to asphyxiation."[92]

Fortunes improved in 1929. Toll revived publication of the association's journal, the *Legislator,* and the fourth annual meeting, though attracting only about fifteen representatives from nine states, did generate more stimulating discussions than earlier gatherings.[93] Moreover, the organization won favorable press notice. "As things stand now the forty-eight State Legislatures rattle around like peas in a gigantic pod," the *New York World* observed. "Maine knows very little of what is being done in South Dakota." Consequently, the American Legislators' Association deserved "wide interest and support."[94]

The year 1930 marked the beginning of a new era in the history of the association. In January Toll secured a $40,000 grant from the Spelman Fund, a Rockefeller family philanthropy, and later that year the Rosenwald Foundation of Chicago gave an additional $15,000 for the support of the American Legislators' Association.[95] This was only the first of many grants from the Spelman Fund, which was to prove the great benefactor of Toll's experiment in interstate cooperation. Exploiting this financial windfall, Toll transformed his semi-mythical organization into an increasingly potent organ for the betterment of state government. He replaced the *Legislator,* which had been little more than a newsletter, with a full-fledged magazine, *State Government.* Beginning with its first issue in April 1930, *State Government* dedicated itself to presenting articles on a wide range of topics of interest to state officials. In its pages both legislators and administrators could learn of the latest policy developments and what was happening in other states.

Toll also used his Spelman grant to open a new association headquarters in Chicago, adjacent to the University of Chicago campus. Initially it consisted of two small rooms with packing boxes for desks and a few borrowed chairs. The original staff comprised Toll, his secretary, and one other employee imported from Denver. Yet with characteristic promotional flair, Toll dubbed the cramped quarters the association's "secretariat" and announced that the Chicago office would also serve as the Interstate Reference Bureau. This bureau was to realize the association's goal of providing a clearinghouse for legislative information. The association promised that the Chicago office would "assist the directors of [state reference] bureaus, and individual legislators, to locate the best sources of information and advice."[96] If lawmakers needed to know what legislation was being enacted elsewhere in the nation or what studies had been conducted on a certain policy question, they could contact this new interstate bureau, and Toll and his colleagues would attempt to provide the answers.

During the early 1930s this bureau was the focus of much of the association's activity. Meanwhile, Toll's staff and quarters expanded to meet the demands for information. In 1932 a staff member reported that "requests for information [were] continually pouring into" the bureau, and by 1933 Toll was claiming that the bureau's staff "at all times" had included "at least ten or twelve college graduates."[97] In 1934 the bureau answered 537 inquiries, with requests for information coming from every state but Nevada.[98]

Toll's work was winning the appreciation of many lawmakers; and during the early 1930s, state legislatures finally afforded the American Legislators' Association official recognition and some welcome, if meager, funding. Beginning in January 1931, a "Uniform Resolution of Endorsement of the American Legislators' Association" circulated among the states, and by March 1932 fifty-four houses of the legislature in thirty-two states had adopted this measure, which officially commended the association and its Interstate Reference Bureau "as legitimate and constructive efforts to assist the legislatures of the various States in the efficient performance of their work."[99]

Meanwhile, the American Legislators' Association was embarking on new initiatives that justified the demands for greater state support. For example, in September 1932 the association organized a regional conference for legislators and state officials from North Carolina, South Carolina, Georgia, West Virginia, Virginia, and Tennessee. The conference was held so that these leaders could exchange information on pressing issues of mutual concern before the convening of the next session of their legislatures. Given the dire economic circumstances prevailing in the fall of 1932, preparation for some tough decision making seemed especially warranted. Explaining the need for the conference, Henry Toll commented: "Definite planning of legislative work in advance of sessions . . . is a promising method. Much time which should be devoted to major legislation is now wasted on petty bills."[100]

At the same time, Toll was taking further steps to advance the cause of interstate cooperation and increase the stature of the American Legislators' Association. By 1932 federal finances were in shambles, with an awesome budget deficit forcing members of Congress to search for new revenues. Simultaneously, the states were also scrambling for funds and were dedicated to keeping the federal government from poaching on what they regarded as their tax domain. Given this tension between the state and federal governments and the mutual need for money, the 1932 annual meeting of the American Legislators' Association discussed calling an interstate conference to deal with the problem of conflicting taxation. State senator George Woodward of Pennsylvania proposed that "state legislatures make common cause in negotiating with Congress," and he offered to donate two thousand dollars to help finance the cost of an assembly of lawmakers from throughout the nation.[101]

Responding to this discussion, the Board of Managers of the American Legislators' Association made plans for an interstate conference on conflicting taxation. In its call for this interstate assembly, the association explained, "It has long been apparent that substantial benefits would result to the citizens of all states from a closer contact between the various legislatures, and that many governmental difficulties are aggravated by the absence of adequate facilities for conference between these lawmaking bodies." But the states could no longer tolerate this lack of interaction. "The present economic emergency creates an imperative necessity for joint counsel and concerted action," proclaimed the association. "It is time for the states to make common cause." To achieve such joint action, each state was asked to select one member of its lower house and one from its upper house to serve as delegates to the conference that would meet in Washington in early February 1933. In addition, each governor was invited to send "one or more principal fiscal officers of the state" to participate in the interstate conclave.[102]

Eighty-seven official participants from thirty-one states attended the Washington conference, which opened with remarks from outgoing president Herbert Hoover. After two days of deliberation, this first interstate assembly endorsed the creation of a permanent commission on conflicting taxation composed of legislators from various states and called for the "continuing cooperation between all the states through the medium of the American Legislators' Association." Moreover, it resolved that a second interstate assembly should be held at a time determined by the association's Board of Managers.[103] In other words, this was not to be the last time state legislators met in common cause. Instead, the 1933 meeting was expected to set a precedent to be followed in years to come.

Carrying out the delegates' wishes, the president of the assembly appointed a Commission on Conflicting Taxation consisting of seventeen state lawmakers from thirteen states, with the ubiquitous Henry Toll as secretary of the commission.[104] During the remaining years of the decade, the commission issued a series of research reports and recommendations but failed to eliminate the duplication of federal and state taxes or divide the tax field so that some revenue sources would be assigned exclusively to the national government and others to the states. It did defend the states' right to levy certain taxes and perhaps curbed federal encroachment on state revenue sources. Its chief legacy, however, was that it set a precedent for collaborative state investigation of policy questions and was a model for later interstate initiatives.

Building on this pioneering effort, the Pennsylvania legislature asked the American Legislators' Association to call an interstate bus and truck conference to frame uniform legislation regarding the width, length, height, and weight of motor vehicles. Each state had different laws limiting the size of trucks, leading to confusion and discord. The conference met in October 1933 in Harrisburg, Pennsylvania, with Henry Toll as presiding officer. Lobbyists representing transportation interests voiced conflicting views before the assembled delegates from seventeen states, and the conference arrived at no consensus other than a recommendation that regional meetings be called to discuss the subject. In June 1934 a Western Bus and Truck Conference attended by eighty delegates from eleven western states proved more successful. The participants agreed to a series of future meetings to work toward the goal of harmonious motor vehicle laws.[105]

Although these conferences produced no immediate dramatic results, Henry Toll was not discouraged. Instead, on the evening following the Harrisburg conference, he presented to the Board of Managers of the American Legislators' Association a proposal for a league of state governments. Cooperation among legislators alone was no longer sufficient. All state officials needed to be involved in the initiative for interstate cooperation. "It is not only *proper* to have executive and administrative state officials participate with the legislators," Toll announced; "it is absolutely *necessary*." During the following year, Toll made plans for this new organization, and in early 1935 the Council of State Governments was born with Henry Toll as executive director. The American Legislators' Association continued to exist but was in effect indistinguishable from the more comprehensive council. One commentator later noted that during this period the two organizations "were functioning as a pair of Siamese twins."[106]

Basic to the early development of the Council of State Governments were the state commissions on interstate cooperation. The council lobbied vigorously for the passage of a uniform statute in each state calling for the creation of these commissions. According to this statute, the state commission was "to carry forward the participation of this state as a member of the Council of State Governments" and generally to "enable this state to do its part — or more than its part in forming a more perfect union among the various governments in the United States and in developing the Council of State Governments for that purpose."[107] By the close of 1936, seventeen states had created these commissions, and by mid-1937 the figure had risen to thirty-five.[108] As of 1937 twenty-one states had taken an additional step and appropriated funds for the council.[109] Gradually Toll was weaning his experiment from its dependence on the Spelman Fund, though state contributions failed to keep pace with the budgetary needs of the expanding Council of State Governments.

By the second half of the 1930s, Toll's dream of interstate cooperation was much closer to realization than during the dismal days of the late 1920s. At the second interstate assembly, held in 1935, 159 delegates from forty-one states attended, as compared with only 87 delegates and thirty-one states at the first assembly in 1933. Moreover, in 1937 the third assembly drew 265 representatives from forty-six states.[110] In other words, virtually all of the states had joined the movement by 1937. The council and state commissions for interstate cooperation were also making some progress toward the goal of statutory harmony. Perhaps their most notable achievements were in the field of criminal justice. In 1935 the Interstate Crime Conference met in Trenton, New Jersey, and established the Interstate Crime Commission, which drafted four model bills on the subjects of extradition, fresh pursuit, compulsory attendance of out-of-state witnesses, and reciprocal supervision of out-of-state parolees. By mid-1937 twenty-five states had adopted one or more of these bills, thereby reducing the interstate barriers to the capture and prosecution of criminals.[111]

But perhaps more importantly, the Council of State Governments was expanding earlier efforts to facilitate the flow of information among the states. In 1935 it published the first issue of *The Book of the States,* a biennial compilation of data on state government and summary of what was transpiring at the state level in certain policy areas. Together with *State Government,* this reference work was to keep state officials informed about the activities of their counterparts elsewhere. In 1939 a proud Henry Toll correctly predicted that *The Book of the States* was "probably destined to become one of the most important and authoritative reference works in American government."[112]

Yet during the last half of the 1930s, the ambitious Toll was not satisfied simply with larger assemblies, more conferences, and additional publications. He was also encouraging the Council of State Governments to affiliate with national organizations of state officials and serve as their central secretariat. In 1936 the Council of State Governments agreed to become the information clearinghouse for the National Association of Attorneys General. As such it published a weekly report that included selected opinions of the states' chief legal officers as well as comments on significant court decisions and articles on subjects of pertinence to the attorneys general. That same year, the council further expanded its role as a facilitator of interstate cooperation by assuming administrative and research responsibilities for the National Association of Secretaries of State. In this role, it prepared bulletins on such topics as election procedures and registration fees as well as aiding in the arrangement of the national association's meetings.[113] In 1936 the Governors' Conference also began to rely on the council's research services, and in 1937 and 1938 the state executives turned to Henry Toll to help organize their annual gatherings. Finding these services invaluable, in 1938 the conference officially named the executive director of the Council of State Governments as its secretary-treasurer and designated the council as its administrative arm. Henceforth, the council would perform the administrative and research tasks for the national conclave of state executives.[114]

This rapid development of Toll's cooperative empire during the 1930s was in large part a response to the perceived threat of federal aggression. Repeatedly commentators warned of the need for the states to band together to preserve their prerogatives and thwart the forces of centralization. To achieve this task, the states had to become better informed and demonstrate that they could indeed shoulder the responsibilities expected of them. Through cooperation they could enlighten themselves, achieve statutory harmony without intervention by the national government, and maintain their place in the federal system. In early 1935 Toll warned, "If we are not to be subjected to extreme federalization within a short time, it can only be because the states are on the verge of cooperating with each other as they have never cooperated before."[115] In fact, the Council of State Governments viewed intergovernmental cooperation as "a compromise between the tyranny of centralization and the anarchy of decentralization." The council offered a middle way that eschewed chaotic fragmentation but also rejected unitary rule by an all-powerful national government. Cooperation was the means for avoiding these undesirable extremes. "Either the federal government must continue to take more and more of the control from the states until they become vestigial relics of local self-government, or else the state governments must harmonize their activities and must work together," announced a council publication in 1935.[116] That same year, a delegate to the second interstate assembly expressed similar sentiments when he urged the conclave to take strong action "in order that the federal government [might] know the sovereign states [were] not asleep at the switch."[117]

The Council of State Governments was, then, a response to the need for vigorous government action during the crisis-ridden 1930s. Atomistic rule by forty-eight disparate sovereigns appeared to be inadequate. The federal government thus extended its functions and boosted its spending. The states, however, reacted by embracing a new framework of cooperation. Henry Toll's creation was a counterbalance to Franklin Roosevelt's New Deal. And like the New Deal, it was a significant development in the history of the American polity, for the Council of State Governments and its affiliated interstate associations would survive and play significant roles in the future.

In December 1938 Henry Toll stepped down as executive director of his burgeoning conglomerate devoted to interstate cooperation and returned to private practice in Denver. During the previous decade, he had changed the nature of American federalism. In 1929 the *New York World* editorialized, "The

Legislature that meets in Helena might just as well be the Russian Duma so far as its standards and procedures and experience are known to the Legislature that meets in Baton Rouge."[118] At that time there was no central clearinghouse for the exchange of information among the states and their officials. There were no interstate assemblies or commissions for interstate cooperation. There were forty-eight states that generally acted individually vis-à-vis the national government, for there was virtually no mechanism whereby the states could act in unison. The Governors' Conference was in large measure a social gathering that many state executives never attended. Yet by December 1938 such a mechanism for joint action and mutual enlightenment existed. In the course of a single decade, Henry Toll had established a permanent framework whereby the states could join in common cause. The national government was expanding its role, but the states were not passively receding from the scene. They were taking unprecedented action to learn from one another and speak in an amplified voice.

The Legislative Council

As Henry Toll well recognized, the weakest element in state government was the legislature. The American Legislators' Association sought to aid this much-maligned branch, but during the 1930s there were other initiatives as well to remedy the shortcomings of state legislative bodies. The most notable was the legislative council. This was a permanent joint committee of a state's legislature that was intended to investigate vital policy questions and present its findings, and possible recommendations, at the beginning of each legislative session. Unlike the house and the senate, it would operate year-round, considering legislative issues during the many months when the legislature was not in sessions. The supposed result would be an informed legislature prepared to tackle the major issues confronting the state.

During the 1920s many legislators had recognized a need to investigate and debate state issues between legislative sessions. Consequently, there was growing use of interim committees, especially in the busy legislatures of New York, Pennsylvania, Illinois, and California. In 1929, for example, California's legislature authorized twelve interim committees to investigate such issues as county home rule, water problems, the preservation of the coastline, and the "regulation and restriction of bill boards, sign boards and 'hot dog stands.'" Illinois lawmakers also created twelve such committees, including ones to study the marketing of Illinois products, the state's revenue system, and the merits of creating a network of parks along the Mississippi River.[119] According to the director of Nebraska's legislative reference bureau, "legislators everywhere [were] finding it necessary to insist upon information from authoritative sources before they arrive[d] at conclusions and act[ed] upon them."[120] And the interim committees were a means for generating such information. By the 1931–32 biennium, there were 237 interim committees or commissions in 39 of the 48 states, and approximately a thousand state legislators served on them. In other words, lawmakers were attempting to overcome the shortcomings of a part-time legislature by keeping some legislators on the job after the session adjourned. Applauding the interim service of legislators, *State Government* claimed that "this recognition of the need of careful study of legislative questions is a modest rainbow in the legislative heavens."[121]

In the minds of some, however, interim committees were not the best remedy for the problems of the biennial legislature with its short sessions and amateur lawmakers. Ad hoc interim committees had to be authorized in each legislative session and had no permanent, expert staff to carry on their work from one biennium to the next. They were makeshift responses to pressing issues, not continuing bodies that could engage in long-term investigation of state functions or facilities or maintain an ongoing review of state administration. In addition, a number of interim committees were created simply to postpone or prevent action on a controversial question rather than to formulate policy. As *State Government* observed, "some commissions were doubtless authorized in the hope that they would provide a lethal chamber for an unwanted problem."[122] Moreover, with each committee focused on an individual issue, there was no coordinated planning of a legislative program during the interim. There was no overarching committee or commission to determine which questions should have priority in the coming session. The governor's opening message continued in large measure to set the legislative agenda.

Kansas lawmakers sought to change this by creating the first effective legislative council. The father of the Kansas council was Sam Wilson, manager of the Kansas State Chamber of Commerce. A civil engineer, Wilson was a devotee of efficiency and economy in government and had campaigned for the adoption of the city-manager plan in a number of municipalities. Frustrated by the legislature's failure to accept a chamber study group's proposals for tax reform, Wilson concluded that state lawmakers did not have the time to adequately investigate or consider policy. He believed the legislature should follow the example of the chamber of commerce and establish study committees aided by expert staff to formulate proposals before the opening of each session. The speaker of the 1933 Kansas house was a member of the board of directors of the state chamber of commerce, and he used his political clout to secure passage of Wilson's legislative council bill.[123]

This new council was to consist of twenty-five members of the legislature chosen by the presiding officers of each house. In addition, the presiding officers were to serve as ex officio members. During the interim this select body of legislators was to investigate state policy issues and at the beginning of each session present pertinent information and a legislative program to incoming lawmakers. To serve as research director, the council selected Frederic Guild, professor of political science at the University of Kansas, whose name was to become synonymous with the concept of the legislative council. "The council movement is what it is largely because of the character of Frederic H. Guild, because of his courage and devotion to an idea," wrote one authority on state government many years later. "It has become standard practice for states working on council legislation to send a delegation to visit 'the sage of Topeka.'"[124]

Basic to Guild's approach was an impartial professionalism and a conscious deference to the authority of the elected legislators. Many lawmakers were fearful that the council and its research staff would seek to dictate policy, and in both the 1935 and 1937 legislative sessions, bills were introduced to abolish the new body. But Guild allayed these fears. He explained, "The Kansas idea of formulating a program has been that the selection of the solution must be reserved for final decision in full legislature." Thus, "even the bills recommended were tentative," and "the council expected them to be subject to amendment and compromise." He emphasized further that it was "imperative that the legislators have an impartial staff under their own control, upon which they [could] fully rely." That is, Guild was careful to avoid charges of usurpation of power or prejudicial consideration of the facts. His staff was to be nonpartisan, impartially serving the council that in turn served the legislature as a whole. As in the case of the earlier legislative reference bureaus, the councils were to ensure greater expertise in the legislative process and put to rest longstanding complaints that the small-town lawyers and farmers congregating in Topeka for two months were ignorant novices unfit to lead the state. Legislative councils were intended to make legislatures more effective; they were not to supplant the elected lawmakers. In Guild's words, the council was "a perpetual interim committee for the legislature, always available to institute a study of a new subject, with full power to secure the necessary information."[125]

Despite some initial misgivings, the council mechanism worked well in Kansas, serving as a model for the rest of the nation. For the special session of 1934, Guild and his staff helped prepare twenty-seven legislative measures, and for the regular session of 1935 it presented studies on forty-two separate policy questions. The 1935 council reports on sales tax, state police, and old-age pensions were in demand nationwide, as legislators elsewhere sought to benefit from the Kansas research. By 1940 the council was a firmly established part of the legislative process and universally accepted by Kansas lawmakers. During the late 1930s, its research department usually employed four trained researchers, and depending on the project undertaken, the total staff numbered as few as nine or as many as fifteen to twenty full-time employees.[126] Though small by later standards, this corps of research personnel was indicative of a new commitment to expert lawmaking.

Others were to follow Kansas's example, with a total of ten states maintaining active legislative councils before 1940. Not all proved successful, however. In 1933 Michigan was the second state to establish a council. Traditionally Republican, Michigan had elected a Democratic legislature in 1932, placing in office scores of inexperienced Democratic lawmakers who previously had never had a chance for victory at the polls. Recognizing the inability of the newcomers to meet the grave crisis of the economic depression, the house speaker pushed through a measure to create a legislative council that could present polished proposals to the anticipated special sessions that would meet during the 1933–34 biennium. During these two years, Michigan's council operated with effectiveness, but legislators who were not fortunate enough to serve on the council resented its authority to formulate legislation and did not necessarily accept its findings. In December 1933, during the first special session, the *Detroit Free Press* observed that the council had "yet to see general and willing acceptance of its views on major issues. . . . There is ample evidence that the members supposed to profit by the experience of these 'elder statesmen' want to do the work all over again, and in their own way."[127]

Clashes with the governor further undermined Michigan's council. After his election in November 1934, incoming governor Frank D. Fitzgerald criticized the lame duck legislative council for presuming to recommend a legislative program. Only three of the council's nine members had been reelected, yet the body proceeded to outline proposals for taxation, state aid to schools, and relief. By the 1937 session, the council was inactive, and two years later the legislature eliminated the moribund institution by repealing the 1933 act.[128]

Michigan's failure did not stymie the movement to ensure greater expertise in lawmaking through year-round consideration of legislative issues. In 1936 both Virginia and Kentucky instituted the reform, the following year Connecticut, Illinois, Nebraska, and Pennsylvania followed suit, and in 1939 Maine and Maryland embraced the concept of a general-purpose permanent interim committee. Although some lawmakers in these states shared the fears of their Michigan counterparts that the council might usurp the prerogatives of the legislature as a whole, none of these states acceded to such doubts and eliminated this new element in the lawmaking process.

The councils of the 1930s, however, were not all cookie-cutter replicas of the Kansas model. The Virginia and Kentucky bodies were not strictly agents of the legislature but instead were dominated by the governor. Other councils differed from the Kansas archetype by focusing solely on research and not assuming responsibility for recommending legislation. This was true of the Illinois body. In 1937 the Illinois legislature created a council that was authorized "to prepare such legislative program in the form of bills or otherwise, as in its opinion the welfare of the State [might] require."[129] During its early years, however, the Illinois council faced the familiar complaints that it was "attempting to do the thinking for the entire body" and "assuming the position of a 'little legislature.'" Consequently, in 1939 the council decided to restrict itself to research and fact-finding and not to draft legislative proposals. The research director observed, "I don't think the council was ever very eager to make recommendations."[130] And henceforth it did not do so. Unlike its Kansas counterpart, the Illinois council was not to present legislative programs for the upcoming sessions. Instead, it was to provide the information necessary for legislators to intelligently consider the issues likely to confront them.

Illinois's council remained a significant part of the lawmaking process, however, and was admired for its research work. By October 1942 it had issued a total of fifty-four formal research reports.[131] Illinois's legislative reference bureau survived, focusing primarily on the drafting of bills, whereas the council answered the lawmakers' requests for information and research. Moreover, the creation of the council did not mark an end to the role of interim committees in the Illinois legislative process. The Illinois institution was, then, perhaps closer to Charles McCarthy's ideal of a legislative reference bureau than it was to the pure council model as created in Kansas. It was a step toward upgrading the expertise of the legislative branch and an attempt to adjust the citizen legislature to the demands of twentieth-century lawmaking. Its research reports usually resulted in legislation, but the Illinois council did not set the legislative agenda for upcoming sessions. In Illinois the governor remained the chief legislator, the single most influential figure in determining the legislative program.

Thus, all legislative councils were not alike. In the future a majority of the states creating legislative councils would follow Kansas's example and establish bodies that recommended legislation and programs. And in these states the legislatures approved a relatively high percentage of the recommendations, though often in amended form. But some states opted for the Illinois alternative, establishing a fact-finding agency to aid the legislative process. All of the councils, however, represented a modification of the citizen legislature ideal. For many years critics of state government had lambasted the amateurish, part-time solons, who by necessity deferred to the full-time, more knowledgeable officials in the executive branch. Proponents of the legislative councils attempted to answer such criticisms. Like the legislative reference bureaus of the early twentieth century, the councils were a stage in the gradual professionalization of the legislative branch. At the close of the 1930s, biennial legislative sessions of sixty or ninety days remained the norm, and the states were not yet ready to fully embrace the notion of professional legislators. Yet through the legislative councils, they could at least strive to provide expert guidance for the amateur lawmakers congregating in the nation's statehouses.

Together with Henry Toll's Council of State Governments, the legislative councils sought to introduce a new level of expertise into state rule. During the 1930s the states expanded their roles, assuming greater responsibility for education and experimenting with novel ideas for boosting their economies. Benefiting from a reformed tax structure, states were picking up the slack for hard-pressed localities and paying an increasing share of the bills. As functions and duties expanded, the need for professionalism in the lawmaking process increased proportionately. Henry Toll and Frederic Guild realized this and through interstate cooperation and interim research contributed to the growing sophistication of state rule.

7

⊷

Working in the Shadows

I N 1958 the chief executives of the states gathered for the fiftieth anniversary
meeting of the Governors' Conference and heard their featured speaker,
United Nations Secretary General Dag Hammarskjöld, expound on international peacekeeping. Given his lack of knowledge on the states or their governments, the renowned Swedish diplomat understandably never once referred
to those topics.[1] Foreign affairs, a responsibility of the federal government, thus
assumed center stage at the semicentennial gathering of state leaders. This incongruous situation reflected the spirit of the age. Foreign policy and national
defense were at the forefront of American consciousness, leaving those units of
government most responsible for domestic affairs in the shadows. Even the
governors themselves chose to mark their anniversary with an address that had
nothing to do with state government or their role as chief executives of the
states. Amid the persistent international tensions of the cold war, questions of
schools, highways, and welfare institutions seemed prosaic and unworthy of
front-page coverage. The nuclear threat and Communism preoccupied Americans, and a foreign diplomat familiar with events in Europe and Asia but ignorant of developments in Topeka and Boise appeared to be an appropriately
significant speaker to highlight the anniversary meeting.

Moreover, the highly distinguished Hammarskjöld lent prestige to the gathering, and prestige was something the governors sorely needed. During the
1940s and 1950s, the only state executives who ever shoved the Soviet threat
from the front page were those loudmouth defenders of racial segregation who
made states' rights synonymous with the oppression of blacks. In the minds of
many journalists and academics, and northerners in general, the states and
their governors too often appeared dedicated only to applying the brakes on
social progress. No matter that executives in Albany and Sacramento were
totally opposed to the views of their fellow governors in Little Rock and
Montgomery; it was the latter who won the most news coverage and tarnished

the image of state government. By the time Dag Hammarskjöld stood before the Governors' Conference, the states seemed insignificant at best and evil at worst. They had no role in curbing the all-important Soviet threat, and a well-publicized minority of the commonwealths appeared firmly aligned against the forces of social justice.

The period from 1940 to the early 1960s was therefore a dark age for the image of state government, an era when the prestige of the states dipped to its lowest point. At no time were they less respected by scholars or commentators in the press. Occasionally they were derided, but more often the states were ignored. The federal government appeared to be the engine propelling the course of American development, and the states seemed vestiges of a horse-and-buggy past that might wither away as policymakers in Washington, D.C., masterminded not only the defeat of fascism and Communism but also the solution of the domestic problems plaguing the nation. Apparently irrelevant to the future of the country, state government remained in the shadows, relatively unnoticed.

What was occurring, however, was that the prevailing obsession with foreign affairs and the media focus on segregation policies in a minority of the states were diverting attention from the continuing expansion and reform of state government. The 1940s and 1950s were not, in fact, decades of state-level lethargy during which small-minded governors and lazy legislators adhered to well-worn ruts and refused to confront social and economic problems. The states were alive and well, and beyond the glare of the public's attention, they were molding the nation's future. If this was a dark age for state government, it was only because observers chose to close their eyes to what was happening in state capitals. A perceptive observer would have seen that states were maintaining the reform momentum of earlier decades, centralizing functions and striving for a more expert, professional government. The states were expanding their roles in elementary and secondary schooling as well as higher education. They were building on Mississippi's BAWI experiment of the 1930s and devoting themselves increasingly to economic development. Moreover, they were adopting reforms aimed at ensuring more efficient and expert legislative, executive, and judicial branches. Certainly, there was no shortage of buffoons or scoundrels in the statehouses, and state government was exasperating to many knowledgeable citizens. But it was neither insignificant nor atrophying.

Amid the tribulation of world conflict and confrontation, then, the states continued to broaden their responsibilities and attempted to cope with the domestic challenges of the nation. Preoccupied with the nation's defense and checked by a generally conservative Congress, the federal government did not greatly expand its domestic role during the 1940s and 1950s. In fact, between

1948 and 1957, the federal government's share of funding for nondefense services dropped from 47 percent to 35 percent, whereas the state and local portion increased from 53 percent to 65 percent.[2] Working in the shadows, the states were taking up the slack, carrying out the less publicized tasks of domestic rule and perpetuating the long-term trends of professionalization and centralization of authority.

The Continuing Tradition of Structural Reform

From the beginning of the twentieth century onward, framers of state constitutional provisions and concerned lawmakers had sought to answer complaints about irresponsible, incompetent government. To bypass the supposedly lobby-dominated legislatures, they authorized the initiative and referendum procedure. Legislative reference bureaus and legislative councils were created to improve the expertise of lawmakers, and plans for administrative restructuring were implemented to ensure a more efficient and responsible executive branch. During the 1940s and 1950s, this tradition of questioning and challenging continued as states attempted to cope with mounting demands and reformers still pursued the elusive goal of effective, efficient government. Structural change did not cease during the supposed dark age of state government. The work of reevaluation and revision continued.

In the early 1940s, a number of studies and commissions proposed reforms to upgrade state government and especially the long-maligned state legislatures. Relying on the wisdom of seventy-five expert consultants, the National Municipal League in 1941 issued a revision of its Model State Constitution. Among the new proposals in this version of the model framework was a provision for a continuous legislative process in place of annual or biennial sessions of limited duration. State legislators would not gather in January of odd-numbered years, meet for two months, and then adjourn with virtually no duties to exercise for the remaining twenty-two months of their terms. Instead, the legislature would meet periodically throughout the biennium and remain in session to answer the needs of the state. The model constitution of 1941 also provided for a strengthened legislative council and improvements in legislative committee procedure. This constitution, if adopted, would promote the professionalization of the legislative process.[3] A continuous legislature together with the research expertise of a legislative council and sound committee procedure would ensure better informed and more professional service, in marked contrast to the supposedly amateurish lawmaking of the past.

Commissions in various states were proposing similar reforms aimed at professionalization of the legislative process. In 1943 Massachusetts's Special

Commission on Legislative System and Procedure issued a comprehensive study, as did the legislative council of Connecticut the following year. Though neither endorsed the continuous legislature proposed by the National Municipal League, both recognized the advantages of annual sessions over biennial sessions. According to the Massachusetts commission, in earlier years when "the tempo of life was slower [and] changes occurred less frequently . . . circumstances might have permitted less frequent meetings of the Legislature." The commission concluded, however, "Today, the rapid pace of life and communal affairs demands a Legislature that is in touch with the pulse of the Commonwealth."[4] To deal with the problems of the mid–twentieth century, all three branches of government had to be on the job.

In 1946 New York joined the group of states preparing comprehensive evaluations of the legislative process. The Empire State already had annual legislative sessions, but the report of the joint legislative committee on methods and practices included other suggestions for upgrading the lawmaking procedures that were to appear on the reform agenda throughout the nation in the 1940s and 1950s. To make the legislative process more efficient and effective, the report recommended a reduction in the number of house and senate committees. Thus, each lawmaker would serve on few committees and would be able to concentrate his or her energies and develop a degree of expertise in the fields covered by those committees. To better compensate lawmakers, whose job was consuming an ever-larger portion of their time, the report also proposed a repeal of the state constitutional provision fixing legislative salaries. The committee urged that salaries be fixed by statute rather than constitutional provision and suggested a doubling of those salaries to five thousand dollars a year. Perhaps most importantly, the New York committee "unequivocally recommend[ed] . . . the establishment of a permanent legislative research agency as an integral part of the legislative process."[5] New York had for decades relied extensively on interim committees to investigate issues between sessions, but it had not embraced the legislative council. This committee was not proposing the creation of an agency modeled on the Kansas example but the establishment of a research arm similar to the research staff of most legislative councils. A permanent corps of experts capable of preparing reports on state issues seemed essential to the future of New York lawmaking. One observer noted, "New York State's Joint Committee on Legislative Methods, in calling for legislative staff, points the way to the technique of modern government—synthesizing the contributions of the expert and the legislator."[6]

More frequent legislative sessions, fewer committees and greater specialization by lawmakers, better compensation, and the creation of expert staffs were, then, emerging as reform goals. Although advocates of these changes generally claimed to be dedicated to the "modernization" of the legislature, modernization, in fact, meant professionalization. The momentum toward expertise and a career legislature was building, and the tradition of the amateur, citizen legislator was slowly eroding. Yet that tradition was deeply rooted in the American mind, and the notion of a "modern" legislature was more marketable than that of a professional one.

In 1946 the Council of State Governments codified the reform agenda of the postwar era when it published the recommendations of the council's Committee on Legislative Processes and Procedures. The committee avoided some politically difficult issues such as reapportionment. Every academic observer included more equitable districting on his or her list of desired reforms, but legislators and the Council of State Governments shied away from this sensitive question. The council committee did, however, present an extensive reform program resembling that suggested in the earlier reports from Connecticut, Massachusetts, and New York. It urged, for example, that legislative sessions be of unrestricted length and that a majority of the legislators as well as the governors be able to call special sessions. Moreover, there should be no "undue restrictions upon the measures to be considered" at such meetings. If restrictions on special sessions were eliminated, then "the question of annual versus biennial sessions [would be] largely resolved." In addition, the council's committee concluded that legislative salaries were too low and should be fixed by statute, not by constitutional provision. Like the New York report, the council's committee recommended that the number of house and senate committees be reduced, and it urged "provision for legislative council or interim committees with adequate clerical and research facilities."[7] In other words, the council and its committee were adding their imprimatur to the notion that legislatures had to become more professional. Lawmakers had to meet more often, receive better pay, focus their attention on fewer committees, and benefit from expert assistance.

Many believed that these reforms were vital, for incompetent state governments were easy prey for centralizers who sought to shift all power to Washington, D.C. Behind the drive for modernization, then, was a nagging fear that inaction would result in further federal encroachment. "I have been one of those who . . . have decried the loss of states' rights and the encroachments of the federal government upon the powers of the state legislatures," admitted a leader of the Massachusetts Legislature in 1944. But he also recognized that "the state legislatures themselves [were] somewhat to blame for this loss of power," and to correct the situation the legislatures should initiate "a general overhauling and modernizing of . . . procedural machinery."[8] That same year, North Carolina governor J. Melville Broughton made much the same argument: "The best answer, indeed the only one, to the alarming and rapid spread of federal encroachment is to give the people a better government through state agencies."[9] Such sentiments were commonplace in the 1940s and 1950s. Procedural reform was not simply desirable; it was necessary to preserve and restore the power of state government.

With Uncle Sam threatening to rob them of their powers and the Council of State Governments providing a blueprint for improvement, many states awakened to the need for change. In January 1947 the council recommendations were fully discussed at the Eighth General Assembly of the States, and in both 1947 and 1948 regional meetings of the council throughout the nation reviewed the reform agenda and state action regarding it. Studies of legislative practices ensued in a number of states, and during the following decade and a half, reformers achieved some success.

For example, states turned to the annual session as fears of legislative excesses yielded to a realization that state lawmaking was a necessity that might actually produce benefits. In 1940 only four states had annual sessions, forty-three had biennial meetings, and one had a quadrennial legislature. Twenty years later, nineteen state legislatures met annually, and thirty-one retained the biennial session. In 1944 Massachusetts was the first to switch, followed by California in 1946, Maryland in 1948, Arizona and Colorado in 1950, and Michigan in 1951. During the next eight years, the reform momentum increased as nine additional states opted for annual meetings of the legislature.

Some states restricted one of the annual sessions in each biennium solely or in large part to fiscal questions. The other session, like the old biennial session, was unlimited in the subjects it could consider. For example, in California the sessions in even-numbered years were limited to financial questions, whereas in Maryland even-year sessions were to deal only with "budgetary, revenue and financial matters of the state government" and bills "dealing with acute emergencies," as well as "those in the general public welfare."[10] In Colorado even-year sessions were restricted to budget, tax, and revenue issues and "subjects designated in writing by the Governor during the first ten days of the session."[11] Maintaining these limitations, however, was not easy. "Much of our time at the fiscal session is wasted arguing and debating over what is fiscal and what is non-fiscal," remarked one critical legislator.[12]

During these same years, legislators were also heeding the Council of State Governments' recommendation that they reorganize and reduce the number of committees. Throughout the first half of the twentieth century, the states had maintained scores of committees in each house of their legislatures, in part so that a maximum number of lawmakers could enjoy the honor of serving as a chair. As a result, legislators served on numerous committees, and because some of their committees met at the same time, they could not participate in the deliberations of all the committees to which they were assigned. Proxy voting was commonplace; the chair could collect proxies from uninformed members and basically do whatever he or she liked with the bills before the committee. In one state after another, the excess of committees meant that there was little informed deliberation in the committee chambers. In the late 1940s and early 1950s there were 46 committees in the 49-member Mississippi senate, and the average senator served on 9. With 51 committees and 140 lawmakers, the situation in the Mississippi house was not quite as bad. Nonetheless, with an average of 5 committee assignments, house members were unlikely to develop specialized knowledge of the subject matter of each of their committees.[13]

In the 1940s and 1950s, legislative reformers were able to rectify the situation in a number of states. Between 1946 and 1959, the median number of house standing committees fell from 39 to 23, and the figure for senate committees dropped from 31 to 20. In 1946 there were over 50 committees in nine houses and three senates. Thirteen years later only two houses and no senates maintained this number. Since the number of legislators did not decline, this meant fewer committee assignments per lawmaker and a greater focus to the lawmaker's work. The reform tide did not sweep uniformly across the nation, and as late as 1961 the Arkansas house still could claim a record total of 69 committees. Overall, however, there was change.[14]

The impact of the reform agenda was, for example, evident in New Mexico. Influenced by the meetings of the Western Interstate Committee on Legislative Procedures sponsored by the Council of State Governments, a group of New Mexico senators met in the fall of 1954 to discuss the reorganization of their branch of the legislature. They proposed the establishment of only seven senate standing committees in the forthcoming session; and on the opening day in January 1955, this proposal was adopted unanimously. Each senator served on only two committees, except for the majority leader, who was assigned to only one but was an ex officio member of every other committee. Moreover, to ensure an orderly procedure, each committee was to hold two regular meetings each week at permanent times fixed by the senate leadership. By arranging permanent meeting times, the leaders could avoid schedule conflicts and ensure that senators could participate on both of their committees. At the close of the 1955 session, the New Mexico house followed the senate's example, adopting a structure of only sixteen standing committees, in place of the existing twenty-four. No member was to serve on more than three of these reorganized committees.[15]

Yet another sign of modernization was the increase in legislative compensation as recommended by the Council of State Governments. A growing number of states were recognizing that the office of legislator entailed yearlong duties and thus deserved a salary rather than a per diem payment for time served during the legislative session. Whereas in 1946 twenty-six states paid a salary to legislators, by 1959 thirty-four did so. And these salaries rose markedly. In 1946 the median figure was $1,000 per biennium; thirteen years later it was $3,600, a 260 percent increase during a period when the cost of living increased only 49 percent.[16] In Mississippi during the early 1940s, the salary had been $1,000 per regular session; it rose to $1,500 in 1946, $2,000 in 1950, and $3,000 in 1956. Then in 1960 Mississippi's legislators acknowledged their year-round duties when they approved an additional $100 per month for the time between the legislative sessions.[17] The salary range among the states was great, with New York allotting $15,000 per biennium for each lawmaker and New Hampshire paying each legislator only $200 every two years. But generally at the beginning of the 1960s, legislators remained underpaid. In 1961 the Committee on Legislative Processes and Procedures of the National Legislative Conference summed up a commonly held opinion: "From the viewpoint of good public service, and in light of the increasing amounts of time that legislators must devote to their duties both during and between sessions, their compensation in most states is now much too low."[18]

Expert staffing was another goal that many states sought to realize and did so to varying degrees. This was apparent in the increasing popularity of the legislative council and its research function. Whereas in 1940 only nine states maintained legislative councils to research issues and to possibly recommend solutions, by 1959 thirty-nine states had such agencies. Among the converts were some long-standing leaders in state government such as Wisconsin and Massachusetts, but a number of southern states that had traditionally lagged behind their northern counterparts also joined the fold. In 1945 Alabama established a legislative council and a legislative reference service to act as the council's research arm. Explaining the reform, one Alabaman noted: "The state legislature, which was originally designed to be a body of intelligent amateurs in the business of government, is today expected to act as a body of trained experts. But no method has been devised for giving legislators the training of experts."[19] The answer to this dilemma was the newly created legislative research agency. In 1949 neighboring Florida also opted for expertise, establishing a council and reference bureau similar to those of Alabama. In justifying the need for these institutions, a Florida academic asserted, "Legislators . . . have been fumbling unsuccessfully with the increasingly bewildering and complex problems of lawmaking without the expert assistance which they as ama-teurs and part-time lawmakers so clearly require."[20] By the mid–twentieth cen-tury, this was the consensus. Lawmaking required expert assistance, and the states had to provide such aid.

Not every state created a legislative council. The large states of New York and California continued to prefer interim committees with generally well-funded research staffs. In 1951–52 New York maintained twenty-eight such committees and appropriated $1.1 million to finance their investigations; ten years later it was spending more than $2.1 million on interim research activi-ties.[21] A number of states relied on both interim committees and legislative councils to investigate questions and prepare legislation. For example, Min-nesota maintained a council but supplemented it in 1951–52 with eleven in-terim committees, including the Legislative Interim Commission on Taxation of Iron Ore, which was appropriated $150,000.[22] By the 1950s the notion of a part-time legislature of unaided amateurs was largely a myth. The months between sessions were not devoid of legislative action. Investigations pro-ceeded year-round, and the states were funding research into major issues con-fronting them.

Some state legislatures, however, seemed reluctant to avail themselves of expert advice. From 1946 through 1957, the Mississippi legislature maintained a General Legislative Investigating Committee to inquire into state operations during the legislative recesses as well as appointing a total of fourteen tempo-rary interim committees. But a study of legislative staff in Mississippi found that "usually these interim committees . . . employed secretarial but no techni-cal assistants." The study concluded that the effectiveness of the committees had been impaired by the failure of the state's lawmakers "to think in terms of employing specially trained research" staff. To remedy this, bills were intro-duced in the state senate in 1950, 1952, 1954, 1956, and 1958 to create a legisla-tive council aided by professional researchers. Each year the senate approved the council bill, but just as consistently the speaker of the house of representa-tives contrived to kill it. Some Mississippi legislators repeated the hoary argu-ment that the council "would develop into a little super-legislature." This attitude prevailed, and at the close of the 1950s, investigators were still forced to conclude that Mississippi had "a drastic need for a comprehensive program of legislative research."[23]

Yet the general trend was toward an increase in legislative staff assistance. Especially significant was the growing number of fiscal analysts aiding law-makers to review budgets and investigate finances. In 1941 California's legi-slature created the Joint Legislative Budget Committee, a permanent interim committee that was expected "to ascertain facts and make recommendations to the legislature . . . concerning the State Budget, the revenues and expenditures of the State, and of the organization and functions of the State, . . . with a view of reducing the cost of State Government, and securing efficiency and economy." To provide professional assistance to the committee, the legislature also established the full-time position of legislative auditor. In 1948 the legislative auditor's office had a technical staff (excluding clerical workers) of ten, but by the late 1950s and early 1960s it had developed into a small bureaucracy with an average of thirty technical employees.[24] Other states followed California's example, and by 1960 twenty-six provided their legislators with staff specializing in the review of fiscal matters.[25]

The postwar period was, then, characterized by incipient professionalization. Indicative of the emerging importance of research services was the creation of a national organization of legislative staff members. In 1947 the Council of State Governments called a National Conference of State Legislative Reference Agencies, and the following year this resulted in the creation of a permanent organization originally known as the Legislative Service Conference. Its annual meetings attracted an increasing number of attendants, and in 1955 it was rechristened the National Legislative Conference. This new name reflected the organization's desire to attract the involvement of legislators as well as legislative service staff members.[26] By the close of the 1950s, it was firmly established and actively disseminating the gospel of a modernized legislature. The cause of professionalism in the lawmaking process now had a national voice.

While the legislatures were gradually responding to the reform agenda, the executive branch was also undergoing some changes. Demands for administrative reform continued, and the message in the 1940s and 1950s was much the same as it had been during the second and third decades of the century. Authority should be concentrated in the hands of the governor, and the scores of state boards and commissions should be reorganized into a manageable number of departments directly responsible to the chief executive. Inspired by the federal government's Hoover Commission of the late 1940s, about two-thirds of the states created little Hoover commissions, whose reports repeated these precepts of administrative reform. The result was some reorganization but no comprehensive restructuring of the executive branch. In 1953 one student of the little Hoover commissions found "a rather general resistance on the part of legislatures to the full acceptance of the executive management theme," but two years later a more optimistic observer concluded that the movement had "produced some concrete results."[27]

Actually, administrative reform was less significant than another change that was enhancing the position of governor. This was the increase in the number of long-term chief executives. Only 10 percent of governors during the first decade of the twentieth century served more than four years in office, and this figure rose to just 16 percent in the 1920s. During the 1950s, though, 29 percent of all governors were in office for more than four years.[28] Eight-year stays in the governor's mansion were becoming more common; thus, the governors were less likely to be transitory figures who affected their states' history for only a couple of years and then passed into oblivion. They were accumulating more on-the-job experience and developing greater expertise as state executives. In addition, they were better able to establish long-term policies. The durability and electoral success of some long-term governors also enhanced their clout among state officials and legislators. A chief executive who was expected to be around for eight years had to be regarded more seriously than one who would pass from the scene after a two-year stint.

This increased longevity was in part a consequence of longer gubernatorial terms. In 1940 twenty-four states still elected governors to two-year terms, and during the previous four decades there had been no marked tendency to lengthen the executive's tenure. By 1964, however, the number of states with two-year terms had dropped to fifteen, the other thirty-five embracing the four-year term.[29] In other words, in 1940 50 percent had two-year terms; in 1964 only 30 percent retained biennial elections.

During the 1940s and 1950s, long-serving and powerful chief executives ruled in both California and New York. Earl Warren presided over California for a record ten years, garnering strong support from the state's electorate. Meanwhile, Governor Thomas Dewey wielded power in New York for twelve years with a mastery equaled by few others in the history of the nation. Not since George Clinton had stepped down from the governor's office in 1804 had anyone served so long as chief executive of the Empire State.

Elsewhere governors were also setting records for longevity. Frank Lausche held the executive's office in Ohio for an unprecedented ten years, G. Mennen Williams accumulated a record twelve years of service in Michigan, and Arthur Langlie of Washington likewise was governor for twelve years. Survival is not synonymous with significance; but at least during the postwar period, governors were less likely to be migratory creatures, alighting for a short time in the state capital and then moving on. This was a trend that would continue in future years. Long-term governors with enough years in office to make an imprint on their states were to become the norm.

From 1940 to the early 1960s, the states did not, then, adhere slavishly to the practices and procedures of the past. This was not a benighted era in which legislators refused to consider all change and the governors were invariably short-lived, forgettable glad-handers. Lawmakers shunned certain controversial reforms, such as legislative apportionment on the basis of population. Yet many states did adapt and reform their governments, embracing a number of the recommendations of the Council of State Governments. The trend toward professionalization accelerated, and calls for expertise in lawmaking mounted.

Reforming the Judiciary

Not only were policymakers of the 1940s and 1950s reconsidering the legislative and executive branches of state government; they were also embarking on a new era of judicial restructuring. Again the cry was for modernization, and again this meant centralization and professionalization. Between 1940 and the early 1960s, a growing corps of judicial reformers rallied behind the cause of court unification, demanding simplification of the court structure and centralization of management and rule-making. They called for a rationalized system of county and district tribunals supervised by the state supreme court and its appointed administrators. In their minds, central administration was an essential ingredient to the efficient provision of justice. Reformers also sought to remove the judiciary from the rough-and-tumble of competitive electoral politics. Competent jurists chosen for their professional qualifications rather than their partisan ties should staff the unified system of state courts. Thus, the dual goals of centralization and professionalism so evident throughout the history of twentieth-century state government were also the primary ends of the campaign for court reform.

The figure most responsible for spreading the gospel of judicial administrative reform in the mid–twentieth century was New Jersey's Arthur T. Vanderbilt. Vanderbilt was a man with a mission, who devoted himself unstintingly to a simplified state court structure headed by a chief justice with sufficient administrative authority to ensure uniform rules of procedure and the assignment of judges appropriate to the needs of each community. As president of the American Bar Association in 1937–38, Vanderbilt was able to secure the association's approval of "Minimum Standards of Judicial Administration" that the states should strive to attain. Predictably, the standards emphasized centralized supervision as essential to the efficient administration of justice.[30]

During the 1940s Vanderbilt realized his dream in his home state of New Jersey. New Jersey's judicial system exemplified all that reformers despised. It was a hodgepodge of seventeen separate classes of courts, with each court operating independently and accruing its own body of procedures and rules. Appalled by New Jersey's archaic, rambling judicial structure, so conducive to delay and confusion, the American Judicature Society named it "the nation's worst court system."[31] In 1947, however, the state adopted a new constitution, with a judicial article strongly influenced by the views of Arthur Vanderbilt. This new charter specified that the chief justice of the supreme court was to "be the administrative head of all the courts of the state" and was to "appoint an administrative director of the courts to serve at his pleasure." Moreover, the supreme court was to make the rules and procedures governing all the courts in the state.[32]

Appropriately, Vanderbilt was appointed the first chief justice under the new constitution, giving him the opportunity to personally realize the goal of a unified, centrally administered state court system. Under Vanderbilt's leadership the supreme court quickly promulgated rules of procedure for the state's courts. Furthermore, at Vanderbilt's behest, the administrative director required a weekly report from every judge in New Jersey, specifying the number of days their courts were in session, the number of motions and cases disposed of, and the amount of litigation still pending. Using this data, Vanderbilt shifted judges from courts with a light workload to those with a clogged calendar. The chief justice took this duty very seriously, demanding prompt completion of the weekly reports from recalcitrant or laggard judges. Vanderbilt claimed that his administrative duties consumed one-third of his time.[33] But he believed it was time well spent. New Jersey was no longer a collection of cacophonous judicial principalities. It was united under the guidance of its formidable chief justice.

New Jersey won laurels from reformers, who praised its new structure of central coordination. Yet the bench and the bar were far from united behind Vanderbilt's campaign. In Pennsylvania judges balked at the loss of autonomy inherent in a scheme of centralized court administration and were especially influenced by what one observer referred to as "reports of the 'czar' system of administration of the neighboring New Jersey courts." Given the scrupulous supervision imposed by Vanderbilt, one Pennsylvania judge claimed that adoption of the New Jersey scheme would require jurists "to ask leave of the court administrator to attend their own mother's funeral."[34] Virginia's chief justice attributed opposition to the creation of a court administrator in his state to fear that "such an office might lead to a regimentation of the judiciary."[35] Many local judges accustomed to unquestioned rule over their courtrooms did not relish the advent of an Arthur Vanderbilt in their state.

Despite such opposition, the cause of court administration won some victories in the 1950s. During that decade eighteen states created court administrative officers modeled on that of New Jersey.[36] Under the supervision of the state chief justice, these officers handled the business affairs of the court system; but more significantly, they also collected the workload data that Vanderbilt deemed so important, using it to recommend the reassignment of judges to areas with crowded court calendars. The notion of a judge as a local official, bound exclusively to the courthouse of one county, was disappearing. According to Michigan's court administrator, "members of the Michigan judiciary [were] viewed under the Court Administrator Act as state, not merely local, judges available to statewide service, and they [were] expected to accept assignments to circuits other than their own as necessity demand[ed]." Each judge shared "the responsibility for the efficient and expeditious handling and disposition of all judicial business throughout the state."[37] Lauding the creation of a court administrator in his state, Virginia's chief justice also emphasized that statewide coordination and uniformity was supplanting the past pattern of parochial anarchy. "We . . . feel that we now have the means to provide for a cooperative integration of the judiciary which will lead to promotion of uniformity of practice and the more expeditious disposal of judicial business," he proudly wrote in 1954.[38] In a number of pioneering states, the chief justice was becoming not only the presiding officer of the highest appellate court but also, as in New Jersey, the administrative chief of the entire judicial department. Assisted by the new corps of court administrators, the chief justices were beginning to impose a new degree of unity on the state judicial systems.

Responding to calls for judicial reform, a number of states were taking other action to overhaul their antiquated courts. In pursuit of professionalism, reformers especially targeted justices of the peace and other minor jurists, who generally had no formal legal training. During the early 1950s, California reduced the total number of its lower courts by almost one-half and established a written qualifying examination for those presiding over justice courts.[39] In 1957 Ohio abolished the office of justice of the peace and substituted a new corps of county court judges, who had to be members of the bar.[40] Two years later Connecticut replaced 66 municipal and 102 justice-of-the-peace courts with 44 state-appointed circuit court judges, all of whom were to be trained in the law and could be assigned duty anywhere in the state.[41] That same year, Wisconsin's legislature reorganized the state's system, abolishing a number of minor courts and robbing the justices of the peace of most of their functions.[42] In 1961 Maine eliminated 50 part-time municipal and trial justices, creating in their stead 13 full-time district court judges.[43] Progress was piecemeal, and reformers often had to bide their time. In 1955 a committee of the Iowa Bar Association won approval for a state court administrator but by the beginning of the 1960s had made no headway in the fight to eliminate the minor judiciary. "We are just beginning to fight that battle," commented the committee's chair.[44] Yet during the 1950s the momentum for a simplified, integrated, and professional court structure was increasing, and in one state after another, the judicial relics of a bygone era were gradually being assigned to oblivion.

Indicative of the growing concern for professionalism was the campaign to reform the selection process for jurists. For decades legal scholars had deplored the partisan election of judges and the detrimental influences of party politics on the courts. Complaints about judicial selection culminated in the formulation of a so-called merit plan, approved by the American Bar Association in 1937. Under this plan the governor would fill vacancies on the bench from a list of qualified nominees prepared by a committee of judges, attorneys, and laypersons. To preserve a popular check on the judiciary, the question of whether to retain the gubernatorial appointee would be placed on the ballot after the judge had served a certain number of years. The judge would not face opposition from another candidate. Instead, the voters would decide simply whether to dismiss the jurist. If they voted dismissal, then the governor would again fill the vacancy from a list submitted by the selection committee.[45] The merit plan combined gubernatorial appointment and popular veto, but it also sought to eliminate competitive races for judicial posts and inordinate influence by political leaders.

Missouri was the first state to adopt this merit plan. Fueling popular indignation over the partisan election of judges in Missouri was the election of a pharmacist who had never engaged full-time in the practice of law to the Saint Louis Circuit Court, where he acquired a reputation for covering up Democratic election frauds. The Missouri State Bar Association organized a successful initiative campaign to place a merit-selection constitutional amendment on the ballot. In November 1940, 54 percent of those casting ballots endorsed the change, placing Missouri in the forefront of judicial reform. Specifically, the Missouri scheme provided for two nominating commissions, one to nominate candidates for the state's supreme and appellate courts and the other to propose persons to serve on the circuit and probate courts of the city of Saint Louis and Jackson County (Kansas City). Elsewhere in the state, localities could continue to elect their jurists in the traditional manner. The governor would appoint jurists from a list of three names submitted by the appropriate commission, and the voters could accept or reject the governor's choice after the new judge had served on the bench for a year.[46] Missouri's plan conformed closely to the American Bar Association proposal and to the idea of selection on the basis of professional merit.

During the 1940s and 1950s, reformers proclaimed the Missouri Plan as a partial remedy to the ills plaguing America's judiciary, though other states at first proved reluctant to swallow this palliative. In 1951 the reform scheme appeared on New Mexico's ballot but won the approval of only 37 percent of those voting. Especially damaging to its prospects for success were the suspicions of New Mexico's large Hispanic population that the elite nominating commission would severely limit the number of Hispanic judges. In New Mexico and elsewhere, reform efforts also suffered from the reluctance of some lawyers to support a scheme that might disturb the status quo, no matter how "unprofessional" that status quo might be.[47] In November 1958, however, Kansans lined up behind the Missouri Plan, expressing their disgust over a political ploy labeled the "Triple Play." The governor, who had recently been defeated for renomination, and the chief justice both resigned, and upon assuming the gubernatorial office, the former lieutenant governor obligingly appointed the ex-governor to the vacant post of chief justice. This proof of political chicanery in the selection of judges was sufficient to convince 60 percent of Kansas voters to cast their ballots for the merit plan.[48] The following year Alaska was admitted to the union with a constitution that provided for gubernatorial appointment of supreme and superior court judges from lists of nominees selected by a panel. Then in 1962 both Iowa and Nebraska adopted constitutional amendments providing for similar selection schemes.[49] Missouri's experiment with merit selection was gradually bearing fruit.

Adding strength to the slowly mounting wave of reform was the Conference of Chief Justices. Founded in 1949, this group was the judicial analogue of the Governors' Conference and, like that older body, relied on the ubiquitous Council of State Governments to serve as its secretariat. From its beginning the conference was deemed a mechanism by which the reform agenda could be disseminated and realized. For example, at the first meeting in September 1949, the assembled jurists discussed the need for judicial reorganization and the integration of the state court system so that lower courts would operate under the supervision of the state supreme court. The Missouri Plan for judicial selection was also a major focus of attention at the initial meeting. Indicative of the general tenor of the conference, the jurists elected Chief Justice Laurance Hyde of Missouri, a product and leading proponent of merit selection, as the first chair of the group's executive council. In his address before the first conference, Hyde specifically discussed administrative centralization and merit selection as "matters of outstanding importance in improving the administration of justice."[50] Another principal participant of the early conferences was Arthur Vanderbilt, who took full advantage of the gatherings to spread his reform message. On the tenth anniversary of this organization of state jurists, the chief justice of Michigan summed up its history and correctly observed that "formation of the Conference was prompted by the belief that it could become a forum of consultation at the highest level on means for overhauling and modernizing state court systems."[51] Throughout the 1950s it served that function, informing jurists of the advantages of centralized court administration and a rationalized, professional system of state courts.

The Challenge of Schooling

Probably the greatest challenge facing states in the postwar era was the task of educating the millions of youngsters produced in the baby boom of the 1940s and 1950s. Public school enrollments soared 55 percent from 1946 to 1960; by comparison, the increase from 1900 to 1946 was only 50 percent. At no other time during the twentieth century did the demand for schooling increase at such a rapid rate, imposing a heavy burden on local school districts and state governments alike.

Some believed that the states and localities could not shoulder this burden and that the federal government would have to intervene to save America's schools. "Our educational systems face a financial crisis," President Harry Truman told Congress in January 1948. "The Federal Government has a responsibility for providing financial aid to meet this crisis." Therefore, he urged the nation's lawmakers "to consider a comprehensive program of federal aid to education and to enact immediate assistance to elementary and secondary schools."[52] The Senate was already considering a bill "to authorize the appropriation of funds to assist the states and territories in financing a minimum foundation education program . . . and in reducing the inequalities of educational opportunities."[53] Writing in the *Harvard Educational Review*, one specialist in education summed up the opinion of many in the nation's capital when he asserted, "Probably never before have the problems of providing adequate financial support for the Nation's schools been so important or their solution so urgent as now."[54]

Yet the federal funding proposals of the late 1940s were to fail just as those of the late 1930s had. Again there was controversy over whether to aid private as well as public schools. But fear of federal control was perhaps the greatest obstacle to approval of a program of general aid. "Equalization as a matter of fact, cannot be secured except by complete federal control and direction," concluded a group of conservative senators in their report on one funding bill. These critics of federal aid further asserted, "Everyone agrees that complete federal control and direction are worse than the inequality which now exists." In addition, some believed the supposed crisis was not so critical as President

Truman assumed. "There is no real evidence that the states, with the exceptions of [a] few areas, are unable to finance adequately their own educational programs," commented one Pennsylvania official. "Moreover, in comparison with the national government's treasury, the state treasuries are in good condition."[55]

These state treasuries, together with the local school districts, were left to finance the expansion of education. Congress continued to subsidize vocational education and provided aid to federally impacted districts, that is, districts that educated a large number of children whose parents worked at federal facilities. But in the 1950s, as in the 1930s and 1940s, proposals to provide general aid to state school systems failed repeatedly. In the school year 1959–60, the federal government accounted for only 4.4 percent of the public school revenues. The states and localities contributed more than 95 percent.[56]

The states and school districts did prove able to bear the burden of the expanding educational system. During the prosperous 1940s and 1950s, the states did not shed the financial responsibilities assumed owing to the fiscal emergency of the depression-ridden 1930s. In fact, the state share of school revenues increased modestly over the two decades, rising from 30.3 percent in 1939–40 to 39.1 percent in 1959–60. In constant dollars, state spending for elementary and secondary schools soared fourfold between 1940 and 1960, permitting per pupil expenditures in constant dollars to more than double over the two decades.[57]

But the states not only met the challenge of schooling through a large-scale infusion of cash; they also took action to reorganize local school districts. For decades educators had criticized the excessive number of small rural school districts that cluttered the map of America and had urged the elimination of these redundant units. Some states had begun to consolidate the minuscule rural units, and the total number of school districts in the United States had dropped from 127,531 in 1932 to 117,108 in 1940. Many believed that further action was necessary, however, especially in the midwestern states, where school governments were inordinately numerous. Kansas, for example, had one school district for every 220 people, and in Nebraska the ratio was one per 180 inhabitants. Most of these units were remnants of the horse-and-buggy era when children had to walk to school and there was a school district for every rural neighborhood. Consequently, many of the districts maintained only a one-room school; and as long as the small districts persisted, so would one-teacher schools. In 1940 there were still 113,600 such schools in the United States, a fact abhorrent to educators who were dedicated to modernization.[58]

In one commission report and research study after another, the authors attacked the superfluity of small, rural school districts as a bane to education.

According to critics, these districts provided inadequate education opportunities, employing the least educated teachers, who focused largely on routine training in the traditional three R's. Yet because of their low enrollments, these same one-teacher schools spent more per pupil than their larger counterparts: they offered less for more. In the 1940s an Illinois study reported, "Communities which support the smaller schools, rarely, if ever, get the quality of education which their money would buy in well-organized schools of larger size." A California commission concluded, "California's school district organization system is expensive to the state and to local communities. It contributes to state and local inefficiency in the assignment of professional personnel, in the building of school buildings, and in any attempt to provide equal educational opportunity for children."[59] And two investigators of Nebraska's wasteful school system summed up this viewpoint graphically: "Inadequate school district organization is causing thousands of Nebraska boys and girls to get a skimpy, educational diet; they are not getting their fair share of educational calories and vitamins."[60]

Responding to these criticisms, the states initiated programs that drastically reduced the number of school districts and created larger units of school government better suited to the era of the school bus and broad curricula. Whereas in 1940 there were about 117,000 school districts nationwide, by the school year 1960–61, the number had dropped by more than two-thirds to 37,000. In no comparable period in the nation's history had there been such a rapid and far-reaching reorganization of local units of government. Moreover, accompanying this change was an even sharper decline in the number of one-teacher schools: in 1961 only 19,800 survived, as compared to 113,600 twenty-one years earlier.[61] In two decades the states largely brought a close to the horse-and-buggy era in education and restructured local school government.

For decades most states had permitted the merger of school districts. This permissive legislation, however, had left the initiative with the localities. Local units could decide to reorganize, but the state did not require or oversee grassroots action. Given the pressure for change, many states recognized that this was not sufficient and during the 1940s enacted what was referred to as semipermissive legislation. These new statutes required or pressured localities to draw up plans for reorganization under the guidance of state officials, but the local electorate retained the power to accept or reject reorganization schemes. In other words, the states were taking one more step toward centralization of authority, though at the same time they were bowing to the long-standing American tradition of local self-rule. As in earlier decades, the states were pulling the reins on local power, yet they were not bringing a halt to local rule.

Washington state provided the model for this semipermissive campaign for reorganization. In the late 1930s a study conducted by the State Planning Council concluded that "the first prerequisite to equalization of educational opportunities in the common schools of Washington [was] a fundamental reorganization of the school district system."[62] Responding to this study, in 1941 the Washington legislature enacted a reorganization law that required the creation of a redistricting committee in each county. These committees were charged with drafting a comprehensive plan for redistricting within the county and were expected to produce larger government units that would be better able to meet the educational needs of the mid–twentieth century. State-employed field workers were available to provide expert assistance to the county committees. Once they had completed the remapping of the school units in their counties, these committees had to submit their plans to a state reorganization committee appointed by the state board of education. This state committee could accept or reject the county plans. If rejected, the plan was returned to the county committee with suggestions for revision. If accepted, the plan would be submitted to local voters for approval. The reorganization plan did not need to win the support of a majority of the voters in each of the existing districts that composed the new unit of government but only had to garner a majority vote from the entire proposed district.[63] By refusing to grant a veto to each existing district, the Washington law stacked the electoral deck in favor of reform. Basically, then, although there was recognition of local prerogatives, state authorities guided the reorganization process and could veto undesirable plans. And the state mandated that counties had to reconsider the existing system of school government.

The Washington program proved successful. Whereas in 1941 there were 1,323 school districts in the state, by early 1946 there were 672. The state had achieved a thorough redistricting of school government and eliminated half of the local units. Some complained that the program was "taking schools away from the people," though others believed that the number of districts in Washington was still excessive.[64] Yet, regardless of these criticisms, the state of Washington had set an example for other commonwealths seeking to slash the surplus in school governments.

By 1950 eleven additional states had adopted semipermissive procedures similar to that of Washington and were achieving comparable results. For example, at the close of the 1930s Illinois maintained about 12,000 school districts and nearly 10,000 one-room schools, more than any other state. There were an average of 118 districts per county and an average of only four teachers per school district.[65] To reduce the excessive number of districts, in 1945 the legislature authorized the creation of a reorganization committee in each county to draw up redistricting plans that were to be submitted to a state advisory commission. By 1954 the number of districts had fallen to 2,349.

Some states, however, eschewed local participation and imposed a new form of school government without consulting the local electorate. In 1947 the Florida legislature abolished the state's 720 local school districts and replaced them with 67 countywide units.[66] Similarly, in 1955 the Nevada legislature, responding to a study conducted by the George Peabody College of Teachers, eliminated the existing 186 school districts and replaced them with seventeen units, one per county.[67] In both Florida and Nevada, lawmakers did not submit the reorganization proposals to local voters. Instead, they imposed the reform scheme without referenda.

Mississippi and South Carolina also opted for mandatory reorganization, though there was some local input in the redistricting process. In 1951 South Carolina created a State Education Finance Commission to supervise reorganization and force redistricting by withholding state school building funds from counties that failed to act. County boards were charged with actually consolidating school districts, but the approval of local voters was not required. The result was a drastic reduction in school districts: the number plummeted from 1,680 in 1947 to 103 in 1955.[68] In 1953 Mississippi's legislature adopted a similar scheme, establishing the Educational Finance Commission and requiring county boards to submit reorganization plans to this commission for its approval. The commission could cut off state school funds to any county that did not implement a redistricting scheme. As in South Carolina, local voters exercised no veto but had to accept the mandated plans. Faced with denial of funds, the county boards obeyed the will of the state, and the number of districts fell from 1,417 in 1953 to 151 in 1957.[69]

Whether by mandatory action of the state legislature or through voter approval of state-endorsed schemes, the result was generally the same. School districts were disappearing by the thousands, and one-room schools were vanishing at an equally rapid rate. The supposedly lethargic and backward states were transforming education. They were appropriating billions of dollars for schools and not backing away from the awesome financial burden imposed by the baby boom generation. Moreover, they were dismantling the antiquated school districts inherited from the nineteenth century and forcing a notable change in school government. As in earlier decades, centralization of state authority over education to achieve professional standards remained the prevailing trend.

Coping with the Challenge of Higher Education

Meanwhile, the states were also reevaluating their systems of higher education. In the early 1950s state leaders began to realize that the existing flock of students at the elementary school level would deluge colleges and universities within a decade. But even before the baby boomers descended on public university campuses, institutions of higher education had to accommodate the rising demand for postsecondary education. More people in the 18 to 22 age range were seeking a college education, and the states needed to provide them that opportunity. This combination of increased population and rising educational expectations resulted in a marked expansion of public universities and colleges that began in the 1950s and peaked in the 1960s. Preparation for this expansion dominated thinking in higher education circles, but budget-conscious lawmakers continued to be attracted to a second objective, the coordination of educational institutions to avoid costly overlap and bitter competition for funding. This traditional goal remained high on the legislative agenda as solons endeavored to achieve some central direction to the education system and curb parochial rivalries between individual institutions.

As with elementary and secondary education, many believed federal aid was essential to meet the growing demand. During the first years after World War II, the federal government paid the tuition bills for hundreds of thousands of veterans and actually surpassed the states as a source of revenue for colleges and universities. In 1947–48 the national treasury accounted for 34.2 percent of the income of all institutions of higher education, whereas the states' share was 23.1 percent. As the number of veterans on college campuses declined, however, it was apparent that the federal government's contribution to advanced learning would also diminish. To consider whether the federal government should continue its financial support after the veterans graduated, Harry Truman appointed the President's Commission on Higher Education, which submitted its findings in late 1947 and early 1948. The report proposed that "public education through the fourteenth year of schooling be made available, tuition free, to all Americans able and willing to receive it." To further ensure maximum access to higher education, the commission recommended that "immediate steps be taken to establish a national program of Federally financed scholarships and fellowships." Moreover, Congress would also make generous annual appropriations for the current operating expenses of state colleges and universities and over the following twelve years pay one-third of the anticipated cost of capital improvements at public institutions. Underlying its conclusions was

the clearly stated assumption that there was "but one source capable of providing the funds needed to avoid a deficit and to balance the operating budget
for higher education: the federal government."[70]

The commission proposed federal funding only for public institutions, however, stirring opposition especially among Roman Catholic educators. In addition, the whole scheme raised fears that federal control would accompany
federal support. Consequently, no action was taken to realize the commission's
recommendations. Viewed largely as unrealistic, the report did not win much
backing in Congress, and the states were left with the primary responsibility
for meeting the higher education challenge.

Thus, the federal contribution peaked during the heyday of the veterans'
benefits under the G.I. Bill, then declined in the early 1950s. In 1949–50 the federal government allocated $527 million to institutions of higher education, but
in 1951–52 the figure dropped to $452 million and to slightly less than $420 million in 1953–54. Washington increased its spending in the second half of the
1950s, though most of the new expenditure was for contract research as the federal government sought to tap the expertise of major universities for the cold
war defense effort. Moreover, these federal research contracts went dispropor-
tionately to prestigious private institutions and provided the least benefit to
nonelite institutions dedicated to providing first-generation college students
an opportunity for higher education. Although the President's Commission
had strongly recommended an expansion of community colleges, in 1957–58
public junior colleges received only $544 in federal grants or contracts and a
total of only $862,000 from Washington. The latter figure was only a little more
than 0.1 percent of all federal appropriations to institutions of higher education.[71] Federal funds went to privately controlled MIT, for instance, not to
public community colleges charged with educating the masses.

Throughout the 1950s and early 1960s, then, the state governments shouldered the largest share of the burden of funding public colleges and universities. In 1957–58 the federal government contributed 14.8 percent of the current
income of such institutions, and the states provided 42.5 percent. Owing to a
rise in contract research, the federal portion was up to 19.1 percent by 1963–64,
but this was still far surpassed by the states' contribution of 38.8 percent. Even
more noteworthy was Washington's retreat from the financing of college building programs. During the 1930s, various federal make-work programs had paid
for the construction of classrooms and dormitories across the nation, accounting in 1939–40 for 34.7 percent of all plant fund receipts for public and private
institutions. By 1957–58 the federal share was 5.1 percent, one-sixth of the state
contribution.[72] Neither before nor after World War II was support of colleges

and universities a primary concern of Washington policymakers. Instead, higher education was fortunate enough to benefit from programs to enhance employment in the 1930s and to enhance national defense in the 1950s. Contrary to the urgings of the President's Commission, Congress did not assume financial responsibility for providing higher education to millions of Americans. And contrary to the commission's expectations, the states proved able to carry out the task.

The states' commitment to higher education was evident in the figures for enrollments and expenditures. Between 1947 and 1957, enrollment in public institutions rose from 1.15 million to 1.75 million, and then in the next five years the pace accelerated so that in 1962 the figure was 2.57 million. From 1950 to 1959, total state spending on higher education soared from $791 million to $2.24 billion, a 183 percent increase. By comparison, state appropriations for elementary and secondary education rose 136 percent and all state expenditures were up 106 percent.[73] The states were facing a formidable increase in demand for services and stepping up their spending accordingly.

Some states responded to the challenge by making up for past shortcomings and establishing state universities. Whereas the states west of the Appalachians and south of the Mason-Dixon Line had maintained full-scale public universities for decades, the commonwealths of the Northeast had bowed to the pressure of existing private institutions and refrained from creating tax-supported institutions with a broad offering of undergraduate and graduate programs. For example, at the close of World War II, the state of New York supported eleven teachers colleges, an equal number of two-year technical institutes, and a few professional schools at Cornell University, as well as a forestry program at Syracuse University, a ceramics program at Alfred University, and a maritime academy. It was a motley assortment, which had developed without unifying plan over the previous century. The state had never supported an arts and sciences college or an engineering school, essential components of the great public universities of the Midwest, the West, and the South.

In 1946, however, the New York legislature created the Temporary Commission to Study the Need of a State University. Two years later this body recommended that the state organize the existing institutions into a single decentralized public university, take charge of two medical schools, and establish new four-year colleges as well as a number of community colleges. In 1948, with the strong support of Governor Thomas E. Dewey, the legislature adopted the recommendations and created the State University of New York. Within the first two years of the university's existence, the state assumed control of one medical school in Syracuse and another in New York City, established the first two liberal arts colleges ever maintained by the state of New York, and helped finance two new community colleges. The system continued to expand with the opening of a state university center on Long Island in 1957 and the transformation of the formerly private University of Buffalo into the State University at Buffalo in 1962. Meanwhile, in 1961 the university's trustees launched a plan to change the teachers colleges into multipurpose colleges of arts and sciences. The number of community colleges increased as well, reaching ten in 1953 and eighteen by 1964.[74]

Traditionally the New England states had also ranked low in their devotion to public higher education. Yet during the 1940s and 1950s there were signs of change, followed by accelerated action in the 1960s. For example, before World War II Rhode Island maintained a land-grant state college specializing in agriculture but not offering a liberal arts curriculum. Anticipating an influx of returning veterans, in 1944 the college introduced a temporary liberal studies program leading to a bachelor of science degree. The long-term goal, however, was a bachelor of arts degree and university status. The college's student newspaper claimed that "if this B.A. degree were added there should be no prominent barrier to the establishment of the UNIVERSITY OF RHODE ISLAND."[75] In 1948 the college trustees authorized the bachelor of arts degree, and three years later the state legislature took the next step by granting the institution university status. Then in 1956 the state's voters overwhelmingly approved a bond issue to support the first stage of a major building program at the university, and the following year the trustees authorized the awarding of the doctor of philosophy degree, a much-coveted achievement among ambitious educational institutions of the postwar era.[76]

Other states were attempting to remedy past neglect of higher education in urban centers. During the nineteenth century, the states had generally located their universities in small towns, where impressionable young students would not fall prey to the evil influences of the city. By the 1940s and 1950s, though, there was a growing need to enhance access to higher education for urban dwellers, and a number of states responded to this need. In Michigan the Detroit Board of Education operated Wayne University for the city's students, but in the 1940s financially strapped Wayne administrators successfully lobbied for state aid. Then in 1955 the university asked the state to assume full responsibility for the institution and relieve Detroit of the burden of maintaining it. The chair of a commission to study this proposal endorsed the transfer of authority, observing: "The people of Michigan—all of its people—need Wayne University. If the Russians should drop a bomb on Wayne University, there is no question whatever but that the state would have to create another university to take its place."[77] The legislature agreed, and in 1956 Wayne became a state university. It was just the first of a series of municipal universities across the country that would become state institutions during the following fifteen years. Localities could no longer shoulder the burden of a full-fledged university. The states had to assume the responsibility and thereby provide urban commuter students with access to the full range of educational opportunities available at a major institution.

Moreover, during the 1950s the states funded expanding systems of junior or community colleges catering especially to a nonelite clientele that otherwise might have been unable to acquire a postsecondary education. For example, the fast-growing state of Florida made community colleges a vital element of its plans to accommodate a flood of new students. In 1953 the state's higher education governing board appointed a study commission to investigate the means by which Florida could "provide the highest quality programs for the greatest number of people at the lowest possible cost." Recognizing that the existing four-year institutions would not be able to handle adequately the expected enormous enrollment increase, the study group proposed "the establishment of public community colleges in strategic centers of population." In response in 1955 the legislature created the Community College Council to "formulate a long range plan for the establishment and coordination of community colleges."[78] The resulting master plan of 1957 was the basis for the rapid development of two-year institutions, the number increasing from five in 1957 to twenty in 1965. The state provided the bulk of the operating funds for these institutions, with the remainder coming from tuition fees and local taxes. For Florida, at least, the community college was the answer to providing the most schooling at the least cost. And it was an answer that Florida quickly implemented. Whereas in 1957 only 20.5 percent of first-time Florida freshmen attended public junior colleges, by 1962 the figure was 50.7 percent.[79]

Other states shared Florida's interest in promoting community colleges. Expressing sentiments similar to those of Florida's policymakers, in 1955 North Carolina's Commission on Higher Education reported, "The community college may be North Carolina's solution for the problem of the large increase in enrollment that is predicted."[80] Two years later, the legislature responded with the Community College Act, which authorized state funds to match local tax support and private contributions for two-year colleges. Four existing institutions soon qualified as the initial elements of the state community college system, and in coming years new campuses appeared in cities across the state. In 1958 the Board of Regents of the University System of Georgia embarked on a junior college program, absorbing two existing institutions in Savannah and

Augusta and founding a new unit in Columbus.[81] That same year, Massachusetts created the Board of Regional Community Colleges, charged with developing a master plan for the establishment of a system of two-year institutions.
The board was also authorized to supervise the operation of the community
colleges created by the state.[82] California had long relied on junior colleges to
provide postsecondary education to those unable or unwilling to attend the
state's four-year institutions. But the state's 1960 Master Plan for Higher Education reiterated California's commitment to the junior college. The plan called
for twenty-two additional junior colleges in areas not then adequately served
by two-year institutions. In addition, the plan pledged the state to increasing
its share of junior college funding from the existing 28 percent to 45 percent by
1975.[83] In California, as in Florida, North Carolina, Georgia, and Massachusetts, the community college seemed to offer a safety valve capable of relieving
the enrollment pressure on four-year institutions. Yet it also provided postsecondary educational opportunities to a broad range of citizens. Consequently,
educational policymakers embraced the junior college and committed a number of states to promoting this two-year alternative.

As state institutions of higher education proliferated and expanded, the
long-standing concern for central coordination became more significant. In
one state after another, policymakers considered how to balance the tradition
of decentralized governance inherited from the nineteenth century and the
twentieth-century need to eliminate wasteful overlapping of functions and
bitter competition for state funds for rival institutions. During the early twentieth century, this need for coordination troubled state lawmakers, and it
would continue to do so in the 1950s. Preferably the growth of higher education
would proceed according to some rational plan rather than as a helter-skelter
response to the disparate demands of different localities and institutions. To
achieve such rationality, however, the states had to ensure some oversight of
educational development.

A number of states attempted to achieve this oversight through the creation
of a formal coordinating agency. In 1941 Oklahoma established the Regents of
the Oklahoma State System of Higher Education to "constitute a co-ordinating
board of control" to "determine the functions and courses of study" at each of
the state institutions and to "recommend to the State Legislature the budget
allocations to each institution."[84] Ten years later, New Mexico likewise created
the Board of Education Finance, which was to "receive, adjust and approve the
budgets submitted by the several institutions," and in 1955 the legislature also
granted the board authority to approve or veto the establishment of graduate-
level programs at the various state colleges and universities. That same year,

the Wisconsin legislature created the Coordinating Committee for Higher Education, "to provide for the co-ordination of the activities of the University of Wisconsin and the state colleges and technical institutions." Specifically, the committee was to "have final authority in determining the single, consolidated biennial budget requests to be presented to the governor" and for delineating "the over-all education programs offered in the state-supported institutions of higher learning."[85] In 1955 Texas also established a Commission on Higher Education with authority to submit budget requests for the state institutions and determine the programs offered on each campus.[86] Basically, each of these co-ordinating agencies was expected to spare the governor and the legislature from the competing budget claims of the various universities and colleges. They were largely to decide what share of state funds each institution received. Moreover, by controlling the distribution of programs, they would supposedly thwart the schemes of every ambitious college to offer Ph.D. and professional programs.

In some states voluntary associations of the state institutions performed much the same function. In 1939 Ohio's state universities joined to form the Inter-University Council, composed of the president and one trustee from each institution, which was to formulate a single combined budget request to the legislature and to determine how much of the lump-sum appropriation each university would receive. In 1940 the council agreed that Ohio State University was "the logical institution among the five state universities for the development and prosecution of graduate work at the Ph.D. level" and for professional training in such fields as law, medicine, and dentistry.[87] In 1945 the University of California agreed to coordinate its efforts with the state colleges and public junior colleges through a body known as the Liaison Committee. This committee, however, was primarily a planning body, dedicated to arriving at a mutually agreeable scheme for development of higher education in the state and to delineating the different functions of the university and the colleges. Then in 1951 Indiana's legislature requested the state's two universities and two teachers colleges to form a conference similar to that of Ohio, primarily in order to collate budget requests prior to submission to the lawmakers.[88]

Yet by the late 1950s, voluntary associations no longer seemed sufficient, and lawmakers were turning increasingly to mandatory councils resembling those of Oklahoma, New Mexico, Wisconsin, and Texas. Ohio's experience exemplified the growing problems with the voluntary bodies. In 1956 Ohio University and Bowling Green State University rebelled against the Inter-University Council's long-standing agreement that Ohio State should enjoy a monopoly on the Ph.D. and embarked on the development of doctoral programs. Five years later, the president of Ohio University attacked the preferential treatment granted the state's flagship institution and blocked a proposal sponsored by the state speaker of the house for a capital improvements bond issue to finance science and engineering facilities at Ohio State. The détente among the state institutions had broken down, and the house speaker and other lawmakers were becoming increasingly dissatisfied with the ineffective council. Consequently, in 1963 the legislature created the Ohio Board of Regents to plan future development of higher education, to approve or disapprove all proposals for branch campuses and new degree programs, and to recommend appropriations for the state universities. The regents would perform the intended functions of the superseded Inter-University Council, but the board of regents was a state agency appointed by the governor, not a gathering of state university presidents allied in a mutual desire to squeeze as much from the state treasury as possible.

Elsewhere in the late 1950s and early 1960s, legislatures were also turning to the mandatory state coordinating council in their desire to ensure some central guidance. In 1959 Utah established a Coordinating Council of Higher Education, exercising the standard planning function and the authority to review budget requests and submit recommendations to the legislature.[89] The following year, California lawmakers created a similar council, which would examine budget submissions, prepare development plans, and determine the location of any new public institutions of higher education. In 1961 Illinois set up a Board of Higher Education, primarily as a planning agency, but it could approve or disapprove any proposed additions to or extensions of programs at the state colleges and universities. That same year, Arkansas followed suit with a Commission on Coordination on Higher Education Finance to consider appropriation requests of the state institutions and formulate spending recommendations.[90] These agencies were not identical in their powers or functions, but like the Ohio board and the earlier agencies in Oklahoma, New Mexico, Wisconsin, and Texas, they sought to force state universities to work cooperatively and avoid bloodletting over appropriations and the creation of graduate programs designed primarily to feed the egos of administrators and faculty rather than serve the needs of the taxpayers. These coordinating councils did not supersede the existing boards of trustees at the individual institutions, and a degree of institutional autonomy was preserved. But the states were attempting to require the disparate institutions to operate as a system rather than pursuing their own ambitions without regard for the larger public welfare.

Coordinating councils would become increasingly common in the middle and late 1960s as more states attempted to bring order to their fast-growing institutions of higher education. Similarly, the number of community colleges would rise steadily in the 1960s, and a growing body of urban universities would join the state systems. The trends of the 1950s, then, persisted in the 1960s as the expected flood of students inundated public colleges and universities. Not everyone believed the states' efforts were wholly successful or desirable. Some might have regarded the creation of community colleges as an opportunistic ploy whereby states could foist a cheap substitute on an education-hungry citizenry. Moreover, urban Wayne State never enjoyed the support or the cachet of the older institution in Ann Arbor. And coordination often failed to curb the ambitions of individual institutions and to raise the welfare of the state above the aspirations of faculty and administrators. The states, however, were not ignoring the problems confronting them but instead were relieving localities such as Detroit of a traditional function and centralizing control over the disparate public colleges and universities. Public higher education was not torpid or languishing during the supposed dark age of state government.

Promoting the Economy

During the 1940s and 1950s, the states not only endeavored to meet the educational challenges facing them; they also built on Mississippi's pioneering economic-development initiatives of the 1930s and focused increasing attention on attracting industry. Not willing to rely solely on local chamber-of-commerce boosters, one state after another launched programs of economic promotion to lure new businesses and retain existing ones. Throughout the nation policymakers believed that the states had to expand their marketing efforts and hustle for jobs and investment. State endeavors were modest compared to the broader, more sophisticated, and sometimes more frantic, efforts of the late twentieth century. Furthermore, despite the claims of critics, the states would not sacrifice everything to please tycoons with deep pockets or kowtow mindlessly to industrial giants. But all observers agreed that economic development was emerging as an increasingly significant function of state government.

This was especially true in the South. The South was poor, and its leaders were acutely aware of the fact. Founded in 1937, the Southern Governors Conference focused its energies on economic growth, leading the *New York Times* to describe it as a "conference with the broad objective of industrial development of the Southeastern states."[91] During its first decade, the conference endeavored primarily to revise the prevailing railroad freight rates for manufactured goods, which were lower in the Northeast and the industrial Midwest than in the South. That is, the railroads, with the acquiescence of the federal Interstate Commerce Commission, had established freight rates that raised the cost of manufacturing and distribution in the South relative to the Northeast and the Midwest and had thereby created a barrier to southern industrialization. Expressing the attitude of southern leaders, Governor Bibb Graves of Alabama predicted, "If we can beat these barriers down you will see millions of dollars worth of southern products going into areas north of the Ohio River and west of the Mississippi."[92]

Seeking a remedy, the southern governors appealed to the Interstate Commerce Commission, but that federal agency proceeded to deal with the issue at an excruciatingly slow pace. In 1943 Georgia governor Ellis Arnall told his fellow southern governors that "nothing but cold-blooded politics, waged with relentless unity, would rescue the South from its accepted role as a disfavored tomcat, prowling the political and economic backyards of a nation addicted to sectional snobbery."[93] Tired of waiting, the Georgia governor initiated suit in the U.S. Supreme Court against the nation's railroads, claiming unlawful collusion to fix excessive and discriminatory rates. This bold action stirred the Interstate Commerce Commission to finally take action, and in 1945 it ruled in favor of the southern governors and ordered an equalization of the rail rates. Two years later the Supreme Court sustained the commission's action, awarding Arnall and his colleagues final victory.

But this victory over the railroads was only a first step. Over the next decade and a half, southern governors continued to preach the gospel of industrialization as the path to economic salvation. One of the most popular means for attracting manufacturing was through industrial bond financing. Mississippi's BAWI program had launched this approach in the 1930s, and it continued to serve as a model for its southern neighbors in the postwar era. BAWI was administered by the Mississippi Agricultural and Industrial Board, which summed up its outlook when it reported, "Business is sensitive—it goes only where it is invited and stays only where it is well treated."[94] And Mississippi was dedicated to treating business well, with the state's localities issuing a total of nearly $103 million in industrial development bonds by the end of 1962. In 1948 the Kentucky legislature followed Mississippi's example and authorized the issuance of such bonds, as did Alabama in 1949, Tennessee in 1951, and Louisiana in 1953. By 1962 nine southern states had created industrial bonding programs, permitting cities and counties to borrow funds to finance new manufacturing plants. A number of northern states did likewise, but the use of public bonds to aid in the construction of industrial facilities was much more significant in the South than the North. Of the $441 million in local industrial development bonds issued through the end of 1962, the South accounted for $408 million.[95]

Perhaps just as important as any of these development programs was the promotional activity of state governors. During the 1950s and early 1960s, southern governors eagerly pursued manufacturing corporations interested in opening new plants. Through letters, telegrams, and telephone calls, each governor attempted to sell the advantages of his state to business executives, and a visiting corporate chieftain would be wined and dined at the executive mansion. Moreover, a number of southern governors embarked on "raiding" junkets to the North, where the state executives could meet personally with corporate moguls and hopefully bring home some industrial trophies for their job-hungry states. Southern industrial development agencies discovered that personal intervention by the state's executive was much more effective than a note and enclosed brochure from a development department functionary. "If you send an industrial representative to these places, he talks to his counterpart in the business," explained Georgia governor Ernest Vandiver. "But a governor—any governor—gets to the president and chairman of the board where the final decisions are made."[96]

Possibly the greatest gubernatorial salesman was Luther Hodges of North Carolina. During his seven years as chief executive, from 1954 to 1961, Hodges made economic development his first priority. North Carolina was home to a number of textile mills and tobacco processing plants, but these paid low wages, contributing to North Carolina's rank of forty-fourth among the forty-eight states in per capita income. Hodges later remarked, "It became increasingly apparent to me that low per capita income was North Carolina's major problem—a bread-and-butter problem that affected everyone in the state and every aspect of its future." An unabashed industry hunter, Hodges admitted, "My administration was considered by many to be 'industry hungry.' It was!"[97]

Pursuing his manufacturing prey, Hodges organized a series of hunting trips. In October 1957 the governor and nearly seventy-five community representatives headed north to New York City. Over the course of the six-day junket, Hodges delivered three major speeches, attended five luncheons and four receptions for more than 600 persons, and appeared on twelve radio and television programs. Meanwhile, his companions on the trip were not idle. According to the governor, "the Tar Heel industry hunters combed New York City, talking with industrialists interested in chemicals, electronics, metal working, and the like. The group in that week was able to make personal visits to about 250 prospects in industry, business, and food distribution fields." In April 1958 the North Carolinians made a similar hunting trip to Chicago, and in November of that year Hodges and his fellow boosters hit Philadelphia, presenting what the governor proudly called "The North Carolina Story." Having exhorted corporate leaders in the Northeast and the Midwest, Hodges next cast his eyes toward Europe, and in the fall of 1959 he led a two-week industry hunt in Great Britain, Netherlands, Germany, Switzerland, France, and Belgium. The irrepressible governor claimed that the North Carolinians "made a great impression all over Europe," and at least 276 Europeans contacted during the tour expressed immediate interest in the state. Always ready to exploit such interest, Hodges reported, "Personal letters over my signature were sent to the 276 contacts as well as all of our European friends who attended North Carolina luncheons or dinners."[98] Such "personal" letters to a multitude of corporate friends were becoming standard promotional tools for gubernatorial salesmen. And as the states began to search abroad for business, more of these letters would end up in European hands.

Among Hodges's most important achievements, however, was the creation of the North Carolina Research Triangle. The triangle was intended to be a research center that would draw on the resources of the three institutions of higher education in the Chapel Hill–Durham–Raleigh area, the University of North Carolina, Duke University, and North Carolina State College. Originally the idea of a construction company executive, this project quickly attracted the attention of the governor, who recognized the triangle's potential for attracting higher-technology, higher-wage industries to North Carolina. In 1955 Hodges appointed the Governor's Research Triangle Committee to implement the proposal, and using his unequaled sales ability to raise the necessary funds, the governor was able to realize his dream. By 1962 Hodges was characterizing the Research Triangle as "the heart and hope of North Carolina's industrial future."[99] He was correct, for in coming years the triangle would become one of the most prominent research centers in the nation, attracting scientists and engineers to a state formerly known for its ready supply of ignorant but docile human labor.

The southern initiatives soon provoked countermeasures in the North. Between 1955 and 1962, thirteen states outside of the South authorized localities to issue industrial development bonds, but a number of northern states were to rely more heavily on state aid than local borrowing to promote industrial development. For example, in 1955 New Hampshire created a state agency known as the Industrial Park Authority, with the power to borrow funds for the development of industrial sites. By 1962 this arm of the state government had invested $3.9 million in thirteen projects.[100] In 1956 the Pennsylvania legislature likewise took action, appropriating $5 million for the capital fund of the newly established Pennsylvania Industrial Development Authority. This authority was empowered to loan funds to nonprofit community development organizations to provide up to 30 percent of the cost of new manufacturing facilities or additions to plants. During the first two years of its operation, the authority contributed to the financing of sixty-eight new or expanded factories, which created 11,800 new manufacturing jobs.[101] In 1957 Maine became the first state to establish an industrial mortgage insurance program. The Maine Industrial Building Authority could pledge the full faith and credit of the state to guarantee mortgages issued by local nonprofit industrial development organizations for the construction of new manufacturing facilities.[102]

Throughout the nation, state governments were assuming a larger role in promoting industrial development. The trade missions and raiding parties of southern governors attracted more public attention than New Hampshire's industrial park authority or Maine's mortgage guarantee program, but in both North and South, state government was increasingly in the marketing business. By 1962 there were state economic development agencies in all fifty of the nation's commonwealths, and the pace of their promotional efforts was rising.[103] In future years scores of governors would follow the example of Luther Hodges and embark for Europe to boost their states. Moreover, sales techniques would become more sophisticated as the pressure to win jobs intensified. It was in the 1940s and 1950s, however, that the states ran the first lap of this race for riches. During these years economic promotion won a secure position among the functions of twentieth-century state government.

Most states would not, however, sacrifice everything to attract business. In the late twentieth century, critics of state government often seemed to assume that legislators and governors would aim at the lowest common denominator in their pursuit of jobs. They would reduce taxes, regulations, and services in a mad rush to match their fellow commonwealths in offering a favorable business climate. Yet this is an exaggerated view. As is evident in the right-to-work battle of the 1940s and 1950s, the desire to please prospective investors was not the sole or even the dominant determinant of policy in most states. States wanted to promote business, but lawmakers and voters also responded to countervailing forces that ensured that state policy did not necessarily conform to every wish of the U.S. Chamber of Commerce or the National Association of Manufacturers.

The battle over so-called right-to-work laws divided the nation in the 1940s and 1950s. Many employers lobbied for the enactment of such laws, which would establish open shops and prohibit the closed-shop requirement that all workers in unionized plants belong to the union. Labor groups, of course, sought to preserve the mandatory union membership of the closed shop. Among the first advocates of right-to-work laws were farm organizations that feared unionization of agricultural laborers. Thus, in 1944 Florida adopted the nation's first right-to-work measure, in response to strong pressure from the state's powerful citrus growers. Two years later, the Associated Farmers pushed passage of Arizona's right-to-work constitutional amendment.[104] In fact, of the eighteen states that had mandated the open shop as of 1955, none were major industrial states, all of them being in the South or in the trans-Mississippi Midwest or Rocky Mountain regions.

Yet the movement had strong support from nonagricultural groups such as chambers of commerce and the National Association of Manufacturers. Right-to-work laws were clearly probusiness measures that could possibly lure industry to the southern and western states. Many observers identified right-to-work laws as favorable to industrial expansion. In 1951 a University of North Carolina professor wrote, "Undoubtedly to the plant which seeks a new location free from union restrictions, for a short time at least, the southern states with their right to work laws offer many attractions."[105] A manufacturers' association in a western state claimed, "Several large corporations have located plants in our state and . . . one of the main reasons given was the right to work law."[106] In the right-to-work state of Texas, an engineering contracting firm testified that it received many inquiries from industries "fleeing from union despotism in the Eastern states." According to this firm, "Texas ha[d] gained many more of the migrant industries than such states as Louisiana, for instance, simply because the Texas labor laws [gave] employers some protection whereas Louisiana's [did] not."[107]

Despite a widespread belief that right-to-work laws attracted industry, most states did not opt for the open shop. Between 1944 and 1948, fifteen states adopted right-to-work laws or constitutional provisions, but Maine, New Hampshire, and Delaware quickly repealed them. From 1950 through 1955, just six additional states rejected the closed shop; Louisiana enacted a general right-to-work statute in 1954, only to repeal it two years later and adopt in its place an open-shop law applying solely to agricultural laborers. Then from 1956 through 1963, three states were added to the right-to-work column, bringing the open-shop total to twenty states. Clearly, the pace of adoption slowed after 1950, for in the remaining states, right-to-work forces were able to make little headway. Each year legislatures confronted right-to-work proposals and rejected them. In 1953 lawmakers in Colorado, California, and Oregon defeated such measures. Two years later the Idaho legislature turned down an open-shop proposal, Colorado lawmakers did so once again, and Ohio's right-to-work bill died in committee. Then in 1956 both Kentucky and Missouri rejected proposals.

In 1958, however, the right-to-work forces faced their day of reckoning, for through initiative petitions they secured a place on the ballot for open-shop laws in California, Colorado, Idaho, Ohio, and Washington. In Kansas an act of the legislature referred the question to the voters. Both business and labor mobilized their forces in these states for a right-to-work Armageddon. Open-shop proponents emphasized freedom of choice and the liberation of workers from the dictatorial rule of labor bosses. But they also noted the positive impact on business growth. A California backer claimed that the right-to-work states had "advanced faster than the States without right-to-work" because "their healthy economic climate attract[ed] industry."[108] According to the executive vice president of the Colorado State Chamber of Commerce, the open-shop law had "encouraged a definite move of industry to such states that ha[d] accepted freedom of choice." In addition, right-to-work advertisements presented figures proving that open-shop Arizona had grown much more rapidly than closed-shop Colorado.[109] Opponents of the measures responded with equal vigor. In California Democratic gubernatorial candidate Edmund Brown attacked the proposition as "a call to class warfare," and an African American newspaper in Cleveland said of the Ohio proposition: "No Negro unionist in his right mind is going to vote for this trick-titled bill. It would be the same as committing suicide."[110]

On election day most voters seemed to heed such advice, for in five of the six states, the right-to-work proposals suffered defeat. In Kansas the open shop won the support of 57 percent of those voting; but in California, Colorado, Ohio, and Washington, it garnered only between 36 and 40 percent of the ballots, and the Idaho measure lost by a narrow margin. That same year, right-to-work measures also failed to pass in the legislatures of Kentucky, Louisiana, Maryland, and Rhode Island.[111] Neither lawmakers nor voters seemed ready to side with the National Association of Manufacturers, and in the wake of the electoral defeat, the *Wall Street Journal* reported that "some right-to-work backers said privately they saw no point in continuing the efforts to pass the law on a state-to-state basis."[112]

Though states were investing increasing effort in industrial promotion, most were not willing to kowtow to every probusiness initiative. Desperately poor states with weak unions such as Mississippi might do virtually anything to attract an industrial plant, but not all of the nation's commonwealths were willing to pander so abjectly to business whims. Competition for jobs did not dictate state policy. If it had, by the close of the 1960s every state would have adopted right-to-work laws. Yet in fact only a minority did so. At the state level, labor remained a powerful countervailing force, as the election of 1958 proved.

In the wake of the 1958 referendum, a bitter *Wall Street Journal* editorialized, "The defeat of right to work legislation in five of the six states where it was up for vote is a tribute to the financial resources and organizational skill of unions."[113] In other words, unions could and did mold state policy. The 1958 election results reflected the diversity of factors determining the course of the states. Although some leaders urged the adoption of probusiness policies that would supposedly attract jobs, they did not necessarily have the final say.

Promotion of business was, then, emerging as a major concern of state government but not the only concern or even a prevailing one. In the mind of the media and the general public, state government seemed to pale in significance compared to the actions of Stalin or Khrushchev; nevertheless, the states were expanding their roles and "modernizing" their institutions through centralization and professionalization. The need to provide adequate schooling at the primary and secondary levels preoccupied many governors and legislators. The emerging wave of college applicants placed further pressure on the states and spurred accelerated activity in the field of higher education. Meanwhile, legislators responded to long-standing criticism and gradually reconsidered the practices and procedures of their branch of government. In other words, the 1940s and 1950s was not a long dry spell in the history of state government producing a meager harvest of action. Instead, during these two decades the long-term expansion of state government continued, largely overlooked by contemporary observers but significant to the future of the nation.

8

Reform and Recognition

S PEAKING BEFORE THE 1974 Governors' Conference, Governor Daniel Evans
of Washington predicted that when historians wrote "of the fundamental
changes . . . in the federal system during the last one third of the Twentieth
Century, the reaffirmation of the intended role of the States [would] be the
characteristic most commonly noted."[1] In a commentary on ABC News that
same year, Howard K. Smith delivered a similar message. Claiming that "since
the New Deal, the federal government ha[d] been the fount of reform and
innovation," Smith told his viewers: "Well, that's changed. Suddenly the state
governments are doing relatively much better."[2] Meanwhile, a leading scholar
on federalism, Daniel Elazar, was observing that a "quiet revolution . . . ha[d]
transformed state government . . . into a solid instrument for meeting the complex needs of American society." "Far from being weak sisters," the states and
localities, according to Elazar, had "actually been carrying the brunt of domestic governmental progress in the United States ever since the end of World
War II and ha[d] done so at an accelerated pace since . . . Vietnam."[3]

By 1974 politicians, media sages, and academics were all coming to the same
conclusion. The states were no longer rusty, creaking cogs in the machinery of
government. They had been refashioned and were operating more effectively
than the once-admired federal dynamo. Evans, Smith, and Elazar all recognized the states' emerging prominence based on a new quality of performance.
The developing consensus was that state government was both better and more
significant.

Underlying this new recognition was a perception that the states had finally
reformed. Indeed, the 1960s and 1970s was an era of change in state government, when states made a concerted effort to professionalize their legislatures,
restructure their executive and judicial branches, and expand their fiscal
resources. Moreover, state and federal courts finally forced reapportionment

on legislative bodies throughout the country, ensuring a greater semblance of representativeness in the state lawmaking bodies. The state governments of the late 1970s thus differed from those twenty years earlier because state leaders had sought to redesign and improve the governing mechanism.

Yet the state governments of the late 1930s had also differed from those of twenty years earlier, and those of the late teens had differed from those of the late 1890s. The states did not suddenly step on the gas after idling for decades. They accelerated somewhat during the 1960s and 1970s, but they moved in the same direction as in earlier decades. During this era of renewed recognition, state governments perpetuated the long-standing trend toward professionalism and centralization. Legislative reforms realized the goals set by the Council of State Governments in 1946. Judicial changes followed the course charted by Arthur Vanderbilt in the 1940s, and the states did not invent any major new taxes but simply continued the shift to income and sales taxes begun in the early decades of the twentieth century. The 1960s and 1970s were not so much an era of innovation as one of realization. Laggard states realized reforms pioneered in earlier decades and worked to fulfill goals that had guided state-level reformers throughout much of the twentieth century.

What was new was the public's negative perception of Uncle Sam. Evans, Smith, and Elazar all pronounced their glowing prognoses in 1974, a year when the federal government's fortunes were at a new low. The Vietnam debacle was coming to a close, and the Watergate crisis commanded the headlines. With the defeat of the nation's vaunted military and the disgrace of the presidency, Uncle Sam no longer seemed a benevolent superman, as he had when handing out billions of dollars in relief during the 1930s or whipping the Nazis in the 1940s. Instead, he suddenly appeared shabby and stumbling. By the 1970s the federal government was tarnished, and by comparison the state glowed a bit more brightly. Rarely have Americans ever evaluated the states except in relation to the federal government. The federal government's gain has traditionally been deemed the states' loss, and Uncle Sam's shame during the 1970s was a signal for renewed appreciation for the states.

In other words, state practices and institutions changed, but so did perceptions of the state and federal governments. The result was a supposed resurgence of the states, a quiet revolution that transformed state government. Yet the 1960s and 1970s were simply another stage in a quiet evolution that had been refashioning the states since the close of the nineteenth century. By the 1970s political leaders, journalists, and scholars were finally recognizing the fruits of this evolution and awarding a few laurels to the formerly denigrated states.

Legislative Reform

In 1962 the U.S. Supreme Court handed down its decision in *Baker v. Carr,* thereby opening the question of legislative apportionment to judicial review. The ruling was to begin years of conflict and confusion, as courts ordered state legislatures to reapportion, the legislatures did so, and then the courts found the reapportionment schemes inadequate and mandated further action. The clash over reapportionment lasted through most of the 1960s and was only cooling down when the results of the 1970 census forced legislatures back to the redistricting drawing boards. In every state, however, reapportionment eliminated the population disparities among districts, forcing a "one-man, one-vote" standard on recalcitrant state legislatures. Furthermore, it disturbed the status quo and caused legislative leaders to reconsider existing practices. The legislative reform effort evident in the 1940s and 1950s accelerated, and the cause of "modernization" picked up momentum. Reformers continued to strive for the same goals of annual sessions, fewer committees, higher pay, and additional staff, but in the 1960s and 1970s they won more victories. There was no revolution, but there was heightened interest in professionalizing the newly reapportioned legislatures and a higher rate of success.

In the forefront of the reform movement, and a model for other states, was California. Even before the 1960s, its legislature had developed an unmatched level of professionalism. In 1946 it had switched from biennial sessions to annual meetings, with the even-year session devoted to fiscal matters. In 1951 for the first time, all California legislators were assigned private offices. Elsewhere most lawmakers had to conduct business from their desks in the house and senate chambers; they had no private quarters in which to meet constituents or consider legislation. That same year, the California house constituted its standing committees as interim committees, meaning that the standing committees would remain in business year-round.[4] Committee staffing increased during the 1950s; and beginning in 1959, each state senator was authorized to hire an administrative assistant and at least one secretary. Meanwhile, legislative compensation, including both salaries and expense allowances, increased from about five thousand dollars per year in 1950 to nine thousand dollars in 1960.[5] In 1956 the legislature demonstrated its interest in self-improvement when it created the Citizens' Legislative Advisory Commission to consider reforms in structure and practice.[6] In the 1960s legislatures throughout the country were to establish this type of blue-ribbon advisory body of leading citizens, but as early as the mid-1950s California employed this device to investigate further reform.

The Californian who became most associated with the cause of legislative reform was Jesse Unruh, speaker of the state house from 1961 to 1969. On assuming the speaker's chair, he determined to modernize his chamber and was especially dedicated to increasing staff support. By 1963 every house committee had at least one consultant, and Unruh also ensured that each member of the lower house could staff an office in his or her home district to handle constituent services. As of the early 1970s, there were 767 staff members employed by California's lower house, including 217 professionals who could apply their expertise to the task of lawmaking.[7]

Unruh not only had an impact within California; he also spread the gospel of legislative professionalism throughout the country. During the 1960s and early 1970s, Unruh wrote and spoke repeatedly on the need for independent legislatures that would no longer be manipulated by governors or lobbyists. At the 1965 National Legislative Conference in Portland, Oregon, he told the assembled legislators, "I believe a supine legislature which can be walked on at will by either the executive branch of government or the special interest groups . . . adds nothing to the effectiveness of a representative form of government."[8] With their own expert staff researching issues, legislators would no longer be dependent on the possibly false or misleading data presented by the executive branch or the special interests. They could draw their own conclusions independent of lobbyists or governors. Moreover, professionalism could make the state legislatures competitive with ever-threatening federal lawmakers. "In order for the legislature to survive, it must be aggressive," observed the assertive Californian. "It must compete creatively with the governor and the federal government to meet the needs of the people."[9] Given the threat from these competitors, Unruh had no tolerance for those lawmakers who wanted to drag their feet and preserve the old-fashioned ideal of the citizen legislator. In 1968 he told a presession conference of the Connecticut legislature, "Many legislators have come to regard their lack of professionalism as a positive virtue." But Unruh claimed that "the concept of the part-time citizen-legislator" was "tinged with aristocratic arrogance." According to the California speaker, "the machinery of modern government [was] too intricate to be run by dilettantes."[10] Thus, for Unruh and his supporters, modern legislatures had to be professional. They had to be full-time deliberative bodies, with expert staffing and the facilities and resources necessary to fend off control by governors, lobbyists, or the federal government.

Unruh also spawned a notable reform disciple, Larry Margolis. A former legislative aide of the California speaker, Margolis in 1965 became executive director of the newly established Citizens Conference on State Legislatures, an organization dedicated to mobilizing legislators and concerned citizens in support of legislative reform. Echoing his former master's words, Margolis wrote: "A revitalized legislature is independent. It has independent sources of information on which to base its judgments, it has the independent capacity to innovate." But existing legislatures could not be independent because their sessions were "too short to permit them to get any kind of firm handle on the work before them," and their members were "preoccupied with figuring out how to make most of their living."[11]

Another organization that supported Jesse Unruh in the campaign for legislative reform was the Eagleton Institute of Politics at Rutgers University. In 1963 New Jersey's solons asked the Eagleton Institute to study the legislature's operation and recommend improvements, and over the next decade the lawmakers of Rhode Island, Wisconsin, Maryland, Florida, Mississippi, Connecticut, and Arkansas also commissioned the Eagleton Institute to produce lengthy reports on their legislatures. In the Maryland report, the institute claimed that its aim was "to assist a specific legislature in overcoming particular problems" and that it had "tried to offer proposals that [were] effective and workable—not in California, New York, or New Jersey, but in Maryland."[12] Nonetheless, the institute basically applied the same reform agenda that Unruh and Margolis were preaching nationwide to each state studied. California's pioneering efforts were assumed to represent the vanguard of a better world. This was understandable considering that Jesse Unruh was politician-in-residence at the institute and joined the faculty as visiting professor.[13] The Eagleton Institute investigators conscientiously studied each state legislature and then informed lawmakers how their house and senate deviated from the reform template formulated in the 1940s and 1950s and elaborated upon by Unruh and likeminded critics.

But the ferment for change was not confined to a few reform organizations and the speaker of California's lower house. Throughout the nation legislatures of the late 1960s and the early 1970s were reconsidering their procedures and facilities, and commissions on legislative reform were commonplace. Virginia's Commission on Legislative Process recommended such standard improvements as annual sessions, increased staff, fewer committees, more generous expense allowances, and additional office space.[14] Cochaired by author James Michener, Pennsylvania's Commission for Legislative Modernization issued an epic fifty-eight suggestions for reform.[15] West Virginia's Citizens Advisory Commission on the Legislature concluded that state legislatures were "restricted unduly and unreasonably" and made fifty-three recommendations, which again included higher compensation, more space and staff, and fewer committees. The Iowa Legislative Processes Study Committee, composed of twenty-four lay citizens and eight legislators, made much the same suggestions, and the twenty-five citizens serving on a good-government committee in Minnesota presented a report of seventy-two pages that repeated the reform litany.[16] One journalist described the work of the Illinois Commission on the Organization of the General Assembly as "aimed at a massive overhaul of the operations" of the legislature. Meanwhile, the Idaho Citizens Committee on the State Legislature, composed of thirty leading Idahoans, sought to create a lawmaking body that was "better equipped, better informed, and better staffed."[17] Washington's Citizen's Advisory Committee offered seventy-five suggestions for improvement, and the thirty-six prominent citizens who comprised the Advisory Committee on the Oregon Legislature were "convinced that one session every two years no longer serve[d] the needs of a growing, progressive state. Three-fourths of the time, Oregon is left without a lawmaking branch of government ready to function."[18]

The result was considerable change in legislatures across the country. Yet much of the change was not revolutionary, the product of sudden upheaval. It was simply a continuation of trends evident in the 1940s and 1950s. In 1940 only four states had annual sessions of the legislature, in 1960 there were nineteen such states, and in 1980 the number was forty-three. The annual session was no longer the exception; it was the rule. In fact, by the early 1980s nine legislatures, primarily those in the most populous states, were in session throughout the year and could be classified as full-time.[19] The long-term decline in the number of standing committees also continued. From 1946 to 1963, the median number of senate committees dropped from thirty-one to twenty and then fell to twelve in 1975. The house median was thirty-nine in 1946, twenty-two in 1963, and seventeen in 1975.[20] In some states the changes in committee structure were especially notable. For example, in 1971 the Arkansas house, which had once been notorious for maintaining sixty-nine committees, streamlined its operation by agreeing to cut the number of committees from twenty-four to ten. Henceforth Arkansas representatives would have only two committee assignments, down from the previous average of four, and thus would be better able to concentrate their efforts and become informed on the issues before their committees. A year later the Arkansas senate likewise agreed to maintain only ten standing committees, identical in name and subject matter jurisdiction to those in the house. Moreover, in 1973 the legislature authorized the ten coordinate house and senate committees to meet jointly during the interim between regular sessions.[21] Legislative reformers had long dreamed of this type of procedural simplification and interchamber cooperation, and by the early 1970s the dream was being realized even in once-benighted Arkansas.

Although reformers of the 1940s and 1950s had won some victories in the battle for restructured committees and annual sessions, there were few notable improvements in legislative facilities before 1960. As late as 1963, only four states provided office space for all legislators. Most lawmakers had only their desks in the legislative chambers, which one student of the Connecticut legislature described as "smaller than those provided to many public school children."[22] According to a management consulting firm hired to investigate legislative facilities in Pennsylvania, "except for his assigned desk position in the appropriate legislative chamber, the average Representative [did] not have a desk or telephone and the average senator [found] himself in a room with three other Senators." Supposedly, one representative kept "over twenty regular shopping bags in the back of his station wagon to accommodate his needs to maintain files."[23] In Oregon also, representatives were forced to conduct routine business at their desks in the assembly chamber. "Anyone who has observed the Assembly in formal session is aware of the crowded conditions on the floor," wrote one critic, "with legislators and their secretaries jammed into space which is far below minimum standards set by the state for other public employees."[24] By the early 1970s, this was changing. New York opened a new nine-story legislative office building; Virginia purchased a hotel annex near the capitol to house offices for its legislators, and Maryland and Tennessee completed new facilities for their lawmakers.[25] By the end of 1975, nineteen states provided private offices for each legislator, and eight others supplied shared space.[26] These numbers continued to increase as legislative office buildings became common landmarks in the nation's capital cities.

At the same time, there was also a transformation in legislative staffing. During the late 1960s and 1970s, state legislatures were expanding their staffs dramatically, providing more professional and clerical assistance to the standing committees and individual lawmakers. By 1979 there were 16,930 full-time professional and clerical staff members in the fifty state legislatures, with New York employing the most, 3,100, and Vermont the fewest, 65.[27] Senators were provided personal staff in twenty-six states, and in nineteen states each member of the lower house likewise was given his or her own secretary or administrative assistant. In thirty-nine states all senate standing committees received professional staff assistance, as did all of the committees in thirty-seven of the lower houses.[28] In fact, as staffing of permanent standing committees increased, the significance of the legislative council diminished. In 1967 the legislative council movement peaked with forty-four states maintaining councils. But in the late 1960s and early 1970s, some state abolished their councils, preferring to staff standing committees that met year-round rather than rely on an interim research agency such as the legislative council.[29] With standing committees operating both in session and between sessions and the interim shrinking as legislators remained in the capital for longer periods, some lawmakers deemed the legislative council obsolete.

Another sign of professionalization was the increase in compensation. In 1955 the constitutions of seventeen states fixed salaries of legislators; by 1979 that number had dropped to nine.[30] Consequently, additional legislatures were freed of their constitutional straitjacket, and they proceeded to approve periodic hikes in salaries and expense allowances. In 1964–65 the median biennial compensation of lawmakers in the fifty states, including both salaries and expense allowances, was about $4,650; ten years later it was $18,200, rising 290 percent during a decade when the cost of living increased by 70 percent. The range in compensation, however, was enormous, with the stingiest state, New Hampshire, paying its lawmakers only $200 for the biennium 1974–75 and California, the most generous state, awarding each legislator $64,140.[31] Since the median four-person family income in 1975 was only $15,848, California's annual remuneration of $32,070 could not be deemed part-time pay for civic-minded citizens willing to sacrifice some of their energies for the governance of the state. California's legislators were professional lawmakers with compensation, staff, and offices worthy of a professional.

Throughout the nation the citizen legislator seemed on the road to extinction. Many were reluctant to abandon the concept, but those dedicated to professionalization had made startling progress. By 1980 state legislatures had acquired many of the attributes of modernization identified by the Council of State Governments in 1946 and promoted by Unruh, Margolis, and the Eagleton Institute in the 1960s and 1970s. Reform had triumphed.

The Executive

State governors were also pursuing the goal of modernization. In their case modernization meant longer tenure and greater gubernatorial control of state agencies. These were not new aims. Since World War II, gubernatorial tenure had been increasing. And since the beginning of the twentieth century, governors had been complaining about dispersed executive authority and their inability to assume administrative control of state government. Administrative reform schemes of the second and third decades of the century had sought to remedy this problem, and in the 1960s and 1970s executive branch reorganization again emerged as the preferred panacea for gubernatorial ills. The result was a fresh wave of plans and proposals for administrative restructuring.

In order to enhance the administrative clout of their chief executives, however, states first had to lengthen gubernatorial terms. During the 1940s and

1950s there had been a marked trend away from two-year terms, and this continued during the 1960s and 1970s. Whereas in 1964 fifteen states elected governors biennially, in 1980 only the four relatively small states of Arkansas, New Hampshire, Rhode Island, and Vermont still did so. Four-year terms were the norm. Moreover, those states that had imposed a one-term limit on their governors were abandoning this restriction. In 1960 fifteen states, primarily in the South, forbade governors to succeed themselves; twenty years later, the number was down to four.

As a consequence, governors had a greater opportunity to leave an imprint on their states. Biennially elected governors had often felt that they were perpetually running for office, but four-year terms granted state executives a little breathing space in which to do something other than campaign. Governors no longer needed to fear that they would pass from the scene after only two years without having had time to accomplish anything. Furthermore, now that they could succeed themselves, incumbents no longer had to spend their last two years in office as constitutionally mandated lame ducks. Legislators, lobbyists, and political leaders generally could not ignore a figure who might wield power for another four years. The virtual elimination of the two-year term and the removal of the ban on consecutive succession translated into more clout for the governor.

Not only did the terms of office lengthen; so did the willingness of voters to return some leaders to office for multiple terms. By the 1970s there were an increasing number of governors who could be deemed perennial. Whereas during the first four decades of the twentieth century only two governors, Albert Ritchie of Maryland and George W. P. Hunt of Arizona, served more than ten years in office, in 1973 eight of the fifty chief executives would eventually hold the governor's office at least twelve years. George Wallace of Alabama, Nelson Rockefeller of New York, Robert Ray of Iowa, and William Milliken of Michigan all held office for fourteen or more years, and John Burns of Hawaii, Arch Moore of West Virginia, Calvin Rampton of Utah, and Daniel Evans of Washington each served three four-year terms. In the mid-1950s a leading scholar on the governor's office referred to the limited-tenure state executives of the first half of the twentieth century as birds of passage who roosted for a short while in the governor's mansions and then flew on.[32] By the 1970s a number of governors were not flying on but nesting year after year in the seats of power. They were not a migratory species; they were permanent residents.

During the 1960s and 1970s, governors across the country also strived for greater control over the larger bureaucracy of state government. For more than fifty years, state executives had complained about the multitude of state agencies, many of which operated virtually independently of the governor's authority. During the second decade of the twentieth century, Illinois under Governor Frank Lowden pioneered administrative reorganization, and other states followed Illinois's example. Yet administrative reformers rarely seemed to reach their goal: some states took no action, others pursued piecemeal restructuring, and still others returned to their old ways and spawned a new breed of independent agencies. The little Hoover commissions of the early 1950s had not produced any comprehensive restructuring of state government, but in the mid-1960s another wave of administrative reform began to sweep the nation. Between 1965 and 1979, twenty-one states implemented comprehensive schemes of administrative reorganization, and a number of others combined some departments and rearranged certain lines of authority to achieve partial reorganization.[33]

During the 1960s and 1970s, administrative reformers pursued the same goals that Frank Lowden had embraced in 1917. Writing in 1972, the director of research of the Council of State Governments observed, "The basic reason for reorganization has not changed over the years: that is, improvement of administration through grouping agencies having related functions, and the need of pinpointing responsibility through giving the Governor authority and a manageable span of control."[34] Consolidation of related agencies and enhancement of gubernatorial control were the aims of Lowden, and they remained the goals of reform governors in the 1960s and 1970s. The state's executive branch had to form a neat pyramid with the governor at the apex exercising administrative responsibility for everything below. And the number of agencies had to be reduced so the governor could reasonably keep track of each of them. This was the dream of administrative reformers in 1917 and in 1972.

In 1965 Michigan initiated the new wave of administrative reform, followed by Wisconsin in 1967, and Colorado and Florida in 1968. Each year administrative reformers could claim victory in some part of the United States; one governor after another pushed for reorganization plans that would enhance his or her control over executive branch functions. For example, in 1971 and 1972 Georgia's Governor Jimmy Carter successfully crusaded for a reorganization scheme that consolidated 300 agencies into 22 departments.[35] Following a typical pattern, in 1975 Connecticut's Governor Ella Grasso appointed a four-person study group to present proposals for reorganization to the 1977 legislature. The result was the consolidation of more than 210 agencies into 22 departments.[36] In most states the new department heads were to serve in a gubernatorial cabinet and consult periodically with the governor.

Although proponents of administrative restructuring acclaimed these reforms, the changes often were more apparent than real. Some schemes just grouped existing agencies into so-called departments without affecting the authority or practices of the agencies. One expert on restructuring noted that "in most States some of the existing agencies were located in the new ones with their structure and authority intact and they [could] operate largely independent of the department head."[37] In 1974 Idaho reorganized its executive branch, placing all existing agencies within nineteen departments. But one of these was the Department of Self Governing Agencies, which had no head. It was simply a title under which all the remaining agencies were placed, and those agencies continued to operate independently, not subject to the coordination or supervision of a department chief.[38] A student of Connecticut's reorganization scheme noted that "much of the reshuffling was window dressing." Thirty-two of the preexisting agencies were relocated to departments where the department heads had virtually no authority over them. Moreover, twenty-eight agencies remained outside Connecticut's twenty-two departments.[39] Often, then, the reforms appeared dramatic on paper, but there was little change in the day-to-day operation of scores of boards, commissions, and offices.

Many of the reorganization schemes also did not grant the governors direct authority to appoint all of the department heads, thus perpetuating a fragmented executive. Florida's governor was solely responsible for appointing only six of the heads of the state's twenty reorganized departments. The other fourteen were chosen by gubernatorially chosen boards, the other elected state executive officers, or jointly by these officers and the governor.[40] Idaho's governor selected only nine of the directors of the nineteen reorganized state departments, Louisiana's chief executive appointed eleven of that state's nineteen department chiefs, and Montana's governor chose nine of the nineteen department heads, with boards or commissions responsible for overseeing the administration of most of the rest.[41] In some states governors could directly hire and fire the chiefs of the administrative departments, but most commonwealths retained some boards and commissions that insulated certain agencies from direct gubernatorial control. In addition, such elected state officers as attorneys general, auditors, and secretaries of state survived the reorganization onslaught and remained independent of the governors.

Meanwhile, the governors were taking joint action to enhance their clout on the national scene. The Governors' Conference had considered serious questions in the past, but many observers in the early 1960s regarded it as largely a social gathering. In truth, politicking and parties seemed to have taken priority over policy at many of the conferences. Yet during the late 1960s and early 1970s, as governors grew more discontented with federal categorical grants hamstringing state action and became greedy for unrestricted federal cash, the conferences took on a more serious tone. The governors increasingly felt the need for a stronger, united voice in their struggle with the federal government, and the Governors' Conference was the natural medium for expressing the governors' views. Moreover, the conference stepped up its services to the governors and the states. In 1974 the conference opened a think tank, the Center for Policy Research and Analysis, which investigated policy questions confronting the governors. The following year, the conference authorized the creation of the Hall of States, a headquarters for state offices and lobbying groups in Washington, D.C. Located just fifteen hundred feet from the nation's Capitol, the hall was physical evidence to a sometimes arrogant Congress that the states were powerful entities and their governors were not about to yield passively to big brother in Washington. Then in 1977 the conference changed its name to the National Governors' Association, thus indicating that it was no longer simply an annual meeting but now an ongoing organization pursuing the interests of the state executives 365 days a year.[42]

With increased clout at home and in Washington, governors were attracting the attention of journalists and academics who had once scorned them as irrelevant to the increasingly centralized government of the nation. By the 1970s observers were commenting on the new breed of governors, who seemed markedly different from those of the past. In 1974 the distinguished columnist David Broder wrote of "the astonishing rise in the status of the state executives." "For most of the past two generations, the American governors have been pitiable figures," Broder claimed. "Penniless, powerless, prone to defeat if they sought to push progressive measures on their legislatures, they were — with a few notable exceptions — richly entitled to the contempt they received from the public and the press." But according to Broder, times had changed, for never had he known "a group of 50 governors — from New England to Dixie — as capable [as] the current crop." The leaders of the Governors' Conference were no longer "political pipsqueaks and goodtime Charlies" but executives worthy of respect.[43]

Political scientist Larry Sabato picked up on this theme when he wrote of "the American governorship transformed" in his 1978 book *Goodbye to Goodtime Charlie*. According to Sabato, "governors as a class [had] outgrown the term 'good-time Charlie.' . . . Once ill prepared to govern and less prepared to lead, governors [had] welcomed into their ranks a new breed of vigorous, incisive, and thoroughly trained leaders." In other words, the pipsqueaks of the benighted past had yielded to a corps of skilled dynamos. Sabato admitted that "some governors of the early 1900s could rival in competence" the governors of the 1970s, but still he contended that overall, the "renaissance" executives were a much more impressive lot.[44]

With longer terms and the right to succeed themselves, governors commanded more respect from state-level politicians. A more dynamic governors' conference won the attention of Congress and the president. And syndicated columnists and political scientists were no longer so dismissive of the state executives. The prevailing image of the governors was changing, and the result was new prestige and heightened political clout.

Yet this new image did not totally reflect reality. Contrary to the rhetoric of Broder and Sabato, governors as a group had never been irrelevant pipsqueaks. Nor were the executives of earlier decades grossly inferior in ability to those of the 1970s. Charles Evans Hughes, Woodrow Wilson, and the bulk of their colleagues would not have felt intellectually inferior to the chief executives attending the Governors' Conference of 1974. Earl Warren, Thomas Dewey, Ellis Arnall, and Luther Hodges would not have proved politically maladroit compared with the governors of the 1970s. In the past there had been highly capable executives as well as good-time Charlies, and in the 1970s the same was true. A new class of demigods was not suddenly inhabiting the governors mansions. What had changed was the recognition now accorded the states and their executives. The perceptions of journalists and scholars had changed much more than the governors had. It is noteworthy that David Broder wrote of his new appreciation of the governors in the midst of the Watergate crisis. As the federal government's star was falling, the states seemed to shine brighter. As the image of the president worsened, long-term, straight-arrow governors such as Washington's Daniel Evans and Utah's Calvin Rampton appeared increasingly attractive.

In fact, the governors that Broder lauded were not uniformly impeccable creatures. Five of the fifty chief executives serving in 1974 would eventually be convicted of felonies. Especially scandal-ridden was the reign of Maryland governor Marvin Mandel. Assuming office in 1969, Mandel first proved a popular governor, but during the early 1970s he won some notoriety when he announced his desire to divorce his wife and marry a much younger divorcée. The scorned wife told reporters that Mandel "should see a psychiatrist" and made clear her intention to continue living in the governor's mansion. For a year she remained in the mansion while the governor lived in a hotel. Finally, she agreed to a divorce and the governor remarried. The second wife, however, had expensive tastes, and the first spouse had secured a lucrative divorce settlement with hefty alimony payments. To support his costly lifestyle, Mandel obtained handsome gifts from friends, who in turn received favorable treatment from the state. Unfortunately for Mandel, a jury deemed this arrangement bribery, and in 1977 the governor was convicted and eventually served nineteen months in prison.[45]

Tennessee's Ray Blanton, however, was probably the most notorious governor of the 1970s. Serving from 1975 to 1979, Blanton won fame for his generous pardoning policy, which resulted in the arrest of three key aides for selling pardons and commutations of sentences. But the governor continued to release prisoners; and to stem this flood of pardons, Blanton's successor was sworn in as governor in an emergency ceremony three days ahead of schedule. A country and western song, "Pardon Me, Ray," drew further attention to the scandal, and a leader of Blanton's own Democratic party labeled the governor's actions the "grossest breach of a chief executive's discretionary power in the history of the state." Further investigation found that Blanton had sold state liquor licenses in exchange for 20 percent of the recipients' profits. This latter crime earned the ex-governor a much-deserved prison sentence.[46]

Blanton and Mandel were not typical governors of the 1970s; their malfeasance was the exception to the rule. In the past, commentators had allowed such misbehavior to cloud their vision of the governors, the negative prevailing over the positive. Although relatively few state leaders violated the public trust, state government was labeled corrupt and incompetent. The few governors who stood in schoolhouse doors to bar black students from entering won the publicity. The scores of honest governors who fought successfully for greater school funding were deemed the exception. By the 1970s, however, the attitude was reversed. The Mandels and Blantons were unfortunate anomalies, and finally columnists and political scientists were proclaiming the achievements and competence of state government. The governors of this new age were, for the most part, competent, conscientious figures, but their predecessors had been as well. Some reforms had strengthened the office of governor, but the trend toward longer terms was not a new one, and the idea of administrative restructuring was as old as the century. The greatest change was a change in judgment. Observers now recognized the merits of state executives.

A Renewed Judiciary

Just as the reform agendas for the legislative and executive branches repeated old themes, so the program for judicial change was a familiar one. As in the 1940s and 1950s, there was much talk about centralized court administration, unification of the state court system, and merit selection of judges. But in the 1960s and 1970s the talk produced more action, with an increasing number of states adopting constitutional provisions or legislation to "modernize" their judicial systems. Moreover, this modernized state judiciary, like the legislatures and the state executives, asserted a new sense of independence and self-confidence. By the close of the 1970s, state supreme courts were not necessarily following in the jurisprudential footsteps of the federal government's highest tribunal, and legal scholars were turning their attention to the previously ignored subject of state constitutional law.

Indicative of the reform spirit of the 1960s and 1970s was the increased success of campaigns for unified state court systems and central court administration. By 1976 forty-six states employed administrators charged with such tasks as managing court finances, assembling data on caseloads from courts throughout the state, conducting research on judicial operation and procedure, and recommending reassignment of lower court judges to expedite the administration of justice. The central administrative bureaucracy also expanded markedly during the late 1960s and the 1970s. In 1973 32 percent of the offices of state court administrator had more than ten employees; three years later this figure was up to 51 percent.[47] In the 1940s New Jersey had pioneered state administration of courts, and it remained a bulwark of centralized management. From 1950 to 1982 the number of staff in the New Jersey court administrator's office soared from 9 to 276.[48]

States adopted other facets of the unified court system, too, thereby ensuring a new degree of order and central supervision. Throughout the nation, legislators gradually pushed through measures that abolished a confusing array of petty tribunals presided over by magistrates with no legal training and enacted statutes reorganizing the lower courts and eliminating overlapping jurisdiction. Lawmakers also created state commissions on judicial qualifications to hear complaints regarding judges from throughout the state and determine what, if any, disciplinary measures should be taken. In 1960 California established the first such commission, and by 1978 forty-eight of the states maintained panels for judging the conduct of judges. Wielding new central supervisory authority, these state commissions could remove, suspend, reprimand, or simply monitor county and district judges. In addition, a growing number of states were assuming full responsibility for funding the courts. Rather than to delegate financing to counties or other localities, by 1978 at least twenty states funded virtually all judicial expenses.[49] Legislative appropriations were intended to ensure adequate funding throughout the state, in poor as well as rich localities.

The pace of change was especially dramatic in some states. For example, during the early 1970s, Alabama transformed its court structure. Recognized as one of the nation's worst, the state's system was an embarrassment and badly in need of reform. "When I went to national conferences," an Alabama judge admitted, "I would kind of mumble about where I came from."[50] Alabama's constitution of 1901 permitted the legislature to create courts whenever it deemed necessary, and the result was a confusing patchwork. By the early 1970s,

the inferior courts bore twenty-three different names in different sections of
the state, and the makeshift structure was plagued by overlapping jurisdiction
and a bewildering variety of sometimes clashing procedural rules.[51] No central
authority imposed order on the state's thirty-eight circuits. According to one
observer, the Alabama system was "analogous to a corporation with 38 branch
offices [but] with no board of directors or executive level management."[52]

In 1971 incoming chief justice Howell T. Heflin set to work to impose the
needed executive-level control. As president of the state bar association in the
mid-1960s, Heflin began lobbying for reform; but once he became the state's
highest judicial officer, he stepped up the pressure and achieved his goals. According to *Time* magazine, "as soon as he had assumed office he began sweet-
talking the legislature and electorate into reforming the state's briarpatch of
conflicting jurisdictions and ludicrous rules."[53] In 1971 the legislature responded
by authorizing the supreme court to promulgate simplified rules of procedure
for Alabama's courts. It also assigned the chief justice administrative supervision over all the trial courts in the state. To aid Heflin in carrying out this function, the legislature created a department of court management and authorized
the hiring of a state court administrator. Heflin also won added authority to
reassign judges to cope with overcrowded dockets and to transfer cases among
appellate courts to expedite the handling of litigation. Continuing the reform
momentum, Alabama voters in 1972 approved a constitutional amendment
abolishing justice-of-peace courts, and the next year they ratified a new judicial article for the state constitution that authorized a total reorganization of
the state court system. This new article consolidated the existing hodgepodge
of trial courts into a uniform system of municipal, district, and circuit courts
and required that all judges be lawyers. Following adoption of the article, the
legislature fulfilled another reform desire when it authorized state funding of
the courts. By 1977 the state treasury was financing 90 to 95 percent of judicial
expenditures.[54]

Some Alabamans attacked this centralization of judicial authority. One
lower court judge claimed that Heflin's efforts to strengthen the position of
chief justice "would put the power to . . . run the courts in the hands of one
person located in Montgomery, Alabama," which was "a long way from [the]
little inferior courts and, in all probability, such a person would not understand
and know the real needs of [the] people so far as the local courts [were] concerned." Another local court official warned that under the unified structure
"the entire judiciary system of the state of Alabama would be under an absolute dictatorship of the Alabama Supreme Court and a central court commission." Summing up the feelings of many opponents, a local judge asserted that
the new judicial article of the state constitution was "another step in destroy-

ing local government."[55] Heflin, however, proved victorious and won plaudits from lawyers and jurists nationwide for achieving the agenda of Arthur Vanderbilt in formerly backward Alabama.

Many states further embraced the ideal of professionalism by opting for the Missouri plan of merit selection of judges. During the 1960s and 1970s, this reform scheme won strong support from bar associations, legal scholars, and judges throughout the country. Whereas only two states followed Missouri's lead before 1960, over the next two decades twenty additional states adopted the plan. In each of these states, a nominating commission submitted a short list of qualified candidates for judicial office, and the governor would appoint one of the nominees. Then in the next general election, the voters would decide whether to retain the appointee. The plan seemed to ensure that professional qualifications, not politics, would determine who served on the state courts. Like the elimination of nonlawyer judges, it was a step toward greater expertise on the bench, a goal that was basic to the campaign to modernize state courts.

Typical of the many state campaigns to adopt the Missouri Plan was that in Indiana. A constitutional amendment embodying the merit scheme appeared on Indiana's ballot in November 1970, and backers mobilized to win voter approval. In advertisements and talks, they repeatedly equated the promised nonpartisan professionalism of the merit plan with modernization. Ads read, "Hoosiers! Only YOU can give Indiana its chance for COURT MODERNIZATION!" And supporters of the amendment urged voters, "Take your high court judges out of politics."[56] On election day 58 percent of Hoosier voters opted for modernization, reiterating a sentiment that was sweeping the nation. The horse-and-buggy courts of untrained justices of the peace and the judicial rule of political hacks had to be eliminated. State courts had to be modernized, and modernization meant professionalism.

Thus, by the late 1970s, the states had moved much closer to the goals of judicial professionalism and court unification. Arthur Vanderbilt won the first notable victories in the midcentury, but during the 1960s and 1970s, lawmakers across the country were taking action. Often this took the form of piecemeal change, with creation of an office of court administrator in one legislative session, the abolition of justice-of-the-peace courts during the following biennium, and the approval of a constitutional amendment to reorganize the lower courts in an election five years later. But every state felt the influence of the reform cause: the courts of 1980, like the legislatures, were notably different from their counterparts of 1960.

Also different was the attitude of a number of state court justices toward their state constitutions and the U.S. Supreme Court. Whereas in the 1950s and 1960s, state jurists had applied the federal constitution's First Amendment as interpreted by the Warren Court to freedom of expression cases and the Fourth, Fifth, and Sixth Amendments to criminal justice questions, during the 1970s an increasing number of judges turned to their state constitutions and specifically to the state bills of rights as independent sources of protection for individual liberties. In more than 300 cases decided from 1970 to 1986, state supreme courts based their affirmation of rights solely on state constitutional provisions, often granting broader protection under their state charters than the U.S. Supreme Court was willing to grant under the federal bill of rights.[57] State court justices no longer felt compelled to interpret articles in state bills of rights as the U.S. Supreme Court did parallel provisions in the federal constitution. In other words, guarantees of free speech in a state constitution did not necessarily mean the same thing as those in the federal charter, and one might have greater rights in Sacramento than in Washington, D.C. State jurists awoke to the fact that California and New Jersey, as well as the United States, had constitutions, and each document could be interpreted independently.

This emerging reliance on state constitutions was known as the new judicial federalism, and by the late 1970s and 1980s, it was being discussed in law review articles and bar association addresses throughout the nation. It reflected an awakening sense of confidence at the state level. Just as legislatures and governors were proclaiming a new activism, state courts were rebelling against an unthinking deference to the views of jurists in the nation's capital. The state courts were reformed and ready to assert their authority.

Encouraging this trend was the growing conservatism of the U.S. Supreme Court presided over by Chief Justice Warren Burger. Frustrated by the Burger Court's predilection for chipping away at the federal guarantees regarding criminal procedure and freedom of expression, liberal state jurists recognized that their state bills of rights could provide the protection that the Burger Court was denying. The state constitutions offered alternative guarantees that state jurists could use to defend liberty within their jurisdictions. Moreover, so long as the state decision rested on independent state constitutional grounds, the ruling was not subject to review by the federal Supreme Court. The state supreme courts were the final arbiters of state constitutional questions, and it was established doctrine that the federal court would defer to their judgment on such questions. State courts could not narrow rights guaranteed by the federal constitution. Instead, that constitution as interpreted by the federal Supreme Court ensured a minimum level of rights to all Americans, no matter their state of residence. But the state courts could interpret their own constitutions to add to this federal minimum, and after 1970 some state jurists did so.

Among those encouraging this state activism were the frustrated liberal dissenters on the Burger Court, most notably Justice William Brennan. A former member of the New Jersey Supreme Court who had served under Chief Justice Arthur Vanderbilt, Brennan was aware of the potential of the finest state courts, and in a series of pronouncements he urged the state judiciary to exercise this potential in defense of liberty. In a 1975 dissent from a Court decision weakening the famed *Miranda* ruling, Brennan reminded state jurists that no state was "precluded by the decision from adhering to higher standards under state law. Each State has power to impose higher standards governing police practices under state law than is required by the Federal Constitution."[58] Two years later, Brennan explained this position further in an article in the *Harvard Law Review:* he observed that state constitutions were "a font of individual liberties, their protections often extending beyond those required by the Supreme Court's interpretation of federal law." Assertion of state-protected rights was especially vital given the trend of Burger Court rulings. "With federal scrutiny diminished," Brennan claimed, "state courts must respond by increasing their own."[59]

Brennan was telling state jurists to think for themselves, avoid ill-considered Burger Court arguments, and protect individual rights through reliance on their state constitutions. Brennan's words were not ignored. A New Jersey Supreme Court justice referred to Brennan's article as "the Magna Carta of state constitutional law," and by 1981 it had been cited by appellate courts in more than fifteen states as well as in scores of law review articles written by authors from twenty-eight states.[60] Moreover, Brennan continued to applaud the independence of state jurists in interpreting their constitutions. In 1986 he proclaimed that the "rediscovery by state supreme courts of the broader protections afforded their own citizens by their state constitutions" was "probably the most important development in constitutional jurisprudence" of the 1970s and 1980s.[61] A year later, Brennan proclaimed, "The state laboratories are once again open for business."[62]

Yet the new judicial federalism appealed not only to liberals like Brennan who sought alternative protection for rights. Conservatives, including Chief Justice Burger, also endorsed the revival of federalism and the assertion of state rights in the defense of liberty. In 1976 Burger wrote, "The 50 states cannot exercise leadership in a national sense, but this does not mean they should not be allowed the independence and freedom that was plainly contemplated by the concept of federalism."[63] Four years later, the U.S. Supreme Court unanimously upheld a California Supreme Court decision that interpreted the free speech provision of California's constitution as granting protection that the federal Supreme Court had earlier denied under the federal constitution. In an opinion written by the conservative Justice William Rehnquist, the Court held that the federal precedent did not "limit the authority of the State to exercise its . . . sovereign right to adopt in its own Constitution individual liberties more expansive than those conferred by the Federal Constitution."[64] Both right and left were ready to support the new judicial federalism, though their motives differed. A California Supreme Court justice noted, "The conservatives' concern over federalism and states' rights intersects—at least for the moment— with the liberals' concern over safeguarding individual rights."[65] Conservatives favored reestablishing the proper balance between state and federal power. Liberals wanted to ensure a proper balance between individual rights and government authority. The new judicial federalism served both their purposes.

Fear of eroding individual and states' rights, however, was not the only factor encouraging independent state action. Declining respect for the federal courts also spurred state independence. The members of the Burger Court rarely agreed on anything, and their rulings usually were accompanied by an array of concurrences and dissents. To an even greater degree than in the past, there was confusion as to Court doctrine. One state supreme court justice summed up the feelings of many when he complained: "A lot of Supreme Court doctrines are no longer persuasive, but filled with fuzzy, soft terminology which has no cutting edge. When the Court's doctrinal cogency begins to fall apart, we have states saying, in effect, 'We don't have to do it that way.'"[66] In other words, the U.S. Supreme Court was not doing a very good job of interpreting the federal constitution, so there was no compelling argument for the state courts to interpret parallel state constitutional provisions in accord with federal rulings. Frankly, an increasing number of state supreme court justices felt they could do better than Burger and his colleagues.

Consequently, during the 1970s and early 1980s, a number of state jurists cast their lot with the new judicial federalism. Perhaps the most dedicated advocate of independent state action was Oregon Supreme Court justice Hans A. Linde. As early as 1970, Linde was arguing that "claims raised under the state constitution should always be dealt with and disposed of before reaching a fourteenth amendment claim of deprivation of due process or equal protection." Furthermore, he was challenging as "too facile" the "customary assumption that the guarantees in the state constitution [were] intend[ed] to protect the same interests against the same abuses as those in the federal Constitution."[67] In a series of articles and addresses over the next two decades, he was to repeat these same two contentions. State judges should rule on state constitutional claims first and only if necessary then proceed to federal claims. And similarly worded state and federal provisions should not be assumed to mean the same thing. These were the basic precepts of Linde's judicial federalism, and he believed both the bar and the bench had to wake up and take notice of the state constitutions. In 1981 Linde made this clear when he remarked, "A lawyer today representing someone who claims some constitutional protection and who does not argue that the state constitution provides that protection is skating on the edge of malpractice."[68]

Some state judges, however, not only expounded the virtues of the new judicial federalism; they were also applying it in their court opinions. In the vanguard was the California Supreme Court. In a series of cases, the liberal state court interpreted the protections afforded by the California constitution more broadly than the U.S. Supreme Court construed parallel sections in the federal constitution. Whereas the Burger Court had held that a confession obtained in violation of the *Miranda* ruling could be used in cross-examination to impeach the credibility of the defendant, in 1976 the California court held that such a reference to an inadmissible confession violated the state's guarantee against self-incrimination. The California jurists declared that the U.S. Supreme Court's ruling was "not persuasive authority in any state prosecution in California," and they reaffirmed "the independent nature of the California Constitution" and their "responsibility to separately define and protect the rights of California citizens despite conflicting decisions of the United States Supreme Court interpreting the federal Constitution."[69] In 1973 the U.S. Supreme Court rejected an equal-protection challenge to inequitable school funding resulting from differences in the property tax bases of local school districts. The federal equal-protection clause did not mandate equal funding for poor and rich districts. But three years later, the California Supreme Court struck down such inequities in school funding on the basis of a state provision guaranteeing equal privileges and immunities to citizens of California.[70] Then in 1979 the California court held that the state's guarantee of free speech protected a person's right to solicit signatures for a petition in a privately owned shopping center. Seven years earlier the federal Supreme Court had held that the First Amendment to the federal constitution did not guarantee such a right.[71] California's most vocal proponent of such independent action was Justice Stanley Mosk, who in 1976 wrote of the "new states' rights" and proclaimed "a phoenix-like resurrection of federalism . . . evidenced by state courts' reliance upon provisions of state constitutions."[72] Mosk, like Linde, was telling his fellow justices and the legal profession as a whole that a new era had arrived, and California's highest court appeared to be the harbinger of this age of independence.

Other state supreme courts also opted for an independent course in a number of rulings. The Hawaii and Pennsylvania supreme courts joined California in interpreting their state guarantees against self-incrimination more broadly than the protection afforded by the U.S. Supreme Court under the Fifth Amendment.[73] Moreover, the Hawaii high court granted that state's citizenry broader protection against unreasonable search and seizure than the federal tribunal was willing to guarantee under the U.S. Constitution. Declaring its independence, the Hawaii court noted, "[An] opinion of the United States Supreme Court . . . is merely another source of authority, admittedly to be afforded respectful consideration, but which we are free to accept or reject in establishing the outer limits of protection afforded by the Hawaii Constitution."[74] The New Jersey, Pennsylvania, and Washington supreme courts followed California's example and rejected the federal argument when ruling on freedom of expression on private property. Oregon's highest tribunal went so far as to grant obscenity protection under its constitution's guarantees of free expression, thus deviating from the U.S. Supreme Court's long-standing refusal to extend First Amendment protection to obscene speech.[75]

Not all state courts joined in the new states' rights cause. In some states jurists hardly seemed to realize that there was any such phenomenon as the new judicial federalism.[76] According to one study, during the period 1981 to 1985, judges relied exclusively on state constitutional law in less than 20 percent of state criminal justice and bill-of-rights cases, and in only 20 percent more did they base their rulings on a combination of state and federal guarantees.[77] Moreover, in some states the voters were undoing the work of the liberal proponents of this new federalism. For example, in 1982 an initiative measure amended Florida's constitution so that the state's search and seizure clause would "be construed in conformity with the 4th Amendment to the United States Constitution, as interpreted by the United States Supreme Court." That same year, an initiative proposition curbed the liberalism of justices like Stanley Mosk by amending the California constitution to read, "Except as provided by statute . . . relevant evidence shall not be excluded in any criminal proceeding."[78] Yet, by the mid-1980s, state constitutional law had come a long way. Just as the state legislative and executive branches seemed infused with a new confidence and activism, so the judiciary was awakening and redefining the rights of state citizens.

Financing the Reformed State

As the state legislative, executive, and judicial branches were gaining a reputation for newfound dynamism, the state taxing structures were also undergoing renovations that enabled them to better shoulder fiscal burdens. During the 1960s and 1970s, state revenues rose rapidly: legislatures approved new sales and income taxes and hiked the rates of existing ones. In addition, state governors launched an assault on the federal treasury to win a share of Uncle Sam's tax receipts. In the end, however, the states proved better able to balance their budgets than the federal government, casting doubt on gubernatorial plaints of poverty. During the 1960s and the 1970s, the states proved that they were able to fund the public's growing demands and were not fiscal incompetents that had to be propped up by an omnicompetent federal treasury.

These were grim decades for foes of taxation. Each legislative session, governors asked for tax hikes; and especially during the 1960s, lawmakers generally granted such increases. About half the states raised taxes in the 1962–63 biennium, and more than three-fourths did so in 1964–65. Throughout the remainder of the 1960s, the proportion fluctuated between these figures, as one state after another felt compelled to expand revenues.[79] Between 1959 and 1970, states enacted a total of 410 new taxes or increases in their sales, income, or excise levies.[80] In the late 1970s, a tax revolt slowed the rate of expansion, but overall the trajectory was definitely upward. Whereas in 1962 state own-source revenue amounted to only 6.6 percent of the total personal income in the United States, by 1975 this figure was up to 9.1 percent. By comparison, the figure for federal revenues remained almost constant, dipping slightly from 23.5 percent in 1962 to 23.1 percent in 1975. Yet states were not only taxing more; they were also borrowing more. From 1959 to 1975, state debts rose more than fourfold, from $16.9 billion to $72.1 billion, whereas the federal debt did not quite double.[81]

Increased spending on education accounted for the largest share of the rise in state expenditures. Parents desired better schools and expanded systems of higher education, and teachers demanded increased salaries. Consequently, the states felt compelled to raise more money for schooling. Moreover, the state share of the total education bill climbed gradually as state lawmakers continued to relieve localities of some of the funding burden. In 1959–60 states accounted for 39.1 percent of school revenues; in 1979–80 this was up to 46.8 percent.[82] By increasing their share of school funding, the states also were able to respond to the mounting clamor for relief from local property taxes in support of education. Always hated, the property tax was once again a popular target for attack during the 1960s and 1970s. Virtually every lawmaker seeking reelection promised state action to limit property levies. By 1975 all of the states had adopted some property tax relief measures, with homestead exemptions and relief for the elderly proving especially popular. Twenty-five states also financed circuit breaker programs. These schemes granted relief when the property tax bill exceeded a certain percentage of the taxpayer's household income.[83] But no matter what form the relief took, all of the programs in effect required the states to assume greater financial responsibility for local functions.

The bottom line, then, was that the states had to raise more revenue. They generally did so by exploiting the two forms of taxation that had dominated state financing since the 1930s—the income tax and the sales tax. A number of states that had previously failed to exploit one or the other of these sources now yielded to fiscal pressure and embraced them. And other states simply raised their rates.

For example, between 1959 and 1969, twelve states abandoned their misgivings about the general sales tax and adopted such levies. Among the converts were Wisconsin, New York, and Massachusetts, all of which had pioneered the income tax and relied heavily upon it for decades. By 1970 forty-five of the fifty states profited from the general sales tax, and the five holdouts were the less populated states of Delaware, New Hampshire, Alaska, Montana, and Oregon. Thus, an estimated 98 percent of the American population lived in sales tax states. Furthermore, between 1959 and 1977, state lawmakers approved a total of seventy-six sales tax increases as rates inched upward from 2 or 3 percent to 5 or 6 percent.[84]

Advocates of the sales tax justified it as necessary to stave off fiscal crisis and to finance expanded services, especially improvements in education. In addition, it was sold as a remedy for the pain inflicted by local property taxes. In his campaign for adoption of a sales tax in Massachusetts, Governor John Volpe successfully exploited each of these arguments. Adoption of the sales tax had been debated in Massachusetts for decades. A state tax commissioner suggested it in 1935, a special taxation committee recommended it in 1947, and Governor Foster Furcolo failed three times to win approval of the new levy in 1957 and 1959. In 1965 Volpe renewed the fight when he asked for legislative approval of a 3 percent sales tax with revenue designated for distribution to the state's cities and towns. In his budget message to the legislature, he claimed that the state "had to face up to the multi-million dollar deficit" and "make up for the previously employed financial 'gimmicks'" that had brought it "to the end of the fiscal road." Specifically, Volpe presented his proposed levy as an "education tax" that would provide needed funds to local schools and head off local property tax hikes. "Forty-six of our sister states assume a higher percentage of the education expenditures of local government than we do," Volpe told the lawmakers. "Therefore, unless we increase state aid to our municipalities, the bulk of our ever-increasing education costs must continue to be borne locally." And reliance on local government meant reliance on property taxes, which, the governor noted ominously, had "been increasing at alarming rates."[85] The sales tax would supposedly aid schools, rein in the property tax, and provide new fiscal hope for Massachusetts. The *Boston Globe* agreed, claiming that "the financial crisis of the state [was] ever more pressing." Massachusetts had the highest per capita tax burden in the nation, and consequently the *Globe* concluded, "The cities and towns must have relief."[86] Despite opposition from labor groups and many Democrats, Volpe and the *Globe* prevailed, and in March 1966 the governor signed a sales tax bill into law, thereby opening a new source of revenue.

Debate over the sales tax in other states repeated some of the same themes heard in Massachusetts. In 1966 Virginia's Governor Mills Godwin pushed a sales tax measure through his legislature, and again local aid and concern for school funding eased passage. The act authorized the state to impose a 2 percent sales tax and gave localities the option of imposing an additional 1 percent tax to be collected by the state and then returned to the localities. Half of the state's sales tax revenues were to be distributed to localities on the basis of school-age population.[87] The result was more money for the state and relief for burdened local units. Vermont was the last state in the twentieth century to add a sales tax, and like Massachusetts's Volpe, Vermont's incoming governor, Deane Davis, sold the new levy by stressing the state's dire fiscal straits. In his inaugural address delivered in January 1969, Davis told the state legislature, "After exhausting all other possibilities and only as a last resort, I must ask you to face together with me the prospect of a tax program adequate to meet our needs." According to Davis, Vermont already had the highest income tax in the nation, so he deemed a sales tax the only alternative. The legislature acceded, passing the levy in April 1969. Writing of the new fiscal era in his autobiography, Davis emphasized that the state "substantially raised the level of state support for public education" and thus gave "some relief to property owners from skyrocketing property taxes in the towns and cities."[88] In Vermont, as in Massachusetts, state aid to schools and property tax relief were achievements a governor was anxious to boast about.

While Volpe, Godwin, and Davis were securing passage of sales taxes, other governors were forced to embrace the income tax. Between 1959 and 1977 eleven additional states adopted the personal income tax, bringing the total to forty-two states with broad-based income levies and two states with limited taxes on income from interest and dividends. Moreover, the newcomers to the income tax ranks included some of the nation's largest industrial states. For example, Michigan adopted the new revenue source in 1967, Illinois in 1969, Ohio and Pennsylvania in 1971, and New Jersey in 1976. The only large states holding out in the late 1970s were Florida and Texas, and in the latter the absence of both personal and corporate income taxes was an article of faith that no governor in the late twentieth century would be able to break. Between 1959 and 1977, states had also enacted seventy-five increases in their personal income taxes. As a result of the new adoptions and the increases, the share of state tax revenues contributed by the individual income tax rose from 12.2 percent in 1960 to 28.1 percent in 1982.[89]

Advocates of the new income taxes used some of the same sales pitches as did proponents of the sales levies. For example, in 1969 Republican governor Richard Ogilvie of Illinois shocked the state's residents and lawmakers by proposing a 45 percent leap in appropriations, to be funded in part by a 4 percent flat-rate income tax. Like most tax-seeking governors, Ogilvie told the legislature that the state was "on the brink of bankruptcy." Despite this insolvent state, the governor claimed the state had to spend far more for its services, especially for education. "Our first priority is elementary and secondary education," he announced in his budget message. Repeating a theme heard throughout the nation, he proclaimed: "Local property taxpayers are presently bearing a disproportionate share of the cost of education. Further increases in property taxes must be prevented — and that is our objective." Consequently, his proposed budget nearly doubled the state funds to be distributed to school districts. To further aid localities, the governor proposed that one-eighth of the revenues from the new state income tax be distributed to local governments with no strings attached. They could spend the money for any service. This latter proposal was designed to appeal especially to Chicago's powerful mayor, Richard Daley, for his city was expected to receive $47.5 million the first year the income tax was levied.[90] After three months of legislative battle, the income tax passed, though Ogilvie had to accept a flat rate of only 2.5 percent. The governor had originally proposed a flat-rate tax because he felt the Illinois Supreme Court would find a graduated income tax in violation of Illinois's constitution. Even the flat-rate levy was deemed constitutionally dubious, given the court's past strictures on the state's taxing power. But within a month after Ogilvie signed the tax act, the state's highest tribunal upheld the new measure, permitting Illinois to profit from a balanced revenue structure based on both sales and income levies.

Two years later, Ohio was to follow Illinois's example and finally embrace the income tax. In a familiar scenario, in March 1971 Democratic governor John Gilligan presented a budget described as "colossal" and "monumental" by both friends and foes. Once again educational funding and property tax relief were key components of the governor's proposal, with Gilligan recommending a marked increase in the state allocation to local school districts. "This education program provides enough new assistance to many districts with very high tax rates to make possible a rollback in property taxes," Gilligan told the legislature.[91] To finance this shift in the school funding burden and the expansion of other programs as well, Gilligan proposed a graduated income tax. By the close of a record-long legislative session, Buckeye lawmakers had approved a state income tax and appropriations that boosted aid to elementary and secondary education by about 35 percent and support for higher education by 25 percent.[92] A lobbyist for the Ohio Education Association hailed the adoption of the tax, saying, "This gets us back in the black." The admiring *Cleveland Plain Dealer* editorialized, "The poor-mouth, pinch-penny days are over. Ohio has been turned around."[93]

The pinch-penny days were over in states across the country. Governors of the 1960s and early 1970s sought more funds, and they succeeded in obtaining them from a balanced system of taxation based on both sales and income. In 1959 only nineteen states had both a broad-based income tax and a general sales tax; by 1977 this number had doubled to thirty-eight as more than three-fourths of the states had opted to exploit both of the principal mainstays of state government. The wave of new levies and tax hikes in the 1960s and early 1970s was, in part, a response to fiscal stress at the state level. Yet the gubernatorial wailing about impending bankruptcy was sometimes exaggerated. Elliot Richardson, Volpe's lieutenant governor and a key figure in securing the Massachusetts sales tax, later admitted, "There was no fiscal crisis as such, we just wanted to be able to do more."[94] This was also the situation in other states where governors proposed to step back from the brink of bankruptcy by increasing expenditures 45 percent. State officials did not sponsor higher taxes simply to meet existing obligations; they did so to assume new obligations. And these new obligations often took the form of aid or relief to local governments, especially for education. By extending further aid to education and property tax–dependent local units, the states were perpetuating a trend evident since the early twentieth century. Throughout the century, Americans sought relief from the shortcomings of the property tax, and this encouraged state assumption of local responsibilities. The pattern persisted in the 1960s and the early 1970s as "bankrupt" states aggressively expanded their roles. The wave of tax reform was not a symptom of the inherent fiscal weakness of the states; it reflected a prevailing desire among policymakers to more fully exploit the states' financial potential and centralize responsibility for services.

But income and sales taxes were not the only revenue sources attracting the governors' attention. Another trove of riches was the federal treasury. Between the end of World War II and the close of 1964, Congress authorized fifty-seven new federal grant-in-aid programs benefiting state and local governments, bringing the total for such aid schemes to eighty. In 1955 Washington, D.C., funneled $3.1 billion to states and localities; by 1964 the figure was over $10.1 billion, and the sum was increasing rapidly as Lyndon Johnson's Great Society spawned a bevy of new programs.[95] Each of these federal grants was for a specific purpose, such as highway construction, vocational education, urban redevelopment, or the building of hospitals. State leaders appreciated the cash, but by the mid-1960s they were rebelling against the confusion bred by such multitudinous grants. In addition, they did not like the many strings attached to the money that severely limited the discretion of state and local officials. In 1966 Governor Robert Smylie of Idaho expressed the view of most of his fellow state executives when he complained that "the growth in number and magnitude of federal grants-in-aid programs" had "produced a jungle of conflicting purposes and administrative chaos." Presenting the solution favored by virtually all of his colleagues in statehouses across the nation, Wyoming's Governor Clifford Hansen declared, "Greater latitude should be given state administrators in implementing programs so as to fit specific needs, through the device of general, noncategorical aid."[96] "No strings attached" was to become the battle cry of the nation's governors. The federal government should hand over the money and then leave the states alone.

Supporting the states in their proposed raid on the federal treasury was the chair of the President's Council of Economic Advisors from 1961 to 1964, Professor Walter Heller of the University of Minnesota. Aided by fellow economist Joseph Pechman, Heller formulated a scheme for revenue sharing whereby the federal government would automatically distribute a percentage of its tax revenues to states and localities with no restrictions on how the funds were to be spent. In 1965 Heller presented the case for such revenue sharing before the National Governors' Conference. The economist explained that "the essence of the case [was] a fiscal mismatch." According to Heller, "the supply of readily available federal revenues in the years ahead [would] rise faster than the demands on the federal purse." But the state and local situation was reversed: "Expenditure demands will rise faster than the readily available revenue supply." Given the coming federal surpluses and the impending state and local debacle, the solution was obvious. The fiscally superior federal government should share its largesse with the fiscally inferior states and localities. "When all is said and done," Heller remarked, "in an era when painful fiscal pressures at the state-local level coexist with pleasant fiscal dividends at the federal level, state and local governments have a commanding case for stronger federal financial support."[97]

Gubernatorial support for general revenue sharing mounted during the late 1960s, and when Richard Nixon assumed office in 1969, revenue sharing was a key plank in his program for changing American government. After almost four years of struggle, Nixon finally secured passage of the State and Local Fiscal Assistance Act on October 1972 and signed it into law at a ceremony at Independence Hall. The site was symbolic, for Nixon asserted that general revenue sharing was "the first step in a comprehensive program of reform" that he described as "a New American Revolution."[98] Secretary of Treasury George Shultz claimed that it marked "the beginning of a new partnership between the federal government and the States and localities," which presented "a reversal of the flow of power and resources from the people to the government in Washington and start[ed] power and resources flowing back to the States and communities."[99] Similarly, the executive director of the Council of State Governments said of general revenue sharing, "Its enactment, hopefully, marks a turning point in the flow of power and decision-making to Washington."[100]

As it turned out, the fiscal assistance act was a small beginning to a short-lived program. It distributed about $6 billion per year, with minimal restrictions as to use. One-third went to the state governments and the remainder to localities. During the early 1970s, this amounted to only about 2 percent of state revenues, and as state tax receipts rose during the inflation-ridden 1970s, the federal government's fixed donation represented an ever-dwindling share of state income. Moreover, federal grants-in-aid to the states totaled $28 billion in 1971–72 and thus far exceeded general revenue-sharing funds.[101] General revenue sharing provided welcome money, but it did not have a marked impact on state receipts.

It was a burden on an overextended federal government, however, and during the late 1970s, congressional opposition to general revenue sharing mounted. Much criticism focused on the fact that the federal government was persistently running a deficit whereas the states enjoyed surpluses and were even reducing taxes. In 1979 Texas senator Lloyd Bentsen noted that nineteen states had cut taxes since the beginning of 1978. Although he recognized that this was "great fun for the Governors because they had surpluses," he argued that it made "little sense for the federal government to worsen its deficit position by paying billions of dollars in revenue sharing funds to states that [were] cutting taxes and running large surpluses." Representative David Obey reported that the legislators in his state of Wisconsin had approved over $900 million in tax relief. "They did that in part because Uncle Sugar sits out here borrowing $2.5 billion to send back to the states; only, we have to pay in interest over $200 million to do it." According to Obey, "That is just nuts." Senator Alan Cranston of California agreed. "The States have been piggy-backing on the federal deficit long enough," Cranston complained.[102] Like many of his fellow lawmakers on Capitol Hill, he could not ignore the deepening federal deficit and the piles of cash in state treasuries.

Responding to such complaints, Congress in 1980 cut off any further revenue sharing to state governments, and in 1986 it halted general revenue sharing with localities. The great experiment in intergovernmental partnership had come to a close. Ultimately, revenue sharing with state governments failed because it was predicated on the false assumption that the federal government would invariably be in better financial shape than the states. Walter Heller and other economists had predicted that the states would topple without a healthy infusion of money from Washington, D.C. The federal income tax was supposedly a limitless source of cash, and the states could never match the fiscal competence of the federal government. Thus, the states could survive only if general revenue sharing supplemented categorical grants.

Yet the fiscal history of the 1970s proved the relative weakness of the federal government and undermined at least part of the rationale for revenue sharing. By 1980 the states remained ready to accept additional money from Washington, D.C., but they no longer accepted the assumption of federal superiority inherent in the thinking of Walter Heller and other "experts" of the 1960s. At the 1980 Eastern Regional Conference of the Council of State Governments, Governor Richard Snelling of Vermont expressed the new confidence in the ability of the states when he asserted, "States today are better at fiscal management, targeting resources, and planning for the future than the federal government, which now stands as the worst example of uncontrolled growth and bad management in the intergovernmental system."[103] Revenue sharing seemingly foundered not because of the incompetence of the states but because of the ineptitude of the federal government. And state leaders like Snelling were willing to express their contempt for the faltering rulers in Washington. Uncle Sam could no longer play sugar daddy, and this earned him the scorn of states that had once prostituted their sovereignty for cash.

In the field of finance, as in jurisprudence and executive and legislative procedure, the states had thus acquired a new self-confidence. By 1980 governors and legislators were no longer so apologetic, and liberal jurists and budget directors were no longer looking to the federal authorities for salvation. State governments had continued to grow more professional, assume expanded responsibility for local functions, and adopt new sources of revenue. In the process they had acquired unwonted recognition as able and dynamic elements of the American system.

Epilogue

‿o‿

The Continuing Evolution

DURING THE 1980s, the states assumed a new significance in the cast of American government. No longer perceived as no-talent spear carriers worthy only to serve the federal prima donna, they were moving to center stage and winning an unaccustomed share of the limelight. President Ronald Reagan touted a New Federalism that seemed to promise a heightened role for the states. Increasingly professional and enjoying favorable reviews from scholarly observers, the reformed legislatures were performing with new confidence, refusing to play a supporting role or yield star status to their governors or the policymakers in Washington, D.C. Assertive state jurists were writing their own scripts and eschewing the lines penned by the U.S. Supreme Court. Meanwhile, the National Governors' Association was drafting authoritative policy statements on education, job creation, and state-federal relations that drew greater attention to the state executives and trumpeted their importance as policy leaders. Moreover, a multitude of governors were taking their show on the road, dramatizing the merits of their states to audiences of deep-pocketed investors in Europe and Asia as well as North America. Once dismissed as insignificant bit players, the states and their leaders were raising their voices and making themselves heard.

By the 1990s, in fact, one of the buzzwords of political discourse was devolution, as scholars, journalists, and political leaders seriously discussed decentralizing government and shifting functions from the national to the state level. Throughout most of the twentieth century, the flow of authority to Washington, D.C., seemed irreversible, and commentators in each decade wrote with tiresome regularity of the withering of the states and the expansion of the federal behemoth. At the close of the century, however, the rhetoric shifted. Frustrated by the seeming ineffectiveness of federal efforts, Americans appeared willing to rely more heavily on the states. Despite the prognostications of pundits throughout the century, people were turning back to Topeka and Boise for solutions and questioning the ability of federal institutions to achieve policy goals. And many state leaders were eager to assume new authority and demonstrate state-level competence.

Yet, as in earlier decades, the states confronted doubters and critics, and state government continued to evolve in response to the demands and indignation of the electorate. The newly appreciated states were not able to bask in the limelight undisturbed by proponents of change. Although they were earning the applause of many commentators, a chorus of catcalls was still to be heard, forcing some changes in the script. The reformed state governments had not achieved immutable perfection.

In some states this continuing evolution entailed the reversal of a trend evident through much of the century. To the shock and dismay of many advocates of professionalization, a movement arose to curb the newly professional legislatures and to limit the prerogatives of their members. Step by step, from Charles McCarthy in Wisconsin, through Frederic Guild in Kansas, to Jesse Unruh in California, state officials had endeavored to achieve more expert, professional legislatures and remedy the faults inherent in the citizen assemblies of farmers and lawyers sojourning in the state capitals for sixty days each biennium. Through improved legislative research services and expert staffing, reformers had sought to transform an uninformed collection of short-term solons into knowledgeable lawmakers capable of determining policy questions. By 1980 they had succeeded to a large degree, yet the general public was not impressed. According to one survey conducted in six states in 1968, 50 percent of the respondents gave positive ratings to the performance of their legislatures. In 1990 a similar survey in seven states received positive replies from only 30 percent of those questioned. In 1968 the unreformed Alabama legislature, ranked the worst in the nation in one reform-minded survey, secured a favorable rating from 65 percent of the Alabama respondents. Twenty-two years later that state's updated, modernized legislature won the approval of only 24 percent.[1] Although other surveys reaped more encouraging results, most observers recognized that reform had not earned the legislatures universal favor.[2] In 1985 a report of the National Conference of State Legislatures concluded: "The modern full-time legislature envisioned by the reformers of the 1960s and 1970s has not fulfilled its promise. A lack of trust has created a gap between legislatures and the public." Legislative reformer Alan Rosenthal of the Eagleton Institute lamented the public's lack of appreciation. "Legislatures really did transform themselves," he observed. "They are an institutional success story, in terms of where they were 20 years ago and where they are now.... It's quite ironic."[3] Apparently everyone was impressed by the modern professional legislatures except the people, a notable exception in a government of the people and for the people.

Indicative of this disenchantment was the increased success of interest groups in avoiding the representative bodies and making law through the initiative process. Use of the initiative procedure had declined after World War II, reaching a low point in the 1960s. Throughout the nation in 1968 there were only ten initiative measures on statewide ballots.[4] During the 1970s, however, the number of initiative proposals rose sharply, and the well-publicized adoption of California's Proposition 13, an initiative tax limit, ushered in a new era of direct legislation. Americans were increasingly willing to obviate their elected representatives and opt for direct democracy. Whereas from 1940 to 1980, 248 initiatives appeared on state ballots, from 1981 to 1992 voters decided the fate of 346 such measures. And the trend was steadily upward. In 1986 there were 41 initiative measures on state ballots, two years later the figure was up to 55, in 1990 it was 65, and in 1992 69.[5] During the 1990s, the success rate of initiative proposals also reached a record high, as the electorate more frequently voted yes on direct legislation. Only twenty-four of the fifty states authorized lawmaking through the initiative procedure, but in such states as California and Oregon, it was a much-exploited means for avoiding representative rule.

The increasing incidence of direct legislation was in part a product of a sophisticated initiative industry that exploited the desire of special interests to secure what state legislatures would not grant them. For a hefty fee, firms specializing in initiative campaigns would collect the requisite number of petition signatures and market a ballot proposition to a sometimes gullible public. Rather than face the informed scrutiny of state legislators, special interests could achieve their ends by selling a proposition to the voters. But the increase in initiative measures also reflected a lack of faith in the elected representatives specifically charged with lawmaking. Reporting on direct democracy in Oregon at the close of the century, columnist David Broder found that "legislators were seen as interlopers, busybodies who had interfered with the sovereign right of the people to make their own laws."[6] Quite simply, many Americans were willing to trust in the amateur judgment of voters rather than rely solely on the professional opinion of career lawmakers aided by expert staff.

In the early 1990s, disgruntled citizens used the initiative to strike at the heart of careerism in the newly professional legislatures. In 1990 voters in Oklahoma, California, and Colorado approved initiative measures limiting the number of years legislators could serve. Two years later the electorate in four-teen additional states endorsed similar initiatives, and by 1995 a total of twenty-two states had adopted legislative term limits. As service in the legislature became a full-time task, the number of career solons increased. Lawmaking was their job, and they intended to remain on the job as long as possible, devel-oping the supposed expertise that resulted from lengthy tenure. By adopting six-, eight-, or twelve-year limits on legislative service, voters sent a definite message to such career lawmakers. The people wanted citizen legislatures; they did not want a body of entrenched lawmakers who spent most of their time in the state capital and knew statehouse lobbyists better than their own con-stituents. Too often professional lawmakers were deemed expert servants of the interests rather than responsive representatives of the people.

This attitude was evident in the campaigns to adopt term limits. Arch-con-servative oilman Lloyd Noble II sponsored and largely financed Oklahoma's initiative campaign. But the proposal won the backing of the incumbent Republican governor, who sought to cure the "electoral rigor mortis" that resulted from the advantages of incumbency. The Democratic candidate for governor also favored limits, emphasizing the close links between lawmakers and special-interest lobbyists.[7] Meanwhile, the California campaign was at-tracting attention nationwide. Not only did the California initiative limit state senators to eight years in office and members of the lower house to six years; it also cut the budget for legislative staff by nearly 40 percent and eliminated pensions for legislators. It boldly aimed to transform the nation's model pro-fessional legislature into a citizens assembly such as was commonplace earlier in the century. Its proponents asserted that the proposal would "put an end to the lifetime legislators," who had "developed cozy relationships with special interests." The measure's backers complained, "A stench of greed and vote-selling hangs over Sacramento because lifetime-in-office incumbents think it's *their* government, not yours."[8]

Such rhetoric appealed to the voters, but the dismantling of the house that Unruh built deeply disturbed defenders of the professional legislature. "I still can't believe it happened here," commented California's speaker of the assem-bly, Willie Brown. "Participating in the electoral process is no longer a career option. It is simply a temporary way station, to be occupied by either those who are marginal or those who are extremely wealthy and idle."[9] Brown's counter-part in Oklahoma claimed that long-serving, experienced bureaucrats and lob-byists would benefit from the reform because they would be able to manipulate the increased number of novice lawmakers. "Entrenched interests will gain from term limits," the Oklahoma speaker succinctly concluded.[10] The Eagleton

Institute's Alan Rosenthal agreed. "The government will be ruled by bureau-crats building up their programs and their budgets without having to contend with strong legislatures," Rosenthal predicted. "That will be a splendid irony for those advocates of term limits who prefer a small government."[11]

Whatever the consequences of this new challenge to state lawmakers, it was clear that voters were not as enamored of professional legislatures as were political scientists such as Rosenthal or politicians such as Brown. Columnist David Broder summed up the message that voters were sending to the legisla-tures: "In that combination of initiatives and term limits, we have seen the clearest expression of the revolt against representative government. It is a com-mand to 'Clear out of there, you bums. You're none of you worth saving. We want to clean house of the lot of you. And we'll take over the job of writing the laws ourselves.'"[12] To the despair of many pundits, a supposedly unthinking electorate seemed dedicated to undoing the advances of the recent past and in the process undermining representative government at the state level.

The revival of the initiative and the term-limits campaign might have rep-resented a setback for those seeking a professional legislature of career law-makers, but there was little indication that the course of state government had shifted into reverse. As parents and concerned citizens worried about edu-cation, the states stepped up their supervision of local school districts, pump-ing in more money and setting additional standards. A number of states were not only funding highways but also subsidizing rail transportation in an effort to divert travelers from the overcrowded pavements. Health and welfare pro-grams filled the agendas of state legislatures, and governors were still stalking the world in search of jobs and industry. Although there was discontent, the states were major players in American government, and there was little doubt that they would remain so in the early decades of the twenty-first century.

Term limits would not derail the states, for the states' rise in the American system was not an overnight occurrence tied simply to the reform efforts of the Eagleton Institute or Jesse Unruh. Instead, it had transpired over many decades as state government adapted to a mounting belief in expertise and centralized administration and a growing skepticism of the partisan amateur and unfettered local rule. During the Progressive era, crusaders for economy and efficiency achieved a greater degree of state-level administration and supervision. The motorists of the 1920s reinforced this trend as they rallied in support of the professional engineers in the state highway departments and the gasoline levies necessary to fund thousands of miles of new pavements. Then during the 1930s, tax-weary voters chose to curb the hated property tax, and states responded with new imposts that filled state treasuries, leaving localities ever more dependent on the states. In the postwar era, the state met the heightened demand for better and more schooling with still more taxes and further intervention. The general trajectory was consistent throughout the decades. When confronted with a problem, state policymakers of the twentieth century, unlike their nineteenth-century counterparts, assumed that state-level administrators and the state treasury could best meet the crisis. Nineteenth-century lawmakers had delegated authority to county and township officials, boards of trustees, and corporate directors. Twentieth-century lawmakers opted for greater central supervision or direct state action.

The prevailing forces of centralization likewise strengthened the federal government, but a countervailing belief in dispersed power kept the states very much alive. Repeatedly, Congress eschewed a total federal takeover of responsibility, opting instead for cooperative effort with the states. Although many commentators thought the states were dead or dying, devotion to traditional notions of federalism kept the nation's lawmakers from actually leveling a fatal blow. Moreover, recurrent wars, foreign crises, and economic depression saddled the federal government with mounting expenses and a burdensome debt that made it reluctant or unable to take on additional tasks. In the wake of World War I, it left the funding of highways primarily to the states; and in the aftermath of World War II, it refused to assume responsibility for education. Finally, in the 1980s the federal government abandoned general revenue sharing because it could no longer afford a policy of unrestricted handouts.

The states and their leaders, then, were never irrelevant ciphers in the story of American government. Twentieth-century American history was made in Albany and Sacramento as well as Washington, D.C.: what happened in statehouses was important. At the close of the century, special interests were investing millions of dollars in initiative campaigns because they knew that state laws counted. State measures could enrich or burden a corporation, protect the environment or ravish it, relieve a class of taxpayers or drain them, perpetuate traditional morality or foster alternative lifestyles. Likewise, term limits were an issue because the electorate knew that legislators affected their lives. Consequently, voters wanted to ensure that lawmakers were not indifferent, life-tenure careerists but responsive representatives of the people. Over the course of the twentieth century, the states had largely shed their role as delegators of authority and become increasingly significant actors in American government. They had risen to new prominence, and at the close of the century their continuing vitality proved wrong earlier prognostications of death. In the 1980s and 1990s, as in the 1920s and 1930s, the states were alive and deserving of attention.

Notes

Chapter 1. A Flawed Prognosis

1. James Bryce, *The American Commonwealth*, 2d ed., rev., 2 vols. (London: Macmillan, 1891), 1:537; Elihu Root, "How to Preserve the Local Self-Government of the States," in *Selected Articles on States Rights*, comp. Lamar T. Beman (New York: H. W. Wilson, 1926), p. 68; Luther Gulick, "Reorganization of the State," *Civil Engineering* 3 (August 1933): 421; Donald C. Sampson, "State Accomplishments during the Past Twenty Years," *State Government* 41 (autumn 1968): 244; *New York Times*, 8 August 1965, sec. 4, p. 2.

2. Harold J. Laski, "The Obsolescence of Federalism," *New Republic*, 3 May 1939, p. 367.

3. Robert S. Allen, "The Shame of the States," in *Our Sovereign State*, ed. Robert S. Allen (New York: Vanguard Press, 1949), pp. vii, xi–xii.

4. Terry Sanford, *Storm over the States* (New York: McGraw-Hill, 1967), pp. vii, 8.

5. The chief work on the states and the New Deal is James T. Patterson, *The New Deal and the States: Federalism in Transition* (Princeton, N.J.: Princeton University Press, 1969).

6. Ira Sharkansky, *The Maligned States: Policy Accomplishments, Problems, and Opportunities* (New York: McGraw-Hill, 1972), pp. 1–2.

7. John E. Bebout, "The Emerging State Governments: A Challenge to Academia," *State Government* 45 (summer 1972): 165–79.

8. Dan W. Lufkin, *Many Sovereign States* (New York: David McKay, 1975), p. v.

9. Carl E. Van Horn, "The Quiet Revolution," in *The State of the States*, ed. Carl E. Van Horn (Washington, D.C.: Congressional Quarterly Press, 1989), p. 1.

10. Mary Graham, "Why States Can Do More," *American Prospect*, no. 36 (January–February 1998): 63–64, 66–70; Richard Rothstein, "When States Spend More," *American Prospect*, no. 36 (January–February 1998): 72–79.

11. John D. Donahue, *Disunited States* (New York: Basic Books, 1997); Daniel Mc-Groarty, review of *Disunited States*, by John D. Donahue, *Spectrum* 70 (summer 1997): 36.

12. Larry Sabato, *Goodbye to Good-time Charlie: The American Governorship Transformed*, 2d ed. (Washington, D.C.: Congressional Quarterly Press, 1983), pp. 1–2.

13. Morton Keller, "State Power Needn't Be Resurrected Because It Never Died," *Governing* 2 (October 1988): 53–57.

Chapter 2. A New Era in State Government

1. Actually, local interests had virtually always framed the charters and local legislation relating to municipalities. Home-rule laws did not, then, really shift power from the state to localities. Instead, they rationalized the system of charter making, allowing the local electorate a larger voice in the process and encouraging a broader representation of local interests. In other words, they shifted power at the local level rather than denying the state a traditional role. See Jon C. Teaford, *The Unheralded Triumph: City Government in America, 1870–1900* (Baltimore: Johns Hopkins University Press, 1984), pp. 103–22.

2. Paul S. Reinsch, *American Legislatures and Legislative Methods* (New York: Century, 1907), p. 132; George H. Haynes, "Representation in State Legislatures," *Annals of the American Academy of Political and Social Science* 15 (March 1900): 70–71; George H. Haynes, "Representation in State Legislatures III — The Southern States," *Annals of the American Academy of Political and Social Science* 16 (July 1900): 105.

3. George H. Haynes, "Representation in State Legislatures IV — The Western States," *Annals of the American Academy of Political and Social Science* 16 (September 1900): 75.

4. E. L. Godkin, "The Decline of Legislatures," *Atlantic Monthly,* July 1897, p. 51.

5. Samuel P. Orth, "Our State Legislatures," in *Readings on American State Government,* ed. Paul S. Reinsch (Boston: Ginn, 1911), p. 52.

6. Emmet O'Neal, "Distrust of State Legislatures — The Cause; The Remedy," *Proceedings of the Sixth Meeting of the Governors* (1913): 216.

7. Orth, "Our State Legislatures," p. 55.

8. Godkin, "Decline of Legislatures," p. 45.

9. George H. Hodges, "Distrust of State Legislatures. The Cause; The Remedy," *Proceedings of the Sixth Meeting of the Governors* (1913): 252.

10. Henry Jones Ford, "The Reorganization of State Government," *Proceedings of the Academy of Political Science* 3 (1912–13): 33.

11. Hodges, "Distrust of State Legislatures," p. 252.

12. Godkin, "Decline of Legislatures," pp. 43, 52.

13. Orth, "Our State Legislatures," p. 48.

14. Ibid., pp. 42–47.

15. Charles F. Ritter and Jon L. Wakelyn, *American Legislative Leaders, 1850–1910* (New York: Greenwood Press, 1989), p. xl.

16. George H. Haynes, "Representation in the Legislatures of the North Central States," *Annals of the American Academy of Political and Social Science* 15 (May 1900): 102; Haynes, "Representation in State Legislatures," p. 77.

17. Ritter and Wakelyn, *American Legislative Leaders,* pp. xlv, xlvii.

18. George H. Haynes, "Representation in New England Legislatures," *Annals of the American Academy of Political and Social Science* 6 (September 1895): 64–67; Haynes, "Representation in State Legislatures," pp. 68–69.

19. George P. McLean, "Legislative Apportionment in Connecticut," in Reinsch, *Readings on American State Government,* p. 128.

20. Edgar L. Murlin, *The New York Red Book* (Albany, N.Y.: James B. Lyon, 1896), p. 317.

21. Elihu Root, "Legislative Apportionment," in Reinsch, *Readings on American State Government,* p. 126.

22. Haynes, "Representation in State Legislatures — The Southern States," p. 116.

23. James Bryce, *The American Commonwealth,* 2d ed., rev., 2 vols. (London: Macmillan, 1891), 1:509.

24. "Remarks of Ambassador Bryce," *Proceedings of the Second Meeting of the Governors* (1910): 87.

25. Gamaliel Bradford, "The Growth of Executive Influence," in *Readings in American Government and Politics,* ed. Charles Beard (New York: Macmillan, 1921), p. 443; Gamaliel Bradford, "Governors and Legislatures," in Reinsch, *Readings on American State Government,* p. 18.

26. John M. Mathews, "The New Role of the Governor," *American Political Science Review* 6 (May 1912): 216, 222, 226.

27. Theodore Roosevelt, *Autobiography* (New York: Scribner's, 1920), p. 282; Leslie Lipson, "Influence of the Governor upon Legislation," *Annals of the American Academy of Political and Social Science* 195 (January 1938): 73.

28. "Executive Usurpation," in Reinsch, *Readings on American State Government,* pp. 14–15; John A. Fairlie, "The State Governor," *Michigan Law Review* 10 (March 1912): 378.

29. David Carley, "Legal and Extra-Legal Powers of Wisconsin Governors in Legislative Relations—Part I," *Wisconsin Law Review* 1962 (January 1962): 11.

30. Ibid.

31. John H. Finley and John F. Sanderson, *The American Executive and Executive Methods* (New York: Century, 1908), pp. 181–83.

32. John A. Fairlie, "The Veto Power of the State Governor," *American Political Science Review* 11 (August 1917): 477, 483; Niels H. Debel, *The Veto Power of the Governor of Illinois* (Urbana: University of Illinois, 1917), p. 23.

33. Frank W. Prescott and Joseph F. Zimmerman, *The Politics of the Veto of Legislation in New York State,* 2 vols. (Washington, D.C.: University Press of America, 1980), 2:1168.

34. Debel, *Veto Power of the Governor,* pp. 87–88.

35. Leslie Lipson, *The American Governor from Figurehead to Leader* (Chicago: University of Chicago Press, 1939), p. 210.

36. David J. Danelski and Joseph S. Tulchin, eds., *The Autobiographical Notes of Charles Evans Hughes* (Cambridge, Mass.: Harvard University Press, 1973), p. 141.

37. *New York Times,* 13 March 1907, p. 4.

38. Edward F. Dunne, "The Growth of Public Control of Utilities," *Proceedings of the Sixth Meeting of the Governors* (1913): 339.

39. Winston Allen Flint, *The Progressive Movement in Vermont* (Washington, D.C.: American Council on Public Affairs, 1941), p. 49.

40. Dunne, "Growth of Public Control," pp. 347–48.

41. Charles E. Merriam, "The Case for Home Rule," *Annals of the American Academy of Political and Social Science* 57 (January 1915): 170.

42. Stiles P. Jones, "State versus Local Regulation," *Annals of the American Academy of Political and Social Science* 53 (May 1914): 96.

43. Ira W. Stratton, "State and Local Regulation in Pennsylvania," *Annals of the American Academy of Political and Social Science* 57 (January 1915): 177.

44. John Purroy Mitchel, "Local and State Regulation of Municipal Utilities," *Annals of the American Academy of Political and Social Science* 57 (January 1915): 122.

45. Balthasar H. Meyer, "Central Utilities Commissions and Home Rule," *American Political Science Review* 5 (August 1911): 377–78; Dunne, "Growth of Public Control," pp. 342–43.

46. Halford Erickson, "The Advantages of State Regulation," *Annals of the American Academy of Political and Social Science* 57 (January 1915): 146–49.

47. Milo R. Maltbie, "The Distribution of Functions between Local and State Regulation," *Annals of the American Academy of Political and Social Science* 57 (January 1915): 163.

48. Dunne, "Growth of Public Control," p. 343.

49. Adolph O. Eberhart, "State Control of Public Utilities," *Proceedings of the Sixth Meeting of the Governors* (1913): 353, 359.

50. *New York Times,* 7 March 1907, p. 8.

51. *Twelfth Biennial Report of the Bureau of Labor, Industries and Commerce of the State of Minnesota 1909–10* (Saint Paul: State of Minnesota, 1910), pp. 147, 146, 148–49.

52. Charles McCarthy, *The Wisconsin Idea* (New York: Macmillan, 1912), p. 159; Frederic C. Howe, *Wisconsin: An Experiment in Democracy* (New York: Scribner's, 1912), p. 103.

53. Robert F. Wesser, "Conflict and Compromise: The Workmen's Compensation Movement in New York: 1890s–1913," *Labor History* 11 (summer 1971): 350–51.

54. Robert Asher, "The Origins of Workmen's Compensation in Minnesota," *Minnesota History* 44 (winter 1974): 145–46.

55. *Thirteenth Biennial Report of the Bureau of Labor, Industries and Commerce of the State of Minnesota 1911–1912* (Saint Paul: State of Minnesota, 1912), p. 52.

56. "Workmen's Compensation Legislation in the United States," *Monthly Review of the U.S. Bureau of Labor Statistics* 1 (September 1915): 45; "Workmen's Compensation Laws—1920," *American Labor Legislation Review* 10 (March 1920): 7.

57. "Workmen's Compensation Legislation in the United States," p. 45.

58. "Three Years under the New Jersey Workmen's Compensation Law," *American Labor Legislation Review* 5 (March 1915): 34–35.

59. Robert Asher, "Radicalism and Reform: State Insurance of Workmen's Compensation in Minnesota, 1910–1933," *Labor History* 14 (winter 1973): 40.

60. Domenico Gagliardo, "The First Kansas Workmen's Compensation Law," *Kansas Historical Quarterly* 9 (November 1940): 384, 396.

61. *First Annual Report of the Commissioner of Public Roads for 1894* (Trenton, N.J.: MacCrellish and Quigley, 1895), p. 20.

62. *Report of the Commission to Improve the Highways of the Commonwealth* (Boston: Wright and Potter, 1893), p. 35.

63. John Hamilton, "Pennsylvania's Road System," in *Proceedings of the International Good Roads Congress, 1901* (Washington, D.C.: Government Printing Office, 1901), p. 26.

64. *First Annual Report of Commissioner of Public Roads,* p. 7.

65. *First Annual Report of the State Board of Public Roads of the State of Rhode Island, January 1903* (Providence, R.I.: E. L. Freeman, 1903), pp. 25–26.

66. *Biennial Report of the Bureau of Highways 1895–1896* (Sacramento, Calif.: A. J. Johnson, 1896), p. 21.

67. *Fifth Annual Report of the Highway Commissioner for 1899* (Norwich, Conn.: Press of the Bulletin Co., 1901), pp. 5, 8.

68. *First Annual Report of Commissioner of Public Roads,* p. 19.

69. *Sixth Annual Report of the Highway Commissioner 1900* (Norwich, Conn.: Press of the Bulletin Co., 1901), p. 87.

70. *First Annual Report of the Iowa State Highway Commission 1905* (Des Moines, Iowa: B. Murphy, 1905), pp. 53–54.

71. C. O. Gardner, "A Report on State Administration of Public Works, Parks and Build-

ings," in *Report of the Efficiency and Economy Committee State of Illinois* (Chicago: Windermere Press, 1915), pp. 760–65.

72. *Second Annual Report of the Iowa State Highway Commission 1906* (Des Moines, Iowa: Emory H. English, 1907), p. 8.

73. Henry R. Trumbower, "Motor Vehicle Fees and Gasoline Taxes," *Public Roads* 5 (September 1924): 1–2; Henry R. Trumbower, "The Incidence of the Highway Tax Burden," *Public Roads* 5 (June 1924): 9.

74. *Fifth Annual Report of the State Highway Department of Ohio* (Springfield, Ohio: Springfield Publishing, 1909), p. 5.

75. *First, Second, Third, and Fourth Annual Reports of the State Roads Commission for the Years 1908, 1909, 1910 and 1911* (Baltimore: State of Maryland, 1912), pp. 7–8; *The Official Good Roads Year Book of the United States, 1912* (Washington, D.C.: American Association for Highway Improvement, 1912), pp. 75–77; *The Official Good Roads Year Book of the United States, 1914* (Washington, D.C.: American Highway Association, 1914), pp. 252–54, 297; *Report of the Commission for the Revision of the Taxation System of the State of Maryland and City of Baltimore* (Baltimore: State of Maryland, 1913), pp. 40, 381.

76. *State of New York Report of the State Commission of Highways, 1910* (Albany, N.Y.: J. B. Lyon, 1910), pp. vii–viii; *State of New York Report of the State Commission of Highways 1912* (Albany, N.Y.: Argus, 1912), pp. 6, 14–15; *State of New York Report of the State Commissioner of Highways, 1917* (Albany, N.Y.: J. B. Lyon, 1917), pp. 18–19; *Report of the Special Tax Commission of the State of New York* (Albany, N.Y.: J. B. Lyon, 1907), p. 67; *Good Roads Year Book, 1914*, pp. 262–63.

77. A. E. Johnson, "History of the Origin, Development and Operation of the American Association of State Highway Officials," in *American Association of State Highway Officials: A Story of the Beginning, Purposes, Growth, Activities and Achievements of AASHO* (Washington, D.C.: American Association of State Highway Officials, 1965), pp. 50–51.

78. *Report of the Director of the Office of Public Roads and Rural Engineering* (Washington, D.C.: U.S. Department of Agriculture, 1917), p. 2. See also Bruce E. Seely, *Building the American Highway System: Engineers as Policy Makers* (Philadelphia: Temple University Press, 1987), pp. 41–43.

79. "State Aid a Preparation for Federal Aid," in *Why Federal Aid in Roads* (n.p.: American Automobile Association, n.d.), p. 19.

80. *Report of Director of Office of Public Roads*, p. 2.

81. *New York Report of Commissioner of Highways, 1917*, p. 21.

82. *A Survey of Educational Institutions of the State of Washington* (Washington, D.C.: Government Printing Office, 1916), pp. 48, 52.

83. Seymour E. Harris, *Higher Education: Resources and Finance* (New York: McGraw-Hill, 1962), p. 325.

84. Charles Richard Van Hise, "Central Boards of Control," *Transactions and Proceedings of the National Association of State Universities* 9 (1911): 64–66.

85. Samuel Paul Capen, *Recent Movements in College and University Administration* (Washington, D.C.: Government Printing Office, 1917), p. 13.

86. Earle D. Ross, *A History of the Iowa State College of Agriculture and Mechanic Arts* (Ames: Iowa State College Press, 1942), pp. 262–63. See also Irving H. Hart, "State Support of Higher Education in Iowa," *Iowa Journal of History* 55 (April 1957): 161–62.

87. Ross, *History of Iowa State College*, p. 263.

88. Capen, *Recent Movements in College Administration*, pp. 14-15; *State Higher Education Institutions of Iowa* (Washington, D.C.: Government Printing Office, 1916), p. 113.

89. Van Hise, "Central Boards of Control," p. 81.

90. *Report of the Commissioner of Education for 1912*, 2 vols. (Washington, D.C.: Government Printing Office, 1913), 1:85-86.

91. Ibid., pp. 90-91; Van Hise, "Central Boards of Control," pp. 82-83; Michael Malone, "The Montana University System: The First Half-Century," *Montana* 44 (spring 1994): 62; John M. Mathews, *A Report on Educational Administration* (Springfield: State of Illinois, 1914), pp. 43-44.

92. Van Hise, "Central Boards of Control," p. 74; *Report of Commissioner of Education 1912*, p. 89.

93. Mathews, *Report on Educational Administration*, p. 47; Lois A. Fisher, "The Role of Politics in the Organization of Public Higher Education in Idaho and Washington," *History of Higher Education Annual* 5 (1985): 121.

94. *Report of Commissioner of Education 1912*, p. 87.

95. Ibid., pp. 94-95.

96. Ibid., p. 91.

Chapter 3. Financing the Emerging State

1. Edwin R. A. Seligman, "Introductory Address," in *National Conference on Taxation* (n.p.: National Civic Federation, 1901), p. 6.

2. Based on figures in U.S. Bureau of the Census, *Historical Statistics of the United States, Colonial Times to 1970, Bicentennial Edition*, pt. 2 (Washington, D.C.: Government Printing Office, 1975), pp. 1129-30.

3. *A Summary of the Reports of Special State Tax Commissions* (Chicago: Civic Federation of Chicago, 1907), p. 4.

4. Kentucky Tax Commission, *Tax Revision State of Kentucky* (Frankfort: State of Kentucky, 1909), p. 14.

5. "Report of Committee on Causes of Failure of General Property Tax," in *State and Local Taxation, Fourth International Conference* (Columbus, Ohio: International Tax Association, 1911), p. 309.

6. Ibid., p. 306.

7. *Report of the Commission on Revenue and Taxation of the State of California, 1906* (Sacramento: Superintendent of State Printing, 1906), p. 57.

8. Seligman, "Introductory Address," p. 9.

9. *Report of Commission on Taxation of California, 1906*, p. 59.

10. *Report of the Efficiency and Economy Committee State of Illinois* (Chicago: Windermere Press, 1915), p. 94.

11. *Report of the Honorary Commission Appointed by the Governor to Investigate the Tax System of Ohio and Recommend Improvements Therein* (Columbus: State of Ohio, 1908), p. 24.

12. *Final Report of the West Virginia Commission on Taxation and Municipal Incorporation, 1902* (n.p.: State of West Virginia, 1902), p. 3.

13. *Report of Commission to Investigate Tax System of Ohio*, p. 21.

14. Samuel T. Howe, "Faults of the General Property Tax," in *Report of Tax Conference, University of Oklahoma Bulletin* (Norman: University of Oklahoma, 1914), p. 67.

15. *Final Report of the Board of Commissioners on Revenue and Taxation for the State of Utah* (Salt Lake City: Arrow Press, 1913), p. 13.

16. *Report of the Special Tax Commission to the Governor of Iowa 1912* (Des Moines, Iowa: Emory English, 1912), p. 23.

17. Charles J. Bullock, "The State Income Tax and the Classified Property Tax," in *Proceedings of the Tenth Annual Conference under the Auspices of the National Tax Association* (New Haven, Conn.: National Tax Association, 1917), p. 375.

18. Robert M. Haig, *A History of the General Property Tax in Illinois* (Urbana: University of Illinois, 1914), p. 217.

19. *Report of Commission to Investigate Tax System of Ohio,* p. 56.

20. *Final Report of West Virginia Commission on Taxation,* p. 3.

21. Kentucky Tax Commission, *Tax Revision,* p. 3.

22. Charles J. Bullock, "A Classified Property Tax," in *State and Local Taxation Third International Conference* (Columbus, Ohio: International Tax Association, 1910), p. 98.

23. "Resolutions and Conclusions Adopted by the Conference," in *State and Local Taxation, First National Conference* (New York: Macmillan, 1908), p. xviii.

24. K. M. Williamson, "The Present Status of Low-Rate Taxation of Intangible Property," in *Proceedings of the Eighteenth Annual Conference on Taxation under the Auspices of the National Tax Association* (New York: National Taxation Association, 1926), pp. 90–128. See also J. G. Arnson, "Two Years' Experience with the Three-Mill Tax on Money and Credits," in *State and Local Taxation, Sixth Annual Conference* (Madison, Wis.: National Tax Association, 1913), pp. 239–48; J. H. Fertig, "The Pennsylvania Tax on Intangibles," in *Proceedings of the Fifteenth Annual Conference on Taxation under Auspices of the National Tax Association* (New York: National Tax Association, 1923), pp. 322–27; Simeon E. Leland, *The Classified Property Tax in the United States* (Boston: Houghton Mifflin, 1928).

25. Bullock, "State Income Tax and Classified Property Tax," p. 369.

26. *Report of the Committee on Tax Investigation of the State of Oregon 1922* (Salem, Oreg.: State Printing Department, 1923), p. 13.

27. Williamson, "Low-Rate Taxation of Intangible Property," pp. 99, 102, 112.

28. Edwin R. A. Seligman, "The Next Step in Tax Reform," in *Proceedings of the Ninth Annual Conference under the Auspices of the National Tax Association* (Ithaca, N.Y.: National Tax Association, 1915), p. 132; Williamson, "Low-Rate Taxation of Intangible Property," p. 113.

29. "Income Taxes and Classified Property Taxes—Round Table Discussion," in *Fifteenth Annual Conference on Taxation,* p. 308.

30. Williamson, "Low-Rate Taxation of Intangible Property," p. 102. In 1929 a special tax committee in Iowa reported, "It does not appear that more than 10 percent to 15 percent of the moneys and credits of the state appear on the tax list." *Preliminary Report of the Iowa Special Legislative Tax Committee and State Board of Assessment and Review* (Des Moines: State of Iowa, 1929), p. 9.

31. James W. Chapman, Jr., *State Tax Commissions in the United States* (Baltimore: Johns Hopkins Press, 1897), pp. 25–26.

32. Harley L. Lutz, *The State Tax Commissions* (Cambridge, Mass.: Harvard University Press, 1918), p. 3.

33. Milo D. Campbell, "The Purpose and Working of the Michigan Tax Commission," *Publications of the Michigan Political Science Association* 4 (June 1901): 9.

34. C. R. Jackson, "The State Board of Tax Commissioners," in *Taxation in Washington, Bulletin of the University of Washington* (Seattle: University of Washington, 1914), p. 247.

35. T. S. Adams, "The Value of a State Tax Commission," in *Report of Tax Conference, Oklahoma,* p. 51.

36. John A. Fairlie, "A Report on Revenue and Finance Administration," in *Report of Efficiency and Economy Committee,* p. 157.

37. Lutz, *Tax Commissions,* pp. 632–33.

38. Mabel Newcomer, *Separation of State and Local Revenues in the United States* (New York: Columbia University, 1917), pp. 31–91; *Report of the New York State Commission for the Revision of the Tax Laws* (Albany, N.Y.: J. B. Lyon, 1932), p. 70.

39. Russell C. Larcom, *The Delaware Corporation* (Baltimore: Johns Hopkins Press, 1937), pp. 167, 169.

40. M. L. Faust, "Sources of Revenue of the States with a Special Study of the Revenue Sources of Pennsylvania," *Annals of the American Academy of Political and Social Science* 95 (May 1921): 113–22; *New York Commission for Revision of Tax Laws,* pp. 67–69.

41. *Report of Commission on Taxation of California, 1906,* p. 77. For tax reform in California, see also Mansel G. Blackford, *The Politics of Business in California, 1890–1920* (Columbus: Ohio State University Press, 1977), pp. 146–60.

42. *Report of Commission on Taxation of California, 1906,* pp. 79, 81.

43. Ibid., p. 81.

44. Carl C. Plehn, "Results of Separation in California," in *Proceedings of Ninth Annual Conference,* p. 52.

45. *Report of the Commission on Revenue and Taxation, 1910* (Sacramento: Superintendent of State Printing, 1910), pp. 9–16; Newcomer, *Separation of State and Local Revenues,* pp. 139–40, 142; Jens Peter Jensen, *Property Taxation in the United States* (Chicago: University of Chicago Press, 1931), p. 257.

46. *Report of the State Tax Commission of the State of California 1917* (Sacramento: California State Printing Office, 1917), p. 9.

47. Newton W. Thompson, "Separation of State and Local Revenues," in *Proceedings of Ninth Annual Conference,* pp. 44–45; Plehn, "Results of Separation," p. 56.

48. Newcomer, *Separation of State and Local Revenues,* p. 89; *New York Commission for Revision of Tax Laws,* pp. 69–70.

49. *Final Report of the California Tax Commission, 1929* (Sacramento: State of California, 1929), p. 52.

50. Clara Penniman and Walter W. Heller, *State Income Tax Administration* (Chicago: Public Administration Service, 1959), pp. 1–4; Delos O. Kinsman, "The Present Period of Income Tax Activity in the American States," *Quarterly Journal of Economics* 23 (February 1909): 296–306.

51. George E. Barnett, "Taxation in North Carolina," in *Studies in Taxation,* ed. J. H. Hollander (Baltimore: Johns Hopkins University Press, 1900), p. 108.

52. Kinsman, "Income Tax Activity in the American States," pp. 299–300.

53. *Summary of Reports of Tax Commissions,* pp. 73–74.

54. *Report of Commission on Taxation of California, 1906,* p. 14.

55. Penniman and Heller, *State Income Tax Administration,* p. 5.

56. Nils P. Haugen, "The Wisconsin Income Tax," in *State and Local Taxation, Sixth Conference,* p. 324.

57. "Discussion—Wisconsin Income Tax," in *State and Local Taxation, Sixth Conference*, p. 334.

58. Haugen, "Wisconsin Income Tax," p. 332.

59. T. S. Adams, "The Significance of the Wisconsin Income Tax," *Political Science Quarterly* 28 (December 1913): 576.

60. *Report of the Special Joint Taxation Committee of the 83rd Ohio General Assembly* (Columbus, Ohio: F. J. Heer Printing, 1919), pp. 97, 104, 106; Rebecca Jean Brownlee, *The Income Tax in Delaware* (Philadelphia: University of Pennsylvania, 1944), pp. 7–9; Robert J. Taggert, "The Modernization of Delaware's School Tax System during the 1920s," *Delaware History* 18 (spring–summer 1979): 156; *New York Commission for Revision of Tax Laws*, p. 69.

61. *Report of Joint Taxation Committee of Ohio*, p. 94.

62. "Preliminary Report of the Committee . . . to Prepare a Plan of a Model System of State and Local Taxation," in *Proceedings of the Twelfth Annual Conference on Taxation under the Auspices of the National Tax Association* (New York: National Tax Association, 1920), pp. 426–70; "Model Personal and Business Income Acts," in *Proceedings of the Fourteenth Annual Conference on Taxation under the Auspices of the National Tax Association* (New York: National Tax Association, 1922), pp. 66–101; *State Income Taxes*, 2 vols. (New York: National Industrial Conference Board, 1930), 2:154–59; Penniman and Heller, *State Income Tax Administration*, pp. 7–9; M. C. Rhodes, *History of Taxation in Mississippi (1798–1929)* (Nashville, Tenn.: George Peabody College for Teachers, 1930), pp. 120–25.

63. Haugen, "Wisconsin Income Tax," pp. 323, 332.

64. Rhodes, *Taxation in Mississippi*, p. 185.

65. Thorstein H. Thoresen, "The Personal Income Tax in North Dakota," in *Proceedings of Twenty-first Annual Conference on Taxation under the Auspices of the National Tax Association* (Columbia, S.C.: National Tax Association, 1929), p. 450.

66. Arthur E. Buck, *Public Budgeting* (New York: Harper, 1929), p. 12.

67. Benjamin Loring Young, "The Budget System as a Preventive Measure against Public Extravagance," in *Proceedings of the Seventeenth Annual Conference on Taxation under the Auspices of the National Tax Association* (New York: National Tax Association, 1925), p. 107; *Report of the Michigan Budget Commission of Inquiry, 1918* (Fort Wayne, Ind.: Fort Wayne Printing, 1918), p. 5: George E. Frazer, "A Report on the Accounts of the State of Illinois," in *Report of the Efficiency and Economy Committee*, pp. 195–96; John A. Fairlie, "Budget Methods in Illinois," *Annals of the American Academy of Political and Social Science* 62 (November 1915): 87.

68. *Report of Tax Commission California 1917*, p. 120.

69. *Report of Michigan Budget Commission*, pp. 4–5.

70. Lester M. Livengood, "A Budget System for the State of Washington," in *Taxation in Washington*, p. 255.

71. Frank W. Prescott and Joseph F. Zimmerman, *The Politics of the Veto of Legislation in New York State*, 2 vols. (Washington, D.C.: University Press of America, 1980), 1:310, 340.

72. Niels H. Debel, *The Veto Power of the Governor of Illinois* (Urbana: University of Illinois, 1917), pp. 118–19, 121–22.

73. John A. Perkins, *The Role of the Governor of Michigan in the Enactment of Appropriations* (Ann Arbor: University of Michigan Press, 1943), p. 57.

74. John Francis Neylan, "California's State Budget," *Annals of the American Academy of Political and Social Science* 62 (November 1915): 69.

75. William F. Willoughby, *The Movement for Budgetary Reform in the States* (New York: D. Appleton, 1918), p. 7.

76. Buck, *Public Budgeting,* p. 13. See also Jonathan Kahn, *Budgeting Democracy: State Building and Citizenship in America, 1890–1928* (Ithaca, N.Y.: Cornell University Press, 1997).

77. Frederick A. Cleveland, "Evolution of the Budget Idea in the United States," *Annals of the American Academy of Political and Social Science* 62 (November 1915): 26–27. See also *Report of Reconstruction Commission to Governor Alfred E. Smith on Retrenchment and Reorganization in State Government* (Albany, N.Y.: J. B. Lyon, 1919), pp. 303–4.

78. Willoughby, *Movement for Budgetary Reform,* pp. 93–94.

79. Ibid., p. 109; E. L. Philipp, "Wisconsin State Budget," *Proceedings of the Eleventh Meeting of the Governors* (1919): 36, 44.

80. Willoughby, *Movement for Budgetary Reform,* p. 84; Neylan, "California's State Budget," p. 71.

81. Neylan, "California's State Budget," p. 71.

82. *Report of Tax Commission California 1917,* p. 121.

83. Philipp, "Wisconsin State Budget," pp. 44–45.

84. *Recommendations of the Committee on Retrenchment and Reform* (Des Moines, Iowa: Robert Henderson, State Printer, 1914), p. 14.

85. Willoughby, *Movement for Budgetary Reform,* pp. 216, 221.

86. Arthur E. Buck, *Budget Making* (New York: D. Appleton, 1921), pp. 9–13.

87. Efficiency Commission of Kentucky, *The Government of Kentucky* (Frankfort, Ky.: State Journal Co., 1924), pp. 204–5.

88. Buck, *Public Budgeting,* p. 285.

89. "The Maryland Proposed Constitutional Amendment for an Executive Budget," *Municipal Research,* no. 73 (May 1916): 32.

90. Ibid., p. 33.

91. Arthur E. Buck, "The Present Status of the Executive Budget in the State Governments," *National Municipal Review* 8 (August 1919): 434.

92. Frank F. White, Jr., *The Governors of Maryland 1777–1970* (Annapolis, Md.: Hall of Records Commission, 1970), p. 253.

93. Willoughby, *Movement for Budgetary Reform,* pp. 49–50.

94. Lloyd M. Short and Carl W. Tiller, *The Minnesota Commission of Administration and Finance 1925–1939: An Administrative History* (Minneapolis: University of Minnesota Press, 1942), pp. 6–7, 11.

95. Efficiency Commission, *Government of Kentucky,* p. 207.

96. *Report of Joint Committee on Administrative Reorganization* (Columbus, Ohio: F. J. Heer Printing, 1921), p. 52.

97. Efficiency Commission, *Government of Kentucky,* p. 84.

Chapter 4. Restructuring State Government

1. Charles Beard, *Readings in American Government and Politics* (New York: Macmillan, 1921), p. 437; Arthur E. Buck, *The Reorganization of State Governments in the United States* (New York: Columbia University Press, 1938), pp. 6–7; *Report of Reconstruction Commission to Governor Alfred E. Smith on Retrenchment and Reorganization in State Government* (Albany, N.Y.: J. B. Lyon, 1919), p. 243.

2. Emmet O'Neal, "Strengthening the Power of the Executive," *Proceedings of the Fourth Meeting of the Governors* (1911): 25, 29.

3. Thomas E. Kynerd, *Administration Reorganization of Mississippi Government: A Study in Politics* (Jackson: University Press of Mississippi, 1978), p. 3.

4. Raymond Moley, "The State Movement for Efficiency and Economy," *Municipal Research*, no. 90 (October 1917): 2. See also *State Commissions on Economy and Efficiency* (Providence, R.I.: Legislative Reference Bureau of the Rhode Island State Library, 1915).

5. Frank E. Horack, "Reorganization of State Government in Iowa," *Applied History* 2 (1914): 23; *Report of Reconstruction Commission*, p. 244.

6. *Message of James F. Fielder Governor of New Jersey Transmitting to the Legislature the Second Report of the Commission upon the Reorganization and Consolidation of Different Departments of the State Government* (Trenton, N.J.: MacCrellish and Quigley, 1914), pp. 1, 13; *Message of the Governor Transmitting Report of the Commission to Consider Best Means to Consolidate State Agencies* (Trenton, N.J.: MacCrellish and Quigley, 1913), p. 19.

7. Horack, "Reorganization of State Government," p. 26. See also Jeremiah S. Young, "Administrative Reorganization in Minnesota," *American Political Science Review* 9 (May 1915): 273–85; and *Final Report of the Efficiency and Economy Commission* (Saint Paul, Minn.: Efficiency and Economy Commission, 1914).

8. *Message of James F. Fielder,* p. 14.

9. Arthur E. Buck, "Administrative Consolidation in State Governments," *National Municipal Review* 8 (November 1919): 640; Moley, "State Movement for Efficiency," p. 131.

10. *Report of the Efficiency and Economy Committee State of Illinois* (Chicago: Windermere Press, 1915), pp. 10, 12, 18, 21, 29; John A. Fairlie, "Governmental Reorganization in Illinois," *American Political Science Review* 9 (May 1915): 252.

11. William T. Hutchinson, *Lowden of Illinois: The Life of Frank O. Lowden,* 2 vols. (Chicago: University of Chicago Press, 1957), 1:311.

12. Buck, "Administrative Consolidation," pp. 647–48; *Report of Reconstruction Commission,* p. 259; John H. Mathews, "Administrative Reorganization in Illinois," *National Municipal Review* 9 (November 1920): 750.

13. Samuel R. McKelvie, "A Responsible Form of Government," *Proceedings of the Eleventh Meeting of the Governors* (1919): 50–54; *Report of Reconstruction Commission,* p. 265.

14. D. W. Davis. "Idaho's New Civil Administrative Code," in *Proceedings of the Eleventh Meeting of the Governors* (1919): 68; *Report of Reconstruction Commission,* pp. 260–65.

15. Frank B. Woodford, *Alex J. Groesbeck: Portrait of a Public Man* (Detroit: Wayne State University Press, 1962), p. 130. See also Harold M. Dorr, *Administrative Organization of State Government in Michigan 1921–1936* (Ann Arbor: Bureau of Government, University of Michigan, 1936), pp. 1–2.

16. Leslie Lipson, *The American Governor from Figurehead to Leader* (Chicago: University of Chicago Press, 1939), pp. 90–99; *The Reorganized State Government* (Albany, N.Y.: J. B. Lyon, 1926).

17. Ronald L. Heinemann, *Harry Byrd of Virginia* (Charlottesville: University Press of Virginia, 1996), pp. 65–67, 70–74; Lipson, *American Governor,* pp. 88–90.

18. Charles V. Chapin, *A Report on State Public Health Work* (Chicago: American Medical Association, 1916), p. 64; William H. Edwards, "The State Reorganization Movement," *Dakota Law Review* 2 (February 1928): 44.

19. Edwards, "State Reorganization," pp. 38, 43.

20. Ibid., pp. 25, 31.

21. Eleanore V. Laurent, *Legislative Reference Work in the United States* (Chicago: Council of State Governments, 1939), p. 2; Marion Casey, *Charles McCarthy: Librarianship and Reform* (Chicago: American Library Association, 1981), p. 28.

22. Charles McCarthy, *The Wisconsin Idea* (New York: Macmillan, 1912), pp. 214, 216, 223–24; Charles McCarthy, "Legislative Reference Department," in *Readings on American State Government*, ed. Paul S. Reinsch (Boston: Ginn, 1911), p. 69.

23. McCarthy, *Wisconsin Idea*, pp. 197, 218.

24. Ibid., pp. 225–26.

25. Casey, *Charles McCarthy*, p. 58; Edward A. Fitzpatrick, *McCarthy of Wisconsin* (New York: Columbia University Press, 1944), p. 72.

26. Fitzpatrick, *McCarthy of Wisconsin*, p. 79.

27. Ibid., p. 84.

28. Laurent, *Legislative Reference Work*, pp. 2–3; Ernest Bruncken, "The Legislative Reference Bureau," *News Notes of California Libraries* 2 (February 1907): 97.

29. C. B. Lester, "Legislative Reference Work and the Law Library," *Index to Legal Periodicals and Law Library Journal* 1 (October 1908): 48. See also Ethel Cleland, "Indiana Legislative Reference Department," *Special Libraries* 1 (October 1910): 58–60.

30. Addison E. Sheldon, "The Legislative Reference Bureau as a Factor in State Development," *Special Libraries* 5 (January 1914): 2.

31. Maud B. Cobb, "Law and Legislative Reference as Parts of a State Library," *Law Library Journal* 10 (October 1917): 52–53.

32. Sheldon, "Legislative Reference Bureau," p. 7; Laurent, *Legislative Reference Work*, p. 16.

33. Laurent, *Legislative Reference Work*, p. 3.

34. Arthur A. Schwartz, "Legislative Laboratories Compared," *State Government* 3 (August 1930): 5.

35. Horace E. Flack, "Scientific Assistance in Law Making," *Proceedings of the American Political Science Association* 10 (1914): 220.

36. *The Initiative, Referendum and Recall* (Springfield, Ill.: Legislative Reference Bureau, 1919), p. 80; John A. Fairlie, "The Referendum and Initiative in Michigan," *Annals of the American Academy of Political and Social Science* 43 (September 1912): 147. See also Samuel E. Moffett, "The Constitutional Referendum in California," *Political Science Quarterly* 13 (March 1898): 1–18.

37. Thomas Goebel, "'A Case of Democratic Contagion': Direct Democracy in the American West, 1890–1920," *Pacific Historical Review* 66 (May 1997): 219–20; Steven L. Piott, "The Origins of the Initiative and Referendum in South Dakota: The Political Context," *Great Plains Quarterly* 12 (summer 1992): 183; C. B. Galbreath, "Provision for State-Wide Initiative and Referendum," *Annals of the American Academy of Political and Social Science* 43 (September 1912): 83.

38. Roger Grant, "Origins of a Progressive Reform: The Initiative and Referendum Movement in South Dakota," *South Dakota History* 3 (fall 1973): 404.

39. Piott, "Origins of Initiative and Referendum," p. 190; Galbreath, "State-Wide Initiative and Referendum," p. 88; Grant, "Origins of a Progressive Reform," p. 403.

40. Piott, "Origins of Initiative and Referendum," p. 190.

41. Alan L. Clem, *Prairie State Politics: Popular Democracy in South Dakota* (Washington, D.C.: Public Affairs Press, 1967), p. 99. See also Galbreath, "State-Wide Initiative and Referendum," p. 89; *Initiative, Referendum and Recall*, p. 103.

42. George A. Thacher, "The Initiative and Referendum in Oregon," *Proceedings of the*

American Political Science Association 4 (1907): 202. See also Douglas Heider and David Dietz, *Legislative Perspectives: A 150-Year History of the Oregon Legislatures from 1843 to 1993* (Salem: Oregon Historical Society Press, 1993), p. 84.

43. James D. Barnett, *The Operation of the Initiative, Referendum, and Recall in Oregon* (New York: Macmillan, 1915), p. 4.

44. Galbreath, "State-Wide Initiative and Referendum," p. 92.

45. Ibid., pp. 94–97; *Initiative, Referendum and Recall*, p. 103; Edwin M. Bacon and Morrill Wyman, *Direct Elections and Law-Making by Popular Vote* (Boston: Houghton Mifflin, 1912), p. 46.

46. Galbreath, "State-Wide Initiative and Referendum," p. 96.

47. W. S. U'Ren, "Results of the Initiative and Referendum in Oregon," *Proceedings of the American Political Science Association* 4 (1907): 193.

48. Barnett, *Operation of the Initiative*, pp. 21–22, 24–25; George H. Haynes, "'People's Rule' in Oregon, 1910," *Political Science Quarterly* 26 (March 1911): 51–52.

49. Alan H. Eaton, *The Oregon System: The Story of Direct Legislation in Oregon* (Chicago: A. C. McClurg, 1912), p. 128.

50. Barnett, *Operation of the Initiative*, p. 188.

51. *Initiative, Referendum and Recall*, pp. 81–82.

52. Steven L. Piott, *Holy Joe: Joseph W. Folk and the Missouri Idea* (Columbia: University of Missouri Press, 1997), p. 124; Steven Piott, "Giving Voters a Voice: The Struggle for Initiative and Referendum in Missouri," *Gateway Heritage* 14 (spring 1994): 28.

53. John M. Allswang, *California Initiatives and Referendums 1912–1990; A Survey and Guide to Research* (Los Angeles: Edmund G. "Pat" Brown Institute of Public Affairs, 1991), p. 10; George E. Mowry, *The California Progressives* (Berkeley: University of California Press, 1951), pp. 140, 149.

54. David Y. Thomas, "Direct Legislation in Arkansas," *Political Science Quarterly* 29 (March 1914): 88.

55. E. K. MacColl, "John Franklin Shaforth, Reform Governor of Colorado, 1909–1913," *Colorado Magazine* 29 (January 1952): 50–52; Thomas E. Cronin and Robert D. Loevy, *Colorado Politics and Government: Governing the Centennial State* (Lincoln: University of Nebraska Press, 1993), pp. 94–95.

56. J. William Black, "Maine's Experience with the Initiative and Referendum," *Annals of the American Academy of Political and Social Science* 43 (September 1912): 177.

57. *Initiative, Referendum and Recall*, p. 103; Winston W. Crouch, *The Initiative and Referendum in California* (Los Angeles: Haynes Foundation, 1950), p. 42.

58. Thomas, "Direct Legislation in Arkansas," p. 110.

59. Barnett, *Operation of the Initiative*, p. 16.

60. Glenn E. Brooks, *When Governors Convene: The Governors' Conference and National Politics* (Baltimore: Johns Hopkins University Press, 1961), pp. 9–10.

61. Charles A. L. Reed, "A Council of States," in *State and Local Taxation First National Conference* (New York: Macmillan, 1908), pp. 20, 27–28, 34.

62. Brooks, *When Governors Convene*, p. 12.

63. "Remarks of President Taft," *Proceedings of the Second Meeting of the Governors* (1910): 9–10.

64. *Proceedings of the Second Meeting of the Governors* (1910): 2.

65. Charles E. Hughes, "Governors' Conferences, Their Scope and Purpose," *Proceedings of the Second Meeting of the Governors* (1910): 14, 16, 18.

66. "Articles of Organization," in *Proceedings of the Fifth Meeting of the Governors* (1912): 5.

67. *Proceedings of the Seventh Meeting of the Governors* (1914); *Proceedings of the Eighth Meeting of the Governors* (1915): 4–5; *Proceedings of the Ninth Meeting of the Governors* (1916).

68. Linna E. Bresette, "History of the Association of Governmental Labor Officials of the United States and Canada," in *Proceedings of the Fifth Annual Convention of the Association of Governmental Labor Officials of United States and Canada* (1918), pp. 8, 11, 13.

69. Allen Ripley Foote, "The Birth, Work, and Future of the National Tax Association," in *Proceedings of the Tenth Annual Conference under the Auspices of the National Tax Association* (New Haven, Conn.: National Tax Association, 1917), p. 27.

70. A. E. Johnson, "History of the Origin, Development and Operation of the American Association of State Highway Officials," in *American Association of State Highway Officials: A Story of the Beginning, Purposes, Growth, Activities and Achievements of AASHO* (Washington, D.C.: American Association of State Highway Officials, 1965), pp. 49–53.

71. *Proceedings of the Twenty-Sixth Annual Meeting of the National Conference of Commissioners on Uniform State Laws* (1916): 1–2; Nathan W. McChesney, "Uniformity of Legislation," *Proceedings of the Fifteenth Conference of Governors* (1923): 120.

72. "Report of the Secretary of the Commissioners on Uniform State Laws," *Proceedings of the Nineteenth Annual Conference of Commissioners on Uniform State Laws* (1909): 88–89; "Secretary's Report," *Proceedings of the Twenty-Sixth Annual Meeting of the National Conference of Commissioners on Uniform State Laws* (1916): 207.

73. *National Civic Federation Review* 3 (September 1910): 1, 2, 3.

74. *Proceedings of the Twenty-Ninth Annual Meeting of the National Conference of Commissioners on Uniform State Laws* (1919), table following p. 159. See also Maurice E. Harrison, "The Adoption of the Negotiable Instruments Law in California," *California Law Review* 6 (November 1917): 23–26.

75. "Address of Hon. Alton B. Parker," *National Civic Federation Review* 3 (1 March 1910): 6.

76. William H. Staake, "President's Address," *Proceedings of the Twenty- Sixth Annual Meeting of the National Conference of Commissioners on Uniform State Laws* (1916): 169. See also Felice Cohn, "Nevada's Divorce Laws," *Women Lawyers' Journal* 6 (November 1916): 11.

77. Staake, "President's Address," p. 170. See also William L. O'Neill, *Divorce in the Progressive Era* (New Haven, Conn.: Yale University Press, 1967), pp. 242–43; Glenda Riley, *Divorce: An American Tradition* (New York: Oxford University Press, 1991), p. 115; Nelson Manfred Blake, *The Road to Reno: A History of Divorce in the United States* (New York: Macmillan, 1962), pp. 140–41.

78. *Proceedings of the Second Meeting of the Governors* (1910): 195.

79. Tasker L. Oddie, "Uniformity of Marriage and Divorce Laws," *Proceedings of the Fifth Meeting of the Governors* (1912): 156, 161–62.

80. *Proceedings of the Second Meeting of the Governors* (1910): 196.

Chapter 5. Adapting to the Automobile Age

1. Marsha Perry Hataway, "The Development of the Mississippi State Highway System, 1916–1932," *Journal of Mississippi History* 28 (November 1966): 298–99.

2. Andrew P. Anderson, "State Highway Mileages and Expenditures in the Year 1918," *Public Roads* 2 (July 1919): 3–4.

3. Bruce E. Seely, *Building the American Highway System: Engineers as Policy Makers* (Philadelphia: Temple University Press, 1987), pp. 46, 52.

4. *American Association of State Highway Officials: A Story of the Beginning, Purposes, Growth, Activities and Achievements of AASHO* (Washington, D.C.: American Association of State Highway Officials, 1965), p. 166.

5. Paul D. Sargent, "The President's Address," *Public Roads* 3 (December 1920): 10.

6. Thomas H. MacDonald, "The Federal Aid Road Law and Changes Suggested by Its Practical Operation," *Public Roads* 1 (January 1919): 3, 6.

7. Thomas H. MacDonald, "Four Years of Road Building under the Federal-Aid Act," *Public Roads* 3 (June 1920): 3.

8. "Secretary Houston Discusses Federal Road Commission Bill," *Public Roads* 2 (June 1919): 3–5.

9. *American Association of State Highway Officials*, p. 166.

10. B. H. Piepmeier, "Is State Supervision of Construction and Maintenance of All Highways Desirable?" *Public Roads* 2 (December 1919): 30.

11. Seely, *Building the American Highway System*, p. 61. See also *New York Times*, 17 April 1921, sec. 7, p. 2.

12. Seely, *Building the American Highway System*, pp. 61–62.

13. Ibid., p. 73.

14. *Report of the Chief of the Bureau of Public Roads, 1927* (Washington, D.C.: Government Printing Office, 1927), p. 7; *Report of the Chief of the Bureau of Public Roads, 1928* (Washington, D.C.: Government Printing Office, 1928), p. 12; *Report of the Chief of the Bureau of Public Roads, 1929* (Washington, D.C.: Government Printing Office, 1929), p. 14.

15. *Report of the Chief of the Bureau of Public Roads, 1927*, pp. 2–3.

16. *Report of the Chief of the Bureau of Public Roads, 1926* (Washington, D.C.: Government Printing Office, 1926), p. 2.

17. "The Problems of Highway Finance," in *Proceedings of the Seventeenth Annual Conference on Taxation* (New York: National Tax Association, 1925), p. 432; Chamber of Commerce of the United States of America, *Referendum 53: On the Report of the Special Committee on Highways and Motor Transport* (Washington, D.C.: Chamber of Commerce of the United States, 1929), p. 8; *Eleventh Biennial Report of the State Highway Commissioner* (Lansing, Mich.: Robert Smith, 1926), p. 141; Grover C. Dillman, "The Building of an Adequate Highway Transportation System for Michigan," in *Proceedings of the Sixteenth Annual Conference on Highway Engineering Held at the University of Michigan* (Ann Arbor: University of Michigan Press, 1930), pp. 31–32.

18. *New York Times*, 31 May 1925, p. 2; 10 December 1925, p. 10. See also *New York Times*, 17 October 1925, p. 17.

19. Frank B. Woodford, *Alex J. Groesbeck: Portrait of a Public Man* (Detroit: Wayne State University Press, 1962), pp. 215, 217–18. See also *Eleventh Report of State Highway Commissioner*, pp. 11–17.

20. *New York Times*, 3 June 1928, sec. 5, p. 10; Woodford, *Groesbeck*, pp. 219–22.

21. Robert P. Howard, *Mostly Good and Competent Men: Illinois Governors, 1818–1988* (Springfield: Illinois Issues, Sangamon State University, and Illinois State Historical Society, 1988), p. 241.

22. *Ninth Annual Report of the Department of Public Works and Buildings, Division of Highways* (Springfield: Illinois State Journal Co., 1927), p. 4.

23. Howard, *Mostly Good and Competent Men*, pp. 237–38.

24. Margaret I. Phillips, *The Governors of Tennessee* (Gretna, La.: Pelican, 1978), pp. 138–39.

25. David D. Lee, *Tennessee in Turmoil: Politics in the Volunteer State, 1920–1932* (Memphis, Tenn.: Memphis State University Press, 1979), p. 58.

26. Frank M. Stewart, *Highway Administration in Texas: A Study of Administrative Methods and Financial Policies* (Austin: University of Texas, 1934), pp. 48, 90, 92.

27. Corey T. Lesseig, "'Out of the Mud': The Good Roads Crusade and Social Change in Twentieth-Century Mississippi," *Journal of Mississippi History* 60 (spring 1998): 69. See also Hataway, "Mississippi State Highway System," pp. 286–303; Bill R. Baker, *Catch the Vision: The Life of Henry L. Whitfield of Mississippi* (Jackson: University Press of Mississippi, 1974), pp. 138–40.

28. B. U. Ratchford, *American State Debts* (Durham, N.C.: Duke University Press, 1941), pp. 383–84.

29. *New York Times,* 26 March 1921, p. 1; 28 March 1921, p. 10.

30. Ratchford, *American State Debts,* pp. 385–95; Timothy P. Donovan and Willard B. Gatewood, Jr., eds., *The Governors of Arkansas: Essays in Political Biography* (Fayetteville: University of Arkansas Press, 1981), pp. 156–58.

31. George S. May, "The Good Roads Movement in Iowa," *Palimpsest* 36 (January 1955): 51.

32. Leonard D. White, *Trends in Public Administration* (New York: McGraw-Hill, 1933), p. 110.

33. Henry J. Bittermann, *State and Federal Grants-in-Aid* (New York: Mentzer, Bush, 1938), p. 97.

34. Thomas H. MacDonald, "Financing Highways," in *Papers Presented at the Highway Conference Held at the University of Colorado on January 16th and 17th 1930* (Boulder: University of Colorado, 1930), pp. 76, 78.

35. Henry R. Trumbower, "Motor Vehicle Fees and Gasoline Taxes," *Public Roads* 5 (September 1924): 1–2; "Report of the Committee of the National Tax Association on Taxation of Motor Vehicle Transportation," in *Proceedings of the Twenty-Third Annual Conference on Taxation* (Columbia, S.C.: National Tax Association, 1931), p. 139.

36. "Increased Motor Vehicle Imposts," *Engineering News-Record* 91 (13 December 1923): 960.

37. A. R. Hirst, "What Car Owners Should Pay for Road Building," *Engineering News-Record* 91 (13 December 1923): 967.

38. Ibid., p. 968.

39. *Part II, Report of the California Highway Commission* (Sacramento: California State Printing Office, 1922), p. 18.

40. John Cynoweth Burnham, "The Gasoline Tax and the Automobile Revolution," *Mississippi Valley Historical Review* 48 (December 1961): 437–44; Finla G. Crawford, *The Administration of the Gasoline Tax in the United States* (New York: Municipal Administration Service, 1930), p. 7; Finla G. Crawford, *The Gasoline Tax in the United States 1934* (Chicago: Public Administration Service, 1935), p. 1.

41. Crawford, *Gasoline Tax,* p. 2; Crawford, *Administration of the Gasoline Tax,* p. 9.

42. Crawford, *Administration of the Gasoline Tax,* pp. 7–9; Emery Fast, "The Growing Gas Tax," *State Government* 3 (August 1930): 8.

43. Crawford, *Gasoline Tax,* pp. 4–5.

44. Burnham, "Gasoline Tax," p. 446.

45. Crawford, *Administration of the Gasoline Tax,* p. 9.

46. W. C. Davidson, "The Five-Cent Gasoline Tax," in *Papers Presented at the Highway Conference Held at the University of Colorado on January 24th and 25th, 1929* (Boulder: University of Colorado, 1929), pp. 37–38.

47. Oliver T. Reedy, "Discussion of Five-Cent Gasoline Tax," in *Papers Presented at Highway Conference at University of Colorado, 1929,* p. 42.

48. "Report of the Committee of the National Tax Association," p. 155.

49. Burnham, "Gasoline Tax," p. 449.

50. Roy A. Klein, "Fundamental Principles Governing the Levying, Collection and Expenditure of Gasoline Taxes," *Highway Topics* 3 (June 1926): 10.

51. Burnham, "Gasoline Tax," p. 447.

52. Crawford, *Administration of the Gasoline Tax,* p. 14.

53. *New York Times,* 10 March 1929, sec. 11, p. 16.

54. P. J. Hoffmaster, "The Relation of State Parks to the Highway System," in *Proceedings of the Sixteenth Annual Conference,* p. 194.

55. Beatrice Ward Nelson, *State Recreation* (Washington, D.C.: National Conference on State Parks, 1928), pp. 3–5; Philip G. Terrie, "The Adirondack Forest Preserve: The Irony of Forever Wild," *New York History* 62 (July 1981): 261–88; Philip G. Terrie, "Forever Wild Forever: The Forest Preserve Debate at the New York State Constitutional Convention of 1915," *New York History* 70 (July 1989): 251–75; Harold W. Lathrop, "Fifty Years of State Parks in Minnesota," *American Planning and Civic Annual* (1939): 195–96.

56. O. G. Libby, "North Dakota's State Park System," *Collections of the State Historical Society of North Dakota* 6 (1920): 213; Russell Reid, "The North Dakota State Park System," *North Dakota Historical Quarterly* 8 (October 1940): 63.

57. John Nolen, "The Parks and Recreation Facilities in the United States," *Annals of the American Academy of Political and Social Science* 35 (March 1910): 6–7; K. L. Schellie, "Wisconsin's System of Recreation Areas," *American Planning and Civic Annual* (1939): 203.

58. John E. Trotter, *State Park System in Illinois* (Chicago: Department of Geography, University of Chicago, 1962), p. 65; James Alton James, "The Beginning of a State Park System for Illinois," *Illinois State Historical Society Transactions for the Year 1936* (1936): 60–61.

59. Nelson, *State Recreation,* pp. 48, 306–9.

60. David M. Silver, ed., "Richard Lieber and Indiana's Forest Heritage," *Indiana Magazine of History* 67 (March 1971): 54–55.

61. Robert Allen Frederick, "Colonel Richard Lieber Conservationist and Park Builder: The Indiana Years" (Ph.D. diss., Indiana University, 1960), pp. 213–14.

62. "Iowa State Parks," *Annals of Iowa* 13 (October 1921): 140. See also T. P. Christensen, "The State Parks of Iowa," *Iowa Journal of History and Politics* 26 (July 1928): 345–52.

63. Charles Landrum, "Michigan War Legislation, 1919," *Michigan History Magazine* 5 (January–April 1921): 261–62.

64. Gilbert C. Fite, *Peter Norbeck: Prairie Statesman* (Columbia: University of Missouri, 1948), p. 76; Nelson, *State Recreation,* p. 248.

65. Robert Shankland, *Steve Mather of the National Parks* (New York: Alfred A. Knopf, 1951), pp. 187–88.

66. Willard B. Gatewood, Jr., "North Carolina's Role in the Establishment of the Great Smoky Mountains National Park," *North Carolina Historical Review* 37 (April 1960):

165–84; Shankland, *Steve Mather,* pp. 282–83; Allen R. Coggins, "The Early History of Tennessee's State Parks, 1919–1956," *Tennessee Historical Quarterly* 48 (fall 1984): 300–301; Nelson, *State Recreation,* p. 253.

67. Shankland, *Steve Mather,* pp. 194–200; Nelson, *State Recreation,* p. 37.

68. Frederick, "Colonel Richard Lieber," pp. 165–72; Nelson, *State Recreation,* pp. 80–81; Robert E. Grese, *Jens Jensen: Maker of Natural Parks and Gardens* (Baltimore: Johns Hopkins University Press, 1992), pp. 122–29; J. Ronald Engel, *Sacred Sands: The Struggle for Community in the Indiana Dunes* (Middletown, Conn.: Wesleyan University Press, 1983), pp. 245–53.

69. Paula Eldot, *Governor Alfred E. Smith: The Politician as Reformer* (New York: Garland, 1983), p. 115.

70. *New York Times,* 28 March 1923, p. 18.

71. Eldot, *Governor Alfred E. Smith,* pp. 149–50.

72. Nelson, *State Recreation,* p. 175.

73. Ibid., p. 37.

74. Ibid., p. 38.

75. Frederick Law Olmsted, *Report of State Park Survey of California* (Sacramento: California State Printing Office, 1929), p. 3.

76. Ibid., p. 4; Nelson, *State Recreation,* p. 40.

77. Olmsted, *State Park Survey,* pp. 54–55, 57–69.

78. Dan R. Hull, "California Park Legislation," *American Planning and Civic Annual* (1937): 225. See also Nelson B. Drury, "State Park Acquisition as Viewed in California," *American Planning and Civic Annual* (1941): 157–60.

79. Norman D. Brown, *Hood, Bonnet, and Little Brown Jug: Texas Politics, 1921–1928* (College Station: Texas A&M University Press, 1984), pp. 137–38.

80. Nelson, *State Recreation,* pp. 259–60.

81. Ibid., pp. 131, 277–78.

82. Frederick, "Colonel Richard Lieber," p. 233.

83. Nelson, *State Recreation,* p. 139.

84. J. H. Fortenberry, "Mississippi," *American Planning and Civic Annual* (1938): 168.

85. Richard Lieber, "A Ten-Year Review," *American Planning and Civic Annual* (1935): 152.

86. Russell Reid, "North Dakota State Parks, " *American Planning and Civic Annual* (1939): 208; Lathrop, "Fifty Years of Parks in Minnesota," p. 198.

87. Page S. Bunker, "Alabama," *American Planning and Civic Annual* (1938): 163; R. A. Walker, "South Carolina," *American Planning and Civic Annual* (1938): 173.

Chapter 6. Economic Depression and Accelerated Change

1. Richard C. Keller, *Pennsylvania's Little New Deal* (New York: Garland, 1982), p. 68; Paul Tutt Stafford, *Government and the Needy: A Study of Public Assistance in New Jersey* (Princeton, N.J.: Princeton University Press, 1941), p. 142.

2. Josephine Chapin Brown, *Public Relief 1929–1939* (New York: Henry Holt, 1940), p. 89; Kenneth S. Davis, *FDR: The New York Years 1928–1933* (New York: Random House, 1985), p. 240.

3. Brown, *Public Relief,* p. 90; Marietta Stevenson, "The Out-of-Work," *State Government* 5 (February 1932): 3–4; Davis, *FDR,* p. 243; Rowland Haynes, *State Legislation for*

Unemployment Relief from January 1, 1931, to May 31, 1932 (Washington, D.C.: Government Printing Office, 1932), pp. 13–14.

4. Haynes, *State Legislation*, pp. 27–28; Stafford, *Government and the Needy*, pp. 103–5, 143; Stevenson, "Out-of-Work," p. 4.

5. Haynes, *State Legislation*, pp. 38–39, 49, 56, 70–72; Brown, *Public Relief*, pp. 95–96; Stevenson, "Out-of-Work," p. 5; John E. Miller, *Governor Philip F. LaFollette, the Wisconsin Progressives, and the New Deal* (Columbia: University of Missouri Press, 1982), p. 21.

6. Davis, *FDR*, p. 242.

7. O. Max Gardner, "Extension of State Operation of Highways and Roads," in *Proceedings of the Governors' Conference Twenty-fourth Annual Session* (Washington, D.C.: Printing Corporation of America, 1932), p. 18; James W. Fesler, "North Carolina's Local Government Commission," in *Readings in American State Government*, ed. Lane W. Lancaster and A. C. Breckenridge (New York: Rinehart, 1950), p. 331.

8. Fesler, "North Carolina's Local Government Commission," p. 333.

9. Joseph L. Morrison, *Governor O. Max Gardner: A Power in North Carolina and New Deal Washington* (Chapel Hill: University of North Carolina Press, 1971), p. 88.

10. *Biennial Report of the Superintendent of Public Instruction of North Carolina for the Scholastic Years 1932–1933 and 1933–1934* (Raleigh, N.C.: State Superintendent of Public Instruction, 1934), p. 11.

11. David T. Blose and Henry F. Alves, *Statistics of State School Systems 1937–38* (Washington, D.C.: Government Printing Office, 1941), p. 31; *Biennial Report of Superintendent of Public Instruction 1932–1933 and 1933–1934*, p. 15.

12. *Biennial Report of Superintendent of Public Instruction 1932–1933 and 1933–1934*, p. 15; George D. Strayer, Jr., *Centralizing Tendencies in the Administration of Public Education* (New York: Teachers College, Columbia University, 1934), pp. 26, 28; *Biennial Report of the Superintendent of Public Instruction of North Carolina for the Scholastic Years 1930–31 and 1931–32* (Raleigh, N.C.: State Superintendent of Public Instruction, 1932), p. 7; Allen J. Maxwell, "North Carolina's Plan of Consolidation, Retrenchment and Control of Expenditures," in *Proceedings of the Twenty-fourth Annual Conference on Taxation under the Auspices of the National Tax Association* (Columbia, S.C.: National Tax Association, 1932), pp. 39–40.

13. Allen J. Maxwell, "After Three Years," *State Government* 7 (January 1934): 21.

14. Blose and Alves, *Statistics of State School Systems 1937–38*, p. 32.

15. A. Steven Gatrell, "Herman Guy Kump and the West Virginia Fiscal Crisis of 1933," *West Virginia History* 42 (spring–summer 1981): 256.

16. David T. Blose and Henry F. Alves, *Statistics of State School Systems 1939–40 and 1941–42* (Washington, D.C.: Government Printing Office, 1944), pp. 22, 24.

17. *Ninety-Third Report of the Superintendent of Public Instruction for the Biennium 1933–1935* (Lansing, Mich.: Eugene B. Elliott, Superintendent of Public Instruction, 1936), p. 50; Ward W. Keesecker, *A Review of Education Legislation 1933 and 1934* (Washington, D.C.: Government Printing Office, 1935), pp. 10–11; Ward W. Keesecker, *A Review of Education Legislation 1935 and 1936* (Washington, D.C.: Government Printing Office, 1937), p. 8.

18. Walter E. Morgan, "State Sales Tax Returns and State General Fund Apportionments for Elementary Schools and High Schools," *California Schools* 7 (December 1936): 384–85; Keesecker, *Review of Educational Legislation 1933 and 1934*, pp. 6–7.

19. I. George Blake, *Paul V. McNutt: Portrait of a Hoosier Statesman* (Indianapolis: Central, 1966), p. 165; Keesecker, *Review of Education Legislation 1933 and 1934*, pp. 8–9.

20. *Eighty-Third and Eighty-Fourth Annual Reports of the Director of Education to the Governor of the State of Ohio* (Columbus, Ohio: F. J. Heer Printing, 1939), pp. 487, 529; Blose and Alves, *Statistics of State School Systems 1939–40 and 1941–42*, p. 24.

21. *Biennial Report of the Superintendent of Public Instruction of North Carolina for the Scholastic Years 1934–1935 and 1935–1936* (Raleigh, N.C.: State Superintendent of Public Instruction, 1936), p. 9.

22. Jerry Bruce Thomas, *An Appalachian New Deal: West Virginia in the Great Depression* (Lexington: University Press of Kentucky, 1998), p. 87.

23. W. S. Deffenbaugh, *Effects of the Depression upon Public Elementary and Secondary Schools and upon Colleges and Universities* (Washington, D.C.: Government Printing Office, 1938), pp. 9–10, 24.

24. U.S. Bureau of the Census, *Historical Statistics of the United States, Colonial Times to 1970, Bicentennial Edition* (Washington, D.C.: Government Printing Office, 1975), pp. 373–74, 1104.

25. John K. Norton, "Status of the Federal Aid Issue," *Teachers College Record* 40 (March 1939): 483.

26. Ibid., p. 490; Advisory Committee on Education, *The Federal Government and Education* (Washington, D.C.: Government Printing Office, 1938).

27. William F. Russell, "Federal Aid—Boon or Bane," *Teachers College Record* 35 (April 1934): 546.

28. Blose and Alves, *Statistics of State School Systems 1939–40 and 1941–42*, p. 22.

29. "Tax Delinquency," *Tax Policy*, no. 7 (May 1934): 1; Robert S. Ford, "Fiscal Policy in Michigan during the Depression," *Tax Policy* 2 (January 1935): 35.

30. Keith D. McFarland, *Harry H. Woodring: A Political Biography of FDR's Controversial Secretary of War* (Lawrence: University Press of Kansas, 1975), p. 41.

31. John F. Sly and George A. Shipman, *Tax Limitation in West Virginia: Relief to the Farm and the Home* (Morgantown: Bureau for Government Research, West Virginia University, 1934), pp. 6–7.

32. L. David Norris, "Pyrrhic Victory: The Campaign for Amendment Nineteen to the Arkansas Constitution," *Red River Valley Historical Review* 1 (autumn 1974): 252.

33. "Overhauling State Revenue Systems," *Tax Policy*, no. 10 (August 1934): 2–3; Rodney L. Mott and W. O. Suiter, "The Types and Extent of Existing Tax Limitations," in *Property Tax Limitation Laws*, ed. Glen Leet and Robert M. Paige (Chicago: Public Administration Service, 1936), pp. 41–47.

34. Harold D. Smith, "Tax Limitation in Michigan," in Leet and Paige, *Property Tax Limitation Laws*, p. 65; Sly and Shipman, *Tax Limitation in West Virginia*, p. 7; John F. Sly and George A. Shipman, "Tax Limitation in West Virginia," in Leet and Paige, *Property Tax Limitation Laws*, p. 80; Joseph P. Harris and Russell Barthell, "Washington Tax Limitation Measures," in Leet and Paige, *Property Tax Limitation Laws*, p. 75.

35. R. C. Atkinson, "Stringent Tax Limitation and Its Effects in Ohio," in Leet and Paige, *Property Tax Limitation Laws*, p. 73.

36. Carroll H. Wooddy, "Tax Limitation in Iowa," in Leet and Paige, *Property Tax Limitation Laws*, p. 54; Richard W. Nelson, "Iowa Fiscal Policies during the Depression," *Tax Policy* 2 (January 1935): 27.

37. Jens P. Jensen, "Kansas Tax Limitations," in Leet and Paige, *Property Tax Limitation Laws*, pp. 59–63; Glenn W. Fisher, *The Worst Tax? A History of the Property Tax in America* (Lawrence: University Press of Kansas, 1996), p. 160.

38. "Historical Review of State and Local Government Finances," *State and Local Government Special Studies*, no. 25 (June 1948): 14.

39. Ibid.; "Trends in State Revenues," in *The Book of the States 1939–40* (Chicago: Council of State Governments, 1939), p. 86.

40. Robert S. Ford and Albert Waxman, *Financing Government in Michigan* (Ann Arbor: University of Michigan Press, 1942), p. 39.

41. J. M. Labovitz, "Government Finance in Illinois during the Depression," *Tax Policy* 2 (January 1935): 16.

42. Francis B. Elwell, "The Decline of a Tax," in Lancaster and Breckenridge, *Readings in American State Government*, pp. 285–86.

43. "The Personal Income Tax and School Support," *Studies in State Education Administration*, no. 8 (February 1931): 20.

44. Donald R. McCoy, *Landon of Kansas* (Lincoln: University of Nebraska Press, 1966), p. 120.

45. "Present Status of State Income Taxes," *Tax Policy* 2 (May 1935): 1–5; *Federal-State-Local Finances: Significant Features of Fiscal Federalism* (Washington, D.C.: Advisory Commission on Intergovernmental Relations, 1974), p. 159.

46. "Present Status of State Income Taxes," p. 7.

47. Ibid., pp. 7–8; Roy G. Blakey and Gladys C. Blakey, *Taxation in Minnesota 1939 Supplement* (Minneapolis: University of Minnesota Press, 1939), p. 4.

48. If one includes the unemployment compensation tax, the figures for 1930 and 1940 are not comparable. "Historical Review of State and Local Government Finances," p. 20.

49. Michael F. Walsh, *Manual for the Use of the Legislature of the State of New York 1939* (Albany, N.Y.: J. B. Lyon, 1939), p. 755.

50. "Historical Review of State and Local Government Finances," p. 20; U.S. Bureau of the Census, *Historical Statistics of the United States*, pp. 1104–5, 1107.

51. *Report of the Connecticut Temporary Commission to Study the Tax Law of the State and to Make Recommendations concerning Their Revision* (Hartford: State of Connecticut, 1934), pp. 573–74.

52. Harold M. Groves, "Review of State Tax Legislation 1931–1932," in *Proceedings of the Twenty-fifth Annual Conference on Taxation under the Auspices of the National Tax Association* (Columbia, S.C.: National Tax Association, 1933), p. 19.

53. James W. Martin, "Rainbow's End," *State Government* 8 (January 1935): 298.

54. "Productivity of State Income Taxes," *Taxbits* 4 (March 1937): 1.

55. "Historical Review of State and Local Government Finances," p. 20.

56. William Winter, "Governor Mike Conner and the Sales Tax, 1932," *Journal of Mississippi History* 41 (August 1979): 215. For a slightly different figure on the amount in the general fund, see *Proceedings of the National Association of State Tax Administrators* (n.p.: National Association of State Tax Administrators, 1934), p. 15.

57. Winter, "Governor Mike Conner," p. 215.

58. Ibid., p. 221; Richard Aubrey McLemore, ed., *A History of Mississippi*, 2 vols. (Hattiesburg: University and College Press of Mississippi, 1973), 2:102.

59. A. H. Stone, "The Mississippi Sales Tax," in *Proceedings of the Twenty-Sixth Annual*

Conference on Taxation under the Auspices of the National Tax Association (Columbia, S.C.: National Tax Association, 1934), p. 228; "State Tax Yield Statistics: 1937," *Tax Policy* 5 (November–December 1937): 4, 10–11.

60. Stone, "Mississippi Sales Tax," p. 232.

61. *Proceedings of the National Association of State Tax Administrators*, p. 31.

62. "Historical Review of State and Local Government Finances," p. 20.

63. "Backward States in Tax Legislation: Florida-Illinois-Michigan-Ohio," *Taxbits* 3 (November 1935): 3–4.

64. Elmer L. Puryear, *Democratic Party Dissension in North Carolina 1928–1936* (Chapel Hill: University of North Carolina Press, 1962), p. 169.

65. Fred E. Stewart, "California's New Revenue System," in *The State Sales Tax,* ed. Egbert Ray Nichols, Marian Murray Nichols, and Egbert Ray Nichols, Jr. (New York: H. W. Wilson, 1938), p. 215.

66. "Remarks of George A. Critchlow at the 1933 Conference of the National Tax Association," in Nichols, Nichols, and Nichols, *State Sales Tax,* p. 297.

67. Alfred G. Buehler, "The General Sales Tax as a Normal State Revenue," in *Proceedings of the Twenty-seventh Annual Conference on Taxation under the Auspices of the National Tax Association* (Columbia, S.C.: National Tax Association, 1935), p. 108.

68. Jordan A. Schwarz, "John Nance Garner and the Sales Tax Rebellion of 1932," *Journal of Southern History* 30 (May 1964): 173.

69. Richard G. Lillard, *Desert Challenge: An Interpretation of Nevada* (New York: Alfred A. Knopf, 1942), p. 354; Nelson Manfred Blake, *The Road to Reno: A History of Divorce in the United States* (New York: Macmillan, 1962), p. 158. See also Frank W. Ingram and G. A. Ballard, "The Business of Migratory Divorce in Nevada," *Law and Contemporary Problems* 2 (June 1935): 302–8.

70. Blake, *Road to Reno,* p. 157.

71. Eric M. Moody, "Nevada's Legalization of Casino Gambling in 1931: Purely a Business Proposition," *Nevada Historical Society Quarterly* 37 (summer 1994): 84.

72. Ibid., p. 87.

73. Ibid., p. 89.

74. Ibid., p. 100; Phillip I. Earl, "The Legalization of Gambling in Nevada, 1931," *Nevada Historical Society Quarterly* 24 (spring 1981): 46.

75. Blake, *Road to Reno,* p. 158.

76. Ibid.; Lillard, *Desert Challenge,* pp. 340–41.

77. Lillard, *Desert Challenge,* p. 81; Russell R. Elliott, *History of Nevada* (Lincoln: University of Nebraska Press, 1973), p. 285.

78. Eric C. Clark, "Legislative Adoption of BAWI, 1936," *Journal of Mississippi History* 52 (November 1990): 285.

79. James C. Cobb, *The Selling of the South: The Southern Crusade for Industrial Development, 1936–1990,* 2d ed. (Urbana: University of Illinois Press, 1993), p. 11.

80. Ibid.; Clark, "Legislative Adoption of BAWI," p. 284; McLemore, *History of Mississippi,* 2:241.

81. Cobb, *Selling of the South,* pp. 14, 21.

82. Ernest J. Hopkins, *Mississippi's BAWI Plan: An Experiment in Industrial Subsidization* (Atlanta, Ga.: Federal Reserve Bank of Atlanta, 1944), p. 61; Cobb, *Selling of the South,* p. 24.

83. Hopkins, *Mississippi's BAWI Plan*, pp. 7–8.

84. Cobb, *Selling of the South*, p. 26.

85. McLemore, *History of Mississippi*, 2:117.

86. Cobb, *Selling of the South*, p. 5.

87. *Legislator* 1 (April 1926): 1.

88. *Legislator* 1 (August–September 1926): 1.

89. Ibid.

90. *The Book of the States 1935* (Chicago: Council of State Governments, 1935), p. 416. Another account said the five attending were four reporters and one lobbyist. *The Book of the States 1937* (Chicago: Council of State Governments, 1937), p. 8.

91. *Book of the States 1937*, p. 8.

92. Henry W. Toll, "Four Chapters concerning the Council of State Governments," *State Government* 11 (November 1938): 202.

93. Frederick L. Zimmermann, "Fourteen Creative Years," *State Government* 32 (summer 1959): 168; *Legislator* 2 (October–November 1929): 7–8.

94. *Legislator* 2 (October–November 1929): 7–8.

95. *Book of the States 1937*, pp. 15–16; Henry W. Toll, "The Founding of the Council of State Governments—Introduction," *State Government* 32 (summer 1959): 162; Zimmermann, "Fourteen Creative Years," p. 168. See "Spending to Save," *State Government* 4 (January 1931): 15, for different figures for the Spelman grant.

96. Toll, "Four Chapters," p. 201; *State Government* 6 (July 1933): inside cover.

97. Rodney L. Mott, "Research Work of the American Legislators' Association," *American Political Science Review* 26 (April 1932): 312; *Book of the States 1935*, p. 193.

98. *Book of the States 1935*, p. 386.

99. *State Government* 4 (February 1931): inside cover; *State Government* 5 (April 1932): 4.

100. *Book of the States 1935*, p. 109.

101. Ibid., p. 71.

102. Ibid., p. 74.

103. Ibid., pp. 77, 79; *State Government* 6 (July 1933): 4.

104. *Book of the States 1935*, p. 84. See also *Book of the States 1935*, pp. 316–31; and *State Government* 7 (July 1934): 135–36.

105. *Book of the States 1935*, pp. 121–26; Zimmermann, "Fourteen Creative Years," p. 170; J. F. Shaughnessy, "On the Road," *State Government* 7 (August 1934): 177–80.

106. Zimmermann, "Fourteen Creative Years," pp. 170, 171.

107. *Book of the States 1937*, pp. 49–50.

108. Ibid., pp. 11, 59.

109. Ibid., p. 34.

110. *Book of the States 1937*, pp. 19, 23.

111. Ibid., pp. 11, 20.

112. Henry W. Toll, "Horizons of the Council," *Book of the States 1939–40*, p. xi.

113. *Book of the States 1937*, pp. 45, 42.

114. Ibid., pp. 39–40; Glenn E. Brooks, *When Governors Convene: The Governors' Conference and National Politics* (Baltimore: Johns Hopkins University Press, 1961), pp. 37–38.

115. *Book of the States 1935*, p. 302.

116. Ibid., p. 93; *Book of the States 1937*, p. 1.

117. *Book of the States 1935*, p. 498.

118. *Legislator* 2 (October–November 1929): 7.

119. Edna D. Bullock, "Before We Enact a Law," *State Government* 3 (May 1930): 12–13; *Legislator* 2 (August–September 1929): 2.

120. Bullock, "Before We Enact a Law," p. 12.

121. "Ad Interim," *State Government* 5 (February 1932): 12, 13.

122. Ibid., p. 13

123. William J. Siffin, *The Legislative Council in the American States* (Bloomington: Indiana University Press, 1959), pp. 62–65; William J. Siffin, "Footnote to the Legislative Council Movement," *State Government* 28 (July 1955): 156–58; William H. Cape and John Paul Bay, *An Analysis of the Kansas Legislative Council and Its Research Department* (Lawrence: Governmental Research Center, University of Kansas, 1963), pp. 26–27.

124. Siffin, *Legislative Council,* 67.

125. Frederic H. Guild, "Development of the Legislative Council Idea," *Annals of the American Academy of Political and Social Science* 195 (January 1938): 145–46, 148.

126. Frederic H. Guild, "Achievements of the Kansas Legislative Council," *American Political Science Review* 29 (August 1935): 637; Roy H. Johnson, "A Review of Legislative Councils," *University of Kansas City Law Review* 8 (February 1940): 71

127. Harold M. Dorr, "A Legislative Council for Michigan," *American Political Science Review* 28 (April 1934): 275.

128. Hubert R. Gallagher, "Legislative Councils," in *Unicameral Legislatures,* ed. E. C. Buehler (New York: Noble & Noble, 1937), p. 93; Siffin, *Legislative Council,* p. 109.

129. Siffin, *Legislative Council,* p. 134. See also T. V. Smith, "Illinois Calls on Kansas," *State Government* 10 (December 1937): 252–54.

130. Siffin, *Legislative Council,* p. 135.

131. "Legislative Councils in Action," *State Government* 16 (February 1943): 47.

Chapter 7. Working in the Shadows

1. *Proceedings of the Governors' Conference 1958* (Chicago: Governors' Conference, 1958), pp. 85–91.

2. *Proceedings of the Governors' Conference 1959* (Chicago: Governors' Conference, 1959), p. 54.

3. Frederic H. Guild, "The Legislature," in *Model State Constitution with Explanatory Articles,* 5th ed. (New York: National Municipal League, 1948), pp. 27–29.

4. *Report of the Nebraska Legislative Council Committee on Annual Legislative Sessions* (Lincoln: Nebraska Legislative Council, 1952), p. 24; Research Department, Kansas Legislative Council, *Annual Legislative Sessions* (Topeka: Kansas Legislative Council, 1953), p. 28.

5. John A. Perkins, "The Legislatures and the Future of the States," *State Government* 19 (October 1946): 256; *Our State Legislatures,* rev. ed. (Chicago: Council of State Governments, 1948), p. 13.

6. Perkins, "Legislature and Future of States," p. 256.

7. Lynton K. Caldwell, "Strengthening State Legislatures," *American Political Science Review* 41 (April 1947): 282–84, 286; *Our State Legislatures,* pp. 4–5, 9, 12.

8. Jarvis Hunt, "How Our State Legislatures Can Be Improved," *State Government* 17 (September 1944): 400.

9. *State Government* 17 (October 1944): 414.

10. Kansas Legislative Council, *Annual Legislative Sessions*, p. 17; *Report of Nebraska Committee on Annual Sessions*, p. 15.

11. *Report of Nebraska Committee on Annual Sessions*, p. 17; Kansas Legislative Council, *Annual Legislative Sessions*, p. 20.

12. Patricia Shumate Wirt, "The Legislature," in *Salient Issues of Constitutional Revision*, ed. John P. Wheeler (New York: National Municipal League, 1961), p. 75.

13. C. N. Fortenberg and Edward H. Hobbs, "The Mississippi Legislature," in *Power in American State Legislatures: Case Studies of the Arkansas, Louisiana, Mississippi, and Oklahoma Legislatures*, ed. Alex B. Lacy, Jr. (New Orleans: Tulane University, 1967), pp. 82–83.

14. *The Book of the States 1960–1961* (Chicago: Council of State Governments, 1960), p. 33; *The Book of the States 1962–1963* (Chicago: Council of State Governments, 1962), p. 38.

15. Jack E. Holmes, "New Mexico Reorganizes Its Legislative Committee," *State Government* 28 (October 1955): 231–32, 240.

16. "Legislative Reorganization since World War II," *State Government* 27 (February 1954): 34; *Book of States 1960–61*, p. 32.

17. Leon A. Wilber, "Mississippi Governmental Development, 1945 to 1963," *Southern Quarterly* 2 (October 1963): 5.

18. *Book of States 1962–63*, pp. 36–37.

19. Hallie Farmer, "Legislative Planning and Research in Alabama," *Journal of Politics* 9 (August 1947): 429.

20. Arthur J. Waterman, Jr., "Research for the Legislature in Florida," in *Studies in Florida Administration* (Gainesville: Public Administration Clearing Service of the University of Florida, 1949), p. 93.

21. "Legislative Research in the States," *State Government* 25 (October 1952): 233; *Book of States 1962–63*, p. 66.

22. "Legislative Research," pp. 233–35.

23. C. N. Fortenberry and Donald S. Vaughan, "Staff Assistance for the Mississippi Legislature," *Public Administration Survey* 5 (July 1958): 5, 7–8.

24. D. Jay Doubleday, *Legislative Review of the Budget in California* (Berkeley, Calif.: Institute of Governmental Studies, 1967), pp. 35, 52.

25. *Book of States 1960–61*, p. 62.

26. "Origin and Development of the National Legislative Conference," *State Government* 34 (winter 1961): 34–38.

27. Bennett M. Rich, "The Governor as Administrative Head," in Wheeler, *Salient Issues of Constitutional Revision*, p. 103.

28. Larry Sabato, *Goodbye to Good-time Charlie: The American Governorship Transformed*, 2d ed. (Washington, D.C.: Congressional Quarterly Press, 1983), p. 104.

29. Ibid., p. 99.

30. Shelden D. Elliott, "Arthur T. Vanderbilt: Administrator of Justice," *State Government* 31 (autumn 1958): 226.

31. G. Alan Tarr and Mary Cornelia Aldis Porter, *State Supreme Courts in State and Nation* (New Haven, Conn.: Yale University Press, 1988), p. 188.

32. Elliott, "Vanderbilt," p. 229.

33. Tarr and Porter, *State Supreme Courts*, p. 192.

34. Sidney Schulman, *Toward Judicial Reform in Pennsylvania: A Study in Court Reorganization* (Philadelphia: University of Pennsylvania Law School, 1962), p. 192.

35. Edward W. Hudgins, "The Judicial Council and Judicial Conference in Virginia," *State Government* 27 (January 1954): 19.

36. *Book of the States 1960-61*, p. 112.

37. Meredith H. Doyle, "The Administrative Officer of the Courts: His Role in Government," *State Government* 30 (December 1957): 263.

38. Hudgins, "Judicial Council," p. 19. See also Frederick W. Invernizzi, "The Office and Work of the Court Administrator," *Journal of the American Judicature Society* 43 (April 1960): 186-89.

39. Benjamin F. Crane and Shelden D. Elliott, "Progress in Judicial Administration— 1953," *State Government* 26 (November 1953): 271.

40. "Justices of the Peace Abolished in Ohio by Legislature," *Journal of the American Judicature Society* 41 (June 1957): 15.

41. I. Ridgway Davis, *Administration of Justice in Connecticut* (Storrs: University of Connecticut, 1963), pp. 27-33; *Book of the States 1960-61*, p. 100; Schulman, *Toward Judicial Reform*, p. 237; "Connecticut Minor Court Reorganization Moves Ahead," *Journal of the American Judicature Society* 43 (February 1960): 169; David Mars, "Court Reorganization in Connecticut," *Journal of the American Judicature Society* 41 (June 1957): 6-14.

42. *Book of the States 1960-61*, p. 100; *Book of the States 1962-63*, p. 117.

43. *Book of the States 1962-63*, p. 118.

44. Schulman, *Toward Judicial Reform*, p. 233.

45. Jack W. Peltason, *The Missouri Plan for the Selection of Judges* (Columbia: University of Missouri, 1945), p. 38.

46. Ibid., pp. 42, 56; Richard A. Watson and Randal G. Downing, *The Politics of the Bench and Bar: Judicial Selection under the Missouri Nonpartisan Court Plan* (New York: John Wiley, 1969), pp. 10-11.

47. Glenn R. Winters, "The New Mexico Judicial Selection Campaign—A Case History," *Journal of the American Judicature Society* 35 (April 1952): 170, 174; Schulman, *Toward Judicial Reform*, p. 220; Philip L. Dubois, "The Politics of Innovation in State Courts: The Merit Plan of Judicial Selection," *Publius* 20 (winter 1990): 37.

48. Schulman, *Toward Judicial Reform*, pp. 233-34; Dubois, "Politics of Innovation," p. 36.

49. *Book of the States 1960-61*, p. 99; *Book of the States 1962-63*, p. 120; Dubois, "Politics of Innovation," p. 29; "Iowa Adopts Society's Judicial Selection and Tenure Plan for all State Judges," *Journal of the American Judicature Society* 46 (June 1962): 1-3; "Greatest State Court Reform Victory in American History; Society's Judicial Selection Plan Wins in Nebraska," *Journal of the American Judicature Society* 46 (November 1962): 117-18.

50. "The Conference of Chief Justices," *State Government* 22 (December 1949): 276-77; "Conference of Chief Justices Is Organized in St. Louis," *Journal of the American Judicature Society* 33 (October 1949): 72.

51. John R. Dethmers, "Ten Years of Progress: The Conference of Chief Justices," *American Bar Association Journal* 45 (January 1959): 47.

52. Charles A. Quattlebaum, "Federal Aid to Elementary and Secondary Education," *Harvard Educational Review* 18 (spring 1948): 86.

53. M. Vashti Burr, "Arguments for and against Federal Aid to Education," *State Government* 20 (December 1947): 307-8.

54. Quattlebaum, "Federal Aid," p. 76.

55. Burr, "Arguments," p. 309.

56. *Digest of Education Statistics 1996* (Washington, D.C.: U.S. Department of Education, 1996), p. 50.

57. U.S. Bureau of the Census, *Historical Statistics of the United States, Colonial Times to 1970, Bicentennial Edition*, pt. 1 (Washington, D.C.: Government Printing Office, 1975), p. 373.

58. Ibid., p. 368.

59. Francis S. Chase and John D. Baker, "Rural Education Today," in *The Fifty-first Yearbook of the National Society for the Study of Education*, pt. 2, *Education in Rural Communities*, ed. Nelson B. Henry (Chicago: University of Chicago Press, 1952), pp. 95, 91.

60. Leslie L. Chisholm and M. L. Cushman, "The Relationship of Programs of School Finance to the Reorganization of Local School Administrative Units and Local School Centers," in *Problems and Issues in Public School Finance*, ed. R. L. Johns and E. L. Morphet (New York: National Conference of Professor of Education Administration, 1952), p. 79.

61. Bureau of Census, *Historical Statistics*, p. 368; *Book of the States 1962–63*, p. 317.

62. Elmer L. Breckner, "Washington Reorganizes Its School Districts for Better Education," *American School Board Journal* 103 (December 1941): 17.

63. Leslie L. Chisholm, "School District Reorganization in the State of Washington," in *Your School District: The Report of the National Commission on School District Reorganization* (Washington, D.C.: Department of Rural Education, National Education Association, 1948), pp. 215–23.

64. Ibid., p. 227; George D. Strayer, *A Digest of a Report of a Survey of Public Education in the State of Washington* (Olympia: State of Washington, 1946), p. 42.

65. *Some Aspects of School Administration in Illinois* (Springfield: Illinois Legislative Council, 1938), pp. 7, 10, 14, 16.

66. Kate V. Wofford, "Better Rural Education through Reorganization of the Administrative Unit and the Curriculum," in Henry, *Fifty-first Yearbook of National Society for Study of Education*, p. 171.

67. *School District Organization* (Washington, D.C.: American Association of School Administrators, 1958), p. 168; Mary Ellen Glass, "Nevada Turning Points: The State Legislature of 1955," *Nevada Historical Society Quarterly* 23 (winter 1980): 224–25.

68. *School District Organization*, pp. 170–71; *The Book of the States 1956–57* (Chicago: Council of State Governments, 1956), p. 255.

69. Thomas H. Naylor, "The Status of Education Reorganization," *Public Administration Survey* 5 (January 1958): 1–2; *School District Organization*, p. 170.

70. Alfred D. Simpson, "Financing Higher Education," *Journal of Higher Education* 19 (April 1948): 195; John D. Millet, *Financing Higher Education in the United States* (New York: Columbia University Press, 1952), p. 425.

71. Henry D. Badger, *Statistics of Higher Education 1957–58: Receipts, Expenditures, and Property* (Washington, D.C.: U.S. Department of Health, Education, and Welfare, 1961), pp. 21, 13, 27.

72. Ibid., pp. 22, 37; Kenneth A. Simon and W. Vance Grant, *Digest of Educational Statistics 1966* (Washington, D.C.: U.S. Department of Health, Education, and Welfare, 1966), p. 83.

73. Simon and Grant, *Digest of Educational Statistics*, p. 64; Seymour E. Harris, *Higher Education: Resources and Finance* (New York: McGraw-Hill, 1962), p. 327.

74. Algo D. Henderson, "New York's State University System," *State Government* 22

(February 1949): 39–41, 52; Alvin C. Eurich, "The State University of New York: A Pioneering Venture in Higher Education," *Higher Education* 6 (1 April 1950): 169–72; Alvin C. Eurich, "State University of New York—Two Years Young," *Educational Record* 32 (January 1951): 56–63; "State University of New York Makes Progress," *Higher Education* 8 (1 September 1951): 1–5; *New York Red Book 1968–1969* (Albany, N.Y.: Williams Press, 1968), pp. 679–81; William Morsch, *State Community College Systems: The Role and Operation in Seven States* (New York: Praeger, 1971), p. 108.

75. Herman F. Eschenbacher, *The University of Rhode Island: A History of Land-Grant Education in Rhode Island* (New York: Appleton-Century-Crofts, 1967), p. 336.

76. Ibid., pp. 342, 346–52, 361, 374.

77. Leslie L. Hanawalt, *A Place of Light: The History of Wayne State University* (Detroit: Wayne State University Press, 1968), pp. 406–7. See also Samuel Halperin, *A University in the Web of Politics* (New York: Holt, Rinehart & Winston, 1960).

78. Doak S. Campbell, "A State Plans for the Future," *Junior College Journal* 26 (September 1955): 4–5; Morsch, *State Community College Systems*, p. 48.

79. Morsch, *State Community College Systems*, pp. 47, 50.

80. Luther H. Hodges, *Businessman in the Statehouse: Six Years as Governor of North Carolina* (Chapel Hill: University of North Carolina Press, 1962), p. 198.

81. Cameron Fincher, *Historical Development of the University System of Georgia: 1932–1990* (Athens: Institute of Higher Education, University of Georgia, 1991), pp. 49–50.

82. S. V. Martorana, "Recent State Legislation Affecting Junior Colleges," *Junior College Journal* 30 (February 1960): 315.

83. Morsch, *State Community College Systems*, pp. 26–27; William P. Niland, "The Master Plan Study and Trends in California Junior Colleges," *Junior College Journal* 31 (April 1961): 429–30.

84. Lyman A. Glenny, *Autonomy of Public Colleges: The Challenge of Coordination* (New York: McGraw-Hill, 1959), p. 37.

85. Ibid., p. 38.

86. Ibid., p. 39.

87. Ibid., p. 29. See also John D. Millett, *Politics and Higher Education* (University: University of Alabama Press, 1974), pp. 8–12.

88. Glenny, *Autonomy of Public Colleges*, pp. 31–33, 29–30.

89. M. M. Chambers, "Changes in the State Administrative Structure for Higher Education during 1959," *Journal of Higher Education* 31 (March 1960): 150–51.

90. *Book of the States 1962–63*, pp. 321–22.

91. H. C. Nixon, "The Southern Governors' Conference as a Pressure Group," *Journal of Politics* 6 (August 1944): 338.

92. Robert A. Lively, "The South and Freight Rates: Political Settlement of an Economic Argument," *Journal of Southern History* 14 (August 1948): 364.

93. Lively, "South and Freight Rates," p. 375.

94. Albert Lepawsky, "Government Planning in the South," *Journal of Politics* 10 (August 1948): 561.

95. *Industrial Development Bond Financing* (Washington, D.C.: Advisory Commission on Intergovernmental Relations, 1963), p. 56; James C. Cobb, *The Selling of the South: The Southern Crusade for Industrial Development, 1936–1990*, 2d ed. (Urbana: University of Illinois Press, 1993), p. 36.

96. Cobb, *Selling of the South,* p. 75; Numan V. Bartley, *The Creation of Modern Georgia* (Athens: University of Georgia Press, 1983), pp. 199–200.

97. Hodges, *Businessman in the Statehouse,* pp. 29–30.

98. Ibid., pp. 58, 74–75.

99. Ibid., p. 203. See also Cobb, *Selling of the South,* pp. 171–76.

100. *Industrial Development Bond Financing,* p. 81.

101. William R. Davlin, "State Development Corporations: The Pennsylvania Experience," *Law and Contemporary Problems* 24 (winter 1959): 89, 92, 94.

102. *Industrial Development Bond Financing,* p. 81.

103. *Book of the States 1962–63,* p. 453.

104. John G. Shott, *How "Right-to-Work" Laws Are Passed: Florida Set the Pattern* (Washington D.C.: Public Affairs Institute, 1956), pp. 18–43; Michael S. Wade, *The Bitter Issue: The Right to Work Law in Arizona* (Tucson: Arizona Historical Society, 1976).

105. *The Case against "Right to Work" Laws* (Washington, D.C.: Congress of Industrial Organizations, 1955), pp. 24–25.

106. Sanford Cohen, "Operating under Right-to-Work Laws," *Labor Law Journal* 9 (August 1958): 576.

107. W. R. Brown, "State Experience in Defending the Right to Work," *Proceedings of the Academy of Political Science* 27 (May 1954): 41.

108. *San Francisco Chronicle,* 28 October 1958, p. 32.

109. *Denver Post,* 21 October 1958, p. 15; 31 October 1958, p. 41.

110. *San Francisco Chronicle,* 23 October 1958, p. 14; *Cleveland Call and Post,* 1 November 1958, sec. D, p. 2.

111. David A. Swankin, "State Right-to-Work Legislative Action in 1958," *Monthly Labor Review* 81 (December 1958): 1380.

112. *Wall Street Journal,* 6 November 1958, p. 6.

113. Ibid., 7 November 1958, p. 10.

Chapter 8. Reform and Recognition

1. Daniel J. Evans, "The Reaffirmation of the States," *State Government* 47 (autumn 1974): 238.

2. *State Actions 1974: Building on Innovation* (Washington, D.C.: Advisory Commission on Intergovernmental Relations, 1975), frontispiece.

3. Daniel Elazar, "The New Federalism: Can the States Be Trusted?" *Public Interest,* no. 35 (spring 1974): 90–91; Richard H. Leach, "A Quiet Revolution 1933–1976," in *The Book of the States 1976–1977* (Lexington, Ky.: Council of State Governments, 1976), 27.

4. Alan J. Wyner, "Legislative Reform and Politics in California: What Happened, Why, and So What?" in *State Legislative Innovation: Case Studies of Washington, Ohio, Florida, Illinois, Wisconsin, and California,* ed. James A. Robinson (New York: Praeger, 1973), p. 60; Ernest A. Engelbert, "Legislative Reorganization in California," *State Government* 36 (winter 1963): 59.

5. Wyner, "Legislative Reform," pp. 61, 73.

6. Engelbert, "Legislative Reorganization," p. 60.

7. Alan Rosenthal, *Legislative Life: People, Process, and Performance in the States* (New York: Harper & Row, 1981), p. 212; Wyner, "Legislative Reform," p. 60.

8. "Rising Tide for Strengthening State Governments Cheer 1500 Delegates at Nation Legislative Conference," *State Legislatures Progress Reporter* 1 (October 1965): 1.

9. C. George DeStefano, "Contemporary Legislative Leadership in a Dynamic Society," *Yearbook of the National Conference of State Legislative Leaders,* no. 2 (November 1967): 14, 16.

10. Jesse M. Unruh, "The Way to Legislative Reform," *State Legislatures Progress Reporter* 4 (May–June 1969): supplement.

11. Larry Margolis, "Revitalizing State Legislatures," *Yearbook of the National Conference of State Legislative Leaders,* no. 3 (November 1968): 12; Larry Margolis, "Some Considerations for Legislative Modernization," *Yearbook of the National Conference of State Legislative Leaders,* no. 4 (November 1969): 7.

12. Alan Rosenthal, *Strengthening the Maryland Legislature* (New Brunswick, N.J.: Rutgers University Press, 1968), p. v.

13. Alan Rosenthal, "Reform in State Legislatures," in *Encyclopedia of the American Legislative System,* 3 vols., ed. Joel H. Silbey (New York: Scribner's, 1994), 2:840.

14. "Trend toward Annual Sessions Grows as 36 Convene This Year," *State Legislatures Progress Reporter* 4 (January–February 1970): 1.

15. John Burns, *Sometime Governments: A Critical Study of the 50 American Legislatures* (New York: Bantam Books, 1971), p. 290.

16. "Ask Modern Methods for West Virginia," *State Legislatures Progress Reporter* 4 (January–February 1969): 1; "Iowa Committees Would Be Reduced," *State Legislatures Progress Reporter* 4 (January–February 1969): 1; "Citizen Committee Studies Legislature," *National Civic Review* 57 (May 1968): 273.

17. Edward Lindsay, "Ways to Achieve Strong Legislature Charted in Illinois," *State Legislatures Progress Reporter* 2 (January 1967): 1; "Idahoans Propose Smaller Legislature," *State Legislatures Progress Reporter* 4 (January–February 1969): 3. See also "Lawmakers Urged by Idaho Citizens to Adopt Reforms," *State Legislatures Progress Reporter* 4 (October 1968): 1–2.

18. "Washington Citizens Group Charts 75 Ways to Upgrade Legislature," *State Legislatures Progress Reporter* 2 (February 1967): 1; "Freedom and Space Asked for Oregon," *State Legislatures Progress Reporter* 4 (January–February 1969): 1.

19. William Pound, "The State Legislatures," in *The Book of the States 1982–83* (Lexington, Ky.: Council of State Governments, 1982), p. 182.

20. Herbert L. Wiltsee, "The State Legislatures," in *Book of the States 1976–77,* p. 34.

21. Cal Ledbetter, Jr., "Legislative Improvements in Arkansas," *State Government* 46 (spring 1973): 110, 112; Ralph Craft, *Strengthening the Arkansas Legislature* (New Brunswick, N.J.: Rutgers University Press, 1972), pp. 11–12.

22. Burns, *Sometime Governments,* p. 64.

23. Wyner, "Legislative Reform," pp. 73–74.

24. Dan P. Allen, "What Ails the Legislature?" *State Legislatures Progress Reporter* 3 (October 1967): supplement.

25. "Many States Act to Give Lawmakers More Adequate Office Space," *State Legislatures Progress Reporter* 5 (May–June 1970): 3; Wiltsee, "State Legislatures 1976–77," p. 38.

26. Wiltsee, "State Legislatures 1976–77," p. 38.

27. Brian Weberg, "Changes in Legislative Staff," *Journal of State Government* 61 (November–December 1988): 191–92.

28. *The Book of the States 1980–1981* (Lexington, Ky.: Council of State Governments, 1980), pp. 128–29.

29. Carolyn L. Kenton, "Modern Legislative Staffing," *State Government* 47 (summer 1974): 167; J. T. Williams, Jr., "Better Staffing Means Stronger Legislature," *Yearbook of the National Conference of State Legislative Leaders*, no. 4 (November 1969): 34–35; Alan Seth Chartock and Max Berking, *Strengthening the Wisconsin Legislature* (New Brunswick, N.J.: Rutgers University Press, 1970), pp. 9–11.

30. Wiltsee, "State Legislatures 1976–77," p. 36; William Pound, "The State Legislatures," in *Book of the States 1980–81*, p. 79.

31. Wiltsee, "State Legislatures 1976–77," p. 37.

32. Coleman B. Ransone, Jr., *The Office of Governor in the United States* (University: University of Alabama Press, 1956), pp. 227, 234.

33. James K. Conant, "Executive Branch Reorganization in the States, 1965–1991," in *The Book of the States 1992–93 Edition* (Lexington, Ky.: Council of State Governments, 1992), pp. 67–69.

34. George A. Bell, "State Administrative Organization Activities, 1970–1971," in *The Book of the States, 1972–1973* (Lexington, Ky.: Council of State Governments, 1972), p. 141.

35. George A. Bell, "State Administrative Organization Activities, 1972–1973," in *The Book of the States 1974–75* (Lexington, Ky.: Council of State Governments, 1974), p. 137.

36. Douglas Fox, "Reorganizing Connecticut State Government," *State Government* 52 (spring 1979): 80–84; Judith Nicholson, "State Administrative Organization Activities, 1976–1977," in *The Book of the States 1978–1979* (Lexington, Ky.: Council of State Governments, 1978), p. 105.

37. Bell, "Administrative Organization Activities, 1970–71," p. 143.

38. George A. Bell, "State Administrative Organization Activities, 1974–1975," in *Book of the States 1976–77*, p. 105.

39. Fox, "Reorganizing Connecticut State Government," p. 82.

40. George A. Bell, "State Administrative Organization Activities, 1968–1969," in *The Book of the States 1970–71* (Lexington, Ky.: Council of State Governments, 1970), p. 135.

41. Bell, "Administrative Organization Activities, 1974–75," p. 105; Bell, "Administrative Organization Activities, 1970–71," p. 142; Conant, "Executive Branch Reorganization," pp. 68–69. See also Thad L. Beyle, "From Governor to Governors," in *The State of the States*, ed. Carl E. Van Horn (Washington, D.C.: Congressional Quarterly Press, 1989), p. 41.

42. Larry Sabato, *Goodbye to Good-time Charlie: The American Governorship Transformed*, 2d ed. (Washington, D.C.: Congressional Quarterly Press, 1983), pp. 173–74; Carol S. Weissert, "The National Governors' Association: 1908–1983," *State Government* 56 (1983): 50; Beyle, "From Governor to Governors," p. 57.

43. *Washington Post*, 12 June 1974, p. A28.

44. Sabato, *Goodbye to Good-time Charlie*, pp. 1–2.

45. George H. Callcott, *Maryland and America 1940 to 1980* (Baltimore: Johns Hopkins University Press, 1985), pp. 289–96; John W. Raimo, ed., *Biographical Directory of the Governors of the United States 1978–1983* (Westport, Conn.: Meckler Publishing, 1975), pp. 125–26.

46. Raimo, *Biographical Directory of Governors*, pp. 292–93.

47. Robert A. Shapiro and Rachel N. Doan, "A Profile of State Court Administrators," *Judicature* 60 (October 1976): 119, 120.

48. Robert G. Nieland and Rachel N. Doan, *State Court Administrative Offices*, 2d ed. (Chicago: American Judicature Society, 1982), p. 9.

49. Jag C. Uppal, "The State of the Judiciary," in *Book of the States 1978–79*, p. 81.

50. G. Alan Tarr and Mary Cornelia Aldis Porter, *State Supreme Courts in State and Nation* (New Haven, Conn.: Yale University Press, 1988), p. 69.

51. William H. Stewart, Jr., *The Alabama Constitutional Commission: A Pragmatic Approach to Constitutional Revision* (University: University of Alabama Press, 1975), p. 85.

52. Larry Berkson and Susan Carbon, *Court Unification: History, Politics and Implementation* (Washington, D.C.: National Institute of Law Enforcement and Criminal Justice, 1978), p. 47.

53. Tarr and Porter, *State Supreme Courts*, p. 90.

54. Berkson and Carbon, *Court Unification*, p. 49. See also M. Roland Nachman, Jr., "Alabama's Breakthrough for Reform," *Judicature* 56 (October 1972): 112–14.

55. Stewart, *Alabama Constitutional Commission*, pp. 96, 105, 110.

56. James E. Farmer, "Indiana Modernizes Its Courts," *Judicature* 54 (March 1971): 327.

57. Ronald K. L. Collins, Peter J. Galie, and John Kinkaid, "State High Courts, State Constitutions, and Individual Rights Litigation since 1980: A Judicial Survey," *Publius* 16 (summer 1986): 142.

58. *Michigan v. Mosley*, 423 U.S. 120; A. E. Dick Howard, "State Courts and Constitutional Rights in the Day of the Burger Court," *Virginia Law Review* 62 (June 1976): 874.

59. William J. Brennan, Jr., "State Constitutions and the Protection of Individual Rights," *Harvard Law Review* 90 (January 1977): 491, 503.

60. Stewart G. Pollock, "State Constitutions as Separate Sources of Fundamental Rights," *Rutgers Law Review* 35 (summer 1983): 716; Ronald K. L. Collins, "Reliance on State Constitutions—Away from a Reactionary Approach," *Hastings Constitutional Law Quarterly* 9 (fall 1981): 1–2.

61. G. Alan Tarr, *Understanding State Constitutions* (Princeton, N.J.: Princeton University Press, 1998), p. 165.

62. William J. Brennan, Jr., "The Bill of Rights: State Constitutions as Guardians of Individual Rights," *New York State Bar Journal* 59 (May 1987): 18.

63. Shirley S. Abrahamson, "Reincarnation of State Courts," *Southwestern Law Journal* 36 (1982): 971.

64. *Pruneyard Shopping Center v. Robins*, 447 U.S. 81; Stanley Mosk, "State Constitutionalism: Both Liberal and Conservative," *Texas Law Review* 63 (March–April 1985): 1090.

65. Mosk, "State Constitutionalism," p. 1092.

66. John Kinkaid, "The New Judicial Federalism," *Journal of State Government* 61 (September–October 1988): 166.

67. Hans A. Linde, "Without 'Due Process': Unconstitutional Law in Oregon," *Oregon Law Review* 49 (February 1970): 135, 183.

68. Ronald K. L. Collins, "Reliance on State Constitutions: Some Random Thoughts," *Mississippi Law Journal* 54 (September–December 1984): 374. See also Hans A. Linde, "First Things First: Rediscovering the States' Bills of Rights," *University of Baltimore Law Review* 9 (spring 1980): 379–96; Hans A. Linde, "E Pluribus—Constitutional Theory and State Courts," *Georgia Law Review* 18 (winter 1984): 165–200.

69. *People v. Disbrow*, 16 California 3d 113, 114–15; Brennan, "State Constitutions," p. 499.

70. *Serrano v. Priest II*, 18 California 3d 728; Linde, "First Things First," p. 387; Mary Cor-

nelia Porter, "State Supreme Courts and the Legacy of the Warren Court: Some Old Inquiries for a New Situation," in *State Supreme Courts: Policymakers in the Federal System*, ed. Mary Cornelia Porter and G. Alan Tarr (Westport, Conn.: Greenwood Press, 1982), p. 14.

71. *Robins v. Pruneyard Shopping Center*, 23 California 3d 899; *State Constitutions in the Federal System: Selected Issues and Opportunities for State Initiatives* (Washington, D.C.: Advisory Commission on Intergovernmental Relations, 1989), p. 52; Joseph Grodin, "The Role of State Constitutions in a Federal System," in *Constitutional Reform in California: Making State Government More Effective and Responsive*, ed. Bruce E. Cain and Roger G. Noll (Berkeley, Calif.: Institute of Governmental Studies Press, 1995), pp. 38–39; Mosk, "State Constitutionalism," p. 1090.

72. Howard, "State Courts and Constitutional Rights," pp. 875–76; Abrahamson, "Reincarnation of State Courts," p. 952; Brennan, "Bill of Rights," p. 19.

73. Brennan, "State Constitutions," p. 499; Stanley H. Friedelbaum, "Independent State Grounds: Contemporary Invitations to Judicial Activism," in Porter and Tarr, *State Supreme Courts*, p. 36.

74. *State v. Kaluna*, 55 Hawaii 369 (1974); Linde, "First Things First," p. 392; Brennan, "State Constitutions," p. 500; Friedelbaum, "Independent State Grounds," p. 35.

75. *State Constitutions in the Federal System*, pp. 52–53, 57; Kincaid, "New Judicial Federalism," pp. 164–65.

76. See Mary Cornelia Porter and G. Alan Tarr, "The New Judicial Federalism and the Ohio Supreme Court: Anatomy of a Failure," *Ohio State Law Journal* 45 (1984): 143–59.

77. Tarr, *Understanding State Constitutions*, p. 167.

78. Linde, "E Pluribus," p. 200; Mosk, "State Constitutionalism," p. 1091.

79. Leon Rothenberg, "Recent Trends in State Taxation," in *The Book of the States 1966–1967* (Chicago: Council of State Governments, 1966), p. 198; Leon Rothenberg, "Recent Trends in State Taxation," in *The Book of the States 1968–1969* (Chicago: Council of State Governments, 1968), p. 196; Leon Rothenberg, "State Budgets—1968," *State Government* 41 (spring 1968): 96.

80. Ira Sharkansky, *The Maligned States: Policy Accomplishments, Problems, and Opportunities* (New York: McGraw-Hill, 1972), p. 68.

81. *Significant Features of Fiscal Federalism*, vol. 2, *Revenues and Expenditures* (Washington, D.C.: Advisory Commission on Intergovernmental Relations, 1994), pp. 46, 12.

82. Allan R. Odden and Lawrence O. Picus, *School Finance: A Policy Perspective* (New York: McGraw-Hill, 1992), p. 6.

83. *State Actions in 1975* (Washington, D.C.: Advisory Commission on Intergovernmental Relations, 1976), p. 32.

84. John F. Due and John L. Mikesell, *Sales Taxation: State and Local Structure and Administration*, 2d ed. (Washington, D.C.: Urban Institute Press, 1994), p. 3; John Shannon and Robert J. Kleine, "Characteristics of a 'Balanced' State-Local Tax System," in *State Government: CQ's Guide to Current Issues and Activities 1986–87*, ed. Thad L. Beyle (Washington, D.C.: Congressional Quarterly, 1986), p. 159.

85. *Boston Globe*, 28 January 1965, morning edition, pp. 12, 34.

86. Ibid., p. 14.

87. J. Harvie Wilkinson III, *Harry Byrd and the Changing Face of Virginia Politics 1945–1966* (Charlottesville: University Press of Virginia, 1968), pp. 289–94.

88. Deane C. Davis and Nancy Price Graff, *Deane C. Davis: An Autobiography* (Shelburne, Vt.: New England Press, 1991), pp. 237, 240.

89. Shannon and Kleine, "Characteristics of a 'Balanced' Tax System," p. 159; Daniel R. Feenberg and Harvey S. Rosen, "State Personal Income and Sales Taxes, 1977–1983," in *Studies in State and Local Public Finance*, ed. Harvey S. Rosen (Chicago: University of Chicago Press, 1986), p. 135.

90. *Chicago Tribune*, 2 April 1969, sec. 1, pp. 8, 1.

91. *Cleveland Plain Dealer*, 17 March 1971, p. 2A; 16 March 1971, p. 6A.

92. *Columbus Dispatch*, 11 December 1971, p. 3; Robert J. Kosydar and John H. Bowman, "Modernization of State Tax Systems: The Ohio Experience," *National Tax Journal* 25 (September 1972): 379.

93. *Cleveland Plain Dealer*, 11 December 1971, pp. 12A, 10A.

94. Richard F. Winters, "The Politics of Taxing and Spending," in *Politics in the American States: A Comparative Analysis*, ed. Virginia Gray and Herbert Jacobs (Washington, D.C.: Congressional Quarterly Press, 1996), p. 343.

95. *Proceedings of the National Governors' Conference 1965* (Chicago: National Governors' Conference 1965), p. 53; *Proceedings of the National Governors' Conference 1966* (Chicago: National Governors' Conference, 1966), p. 36; Richard P. Nathan, Allen D. Manvel, and Susannah E. Calkins, *Monitoring Revenue Sharing* (Washington, D.C.: Brookings Institution, 1975), p. 350.

96. *Proceedings of Governors' Conference 1966*, pp. 37, 41.

97. *Proceedings of Governors' Conference 1965*, pp. 52, 54. See also Sylvia V. Hewitt, "A History of Revenue Sharing," *State Government* 46 (winter 1973): 37–38; Nathan, Manvel, and Calkins, *Monitoring Revenue Sharing*, pp. 347–49.

98. Richard M. Nixon, "Letter from the President," *State Government* 46 (winter 1973): 5.

99. George P. Shultz, "Revenue Sharing—What It Is and Does," *State Government* 46 (winter 1973): 22.

100. Brevard Crihfield, "Foreword," *State Government* 46 (winter 1973): 3.

101. Harvey E. Brazer, "The States and General Revenue Sharing," in *The Economic and Political Impact of General Revenue Sharing*, ed. F. Thomas Juster (Ann Arbor, Mich.: Survey Research Center, Institute of Social Research, 1977), p. 105; Nathan, Manvel, and Calkins, *Monitoring Revenue Sharing*, p. 336.

102. Will Myers and John Shannon, "Revenue Sharing for States: An Endangered Species," *Intergovernmental Perspective* 5 (summer 1979): 12.

103. Richard A. Snelling, "American Federalism in the Eighties," *State Government* 53 (autumn 1980): 169.

Epilogue

1. Alan Ehrenhalt, "An Embattled Institution" in *State Government: CQ's Guide to Current Issues and Activities 1992–93*, ed. Thad L. Beyle (Washington, D.C.: Congressional Quarterly, 1992), pp. 96–97.

2. See Rich Jones, "The State Legislatures," in *The Book of the States 1990–91 Edition* (Lexington, Ky.: Council of State Governments, 1990), p. 115.

3. Ehrenhalt, "Embattled Institution," p. 97.

4. David D. Schmidt, *Citizen Lawmakers: The Ballot Initiative Revolution* (Philadelphia: Temple University Press, 1989), p. 23.

5. David Kehler and Robert M. Stern, "Initiatives in the 1980s and 1990s," in *The Book of the States 1994–95 Edition* (Lexington, Ky.: Council of State Governments, 1994), pp. 279, 284.

6. David S. Broder, *Democracy Derailed: Initiative Campaigns and the Power of Money* (New York: Harcourt, 2000), p. 9.

7. James K. Coyne and John H. Fund, *Cleaning House: America's Campaign for Term Limits* (Washington, D.C.: Regnery Gateway, 1992), p. 147. See also Victor Kamber, *Giving Up on Democracy: Why Term Limits Are Bad for America* (Washington, D.C. Regnery Publishing, 1995), pp. 4–6; Gary W. Copeland, "Term Limitations and Political Careers in Oklahoma: In, Out, Up, or Down," in *Limiting Legislative Terms,* ed. Gerald Benjamin and Michael J. Malbin (Washington, D.C.: Congressional Quarterly Press, 1992), pp. 140–42.

8. "The California Ballot Pamphlet: The Pros and the Cons of Proposition 140," in Benjamin and Malbin, *Limiting Legislative Terms,* pp. 276, 279.

9. Douglas Foster, "The Lame-Duck State," *Harper's,* February 1994, p. 66.

10. Copeland, "Terms Limitations in Oklahoma," p. 154.

11. Alan Rosenthal, "The Effects of Terms Limits on Legislatures: A Comment," in Benjamin and Malbin, *Limiting Legislative Terms,* p. 208; Kamber, *Giving Up on Democracy,* p. 46.

12. Broder, *Democracy Derailed,* p. 21.

Index